IMS/VS Data Communications Programming

Using Message Format Service

Ziep N. Vuong

TAB Professional and Reference Books®

Division of TAB BOOKS Inc.

Blue Ridge Summit, PA

A Petrocelli book

TPR books are published by TAB Professional and Reference Books, a division of TAB BOOKS Inc. The TPR logo, consisting of the letters "TPR" within a large "T," is a registered trademark of TAB BOOKS Inc.

FIRST EDITION
FIRST PRINTING

Library of Congress Cataloging-in-Publication Data

Vuong, Ziep N.
IMS/VS data communications programming using message format service / by Ziep N. Vuong.
p. cm.
ISBN 0-8306-3381-2
1. Data base management. 2. IMS/VS (Computer system) I. Title.
QA76.9.D3V86 1989 89-36366
005.74—dc20 CIP

TAB BOOKS Inc. offers software for sale. For information and a catalog, please contact TAB Software Department, Blue Ridge Summit, PA 17294-0850.

Questions regarding the content of this book should be addressed to:

Reader Inquiry Branch
TAB BOOKS Inc.
Blue Ridge Summit, PA 17294-0214

Vice-President & Editoral Director: Larry Hager
Technical Editor: Roman H. Gorski
Series Design: Jaclyn B. Saunders

Contents

Introduction

This book is written primarily for professional programmers and analysts who are interested in developing interactive programs in an IMS/VS data communication environment. It covers the most useful IMS/VS features needed by the IMS programmer.

MFS stands for "Message Format Service." It is an IMS/VS facility which allows you to take advantage of the full-screen capabilities of the 3270 terminals. You will find that MFS simplifies much of the programming effort because it takes over some of the programming tasks that would have to be handled in the COBOL program.

Learning IMS DC programming from the IBM manuals is quite frustrating since these manuals are mainly for reference. They do not assist you in building up your knowledge in a gradual progression of content and difficulty, related to a specific topic. This book, however, makes your learning easy. It walks you through IMS DC programming step by step from basic to advanced while focusing on the important and practical issues that you need to master.

HOW IS THIS BOOK ORGANIZED?

This book is organized into three main sections.

Section I begins with the IMS/VS concepts and terminology that are crucial to your understanding of the IBM data communication environment. Then, it introduces you to the components of the message format service. You will see how MFS accesses and processes online messages. In-depth coverage is given to the transaction flow in an DB/DC environment; the DL/1 calls to accept and to write messages to terminals. Upon completion of this section, you will be able to code basic MFS formats and to develop simple IMS DC COBOL applications.

Section II deals with MFS programming techniques. This section expands the MFS background that you acquired in the previous section. It includes several commonly-used techniques along with their efficiency considerations and problems that will occur within an IMS/VS DB/DC environment. Each MFS facility is presented with the various alternatives available, followed by a discussion as to which alternate will best serve to achieve a given end. COBOL programming samples related to the MFS techniques are also presented. Upon completion of this section, you will be able to handle complex programming tasks such as using password protection, positioning the cursor on the screen, modifying the attribute bytes of the device fields, and invoking paging on the screen or specifying special hardware features. Design considerations are also covered to assist you in selecting the techniques which will best optimize your MFS applications.

Section III goes over the more challenging topics of IMS DC functions. These include sending messages to alternate terminals, conversational processing (which provides a mechanism for storing data between terminal interactions before processing), batch message processing (that performs batch-type processing concurrently with message processing), and the JCL requirements to invoke a checkpoint/restart facility.

REQUIRED BACKGROUND

To start your IMS DC training, you need to know how to design and code COBOL batch programs. You also need to understand DL/1 database processing. Some knowledge of OS JCL is helpful to set up batch message processing jobs.

REFERENCES

Consult the following IBM reference manuals for additional information not covered in this book:

- IMS/VS Version 1—Application Programming SH20-9026
- IMS/VS Version 1—Message Format Service User's Guide SH20-9053
- IMS/VS Version 1—Utilities Reference Manual SH20-9029
- IMS/VS Version 1—Installation Guide SH20-9081
- IMS/VS Version 1—Messages and Codes Reference Manual SH20-9030

The first two manuals listed above are most useful to you.

Section I

Basic Programming for Message Processing

This section introduces you to basic message processing programming. You will learn

- Important IMS/VS concepts and terminology
- The basic message format service
- Mapping data by MFS
- DL/1 calls to accept and write messages to terminals
- Handling error situations

Upon completion of this section, you will be able to code basic MFS formats and to develop simple IMS DC COBOL applications.

1

IMS/VS Data Communication Concepts and Terminology

Before you can start learning the details of IMS/VS COBOL programming with MFS, you need to know some basic concepts and terminology. These concepts and terminology are crucial to your understanding of the data communication environment.

We will begin with a brief overview of the database and data communication features of IMS/VS, and then we will see how the batch and online environments differ from each other. We will look at the resources that come under the control of IMS/VS. These resources must be defined initially before you can start using IMS/VS, and you will see how IMS coordinates the various resources that are brought under its control.

After that, you will see how data flows through the online system and how IMS supports the application program through the scheduling of messages.

THE IMS/VS FACILITIES

There are two features of IMS/VS: the database facilities and the data communication facilities. Data processing centers may use the database facilities of IMS or the data communication facilities, or may use both.

The IMS Database System

When only the database facilities are used, the system is known as a database (DB) system which can be used independently of the data communication facilities, and is used to store and manipulate IMS databases in a batch mode. In a database system environment, the application programs run in a batch region, and each region where a program is executing must contain all the system components.

FIGURE 1-1 illustrates the IMS/VS batch processing environment.

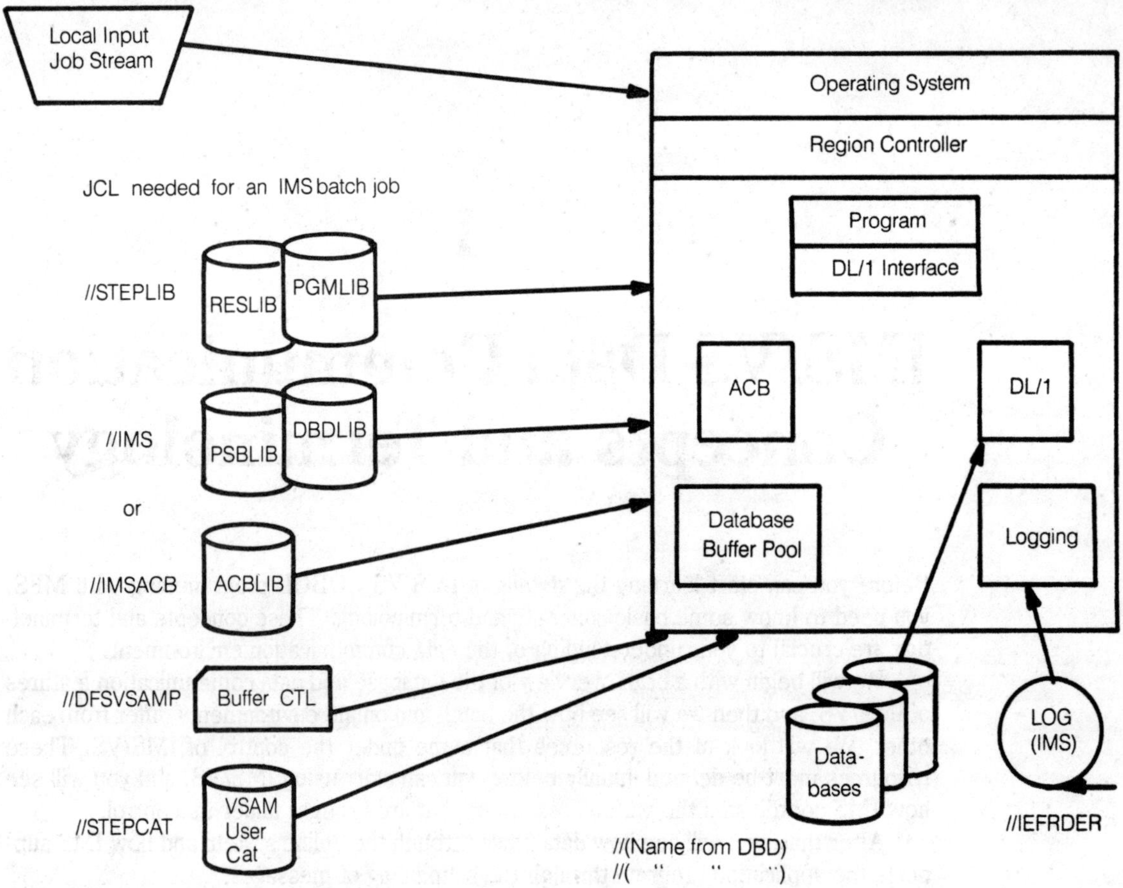

Fig. 1-1. IMS/VS batch processing environment.

In the batch environment, we have to supply the JCL for the execution of a DL/1 application program. Our application program occupies one of the operating system's partitions called "region." The region contains a copy of DL/1. All the components that our program requires for execution are contained within this region and the application program is independent of any other jobs in the system. In a multibatch processing environment, each batch region contains the system components separately; there is no centralized control and, consequently, there is core redundancy.

The IMS/VS Database Data Communication System

When the data communication facilities are used, the system is known as a database/ data communication (DB/DC) system. The data communication system allows the application program to interface with remote terminals via telecommunication lines. In the

DB/DC environment, application programs are automatically scheduled by IMS/VS as a result of messages that are received from remote terminals.

FIGURE 1-2 illustrates the database/data communication environment.

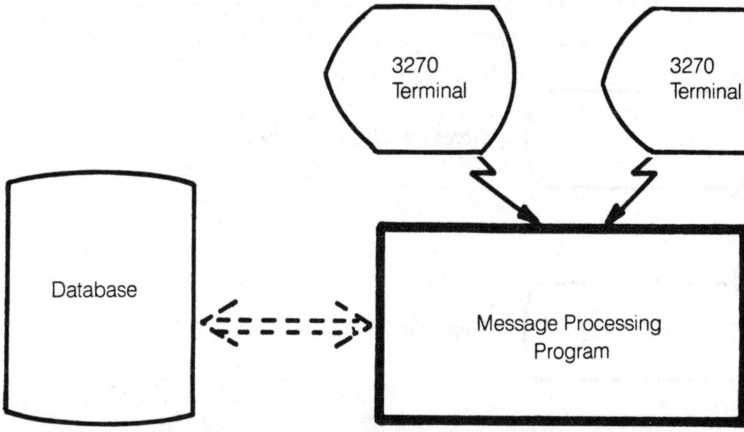

Fig. 1-2. The IMS database communication system.

HOW IMS RESOURCES ARE DEFINED TO THE SYSTEM

To use the database and data communication facilities of IMS/VS, every computer installation has to initially perform the task of system definition (SYSGEN). Let's see how this process is performed.

The System Definition Process

The IMS System Definition is a process in which a number of system control statements are coded and processed

- To describe the IMS facilities that an installation has intended to use, and
- To communicate to IMS information on the hardware and operating system.

During the SYSGEN, various control statements are processed by the Assembler and Linkage editor, and various IMS load modules and control blocks are created and stored in various IMS/VS libraries. These libraries are listed in FIG. 1-3.

DEFINING THE DATABASE SYSTEM

In the batch environment, the application programmers need not be concerned with the SYSGEN process. The system definition is performed once for all users of the installation. After the SYSGEN is done, databases and application programs may be added to the system via the DBDGEN and PSBGEN processes.

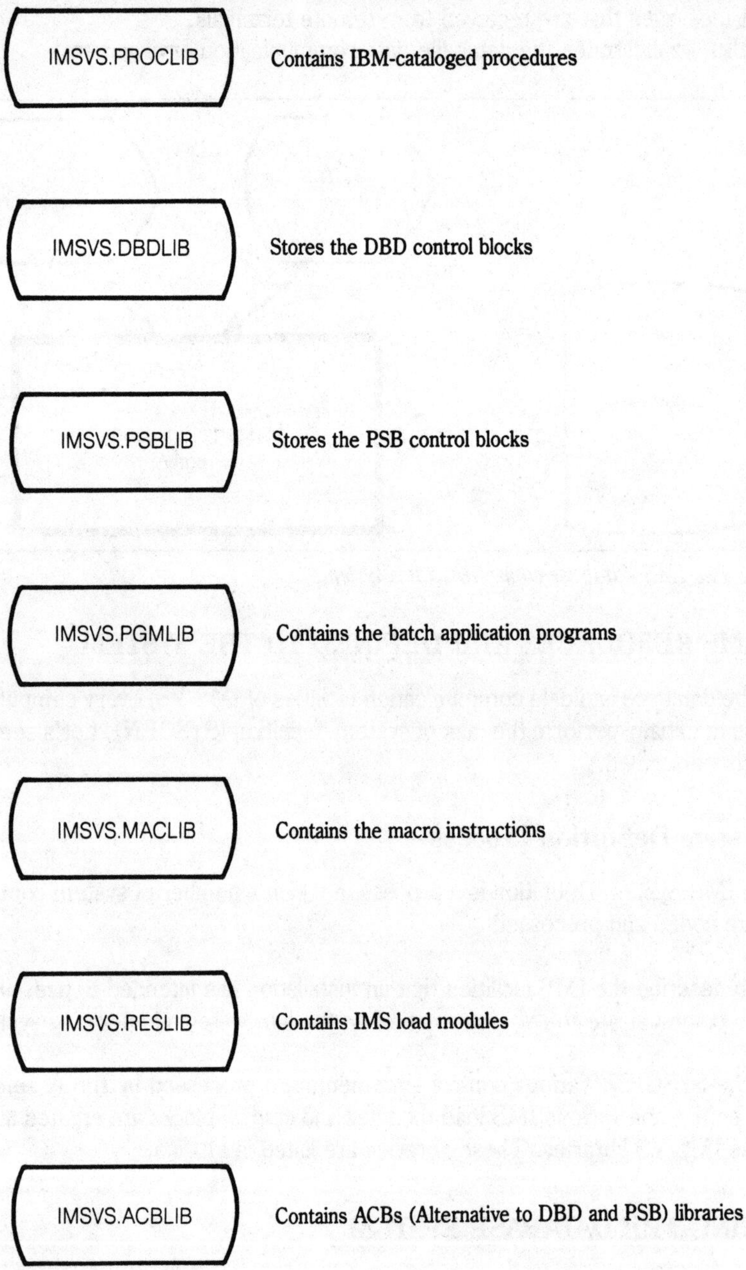

Fig. 1-3. Typical IMS/VS libraries.

Now, let's look at each one of these processes individually.

The Program's View of Data. IMS/VS uses two kinds of control blocks to make it possible for application programs to be independent of the way in which we store the data in the database.

One control block defines the physical structure of the database, the appearance and contents, or fields, that make up each of the segment types in the database; the other control block defines an application program's logical view of the database.

Defining the Database—DBDGEN. The process of describing the physical structure of the database to IMS is called the DBD Generation. A series of control statements are coded by the database administrator and are submitted to the system via a JCL. The DBDGEN control statements are processed by the assembler, producing a load module which is stored in a library called DBDLIB (FIG. 1-4). The DBDGEN is normally performed once for a database. After that, all DL/1 applications can use that DBD to access the database.

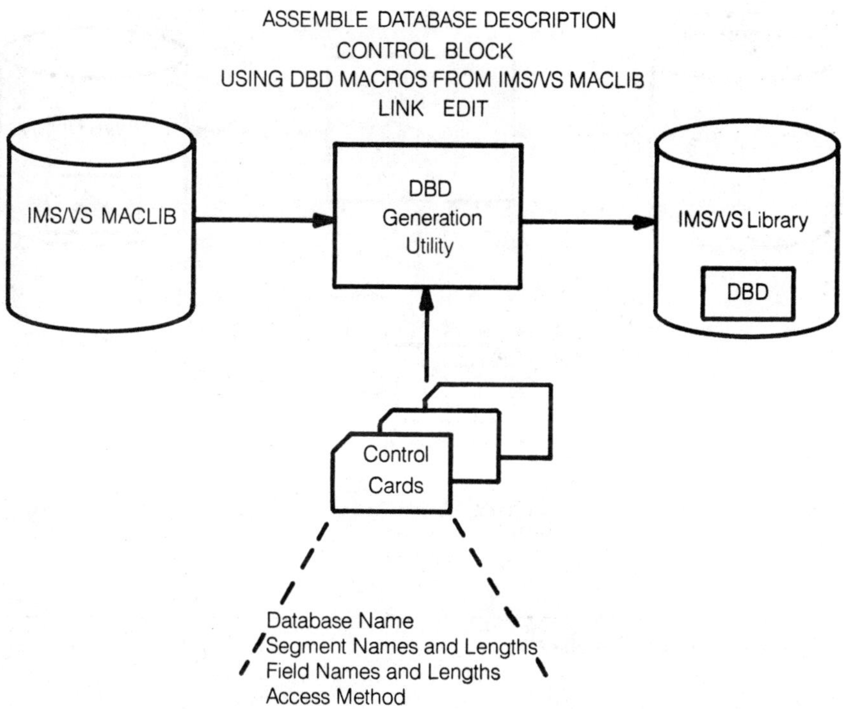

Fig. 1-4. The DBD generation process.

For information on generating DBDs, refer to "Database Description (DBD) Generation" in the IBM "IMS/VS Utilities Reference Manual."

Defining an Application Program's View of the Database—PSBGEN. An application program often needs to access only some of the segments in a database. The application program's view of the database is defined by a database program communication block (DB PCB). A PCB defines which of the segments in the database the program is allowed to access; in other words, the segments to which the program is sensitive.

The PCB also determines how the application program is allowed to process the segments it accesses—whether it can read the segments and whether it can update them as well. An application program may use only one DB PCB (one logical data structure) or several, one for each data structure.

The process of describing the logical view of a database for an application program is called PSBGEN. This process is very similar to the DBDGEN process. PSBGEN control statements are processed by the assembler, producing a load module which is stored in a library called the PSBLIB. Each PSB consists of one or more PCBs (FIG. 1-5). For information on generating PSBs, refer to "Program Specification Block (PSB) Generation" in the IBM "IMS/VS Utilities Reference Manual."

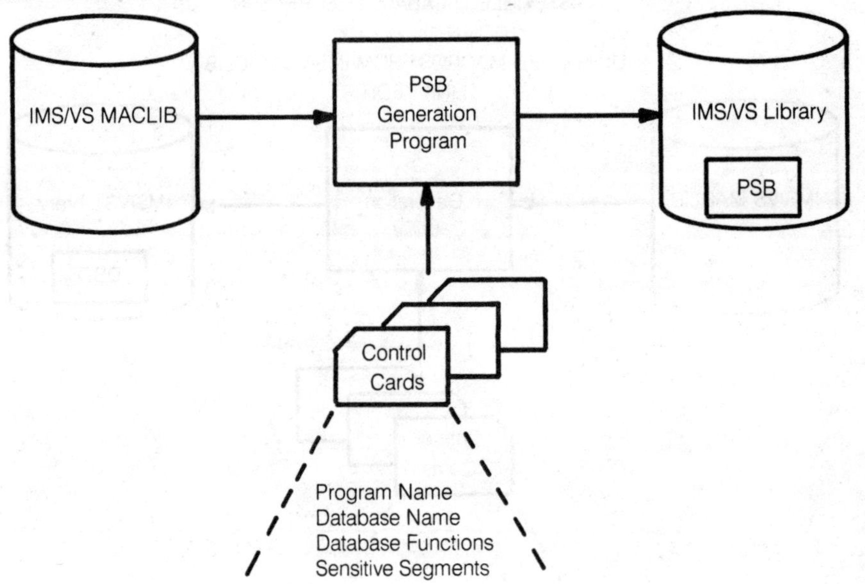

Fig. 1-5. The PSB generation process.

Defining the DB/DC System

The system definition for a DB/DC system is more complex than for the DB system. Unlike the batch environment where we can add new programs and databases to the DB system, in the DB/DC environment, we must have all the resources that come under the control of IMS/VS defined to IMS during the system definition (FIG. 1-6).

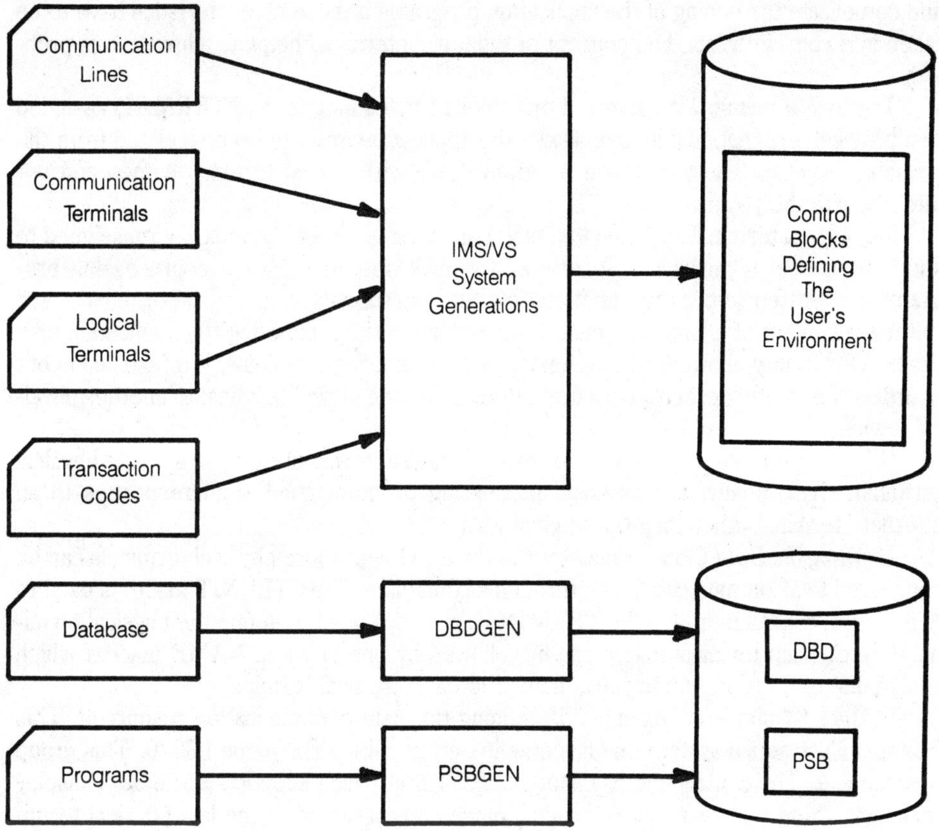

Fig. 1-6. The data communication system definition.

The resources that have to be defined to IMS/VS DB/DC can be divided into two categories:

- Data communication resources and
- Application resources

Let's look at these two categories.

The Data Communication Resources. The data communication resources that must be defined during the SYSGEN include the physical hardware in the data communication network, such as the communication controller, the communication lines, and the remote terminals.

In the IMS/VS DB/DC system, a single communication line can handle several remote terminals of a similar type. Communication lines that connect terminals of a similar type may be grouped together into line groups. Each line group is defined to IMS/VS by the LINEGRP and LINE macros. We will show an example of this later.

The physical characteristics of the remote terminals vary from one type to another and complicate the coding of the application programs if these characteristics have to be taken into consideration. The concept of the logical terminal helps to alleviate this problem.

The logical terminal is a name of one to eight bytes long (e.g., LTERMA1) assigned to a physical terminal, and its use allows the application program to be isolated from the physical terminal. The application program deals with logical terminal names and not directly with the physical terminals.

The logical terminal assigned to a physical terminal can be dynamically reassigned to another physical terminal by the master terminal operator. Message processing programs are written to perform input and output operations against logical terminals, and the reassignment of a logical terminal can be done without affecting the application program. This facility allows for more flexibility in scheduling terminals. If a terminal is out of order, the master terminal operator can reassign the logical terminal to another physical device.

It is also possible to assign more than one logical terminal name to a single physical terminal. Occasionally, the message processing program must send responses to an alternate terminal other than the original terminal.

Defining the Data Communication Resources. One or more physical terminals can be connected to a communication line through a controller. The CTLUNIT macro is used to define each control unit, and the TERMINAL macro is used to define the physical terminal device. Each terminal macro can be followed by one or more NAME macros which assign one or more logical terminal names to each physical terminal.

FIGURE 1-7 shows an example of defining the data communication resources. This example illustrates a system that has one line group with a DD name L3270. This group has one line. The control unit is a Model 2 3271 unit which supports three 3277 display terminals. Note that two logical terminal names are assigned to the last physical terminal.

```
LINEGRP           DDNAME=L3270,UNITYPE=3270  <------ Line Group
 LINE             ADDR=0C9                   <------ Line
  CTLUNIT         ADDR=C1,MODEL=2  <---------------- Control Unit
   TERMINAL       ADDR=40
     NAME         LTERMA1
    TERMINAL      ADDR=C1
     NAME         LTERMA2
    TERMINAL      ADDR=C2
     NAME         LTERMA3
     NAME         LTERMA4
```

Fig. 1-7. Defining the IMS/VS data communication resources.

The Application Resources. The application resources are related to the application programs operating in the IMS/VS DB/DC system. These resources include the databases, the transaction codes, and the application programs.

Online processing is performed by two types of programs:

- Message processing programs (MP programs) and
- Batch message processing programs (BMP programs)

The message processing programs and the batch message processing programs are transaction-driven. They are so defined because the data communication is initiated upon receipt of a transaction. When a transaction is received, IMS/VS determines the resources needed to process the transaction. One of the resources is the application program that processes the transaction. The transaction code identifies the application program needed to process the transaction and causes IMS/VS to load it into core and give it control of the CPU. The program then processes the transaction.

In contrast to the data communication environment, in a database system, the DL/1 batch programs control the operating environment rather than the transactions. In this sense, the database system is program-driven.

The relationship between the various application resources under the control of IMS/VS is shown in FIG. 1-8. This figure illustrates a data communications system which supports three transaction codes: TRANS001, TRANS002, and TRANS003. These three transactions are processed by three programs named UPDATE, INQUIRY, and ADDCUST, respectively, and all three programs access one database.

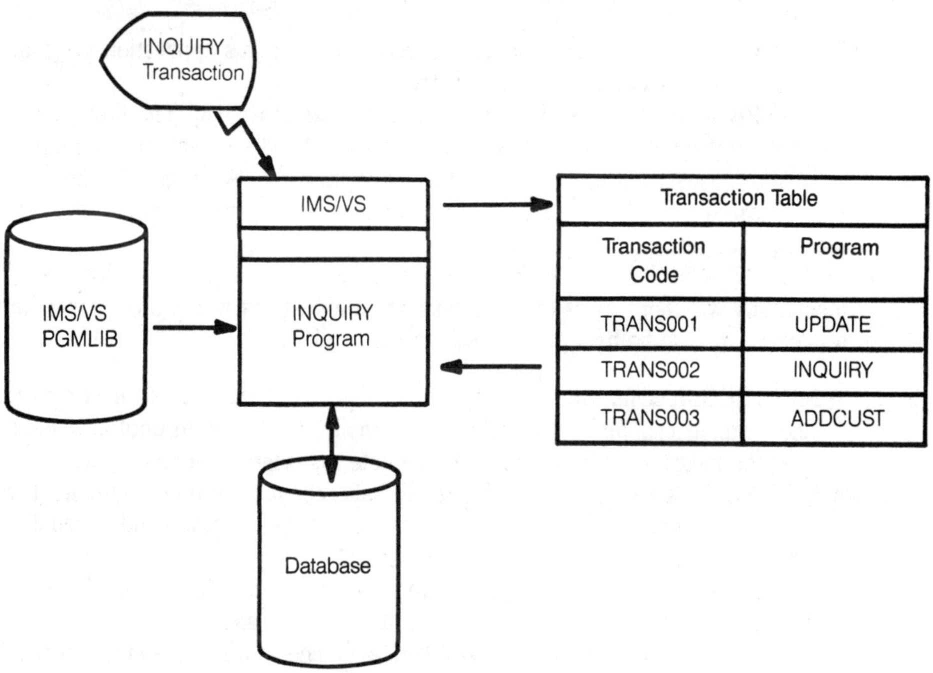

Fig. 1-8. Transaction-driven flow.

Defining the Application Resources. The transaction codes and the programs that process them are defined to IMS/VS with the TRANSACT and APPLCTN macros. The database names that the MP and BMP programs access are defined in a database macro. An example of defining the application resources is:

```
DATABASE         DBD1
APPLCTN          PSB=UPDATE,PGMTYPE=(,,1)
 TRANSACT        CODE=TRANS001,PRTY=(1,1)
APPLCTN          PSB=INQUIRY,PGMTYPE=(,,1)
 TRANSACT        CODE=TRANS002,PRTY=(1,1)
APPLCTN          PSB=ADDCUST,PGMTYPE=(,,1)
 TRANSACT        CODE=TRANS003,PRTY=(3,3)
```

The APPLCTN macro names the application program that processes the transaction code specified in the TRANSACT macro. The TRANSACT macro is used one or more times with each APPLCTN macro instruction to identify the transaction codes that causes the application program named in the preceding APPLCTN macro to be scheduled for execution in an IMS/VS message processing region.

The parameters used to define the application programs and the online transactions are listed in FIG. 1-9. In this section, some of the parameters that define the input message types and the processing modes will be covered. Refer to Appendix C for a detailed explanation of the symbolic parameters specified in the APPLCTN and TRANSACT macro statements.

1. PSB—Specifies the name of the PSB associated with this application program definition. Each local PSB must be unique.
2. PGMTYPE—Specifies the application program characteristics. The first parameter has a default value of "TP" which specifies that IMS/VS schedules the program when messages processed by the program exist. A program defined as BATCH can use DL/1 in the IMS/VS control program region and can refer to the message queues.
3. MSGTYPE—Specifies the kind of the input message (single or multiple segment), and whether or not the communication line, from which the transaction was entered, is to be held until a response is received.

   - MULTSEG:Specifies that the input message might consist of one or more segments. It cannot be scheduled to an application program until an end-of-message indication is received or a complete message is created by MFS.
   - SNGLSEG: Specifies that the input message consists of one segment. The end of the segment is assumed to be the end of the message and scheduling can occur when the first segment is received.
   - NONRESPONSE: Specifies that if the communication line is available for transmission, the terminal can continue to enter messages.
   - RESPONSE: Specifies that the communication line to which the input terminal is attached cannot accept further inputs until a response to this message is received.

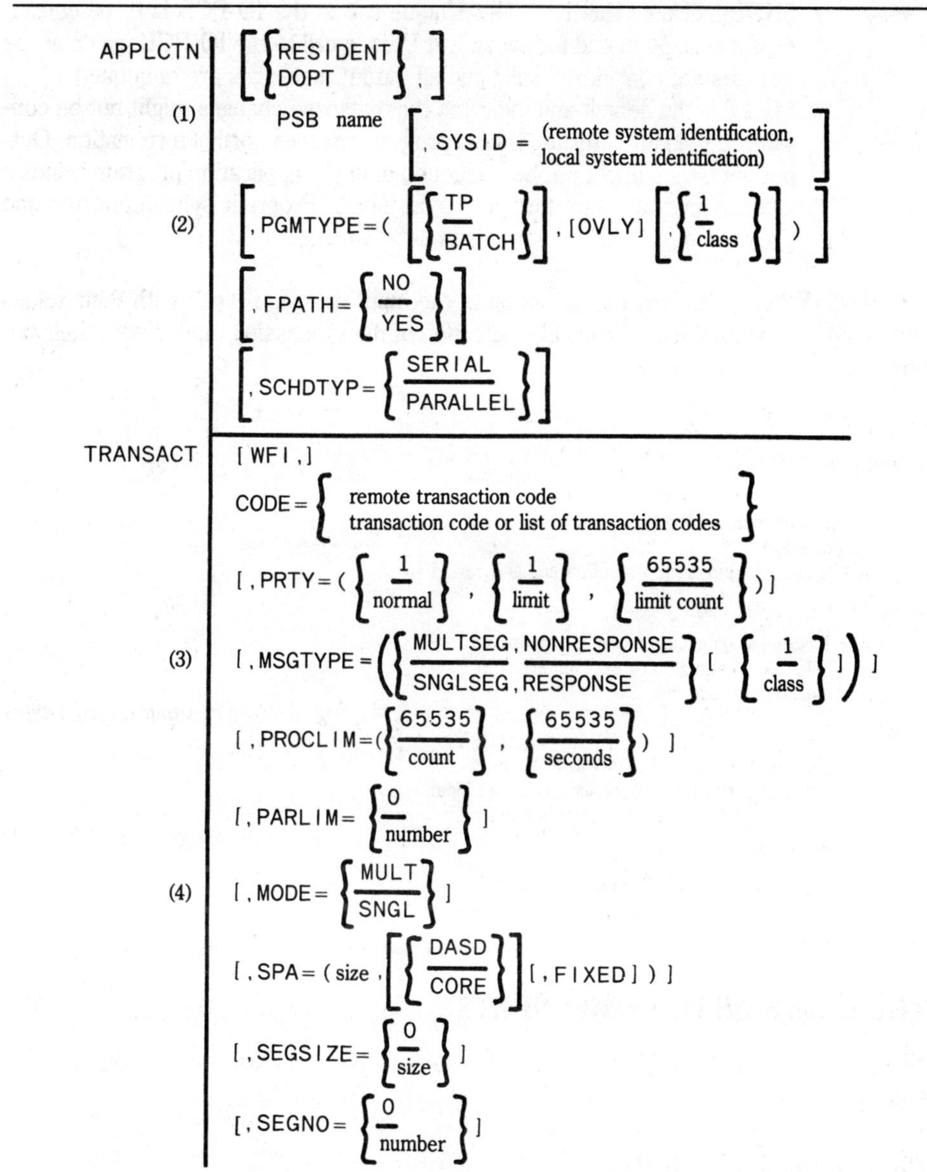

Fig. 1-9. The APPLCTN and TRANSACT macros.

- MODE—Specifies that database buffers are to be written to direct access upon each request for a new message (SNGL) by the processing program or upon program termination (MULT). This operand affects emergency restart.

- SNGL indicates that each Get Unique call to the IO-PCB is to be considered a sync point and for every Get Unique call to the IO-PCB, all database changes are considered valid and all output messages are enqueued.
- MULT is the default and indicates that database changes might not be considered valid until the application program reaches normal termination. Output messages might not be enqueued until the application program issues a Checkpoint call, thus forcing a sync point. Program synchronization and Checkpoint call will be covered in detail in chapter 13.

MSGTYPE determines the definition of the input message types with their values (FIG. 1-10), and MODE determines the definition of the processing modes with their values (FIG. 1-11).

- `MSGTYPE = (SNGLSEG, - , -)`
  - Input message consists of one line
  - End of segment is assumed to mean end of message
  - Scheduling can occur when first line is received
- `MSGTYPE = (MULTSEG, - , -)`
  - Input message consists of one or more lines
  - Scheduling cannot occur until an end of message indication is received
- `MSGTYPE = ( - , RESPONSE, -)`
  - The communication line to which the input terminal is attached cannot accept further inputs until a response to this message is received
- `MSGTYPE = ( - , NONRESPONSE, -)`
  - If the line is available for transmission, the terminal can continue to input messages

Fig. 1-10. The input message types.

THE IMS/VS DB/DC COMPONENTS

Now, let's see how IMS/VS coordinates the various resources that are brought under its control.

Control Region Facilities

In the data communication environment, there are two types of regions: the control region and the message processing regions. The control region contains the system components and coordinates the entire data communication environment. The message processing regions contain the application programs, and each has a resident controller.

Mode = { SNGL / MULT } Alters synch points and output messages

- SNGL
  - Indicates that each get unique (GU) to the 10-PCB is to be considered a synch point.
    For every GU call to the 10-PCB
    - All database changes are considered valid
    - Output messages are enqueued
- MULT
  - Default—Indicates that database changes may not be considered valid until the application program reaches normal termination
  - Output messages are not enqueued until program terminates or issues "CHKP" call, thus forcing a sync point

Fig. 1-11 The processing modes.

The control region provides the interface for terminals that are sending and receiving messages under IMS/VS. It also contains DL/1 and provides interfaces with the databases and the IMS system log for the applications which process the online messages.

Let's examine each component individually (FIG. 1-12).

Control Program. Coordinates all the activities and events in the control region and communicates with the region controllers in the message processing and batch message processing regions.

Physical and Logical Terminals. The application programs in the IMS DB/DC environment do not communicate directly with physical terminals using hardware addresses. They communicate with terminals using one- to eight-character "logical terminal" names defined to IMS during the system definition process.

The logical terminal name can be assigned to any physical terminal and, therefore, provides independence from the physical device.

Master Terminal. At system definition time, one of the logical terminals is designated as a master terminal, the control center of the entire IMS DB/DC system. The terminal controls the system via special commands. With these commands, the master terminal operator can

- Bring up the IMS DB/DC system and take it down when IMS services are no longer required
- Bring the databases online and offline
- Start and stop communication lines
- Monitor system performance
- Make required changes to the IMS environment

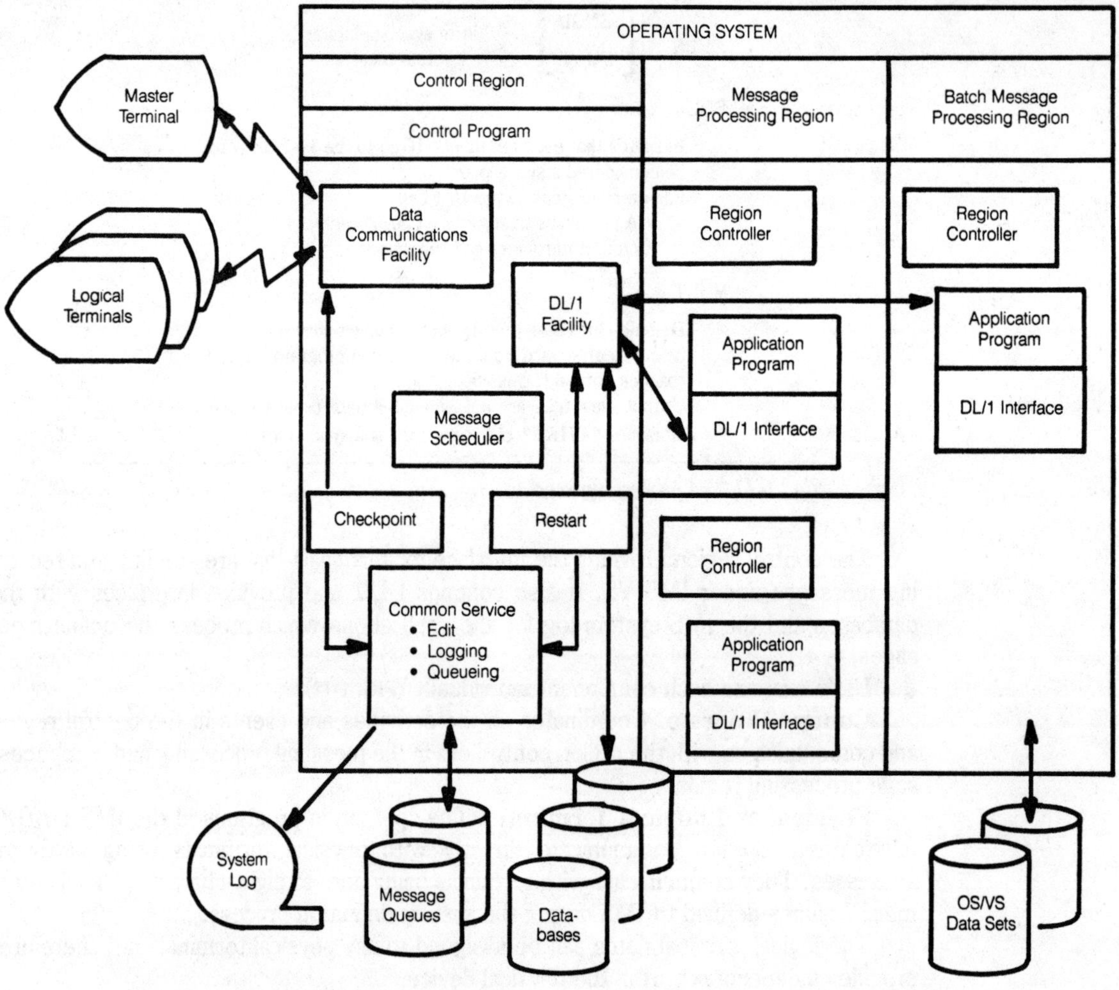

Fig. 1-12. IMS/VS control region system components.

Data Communication Facility. This facility serves as a switchboard for user and master terminals by routing

- Input messages from the terminals to the common service facility
- Output messages from the common service facility to the terminals
- Commands from the terminals to the Control Program

DL/1 Facility. This facility is used to satisfy calls to databases and message queues.

The Scheduling Facility. This facility determines the order in which different transaction types are to be processed from the message queues and schedules the appropriate application programs for the transactions.

Checkpoint Facility. This facility maintains the integrity of the online system. Checkpoints are "snapshots" of the system that are taken after a specified number of transactions have been processed. At appropriate time intervals, checkpoint records that describe the total status of the system are written to the system log. A checkpoint may also be taken at the request of the master terminal.

Restart Facility. This facility allows two types of start: cold and warm.

- A cold start is used to start the online system for the first time, or after a shutdown and no messages left in the queues are to be processed.
- A warm start is used when the system is started after a shutdown and previously-queued messages are to be processed. When a warm start is performed, information stored on the system log is used.

Common-Service Facility. This facility provides a recording of information about all the activity of the system (logging) and uses the information to restart the system and to reverse the effects of an application program that abends. Logging (Recovery) is always active while the Data Communication system is running. The Logging facility records on the System Log all programs that are scheduled and all transactions and responses before and after database updates. Because log information is available, it can be used to restore the system if a failure occurs. If an application program abends, IMS automatically reverses any changes it has made to the databases and to the message queues.

The Message Processing Regions

Besides the control region which coordinates the entire data communication environment, IMS/VS uses several other dependent regions (message processing regions) where online programs and data communication application programs are executed. There are two kinds of message processing regions:

- Message processing regions (MP region) and
- Batch message processing regions (BMP region)

Message Processing Region. Most of the dependent regions in an IMS/VS data communication system are MP regions. All these regions are managed by the IMS control program running in the control region. The MP programs run in the message processing regions. The number of MP regions determines the number of MP programs that are invoked at one time. The MP programs communicate with the terminals and process input transactions against online databases; they cannot access nondatabase files. A MP program normally processes all the input messages that IMS has received for it; then, when it ends, the MP region in which it was running is freed for another MP program to run. The MP programs that run in a given MP region change quickly and this would give the terminal operator instantaneous responses.

Batch Message Processing Region. The other kind of message processing region that is part of the IMS/VS data communication system is the batch message processing region. A BMP region is online and batch-oriented, and is used to run batch message processing programs.

The BMP region provides partial online processing capabilities. It receives and stores messages from terminals in an online manner; however, messages are accumulated and processed against the databases at a later time.

A BMP program can process transactions from the message queues and access online databases just like MP programs. However, the BMP is scheduled through an OS JCL job stream. A BMP is considered an online program by IMS/VS even though it is scheduled through an OS JCL stream.

HOW DOES IMS PROCESS DATA FROM A TERMINAL?

Next, let's see how data flows through the IMS/VS data communication system.

FIGURE 1-13 illustrates the flow of information through the system. This figure shows that:

1. When a transaction is received, it is processed by the data communication.
2. On arrival, it is edited for message validity by performing a security check and by testing the transaction code. The content of the message is also edited. All device-dependent and control characters are removed so that the transactions look the same, no matter what terminal type they come from.
3. If the message is valid, it is written to the system log.
4. Next, the queuing function places it on the message queue.
5. The message scheduler selects messages from the message queue and passes them on to the region for processing. The selection is done on the basis of a priority assigned to each transaction and the number of that transaction type on the queue.
6. When a message is sent to the MP region, the region controller determines whether or not the MP program needed to process the transaction is already in that area. If not, the controller will cause the MP program to be brought in.
7. The MP program then receives control and the input message is retrieved from the message queue and placed in the program's input message area.
8. If a database is to be accessed, this is done via DL/1 calls. The appropriate database segment is retrieved and placed in the program's segment-IO-area for processing.
9. A response is built and placed in the program's output message area and then loaded to the message queue. The response is then transmitted to the interfacing terminal or to an alternate terminal. The response is logged on the system log, another transaction is retrieved, and the process starts again.

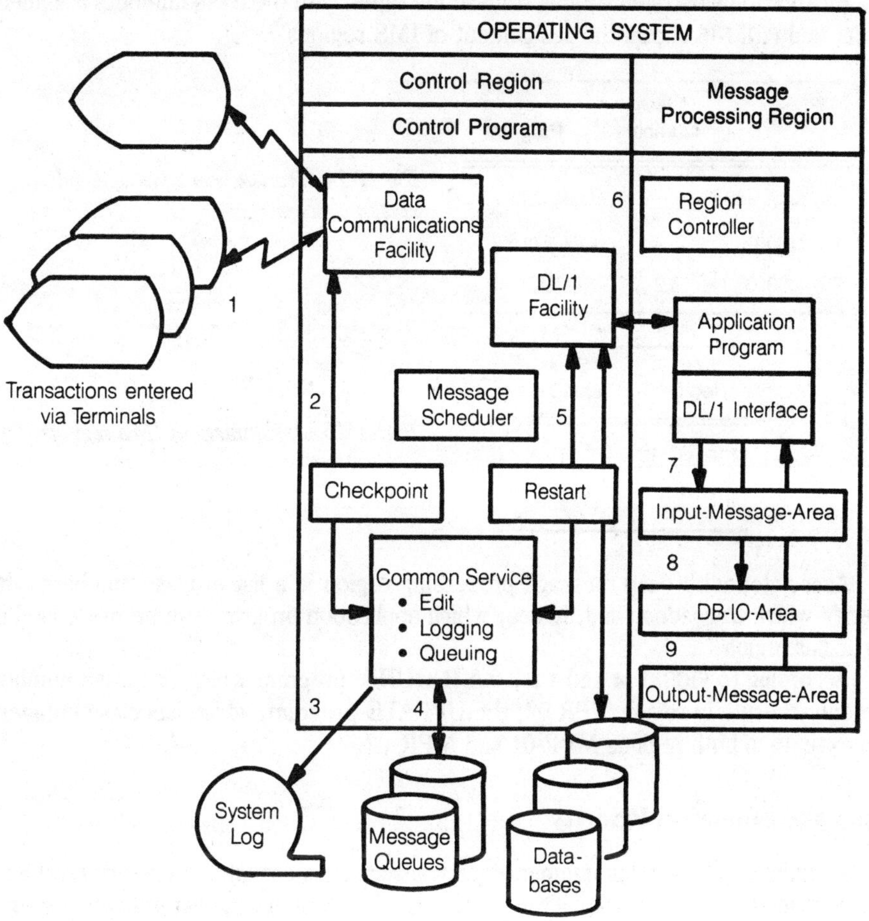

Fig. 1-13. Data communication system flow.

SCHEDULING MESSAGE PROCESSING

You have seen in the previous section that messages received from the remote terminals are placed on the message queue before they are passed to the message processing regions for processing. How does the message scheduler decide which message to select from the queue?

Several factors determine the order in which the applications are scheduled to be executed and the regions into which they are loaded. These factors are explained below.

Class Number

At system definition time, each transaction is assigned a class number which can range from 1 to 255. Several transaction types may be assigned the same number.

FIGURE 1-14 illustrates various transaction types with the class numbers assigned to them, and FIG. 1-15 shows the assignment of IMS regions.

	Class Number	Program
TRANS001	1	UPDATE
TRANS002	3	INQUIRY
TRANS003	2	ADDCUST

Fig. 1-14. Transaction types with related class numbers.

MP Region	Class Number
MRP-01	1
MRP-02	1, 2, 3

Fig. 1-15. Assignment of IMS regions.

Associated with each message processing region is a list of class numbers which specify which transaction and, hence, which application program can be processed in a particular region.

According to FIGS. 1-14 and 1-15, the INQUIRY program which has class number 3 can only execute in region MPR-02; the UPDATE program, which has class number 1, can execute in both regions MPR-01 and MPR-02.

Message Selection Priority

In addition to the class number, each transaction is assigned a priority level which ranges from 0 to 14, with 0 being the lowest and, 14 being the highest priority. For example, when IMS searches for an input message queue to process, it will process the queue with a priority of 9 before that one with priority level of 6 (FIG. 1-16).

	TRANS001	TRANS002	TRANS003
Priority Level	5	6	9
Queue Count	25	9	2
Limit Count	25	15	6
Limit Priority	9	16	12
Processing Limit	10	6	16

Fig. 1-16. Message queues.

If an input queue is assigned a priority level of 0, then the transactions loaded into the queue are forced to accumulate and are then collected for batch processing at a later time in a batch message region.

Queue Count

When selecting input messages for processing, the message scheduler first examines the number of messages of a transaction type in the message queue. This number is the queue count.

The queue count is compared against the limit count and the priority level. If the queue count is less than the limit count, the priority level for the transaction type is used for comparison.

Limit Priority

Sometimes, a limit priority is assigned to input message queues.

Limit Count

Associated with each limit priority is a limit count. If the number of transactions accumulated in a message queue is greater than or equal to the limit count, then the priority level of this queue is temporarily given the value of its limit priority. This will allow the transaction to be processed.

For example, the TRANS003 message queue is assigned a priority level of 9, a limit count of 6, and a limit priority of 12. When six or more TRANS003 transactions are accumulated in the message queue, IMS assigns a priority level of 14 to this queue. This allows processing of the transactions. When all the transactions are processed, the priority level of the queue is reset to 9.

Processing Limit

Sometimes a processing limit is assigned to a transaction type. This limit will prevent the application from executing for an excessive length of time.

When the application program has processed the number of transactions specified by the processing limit, it will receive from IMS a status code indicating that there are no more messages to be processed. Whenever this return code is received, the application program will terminate.

The remaining transactions in the queue will be processed when their queue becomes again the highest priority queue, and the associated program will be rescheduled.

FORMATTING MESSAGES

A message transmitted to the data communication system is called a transaction, and a message sent to the terminal is called a Response. Messages received from or sent to a logical terminal are formatted by the message format service (MFS) which is a facility of IMS/VS DB/DC that handles all horizontal and vertical mapping of data on the CRT terminals. MFS operates as an interface between the message queue and the terminal.

MFS processes incoming messages before they are placed on the message queue, and output messages before they are retrieved from the message queue and sent to the terminal. It is this interface which creates the I-O independence for the application program.

We will talk more about MFS in chapter 2.

ONLINE CONTROL

One of the selling points of IMS/VS is that it provides effective security features. These features can be used for both the database and data communication systems. Let's look at the security features that relate to the online system.

IMS/VS provides two types of security checks to prevent unauthorized use of a transaction:

1. *Password security.*
   A password must be entered as a transaction message. A particular password identifies a person as a legal user of a system and indicates which types of transactions that person may enter. If an invalid password or an unauthorized transaction type is entered, the message will not be processed.
2. *Terminal eligibility.*
   This feature is used to restrict the transaction types that can be entered from a logical terminal. If a transaction type is entered at an LTERM that is not authorized to use that transaction type, the message will be rejected. FIGURE 1-17 shows how programs can be protected by using terminal security.

Transaction Code	Terminal	Password
TRANS001	All	None
TRANS002	All	None
TRANS003	None	None
TRANS004	All	Passwd1
TRANS005	LTERM01	Passwd2
TRANS006	All	Passwd3

Fig. 1-17. Transaction codes, LTERM, and password security.

Messages that violate password security and source terminal eligibility are written to the system log. Review of the system log helps in tracking down attempted security violations. Most installations restrict access to transaction types to only those needed and request the system users to change their passwords frequently.

CONCLUSION

All concepts and terminology presented in this chapter are important to you because they form the foundation of your IMS/VS data communication knowledge. You need to understand them well before you can start learning how to develop basic IMS DC application programs.

2

An Introduction to the Message Format Service

This chapter begins with an overview of the MFS facility. After that, we will describe the components of MFS and their functions, and the linkage between the MFS control blocks.

To enhance your understanding, we will present an example of the MFS processing cycle to illustrate the flow of data from the display format through MFS editing to the IMS DC application program.

As the 3270 terminal is the most commonly-used terminal at many installations, all examples will relate to this type of terminal.

OVERVIEW OF MFS

MFS is a facility of the IMS/VS data communication feature that formats messages to and from terminal devices. MFS handles all horizontal and vertical mapping of data on the CRT terminals. MFS operates as the interface between the message queue and the terminal: MFS processes incoming messages before they are placed on the message queue, and output messages as they are retrieved from the message queue and sent to the terminal. It is this interface which creates I-O device independence for the application program.

MFS DESIGN OBJECTIVES

MFS was developed to simplify the IMS application programmer's job. It frees the programmer from being concerned with creating formats for output messages and also makes the application program itself free of terminal device characteristics. Without MFS, the programmer has to assume responsibility for formatting the program's output; details such as headings, literals, and page numbers have to be set up in the program, and the programmer has to insert varying control characters in the output data stream for each terminal device the application program uses.

By using predefined control blocks, MFS determines where the data is to appear on the screen; it identifies all fields in the output message and will format them in different ways depending on the physical device being used.

MFS makes it possible for the application program to communicate with different types of terminal devices without regard to the physical characteristics of the terminals. With the device independence offered by MFS, one application program can process data to and from multiple device types.

MFS CONTROL BLOCKS

To process a transaction, MFS uses four user-defined control blocks to format input and output messages. By using the control blocks, MFS allows the application program to process data without concern for the actual positioning of data on the terminal screen. The mapping of data by MFS is transparent to the application program.

Four control blocks format input and output messages. These are:

- DIF Device input format
- DOF Device output format
- MID Message input descriptor
- MOD Message output descriptor

The DIF and DOF are device-related control blocks; the MID and MOD are application program-related and are used to show the buffer layout with respect to the application program. The DIF describes the layout of the data fields as they are received from the terminal and the MID describes the layout of the data fields as they are presented to the application program. Working together, the DIF and MID prepare the input message segments before presenting them to the application program.

The MOD defines the output message content that is sent by the application program and the DOF describes the layout of the data fields at the terminal. Working together, the MOD and its related DOF access data in the application program's I-O area and format the output message for display on the terminal.

FIGURE 2-1 illustrates the MFS flow of the input and output messages via the MFS control blocks.

MFS Input Message Flow

To transmit an input message from a terminal device to the message queue, MFS does the following:

1. Based on the specifications in the DIF control block, MFS breaks down the input message from the terminal device into individual fields.

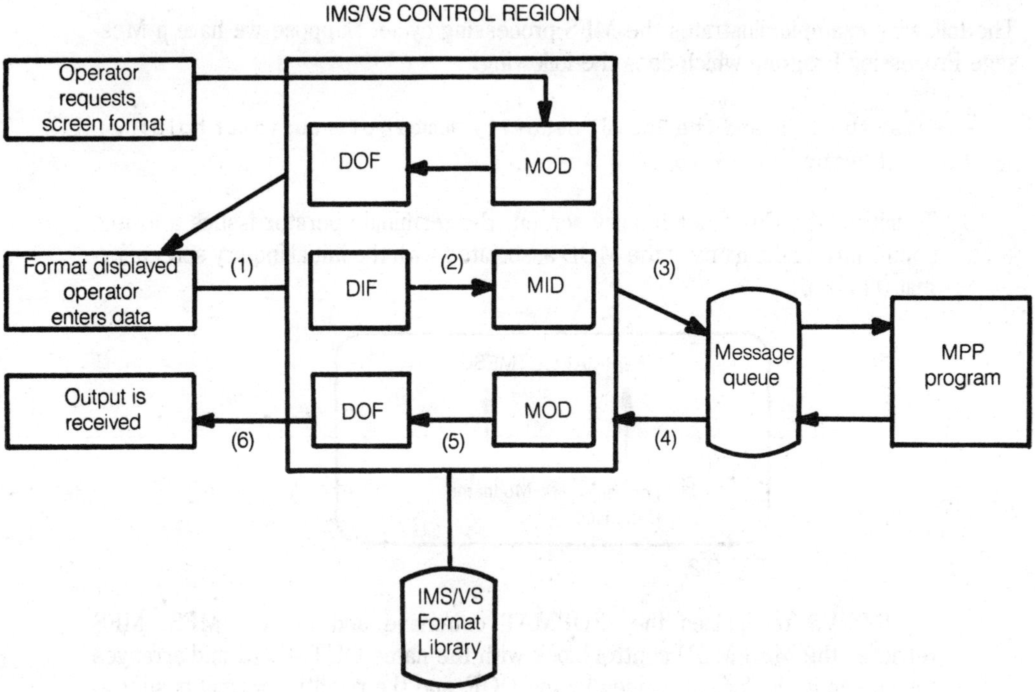

Fig. 2-1. MFS input-output message flow.

2. Based on the specifications in the corresponding MID control block, MFS maps these fields into a message of one or more segments.
3. MFS then loads the input message on the IMS/VS message queue to be accessed by the message processing program for processing.

MFS Output Message Flow

To transmit an output message from the message queue to the terminal device, MFS does the following:

4. MFS accesses the IMS/VS message queue and retrieves the output message which was loaded by the message processing program.
5. Based on the specifications in the MOD control block, MFS maps the output message into separate fields.
6. MFS then formats these fields using the corresponding DOF control block, and transmits them to the interfacing terminal.

THE MFS PROCESSING CYCLE

The following example illustrates the MFS processing cycle. Suppose we have a Message Processing Program which does the following:

```
Display the Name and the Social Security Number of a customer holding
Account number 12345678.
```

1. To initiate the Customer Inquiry screen, the terminal operator issues a format command and the name of the MOD associated with the initial inquiry screen format (FIG. 2-2).

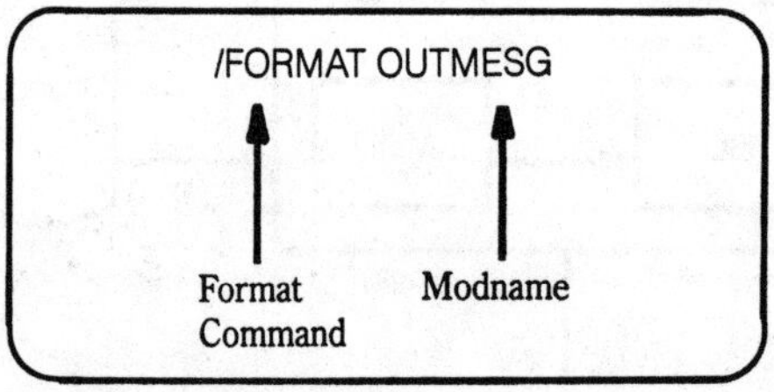

Fig. 2-2.

IMS/VS recognizes the /FORMAT command and invokes MFS. MFS retrieves the MFS MOD control block with the name OUTMESG and arranges the screen in the format defined by the DOF, and the resulting format is sent to the screen (FIG. 2-3, SCREEN 2). The data fields on the screen are blank because no application program has been scheduled and no I-O area has been used.

2. When the operator enters the MOD name, the transaction code associated with the MPP program that processes the request is included in the screen. In our example, the transaction code is 'TRANS001'. The operator does not need to know the name of the program, only the name of the MOD.
3. The operator enters the Account number 12345678 and the letter 'G' in the Action field and presses the ENTER key (FIG. 2-3, SCREEN 3).
4. MFS causes the DIF and MID control blocks to translate the data as it is received from the terminal to the format that the MPP program expects to receive it.

The DIF control block tells MFS how data is going to come from the terminal, and the MID tells MFS how data is to be presented to the application program.

Only the transaction code 'TRANS001' and data actually entered by the operator will be sent. Literals on the screen are not transmitted.

5. The MPP program receives the message, uses the account number as a key to search the customer database, and sends the requested information back to the

terminal. MFS uses the DOF to translate the output message from the MP program to the format to be displayed on the terminal (FIG. 2-3, SCREEN 4).

Now that you have seen that MFS uses the internal control blocks to edit the input and output messages, let's see how the MFS control blocks are defined.

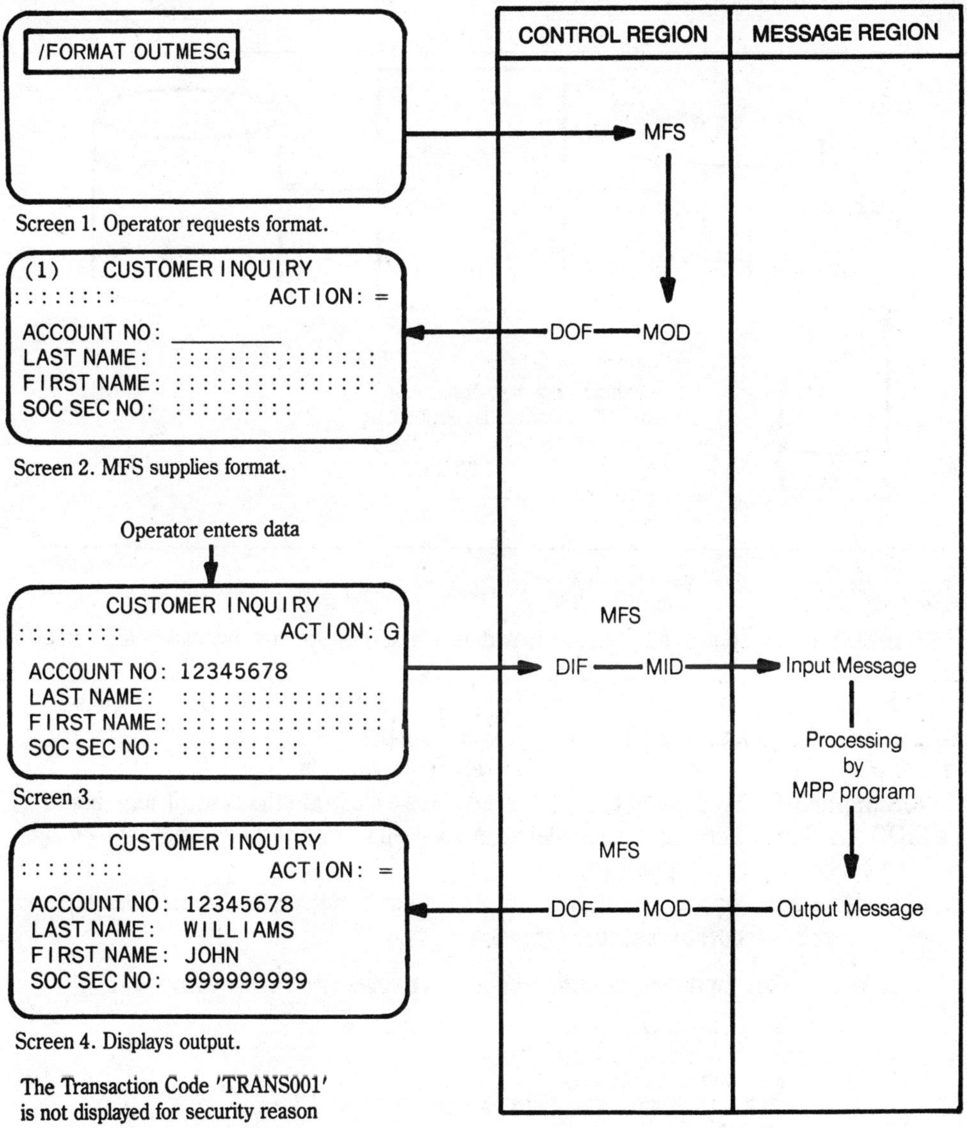

Fig. 2-3. MFS processing cycle.

Defining MFS Control Blocks

The MFS control blocks are defined by utility control statements written by the MFS user. The blocks are generated from these statements during execution of the MFS language utility program and loaded in the IMSVS.FORMAT library. This library must be online during IMS/VS operation. The process of defining the MFS control blocks is illustrated in FIG. 2-4.

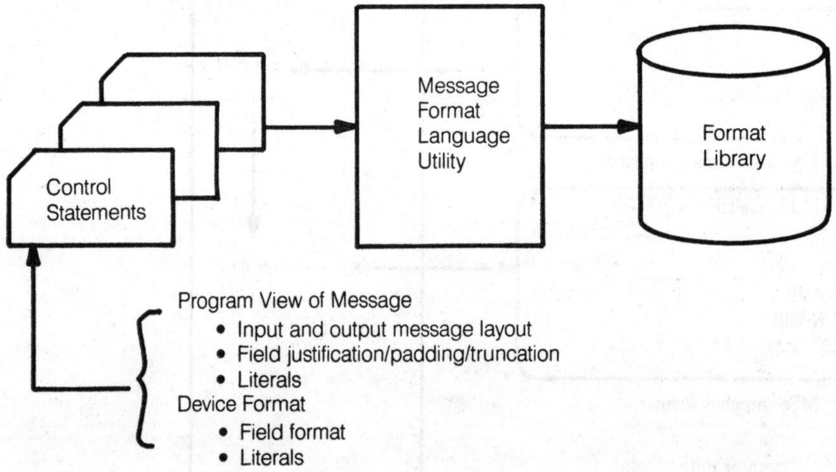

Fig. 2-4. MFS control block generation process.

The MFS utility control statements that define a screen format are called a format set.

The procedure to translate MFS utility control statements into control blocks is called a MFSTEST procedure. It is one of several supplied by IBM to translate format sets. A sample JCL to translate MFS format sets is provided in Appendix B.

A Sample MFS Format Set. FIGURES 2-5 and 2-6 illustrate the control statements of a MOD and DOF. These statements define the screen format of the example shown in the MFS Processing cycle of FIG. 2-3.

```
         MESSAGE OUTPUT DESCRIPTOR (MOD):

OUTMESG  MSG   TYPE=OUTPUT,SOR=(CUSTUP,IGNORE),NXT=INPMESG,OPT=1
         SEG
         MFLD  SOCNUM,LTH=09
         MFLD  LASTNM,LTH=20
         MFLD  FRSTNM,LTH=15
         MFLD  (TRANCD,'TRANS001'),LTH=08
         MSGEND
```

Fig. 2-5. MOD coding.

```
         DEVICE INPUT/OUTPUT FORMATS (DIF/DOF):

CUSTUP   FMT
         DEV   TYPE=(3270,2),FEAT=IGNORE       *** DEVICE TYPE ***
         DIV   TYPE=INOUT
         DPAGE CURSOR=((04,73))                *** CURSOR POSITION***
         DFLD  'CUSTOMER INQUIRY',POS=(02,29),LTH=16,                  *
               ATTR=(PROT,HI)
TRANCD   DFLD  POS=(04,05),LTH=08,ATTR=(MOD,PROT,NODISP)
         DFLD  'ACTION:',POS=(04,65)
ACTION   DFLD  POS=(04,73),LTH=01,ATTR=MOD
         DFLD  'ACCOUNT NO:',POS=(08,05)
ACCTNO   DFLD  POS=(08,17),LTH=08,ATTR=MOD
         DFLD  'LAST NAME:',POS=(09,05)
LASTNM   DFLD  POS=(09,17),LTH=20,ATTR=(MOD,PROT)
         DFLD  'FIRST NAME:',POS=(10,05)
FRSTNM   DFLD  POS=(10,17),LTH=15,ATTR=(MOD,PROT)
         DFLD  'SOC SEC NO:',POS=(11,05)
SOCNUM   DFLD  POS=(11,17),LTH=09,ATTR=(MOD,PROT)
         FMTEND
```

Fig. 2-6. DIF/DOF coding.

The MOD is used to tell IMS/VS the order of the output fields of data as they will appear in the application program's I-O area; the DOF is used to tell IMS where to display the data on the terminal.

The MODs are generated from specifications in the MSG, SEG and MFLD control statements. The DOFs are generated from specifications in the FMT, DEV, DIV, DPAGE and DFLD control statements.

Each MOD and DOF has a name that is referred to it. The MOD name is OUTMESG.

The MSG statement identifies the beginning of a message definition set and names the message input/output control block. In this example, it specifies that this MOD is used to output data to a terminal. The data is contained in four MFLD fields (message fields): SOCNUM, LASTNM, FRSTNM, and TRANCD. The length of each field is specified by the parameter LTH= on the right of each field name.

This MOD tells us that the next logical MFS message descriptor is INPMESG via the NXT= parameter. The SOR= (source) contains a pointer to a device output format named CUSTUP. The DOF name is CUSTUP. (Terminal type 3270, model 2 is being used.)

The IGNORE parameter tells IMS to bypass checking the device features for this device.

DIV TYPE=INOUT signifies that the same format is used for input and output.

The DPAGE parameter specifies where the cursor should be positioned after the format is written to the terminal, at line 4, column 73.

The field names and their lengths correspond with those specified in the MOD. The position of each field is specified in the POS parameter.

The DOF also tells IMS where to place the literals, such as 'CUSTOMER INQUIRY', 'ACTION', and 'ACCOUNT NUMBER', and how many spaces to allow for them.

The ATTR parameter defines the display attributes for each field, such as MOD(ified), PROT(ected), and NODISP(lay).

The MID and DIF are coded the same as the MOD and the DOF. (FIG. 2-7). They vary only as to function. Quite often, the MID and MOD are combined into one control block and the DIF and DOF into another. In this way, one pair of message format descriptors can be used for both input and output.

```
     MESSAGE INPUT DESCRIPTOR (MID):

INPMESG  MSG   TYPE=INPUT,SOR=CUSTUP,NXT=OUTMESG,OPT=1
         SEG
         MFLD  TRANCD,LTH=09               <=== TRANSACTION CODE + 1 FOR IMS
         MFLD  ACTION,LTH=01                    ACTION TO BE TAKEN
         MFLD  ACCTNO,LTH=08                    ACCOUNT NUMBER
         MSGEND
```

Fig. 2-7. MID coding. The MID name is INPMESG, it points to CUSTUP, the same format that OUTMESG points to.

A complete set of MFS coding for our example is given in FIG. 2-9. It shows that a complete MFS coding includes a device format definition set (DIF/DOF), an input message format definition set (MID), and an output message format definition set (MOD).

```
     CONTROL BLOCKS LINKAGE:

CUSTUP   FMT                                                     <=== DIF/DOF
         DEV   TYPE=(3270,2),FEAT=IGNORE
         DIV   TYPE=INOUT
         ...   ....
INPMESG  MSG   TYPE=INPUT,SOR=CUSTUP,NXT=OUTMESG,OPT=1           <=== MID
   ^     ...   ....                           |
   |__________________________________________|_____
                                              |    |
OUTMESG  MSG   TYPE=OUTPUT,SOR=(CUSTUP,IGNORE),NXT=INPMESG,OPT=1 <=== MOD
   ^     ...   ....                           |
   |__________________________________________|
```

Fig. 2-8. Control blocks linkage. For MFS to know which MID is associated with a particular DIF and which MOD is associated with a particular DOF, linkage has been established between corresponding control blocks. Here, both MID and MOD point to DIF/DOF CUSTUP via the SOR parameter, and the MID and MOD point to each other via the NXT parameter.

```
COLUMN
1--------10----16---------------------------------------------------72

         TITLE 'CUSTOMER INQUIRY'              *** TITLE ***
         PRINT NOGEN
CUSTUP   FMT
         DEV   TYPE=(3270,2),FEAT=IGNORE       *** DEVICE TYPE ***
         DIV   TYPE=INOUT
         DPAGE CURSOR=((04,73))                *** CURSOR POSITION***
         DFLD  'CUSTOMER INQUIRY',POS=(02,29),LTH=16,                  *
               ATTR=(PROT,HI)                                          ↑
TRANCD   DFLD  POS=(04,05),LTH=08,ATTR=(MOD,PROT,NODISP)         CONTINUATION
         DFLD  'ACTION:',POS=(04,65)
ACTION   DFLD  POS=(04,73),LTH=01,ATTR=MOD
         DFLD  'ACCOUNT NO:',POS=(08,05)
ACCTNO   DFLD  POS=(08,17),LTH=08,ATTR=MOD
         DFLD  'LAST NAME:',POS=(09,05)
LASTNM   DFLD  POS=(09,17),LTH=20,ATTR=(MOD,PROT)
         DFLD  'FIRST NAME:',POS=(10,05)
FRSTNM   DFLD  POS=(10,17),LTH=15,ATTR=(MOD,PROT)
         DFLD  'SOC SEC NO:',POS=(11,05)
SOCNUM   DFLD  POS=(11,17),LTH=09,ATTR=(MOD,PROT)
         FMTEND
*
INPMESG  MSG   TYPE=INPUT,SOR=CUSTUP,NXT=OUTMESG,OPT=1
         SEG
         MFLD  TRANCD,LTH=09              <=== MFLD NAMES CORRESPOND WITH
         MFLD  ACTION,LTH=01                   DFLD NAMES SPECIFIED IN THE DIF.
         MFLD  ACCTNO,LTH=08
         MSGEND
*
OUTMESG  MSG   TYPE=OUTPUT,SOR=(CUSTUP,IGNORE),NXT=INPMESG,OPT=1
         SEG
         MFLD  SOCNUM,LTH=09              <=== MFLD NAMES CORRESPOND WITH
         MFLD  LASTNM,LTH=20                   DFLD NAMES SPECIFIED IN THE DOF.
         MFLD  FRSTNM,LTH=15
         MFLD  (TRANCD,'TRANS001'),LTH=08
         MSGEND
         END
         THE ABOVE EXAMPLE SHOWS THAT A COMPLETE MFS CODING INCLUDES A DEVICE
         FORMAT DEFINITION SET (DIF/DOF), AN INPUT MESSAGE FORMAT DEFINITION
         SET (MID), AND AN OUTPUT MESSAGE FORMAT DEFINITION SET (MOD).
```

Fig. 2-9. Sample MFS coding.

SYNTAX FOR MFS CONTROL STATEMENTS

This section briefly describes the general syntax rules that apply to MFS control statements. The statements are written in assembler-like language and have the format shown in FIG. 2-10.

- Label — Identifies the statement. Starts in column 1 and may have from one to six characters for FMT statements. For other statements, may have up to eight characters. Must be followed by at least one blank.

```
COLUMN
1--------10----16-----------------------------------------------------72

LABEL    KEY   PARAMETER                    COMMENTS                   *
         WORD
```

Fig. 2-10. Control statement format.

- Keyword — Normally begins in column 10. Must be a valid MFS statement type.
- Parameters — Must be preceded by at least one blank after the statement keyword. Normally begins in column 16. May be in any sequence, and are separated by commas. Cannot go beyond column 71.
- Comments — Can be included in the MFS statements. They must be separated from the last parameter by one or more blanks. A comment card is created by placing an asterisk in column 1 of a card.

Continuation is indicated by placing a nonblank character in column 72. The continued statement must begin in column 16. There is no limit to the number of continuation lines.

MFS Language Utility

The MFS Language Utility consists of two types of control statements—definition statements and compilation statements.

The definition statements are used to define the device format control blocks, the message input/output control blocks, and the operator control table. You will learn how to code the MFS control blocks in this chapter. In chapter 7, we will code the operator control table.

The compilation statements are used to control the way the MFS language utility works. See Appendix A on how to use these statements.

Coding MFS Control Blocks

In this section, we will look briefly at the macros that are required to build the device format control blocks and the message input/output control blocks. For details not covered on this book, refer to IBM's "Message Format Service User's Guide."

Device Format Definition Set. There are 10 MFS source statement types which comprise the full statement set required to build the device format control blocks (DOFs and DIFs). These statements are listed in proper sequence in FIG. 2-11.

Each set of the device control block coding must contain one FMT statement and one FMTEND statement, at least one DEV statement, and one DFLD statement. The other statements are optional.

Message Format Set. There are eight MFS source statement types which comprise the full statement set required to build the message input/output control blocks (MIDs and MODs). These statements are listed in proper sequence in FIG. 2-12.

Statement	Description
FMT	Identifies the beginning of a format definition and names the device format control blocks.
DEV	Identifies the device type used.
DIF	Identifies the format as input/output or output only.
DPAGE	Sets initial cursor position
PPAGE	Identifies a group of logically related records that may be sent to a remote application program at one time.
DO	Requests iterative processing of the subsequent RCD and/or DFLD statement(s).
RCD	Identifies a group of related device fields that are sent to a remote application program as a single record.
DFLD	Defines the device field.
ENDDO	Terminates iterative processing of the previous RCD and/or DFLD statement(s).
FMTEND	Identifies the end of a format definition.

Fig. 2-11. Device format definition set.

Statement	Description
MSG	Identifies the beginning of a message definition set and names the message input/output control block. Specifies whether the control block is for input (MID) or output (MOD).
LPAGE	Identifies a related group fo segments/field definition.
[PASSWORD]	Identifies the fields in the message which constitute an IMS/VS password. This statement is optional and is used only for the MID.
SEG	Defines the beginning of each one of the message segments which make up the entire message.
DO	Requests iterative processing of subsequent MFLD statement(s).
MFLD	Defines the individual characteristics of each field in the message. Message fields are grouped together and form message segments which are defined by the SEG macro.
ENDDO	Terminates iterative processing of previous RCD and/or DFLD statement(s).
MSGEND	Identifies the end of a message definition.

Fig. 2-12. Message format definition set.

With the exception of the PASSWORD statement, the same statements used to create the MOD are exactly the same statements used to build the MID.

The SEG statement divides large input and output messages into segments. Within each group of SEG statements that define a message segment, you can code as many message fields (MFLDs) as you need to identify separate individual fields in the message. There is a one-to-one relationship between the individual MFLDs defined in the format set and the fields defined in the I-O areas of the COBOL program.

The SEG statement is required if multisegment message processing is required by the application program. Each installation has a specified queue buffer length for its online processing, and the length is the limit of the segment size. If the segment size of an input or output message does not exceed the defined queue buffer length, then the SEG statement can be omitted. In this case, MFS will consider the input and output message as a single segment.

The number of segments in an input message does not have to equal the number of segments of the associated output message.

Generally, the size of the output message is greater than that of the input message.

A detailed discussion of the major components of input and output message segments appears in chapter 3.

MFS AND THE APPLICATION PROGRAM

When a message processing program receives an input message from a terminal, the layout of the message as it is stored in the program's input area does not depend on the device characteristics of the terminal; it just depends on the *MFS options* specified for the program. Therefore, if the application program receives input messages which come from a different type of terminal, the program need not be modified to process it. MFS makes it possible for the application program to be independent of the physical device that sends the message.

MFS Control Blocks and Program Components

To use MFS control blocks, your application program must contain a data description and IMS calls that interface with the MIDs and the MODs. The components that the application program must include are

- The message I-O areas,
- The message queue calls, and
- The data area that specifies the name of the MOD.

This area defines the work area where messages are placed when they are received by the application program. It is also the place where messages are created before they are sent to the terminal. The message I-O area is coded in the Working Storage Section of the application program. An example of the message I-O area is shown in FIG. 2-3.

```
     MESSAGE INPUT DESCRIPTOR (MID):
     ---------------------------
INPMESG  MSG   TYPE=INPUT,SOR=CUSTUP,NXT=OUTMESG,OPT=1
         SEG
         MFLD  TRANCD,LTH=09                <=== TRANSACTION CODE + 1 FOR IMS
         MFLD  ACTION,LTH=01
         MFLD  ACCTNO,LTH=08
         MSGEND

     MESSAGE OUTPUT DESCRIPTOR (MOD):
     --------------------------------
OUTMESG  MSG   TYPE=OUTPUT,SOR=(CUSTUP,IGNORE),NXT=INPMESG,OPT=1
         SEG
         MFLD  SOCNUM,LTH=09
         MFLD  LASTNM,LTH=20
         MFLD  FRSTNM,LTH=15
         MSGEND
   --------

      WORKING-STORAGE SECTION.
       .....
     *
     *  INPUT MESSAGE AREA
     *
      01  INPUT-MESSAGE-AREA          PIC X(100).

      01  HEADER-SEGMENT REDEFINES INPUT-MESSAGE-AREA.
          05 HEADER-PREFIX.
             10 HEADER-LENGTH         PIC S999 COMP SYNC.
             10 FILLER                PIC X(2).
          05 HEADER-TEXT.
             10 TRANS-CODE            PIC X(8).
             10 FILLER                PIC X.
             10 ACTION-CODE           PIC X.
             10 ACCOUNT-NUMBER        PIC X(8).
       .....
     *
     *  OUTPUT MESSAGE AREA
     *
      01  OUTPUT-MESSAGE-AREA.
          05 PREFIX-1.
             10 RESP-1-LENGTH         PIC S999 COMP SYNC VALUE +0.
             10 RESP-1-ZZ             PIC S999 COMP SYNC VALUE +0.
          05 RESPONSE-1-TEXT.
             10 RESP-1-SSN            PIC X(9).
             10 RESP-1-LAST-NAME      PIC X(20).
             10 RESP-1-FIRST-NAME     PIC X(15).

         NOTE THAT THE FIELDS IN THE MESSAGE TEXT PORTION OF THE MESSAGE IO
         AREA CORRESPOND WITH THE FIELDS DEFINED IN THE MID AND MOD IN BOTH
         SIZE AND SEQUENCE.
```

Fig. 2-13. MID, MOD, and message I-O areas.

The MOD Name and the Application Program

The application program interfaces with MFS via the MOD name coded in the working storage section. This is an eight-byte field.

```
01 MOD-NAME   PIC  X(08) VALUE 'ERRORFMT'.
```

Let's look at an IMS/MFS call structure (FIG. 2-14). In this call, MOD-NAME is the parameter unique to MFS. The MOD name is also used in the terminal PCB.

During normal processing, the MOD name is specified by control block linkage via the MID, but there are cases when you will want to code the MOD name in the program. For example, you may want to display an error screen to warn the terminal operator of an error condition. This can be done by specifying the MOD name for the error screen. You can override the MOD name by issuing a first ISRT call of a message.

In conversational applications, the MOD name field is used to determine if the operator has cleared the formatted screen prior to entering data. When the operator presses the Clear key, IMS moves blanks to the MOD name field.

SUMMARY

MFS operates as an interface between the message queue and the terminal. By using the DIF, DOF, MID, and MOD control blocks, MFS allows the message processing program to process data without concern for the actual positioning of data on the terminal screen. MFS makes it possible for the application program to be independent of the physical device that sends the message. To be able to use MFS control blocks, the application program must contain message I-O areas which correspond with the fields defined in the MID and MOD in both size and sequence (FIG. 2-13).

```
       01 MOD-NAME                     PIC X(8) VALUE 'ERRORFMT'.


           CALL 'CBLTDLI' USING FUNCTION-CODE
                                TERMINAL-PCB,
                                MESSAGE-IO-AREA,
                                MOD-NAME.
```

Fig. 2-14. IMS/MFS call structure.

3

MFS Data-Mapping

In the last chapter, you learned that the input and output messages processed by MFS are formatted based on the MFS control blocks. You also learned that the message I-O area defined in the application program's data description does not depend on the device characteristics of the terminal but on the MFS options specified for the program.

This chapter deals with the various options that MFS uses to map input and output messages.

The format of the input message is based on the contents of the MID and the DIF. The MID defines how the data should be formatted for presentation to the MPP program and points to the DIF associated with the terminal device. The DIF describes the input data as it is received from the terminal.

The format of the output message is based on the contents of the MOD and the DOF. The MOD defines the output message content and, optionally, the literals that are considered part of the output message. The DOF describes the layout of the data fields to be displayed at the terminal.

There are three options which determine the formatting of input and output messages. Before studying these options, let's review the structure of the IMS/VS message.

TRANSACTION MESSAGE FORMAT

The online input message consists of one or more lines of data. Each line of the message is represented by a message segment. An input message may be considered as a sequence of one or more message segments. The length of the input segment is limited by the line or buffer size of the interfacing terminal.

The first segment in a message is called a *header segment*. The second and subsequent segments are called *trailer segments*.

FIGURE 3-1 illustrates two transactions as multisegment messages.

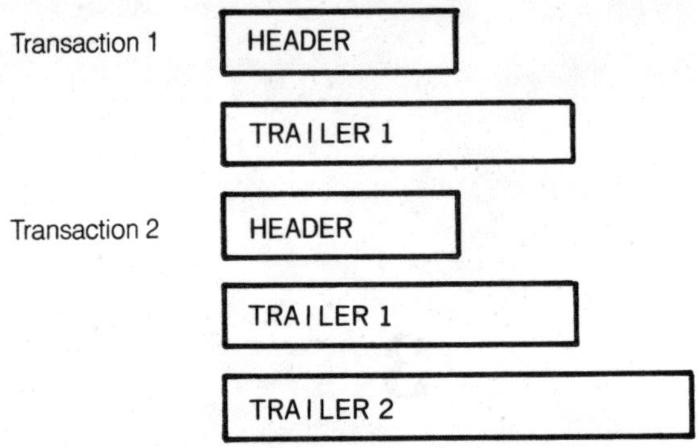

Fig. 3-1. Multisegment messages.

Editing Transaction Messages

Before a transaction is presented to the message processing program, it is edited by IMS/VS. All device-dependent and line-control characters are removed, and the segment text is left-justified.

When IMS/VS places a transaction on the message queue, it adds a message prefix and a segment prefix for each segment. A segment in a message cannot be longer than the LRECL of the long message queue data set defined at IMS/VS system definition.

Because of the processing overhead involved in editing each message segment by IMS/VS and the processing overhead by the application program each time it accesses the message queue, hold the number of segments in a message to a minimum. Single-segment messages should be used whenever possible.

Major Components of a Message Segment

FIGURE 3-2 illustrates the major components of a message segment.

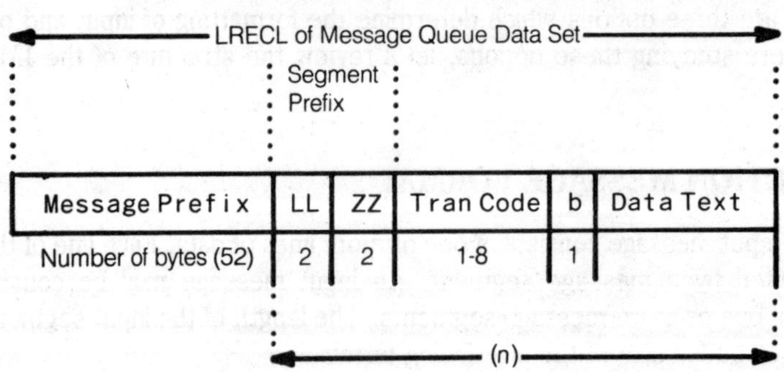

Fig. 3-2. IMS/VS message segment.

A message segment consists of three major components, as described below.

Message Prefix. The message prefix is created by IMS/VS and MFS. It contains the logical terminal name of the originating terminal and the information which uniquely identifies the message:

- The date and time of message arrival, and
- A sequence number (FIG. 3-3).

Fig. 3-3. Message segment prefix.

For the header segment, the size of the message prefix is 52 bytes. For trailer segments, the size of the message prefix is 16 bytes.

The message prefix is not accessible by the application program.

Segment Prefix. The segment prefix consists of two two-byte binary fields:

- LL defines the total length of the segment, including the segment prefix. This amounts to the length of the segment plus four. On input, this field is set by IMS. On output, this field is set by the application program.
- The ZZ field is reserved for IMS use. The individual bytes are referred to as Z1 and Z2. On input, this field is ignored and need not be initialized. On output, Z1 is used by DL/1 routines and is always set to binary zero.

See FIG. 3-4 for an example.

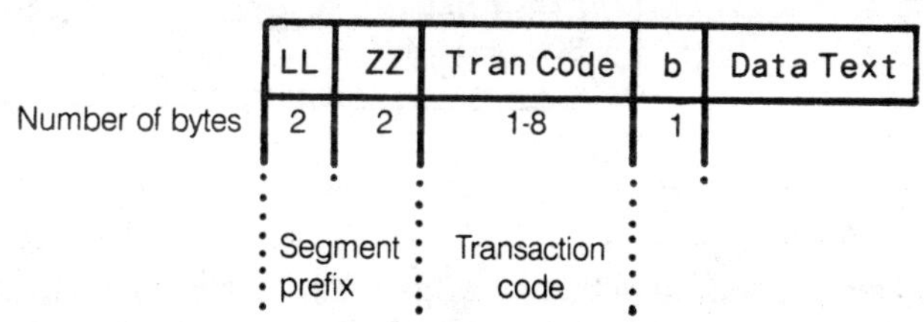

Fig. 3-4. Header segment.

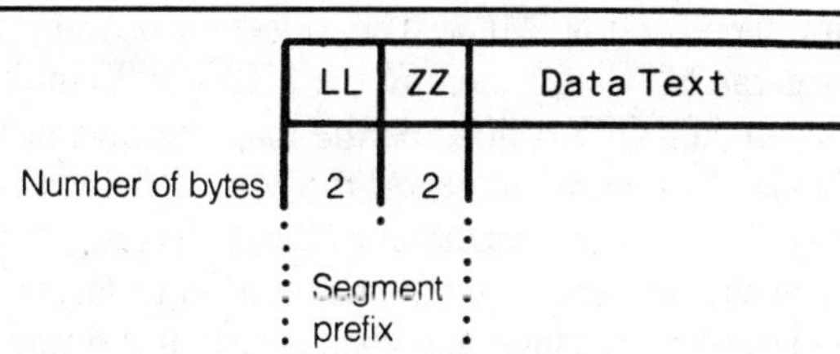

Fig. 3-5. Trailer segment.

Segment Text. This is the information which will be input to or from the application along with the LL and ZZ bytes.

The segment text of the header segment includes a transaction code (one to eight bytes). See FIG. 3-4 for an example. However, trailer segments do not include a transaction code (FIG. 3-5).

INPUT MESSAGE FORMATTING OPTIONS

For an example of a message segment, let's examine the request entered as shown in FIG. 3-6. The operator then enters account number 12345678 and the letter G in the

```
        CUSTOMER INQUIRY
:::::::::                              ACTION:_

ACCOUNT NO:       ____________________
LAST NAME:        ::::::::::::::::::::
FIRST NAME:       ::::::::::::::
SOC SEC NO:       :::::::::
```

Fig. 3-6.

```
        CUSTOMER INQUIRY
:::::::::                ACTION: G

ACCOUNT NO:      12345678
LAST NAME:       ::::::::::::::::::::
FIRST NAME:      ::::::::::::::
SOC SEC NO:      :::::::::
```

Fig. 3-7.

action field and presses the ENTER key (FIG. 3-7). The input message is edited by IMS/VS and is appended with a message prefix as shown in FIG. 3-8.

The order and length of the fields that make up the input message segment depend on the MFS option that the message processing program is using. Three formatting options are supported by MFS. The selection of the option is done via the OPT=n parameter in the MSG statement in the MID (OPT=n can be 1, 2, or 3, see FIG. 3-9).

The parameter OPT= governs the mapping between the DFLD and MFLD statements. It tells MFS how to interpret the MID definitions and to thereby format the data into message fields for presentation to the MPP program. The ZZ field in the message segment contains the option that is being used to format the message to and from the application program. If something goes wrong in the way IMS/VS returns the message to the program's I-O area, we can check the ZZ field to see if IMS/VS is using the correct formatting option. An X'00' in the ZZ field means that MFS did not format the message at all.

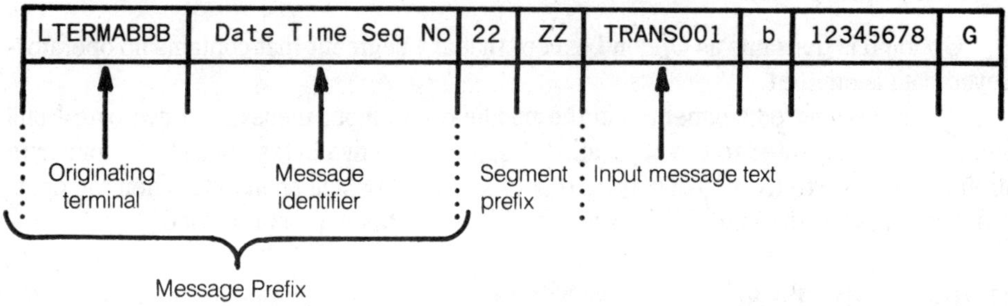

Fig. 3-8. Input data in message queue.

```
     MESSAGE INPUT DESCRIPTOR (MID):
     -------------------------------
INPMESG  MSG    TYPE=INPUT,SOR=CUSTUP,NXT=OUTMESG,OPT=1    <=== OPTION CAN BE
         SEG                                                    1, 2, OR 3
         .....
         MSGEND
```

Fig. 3-9. Input formatting options.

Option I (OPT = 1)

The effect of this option depends on whether or not a FILL = NULL character has been specified in the MFLD statement. FILL = NULL means "do not fill" with spaces.

- If no FILL = NULL character is specified, the input message segment retrieved will contain fields that are of a fixed length and fixed position. Any field not completely filled-in by the operator will be padded with spaces.
- If the FILL = NULL character is specified, compression on input will occur. The length of the input message segment will be shortened and the relative positions of the fields in the segments are altered (FIG. 3-10).

```
INPMESG  MSG    TYPE=INPUT,SOR=CUSTUP,NXT=OUTMESG,OPT=1
         SEG
         .....
         MFLD   NAME,LTH=25,JUST=L,FILL=NULL                 <====
         MSGEND
```

Fig. 3-10. Coding the FILL = NULL character.

In Option I, all segments defined in the MID will be presented to the application program. Segments may contain a combination of operator-keyed data, literals, or fills.

Option II (OPT = 2)

Option II is the same as Option I except that any segment that contains no operator-keyed data is omitted.

When the omitted segment is in the middle of the input message, a five-byte "null segment" is presented to the application program. The five bytes consist of a four-byte prefix plus one byte (X'3F') signifying that this is a pad or null segment. When the omitted segment is at the end of the message, a 'QD' status code is returned.

Option III (OPT = 3)

Option III supplies only the application program with the operator-keyed data and requires the application program to determine the field layouts dynamically. Literals are not mapped to the message queue. This means that the transaction code must be entered by the operator. The format of the message presented to the application program as mapped with Option III will look as in FIG. 3-11.

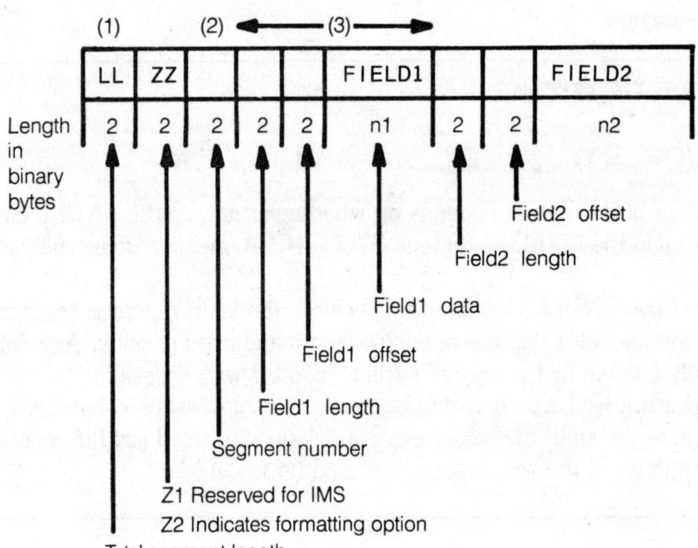

Fig. 3-11. Option 3. Field offsets.

1. The LL and ZZ fields are the same as in other options.
2. A segment in Option III is identified by its relative segment number, that is, what position in the message it occupies. This position is the sequential number of the SEG statement which identifies the segment being mapped. For the first SEG, this number has a value '01'. For the second SEG, this number has a value '02' and so on.

3. The data fields within a segment are identified by their:
   a. Field length, a two-byte binary number which defines the length of the total data field, including the field length and field offset subfields, i.e., field length equal n (data length) + 4.
   b. Offset count within the segment. The offset is a two-byte binary number which defines the relative offset from position 1 which is the first byte of the LL field.

An Example of Field Offsets. Let's examine the SEG statement in FIG. 3-12. In the above example, the ITEMNO field is defined in the MID to start in the fifth position of the third segment, or an offset of 4 from the first byte. DESCR is defined to start in the fifteenth position of the third segment, or an offset of 14 from the first byte.

Thus, the detailed layout of the third segment is as shown in FIG. 3-13.

```
INPMESG  MSG   TYPE=INPUT,SOR=FMT01C,NXT=CUSTIQ,OPT=3
         .....
         SEG                                  <=== THIRD SEGMENT IN MID DEFINITION
         MFLD  ITEMNO,LTH=10
         MFLD  DESCR,LTH=25
         .....
         MSGEND
```

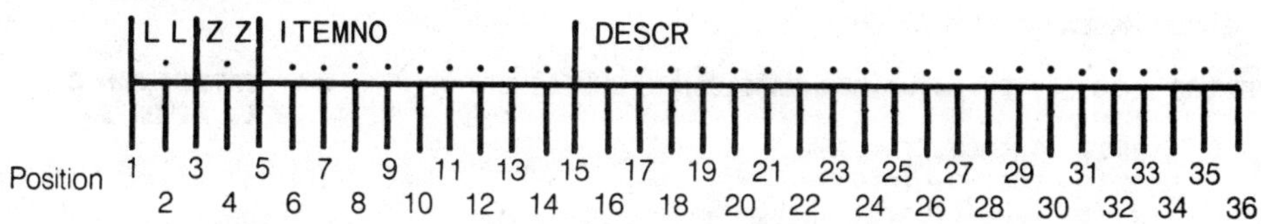

Fig. 3-12.

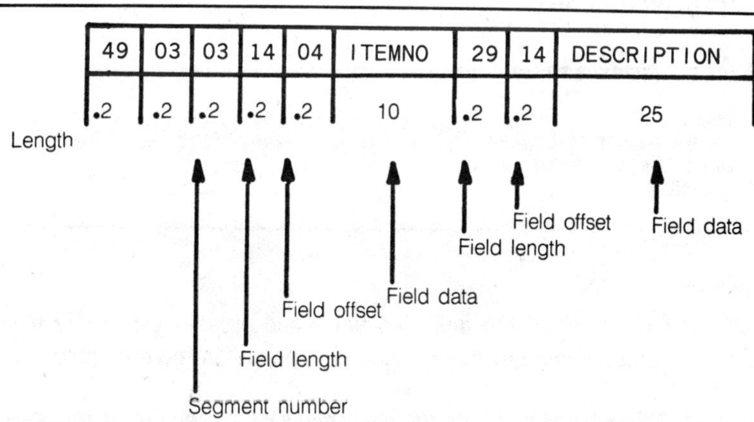

Fig. 3-13.

The following examples explain how each option works.

AN EXAMPLE WITHOUT A FILL=NULL CHARACTER

For a discussion of the MFS mapping options, we will use the CUSTOMER ENTRY screen in FIG. 3-14. Input message definitions of the MID appear in FIG. 3-15. As there are four SEG statements in the MID, the input message will consist of four segments (FIG. 3-16).

```
                         CUSTOMER ENTRY

:::::::::
CUSTOMER NO: __________
NAME: ______________________
ADDRESS: _______________________
CITY: ____________
STATE: _______             ZIP CODE: _________
ITEM NO: _____________     DESCR: _________________________
QUANTITY: ____________     DESTIN: ______________
```

Fig. 3-14.

```
    INPUT MESSAGE DEFINITION:

INPMESG  MSG   TYPE=INPUT,SOR=FMT01C,NXT=CUSTIQ,OPT=N        <=== OPTION CAN BE
         SEG                                                      1, 2, OR 3
         MFLD  TRANCD,LTH=09
         MFLD  CUSTNO,LTH=08
         MFLD  NAME,LTH=25
         SEG
         MFLD  ADDRESS,LTH=25
         MFLD  CITY,LTH=10
         MFLD  STATE,LTH=10
         MFLD  ZIPCODE,LTH=05
         SEG
         MFLD  ITEMNO,LTH=10
         MFLD  DESCR,LTH=25
         SEG
         MFLD  QUANTITY,LTH=10
         MFLD  DEST,LTH=10
         MSGEND
```

Fig. 3-15.

The operator has entered the indicated fields and presses the ENTER key (FIG. 3-16). The data to be presented to the application depends on the option selected in the MID (FIG. 3-18).

FIGURES 3-19 through 3-21 illustrate the input message placed on the message queue. The order and length of the fields that make up the input message segment depend on the MFS option that the message processing program is using.

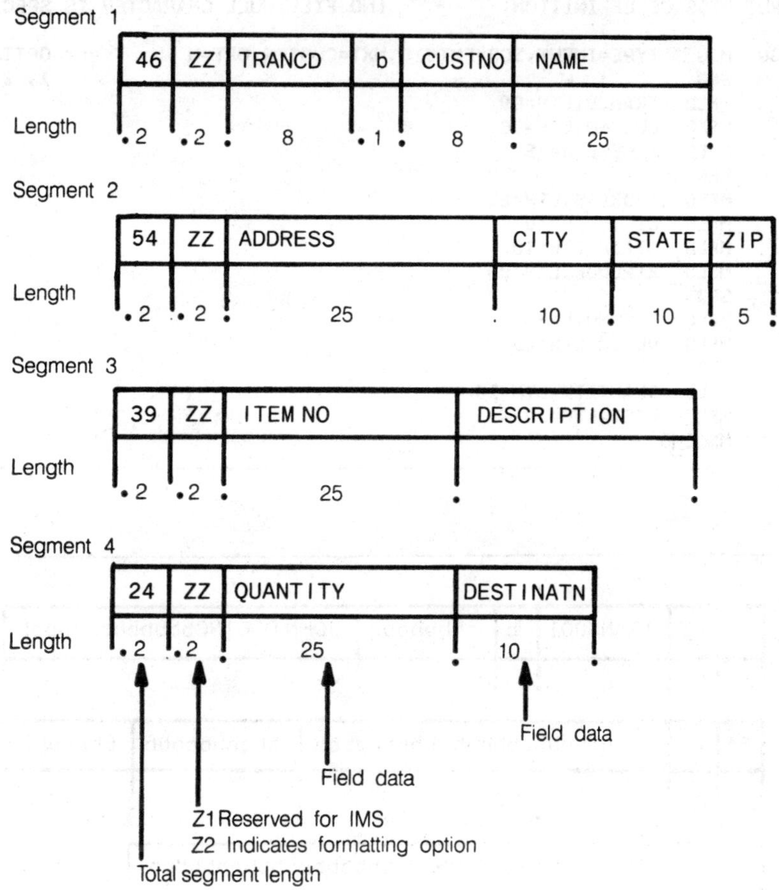

Fig. 3-16. Input message layout.

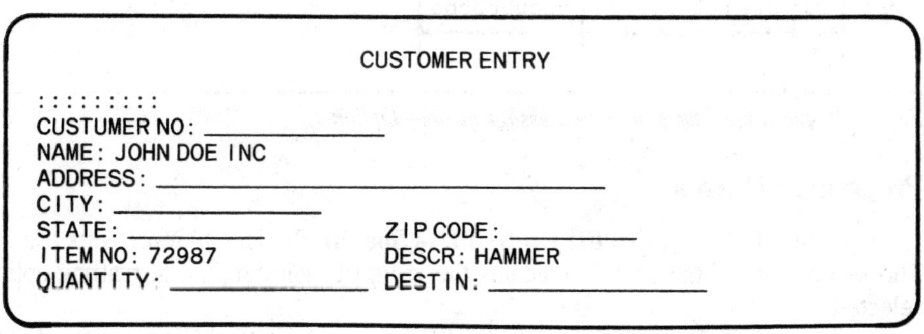

Fig. 3-17.

```
   INPUT MESSAGE DEFINITION:          (NO FILL=NULL CHARACTER IS SPECIFIED)

INPMESG  MSG   TYPE=INPUT,SOR=FMT01C,NXT=CUSTIQ,OPT=N       <=== OPTION CAN BE
         SEG                                                     1, 2, OR 3
         MFLD  TRANCD,LTH=09
         MFLD  CUSTNO,LTH=08
         MFLD  NAME,LTH=25
         SEG
         MFLD  ADDRESS,LTH=25
         MFLD  CITY,LTH=10
         MFLD  STATE,LTH=10
         MFLD  ZIPCODE,LTH=05
         SEG
         MFLD  ITEMNO,LTH=10
         MFLD  DESCR,LTH=25
         SEG
         MFLD  QUANTITY,LTH=10
         MFLD  DEST,LTH=10
         MSGEND
```

Fig. 3-18.

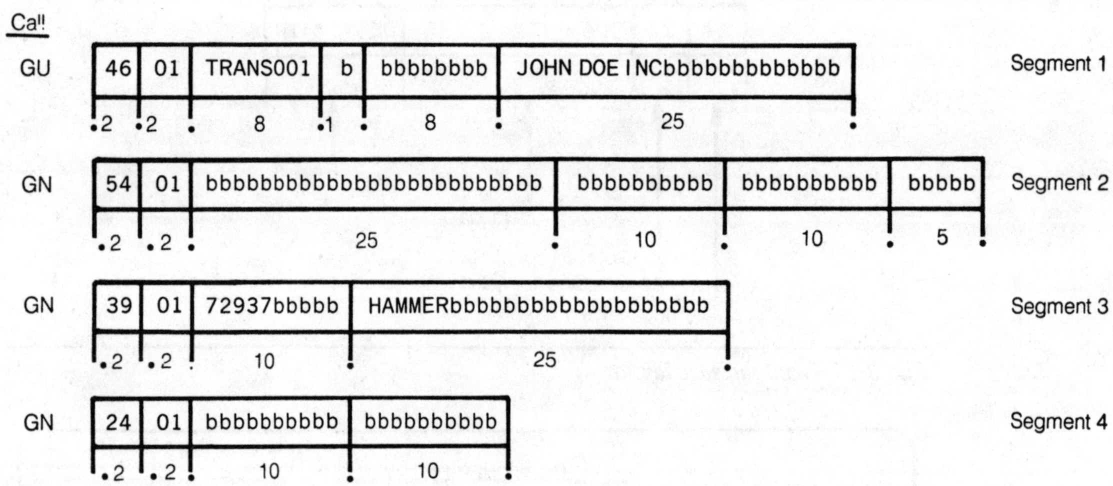

Fig. 3-19. Input message placed on message queue—Option I.

Program I = O Area

Option I (OPT = 1) (No FILL = NULL is Specified). The 'b' represents blanks. The second byte of the ZZ field contains the value 01 indicating the formatting option selected.

In Option I, all segments defined by the SEG statement in the MID are presented to the application program. This occurs whether or not data has been entered into a field and even when no data has been entered for the entire segment (SEGMENT 2).

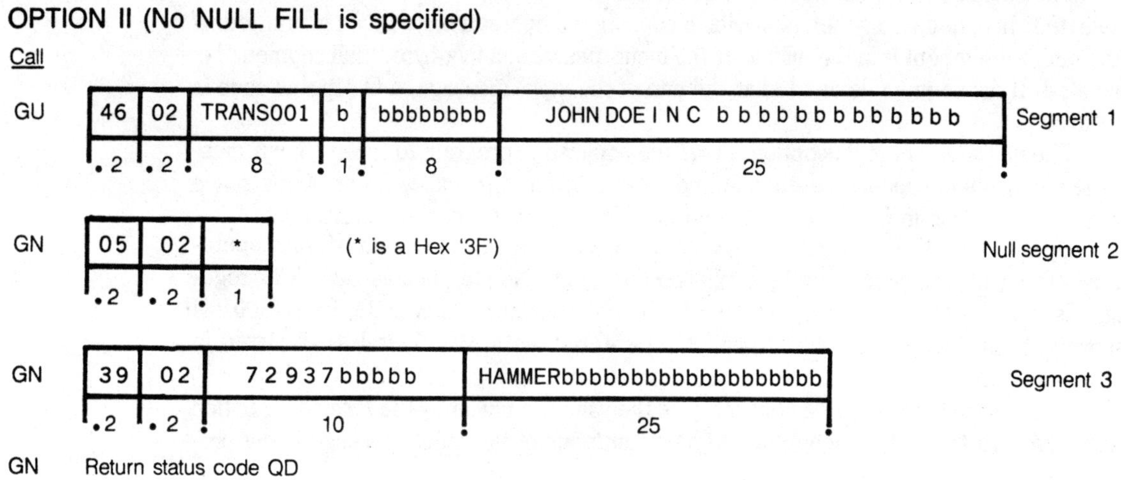

Fig. 3-20. Input message placed on message queue—Option II.

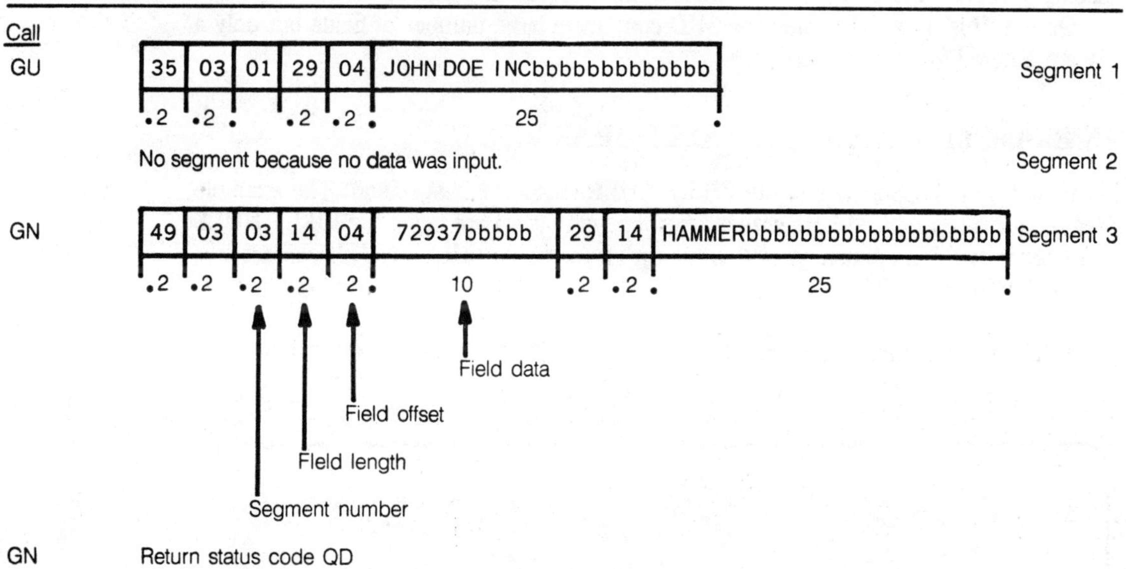

Fig. 3-21. Input message placed on message queue—Option III.

When should you use this option? It is commonly used for applications where data will be entered into most of the fields defined in the MID and the application requires fixed-format input.

One disadvantage of this option is that it maximizes message queue space requirements.

The second byte of the ZZ field contains the value 02 indicting the formatting option selected. In option II, any segment which contains no operator-keyed data is omitted. If the omitted segment is in the middle of the input message, a five-byte "null segment" is created. If the segment is omitted at the end of the input message, a QD status code is returned.

The null segment in this option allows the application program to receive input message segments in sequence even when no data is entered. It makes fewer queue space requirements than in Option I for segments which contain no device-entered data.

Option III (OPT = 3) (No FILL = NULL is Specified). In Option III, only operator-keyed data is presented to the application program. No literal data—default or regular—is mapped to the message queue. Note that the transaction code TRANS001 is missing from Segment 1 since it cannot be entered via a MID literal as occurred in Options I and II.

The second byte of the ZZ field contains the value 03 indicating the formatting option selected; bytes 5 and 6 contain the segment number of the input message being presented.

Each field is identified by its length and by its location in the segment as described in the MID, and each segment contains the segment number. Thus, missing fields and missing segments will present no problem to the application program.

Option III is best used when the MID contains a large number of fields but only a few are entered for any transaction.

AN EXAMPLE WITH A FILL = NULL CHARACTER

Let us see what happens when the FILL = NULL character is specified. The example used earlier is reproduced here with a difference in that we are using the FILL = NULL character in the MID definition (FIG. 3-22). In FIG. 3-23, the FILL = NULL character is specified wherein:

FILL = C'0'	means character zero fill
JUST = L	means left-justify

```
                         CUSTOMER ENTRY

:::::::::

CUSTOMER NO: ____________
NAME: JOHN DOE INC.
ADDRESS: ______________________________
CITY: ____________
STATE: ________           ZIPCODE: ____________
ITEM NO: 72937            DESCR: HAMMER
QUANTITY: _____________   DESTIN: WAREHOUSE
```

Fig. 3-22.

```
   INPUT MESSAGE DEFINITION:           (FILL=NULL CHARACTER IS SPECIFIED)

INPMESG  MSG   TYPE=INPUT,SOR=FMT01C,NXT=CUSTIQ,OPT=N          <=== OPTION CAN BE
         SEG                                                            1, 2, OR 3
         MFLD  TRANCD,LTH=09,JUST=L
         MFLD  CUSTNO,LTH=08,JUST=L
         MFLD  NAME,LTH=25,JUST=L,FILL=NULL                    <=== NULL FILL
         SEG
         MFLD  ADDRESS,LTH=25,JUST=L,FILL=NULL
         MFLD  CITY,LTH=10,JUST=L,FILL=NULL
         MFLD  STATE,LTH=10,JUST=L,FILL=NULL
         MFLD  ZIPCODE,LTH=05,JUST=L,FILL=NULL
         SEG
         MFLD  ITEMNO,LTH=10,JUST=R,FILL=C'0'                  <=== CHARACTER FILL
         MFLD  DESCR,LTH=25,JUST=L
         SEG
         MFLD  QUANTITY,LTH=10,JUST=R,FILL=NULL                <=== NULL FILL
         MFLD  DEST,LTH=10,JUST=L
         MSGEND
```

Fig. 3-23.

JUST=R	means right=justify
FILL=NULL	means do not fill; fields to the right of a missing field will shift to the left to fill the empty spaces

The FILL=NULL character is specified on a field-by-field basis.

The data to be presented to the application depends on the option selected. The order and length of the fields that make up the input message segment depend on the MFS option used by the message processing program.

FIGURES 3-24 through 3-26 illustrate the input message placed on the message queue.

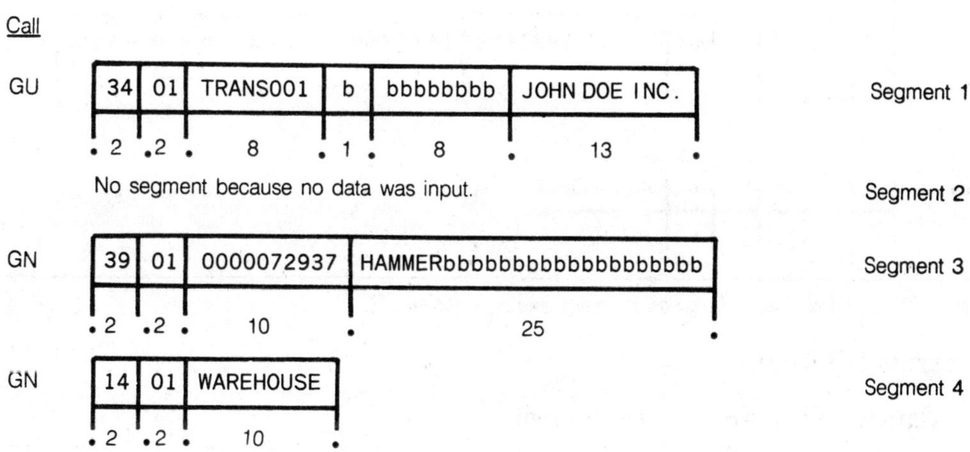

Fig. 3-24. Input message placed on message queue—Option I.

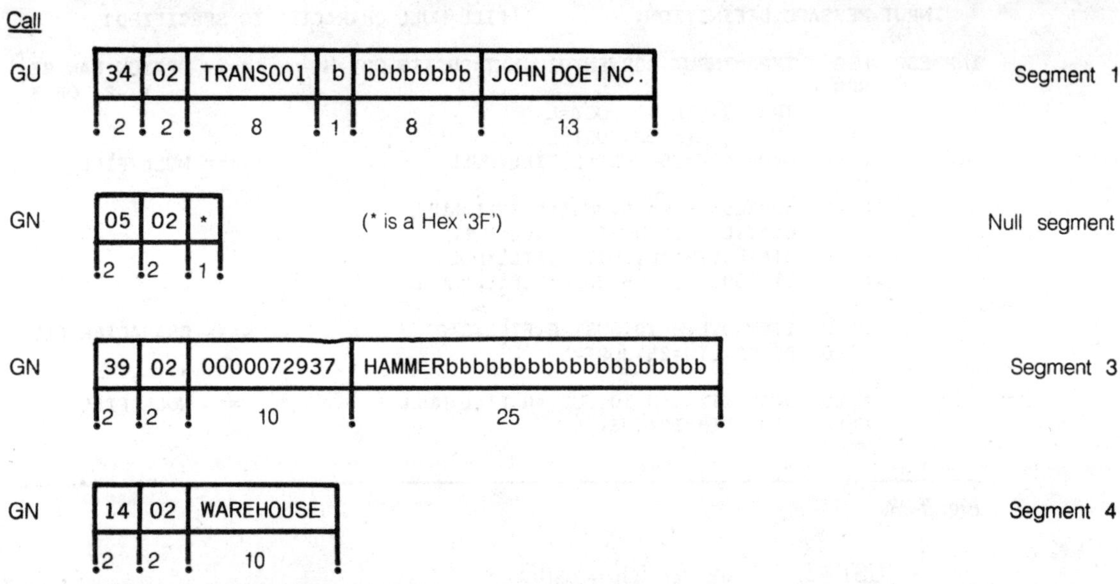

Fig. 3-25. Input message placed on message queue—Option II.

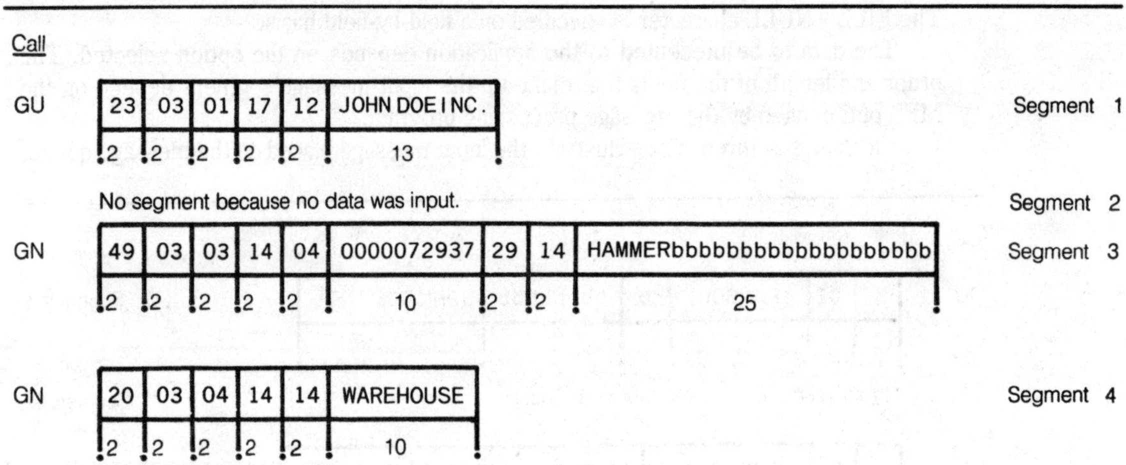

Fig. 3-26. Input message placed on message queue—Option III.

Program I-O Area

Option I (FILL = NULL is specified).

- **In Option I, a segment which contains all nulls—such as Segment 2—is not presented to the application program.**

- A field which has no FILL=NULL specified—such as CUSTNO in Segment 1—will not be compressed.
- The ITEMNO is right-justified and filled with zeroes because FILL=C'0' has been specified for this field.
- When a missing field is in the middle of a segment with FILL=NULL specified, such as in Segment 4, the message segment is compressed to the left by the missing data and the segment length is adjusted.

Option I is normally used to handle a situation in which there are a large number of variable-length fields in the input message. This will save message queue space.

Option II (OPT=2) (FILL=NULL is specified). Option II is the same as Option I except that a segment which contains all nulls, such as Segment 2, is presented to the application program as a five-byte null segment.

If you use Option II, your program will have to account for NULL segments. You can do this by checking the fifth byte in each segment. If it contains an X'3F' you know that you have a NULL segment. (A sample COBOL coding of the NULL segment will be given later in this chapter.)

Option III (OPT=3) (FILL=NULL is specified). In Option III fields with FILL=NULL have their lengths adjusted. Missing fields are not presented to the application program.

If the entire segment is omitted, it is not transmitted to the message I-O area. Since segments and fields may be omitted, we need some way to determine which segment or field we are dealing with. This is done by checking the field length and the field offset fields.

CODING THE NULL SEGMENT—A COBOL TECHNIQUE

You have learned that if segments in the middle of a message are to be omitted, you must specify a NULL segment. A NULL segment has a length of five bytes which consist of a four-byte prefix plus one X'3F' signifying that it is a pad or NULL segment. FIGURE 3-27 gives an example of coding a NULL character in COBOL. Note that NULL-CHARACTER is assigned a numeric value of 3. This is done to ensure that the compiler generates an "F" for the sign. The result is a field which contains a '3F'.

RETRIEVING INPUT MESSAGES

The MPP program uses two Get-Type calls to retrieve input messages from the message queue:

```
GU   GET UNIQUE
GN   GET NEXT
```

The retrieved message is placed in the input message I-O area defined in the call. The format of the call to retrieve an input is shown in FIG. 3-28.

```
         WORKING-STORAGE SECTION.

         01 NULL-CHARACTER.
            05 FILLER                    PIC 9    COMP-3 VALUE 3.

         01 LENGTH-1                     PIC 99   COMP   VALUE 0.
         01 LENGTH-2                     PIC 99   COMP   VALUE 0.

         01 MESSAGE.
            05 NAME-A.
               10 NAME-B                 OCCURS 20 PIC X.
            05 ADDRESS-A.
               10 ADDRESS-B              OCCURS 25 PIC X.

  *   ASSUME THAT ONE SEGMENT OF NAME AND ADDRESS IS TO BE OMITTED

         PROCEDURE DIVISION.
             .....
             MOVE 'JOHN DOE' TO NAME-A.
             MOVE 9 TO LENGTH-1.
             MOVE NULL-CHARACTER TO NAME-B (LENGTH-1).
             MOVE 4 TO LENGTH-2.
             MOVE NULL-CHARACTER TO ADDRESS-B (LENGTH-2).
             .....

    NOTE THAT THE NULL-CHARACTER IS ASSIGNED A NUMERIC VALUE 3. THIS IS
    DONE TO INSURE THAT THE COMPILER GENERATES AN 'F' FOR THE SIGN. THE
    RESULT IS A FIELD WHICH CONTAINS A '3F'.
```

Fig. 3-27.

```
                LINKAGE SECTION.
                    .....
                01  IO-PCB-MASK.
                    .....
                PROCEDURE DIVISION.
                    .....
           *    RETRIEVE MESSAGE FROM ORIGINAL TERMINAL

                      CALL 'CBLTDLI' USING FUNCTION
                                           IO-PCB-MASK
                                           INPUT-MESSAGE-AREA.
```

Fig. 3-28. Call to retrieve input message.

Retrieving the First Segment

The application program should always issue a GU call to the message queue as the first call. Why is this? Well, when IMS/VS schedules the MPP program, it transfers the first segment of the input message to the message processing region; thus, the message is already waiting. If the MPP program does not issue a GU call as the first call, IMS/VS has to transfer the message again and the efficiency provided by message priming is lost.

A status is returned for this call:

- A blank status code means that the GU call is successful
- A 'QC' status code means that there are no more segments to process

Retrieving Subsequent Segments

If the input message has more than one segment, we have to issue GN calls to retrieve subsequent segments of the message. IMS/VS returns one segment at a time to the program I-O area each time we issue a GN call until we have retrieved all the segments of the message. A 'QD' status code means that there are no more subsequent segments to process.

OUTPUT MESSAGE FORMATTING OPTIONS

Online output messages are segmented either automatically by MFS or under control of the message processing program. Output messages do not contain the transaction code: therefore, there is no distinction between the header and trailer segments. Output-message segments, like input-message segments, contain a four-byte segment prefix and a variable-length segment text (FIG. 3-29).

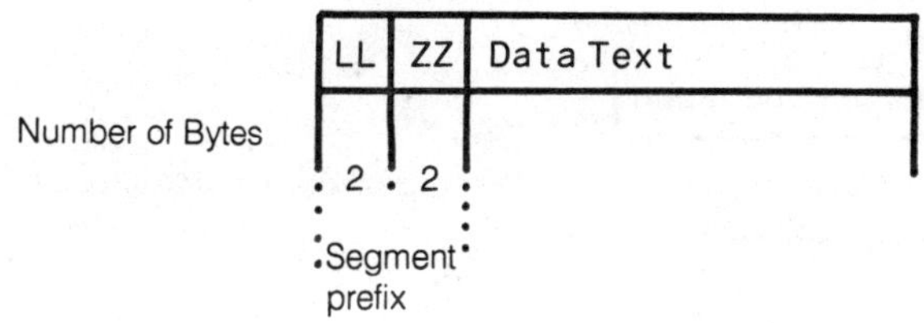

Fig. 3-29. Output-message segment format.

When building an output message, the message processing program has to deal with both the segment prefix and the segment data text:

- For the LL field (length field), the program must determine the length of the segment and add four.
- For the ZZ field, the program is responsible for loading it correctly.
- Z1 is reserved for IMS and is initialized to binary zero.
- Z2 is loaded according to the type of physical terminal receiving the output message.

For output messages, we can specify to MFS what it is to receive from the message processing program. The order and length of the fields that make up the output message depend on the MFS option that the program is using. Selection of the option is done via the OPT=n parameter in the MSG statement in the MOD. OPT=n can be 1, 2, or 3:

```
CUSTIQ  MSG        TYPE=OUTPUT,SOR=(FMT01C,IGNORE),NXT=INPMESG,OPT=1
        SEG
        ....
        MSGEND
```

The only difference with input messages is that the output messages do not contain the option number in the Z2 field.

Options I and II are identical for output mapping. For these, the output format is the same as for input messages. The application program presents all fields and all segments to MFS. All fields in output messages are of fixed lengths and fixed positions based on the structure specified in the MOD. This means that null segments with X'3F' in the fifth position must be inserted for segments with no data to be displayed, except if no more segments follow it.

For Option III, the message processing program submits only those segments and fields which contain data. The program does this by providing the segment number for each segment corresponding to the SEG statements in the MOD.

Each field is identified by its length and field offset. For any field not completely filled, the application program should place an X'3F' at the end of the significant data to tell MFS that there is no valid data to follow (FIG. 3-30).

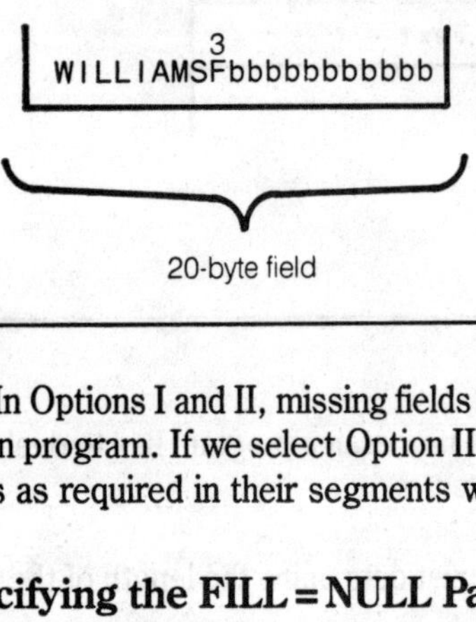

Fig. 3-30. Character X'3F' of a missing field.

In Options I and II, missing fields should have the first byte set to X'3F' by the application program. If we select Option III, the message processing programs will submit all fields as required in their segments with the position information.

Specifying the FILL=NULL Parameter On Output

On output, the FILL= parameter is specified in the MSG statement for the entire message, rather than on a field-by-field basis as on input:

```
OUTMESG  MSG       TYPE=OUTPUT,SOR=(FMT01B,IGNORE),NXT=INPMESG,OPT=1,
                   FILL=NULL
         SEG
         ....
         MSGEND
```

On output, FILL = NULL means that whatever is already in a field on the screen will not be erased. For example, if the name WILLIAMSBURG was displayed on the screen, and now a shorter name SMITH is sent to the terminal, the resulting name is SMITHAMSBURG (FIG. 3-31).

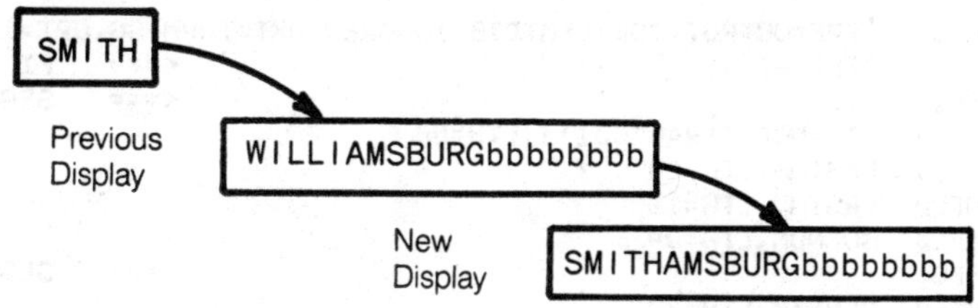

Fig. 3-31. Using FILL = NULL on output.

One way to overcome this problem is to use FILL = PT for output (PT = Program Tab). This will clear the remainder of the field on the screen to nulls if an X'3F' character follows the valid data in the program's output. If the first byte of a field is X'3F', MFS will skip that field.

```
OUTMESG MSG      TYPE=OUTPUT,SOR=(FMT01B,IGNORE),NXT=INPMESG,OPT=1,*
                 FILL=PT
        SEG
        ....
        MSGEND
```

OUTPUT MAPPING EXAMPLE WITH A FILL = PT CHARACTER

The following example will show the mapping of output by MFS when FILL = PT is specified. First we will examine the effects of Option I and then Option III.

Suppose that the following response is to be transmitted to the output message queue and that the message is to be displayed at the terminal as seen in FIG. 3-32.

```
WILLIAMS JOHN 99999999 11713 BASSWOOD DR NOWHERE MD 20708
```

Fig. 3-32.

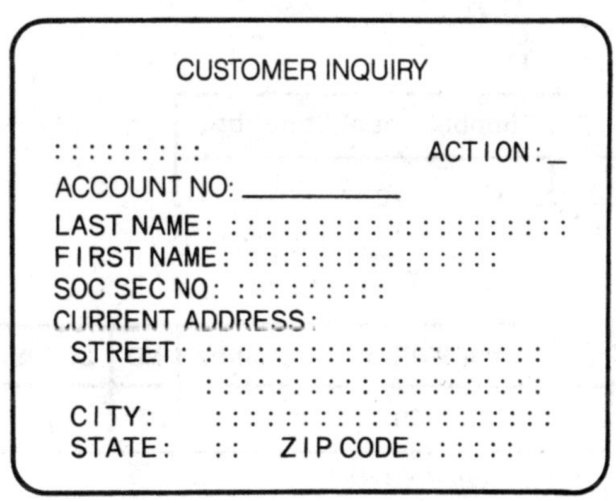

The message output definition for the message is given in FIG. 3-33 wherein the FILL=PT character is specified. According to the MOD in FIG. 3-33 the output message is segmented into four segments as shown in FIG. 3-34.

```
   OUTPUT MESSAGE DEFINITION:                (FILL=PT CHARACTER IS SPECIFIED)
OUTMESG  MSG    TYPE=OUTPUT,SOR=(FMT01B,IGNORE),NXT=INPMESG,OPT=1,        *
                FILL=PT                                 <===   FILL CHARACTER
         SEG                                            <===   SEGMENT 1
         MFLD   (TRANCD,'TRANS001'),LTH=08
         MFLD   LASTNM,LTH=20
         MFLD   FRSTNM,LTH=15
         MFLD   SOCNUM,LTH=09
         SEG                                            <===   SEGMENT 2
         MFLD   OLDSTR,LTH=20
         SEG                                            <===   SEGMENT 3
         MFLD   OLDST2,LTH=20
         SEG                                            <===   SEGMENT 4
         MFLD   OLDCTY,LTH=20
         MFLD   OLDSTA,LTH=02
         MFLD   OLDZIP,LTH=05
         MSGEND
```

Fig. 3-33.

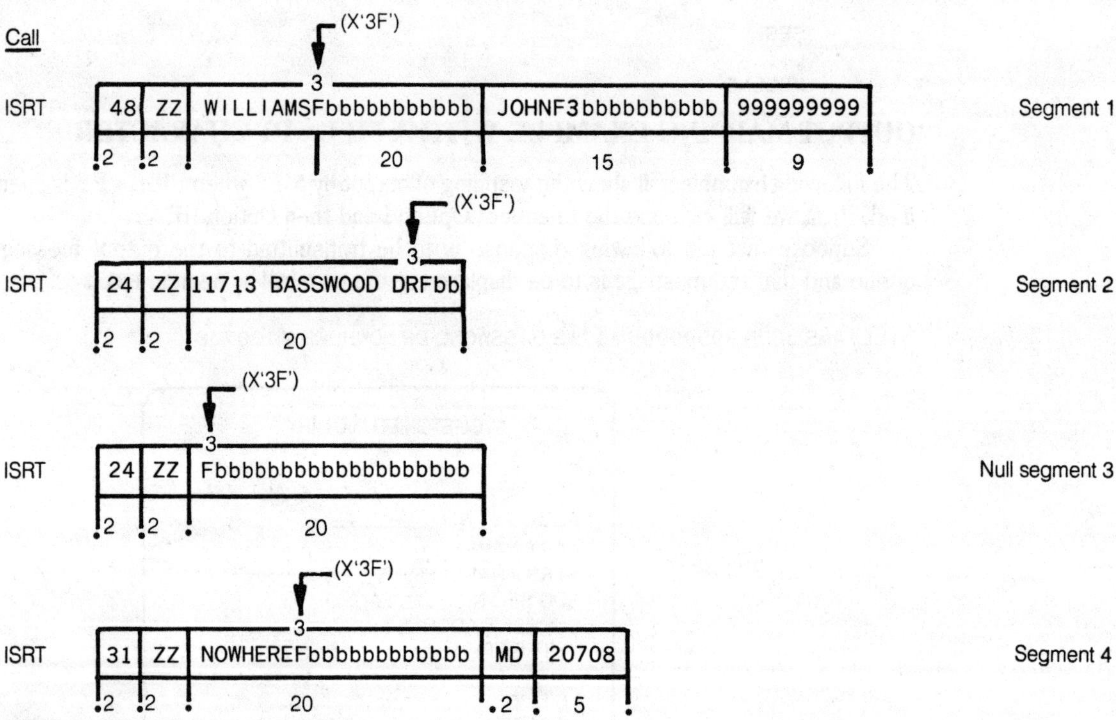

Fig. 3-34. Segmented Output message.

PROGRAM I-O AREA

Option I (OPT = 1) (FILL = PT is specified)

In Option I, all fields are of a fixed length and all four segments are presented to the MFS. Segment 3 is a null segment with an X'3F' in the fifth position. The application program will load the output message area one segment at a time.

The resulting display is shown in FIG. 3-35.

```
              CUSTOMER INQUIRY

:::::::::                        ACTION: _
ACCOUNT NO: ________
LAST NAME: WILLIAMS
FIRST NAME: JOHN
SOC SEC NO: 999999999
CURRENT ADDRESS:
 STREET: 11713 BASSWOOD DR
 CITY:        NOWHERE
 STATE:   MD   ZIP CODE: 20708
```

Fig. 3-35.

Option III (OPT = 3) (FILL = PT is specified)

In Option III (FIG. 3-36), the output field is shown exactly equal to the data contained in it. Character X'3F' is not valid for this option.

Option III with FILL = PT is the best choice if only a few of the specified fields are used for the output message.

SENDING OUTPUT MESSAGES

To send a message to the message queue, the MPP program issues an ISRT call using the IO-PCB. The message is transmitted from the message I-O area referenced in that call. The format of the call to send an output message is:

```
CALL 'CBLTDLI' USING ISRT
                     IO-PCB-MASK
                     OUTPUT-MESSAGE-AREA.
```

After each ISRT call, the related segment is loaded to the message queue. The next GU call will tell IMS/VS to take this response from the message queue and send it to the interfacing terminal.

USE OF CONTROL CHARACTERS

Instead of segmenting the output response, the MPP program can load the entire message into the message output area.

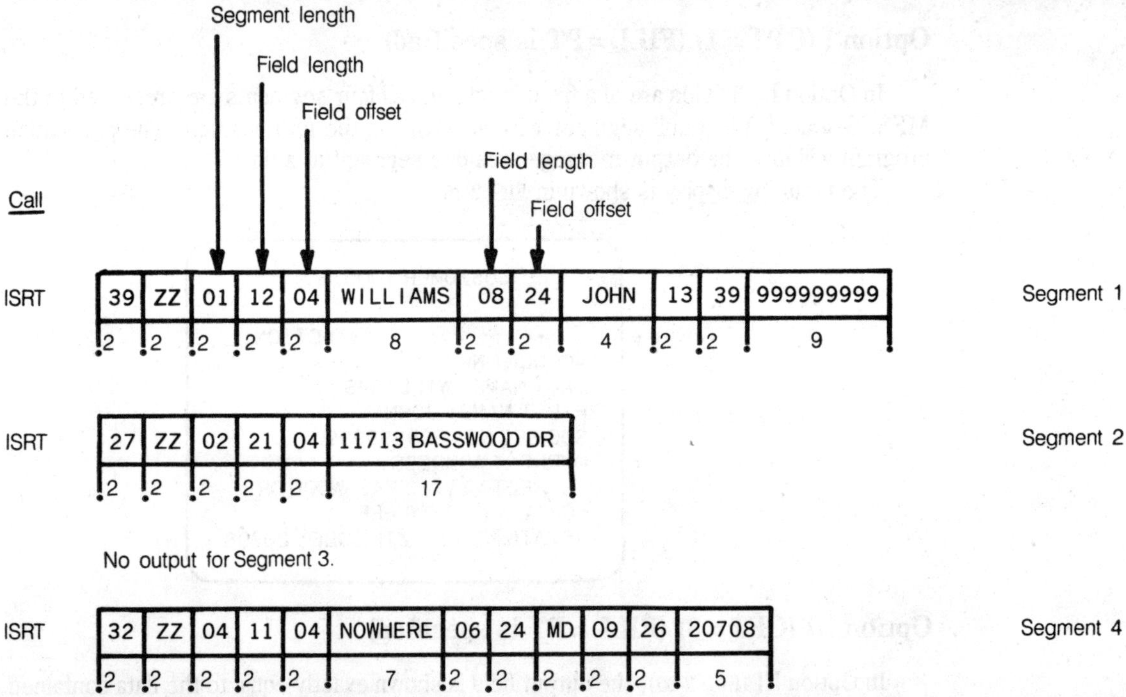

Fig. 3-36. Segmented Output message.

Let's assume that the receiving terminal has a line capacity of 45 characters. IMS would automatically segment the output response and display it on the terminal as shown in FIG. 3-37. This technique is efficient, but has the disadvantage that the output message is not divided into "logical" segments. We can overcome this problem by inserting the NL (new line) control character into the message text where a break is desired. This is shown in FIG. 3-38.

```
WILLIAMS JOHN 999999999 11713 BASSWOOD DR NOW
HERE MD 20708
```

Fig. 3-37. Output message segmented by IMS/VS.

The advantage of using the control character is that it requires only one ISRT call; the disadvantage is that it makes the application program device-dependent.

When considering this technique, consider the difference between device independence and program efficiency.

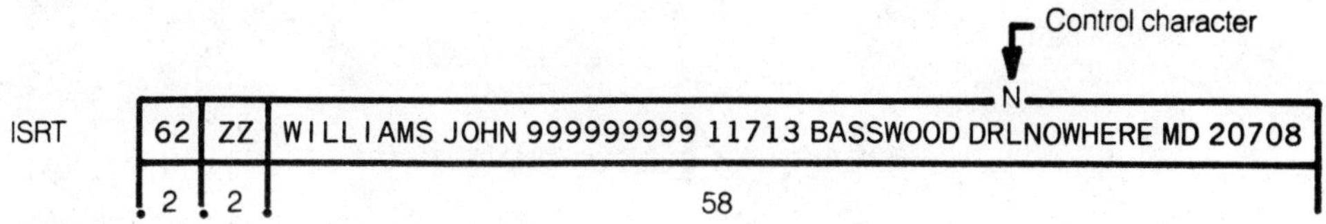

Fig. 3-38. Output message with control character.

The resulting display is shown in FIG. 3-39.

```
WILLIAMS JOHN 999999999  11713  BASSWOOD DR
NOW HERE  MD  20708
```

Fig. 3-39. Formatted output message.

HOW TO SELECT THE PROPER MFS OPTION

You have seen that mapping input and output messages depends on the MFS option specified via the OPT= parameter and on the use of the FILL= character.

Selection of the proper option for an application program is a design consideration based on

- How complex the input data is and how much it will vary
- The complexity of the application program
- The programming language used

Option I is the default and is the most-used option.

Option II may be desired as a performance factor if many segments are absent.

Option III has a significant impact on the application program when fields are added, deleted or changed during maintenance. This option can only be used in an application which uses a small amount of input and output data.

4

Message Processing Programming— COBOL Basics

This chapter is an introduction to the basics of COBOL programming in an IMS/VS data communication environment. First, we will describe the elements of the message processing program; then we will see how the application program interfaces to IMS. After that, we will concentrate on coding the linkage section, the input and output message areas, the DB/DC calls to retrieve input messages and to send output messages, and finally handling error conditions.

Once you understand message processing, we will put these elements together into a complete program.

MESSAGE PROCESSING PROGRAM STRUCTURE

This section describes the portions of the message processing program (MPP) which are required by IMS to support operations in the online mode. An MPP can be written in COBOL, PL/1, or Assembler language, but COBOL is the most-used host language for message processing programs. (All examples in this book are written in COBOL.)

FIGURE 4-1 illustrates a message-processing program. An MPP written in COBOL has four divisions:

1. IDENTIFICATION DIVISION
   ID DIVISION and PROGRAM ID are the only two required statements we need to specify in the IDENTIFICATION DIVISION.
2. ENVIRONMENT DIVISION
   ENVIRONMENT DIVISION is the only statement required in this division. The SELECT statement is not needed because—in the message processing program—the database manipulation is handled by the DL/1 database component; communication between the terminal devices and message processing program is handled by the data communication component of IMS/VS.

```
         IDENTIFICATION DIVISION.
         PROGRAM-ID. PROGRAM1.
         .....

         DATA DIVISION.

         WORKING-STORAGE SECTION.
         01  INPUT-MESSAGE-AREA.
             .....
         01  OUTPUT-MESSAGE-AREA.
             .....
         01  ACCOUNT-IO-AREA.
             .....
         01  IMS-CALL-FUNCTIONS.
             03  GU                           PIC X(4) VALUE 'GU  '.
             03  GN                           PIC X(4) VALUE 'GN  '.
             03  ISRT                         PIC X(4) VALUE 'ISRT'.
             .....
         01  ACCOUNT-SSA.
             .....
         01  ATTRIBUTE-VALUES.
             .....
         LINKAGE SECTION.
         01  IO-PCB-MASK.
             .....
         01  ALTERNATE-PCB-MASK.
             .....
         01  ACCOUNT-PCB-MASK.
             .....
         PROCEDURE DIVISION.

(1)          ENTRY 'DLITCBL' USING IO-PCB-MASK
                                   ALTERNATE-PCB-MASK
                                   ACCOUNT-PCB-MASK.

(2)    *   RETRIEVE MESSAGE FROM ORIGINAL TERMINAL
             CALL 'CBLTDLI' USING GU
                                  IO-PCB-MASK
                                  INPUT-MESSAGE-AREA.

(3)    *   CALL TO ACCESS ACCOUNT DATA BASE
             CALL 'CBLTDLI' USING GU
                                  ACCOUNT-PCB-MASK
                                  ACCOUNT-IO-AREA
                                  ACCOUNT-SSA.

(4)    *   BUILD OUTPUT MESSAGE
           .....
(5)    *   SEND MESSAGE TO ORIGINAL TERMINAL
                CALL 'CBLTDLI' USING ISRT
                                     IO-PCB-MASK
                                     OUTPUT-MESSAGE-AREA.
           .....
(6)    *   SEND MESSAGE TO ALTERNATE TERMINAL
                CALL 'CBLTDLI' USING ISRT
                                     ALTERNATE-PCB-MASK
                                     OUTPUT-MESSAGE-AREA.
           .....
               GOBACK.
```

Fig. 4-1. IMS message processing program.

3. DATA DIVISION
   The DATA DIVISION consists of two sections:

   - WORKING-STORAGE SECTION
   - LINKAGE SECTION

   In the WORKING-STORAGE SECTION, we have to define the following types of areas to be used by the PROCEDURE DIVISION:

   a) INPUT MESSAGE AREA
      This area is used to store the input message after it has been retrieved from the message queue.
   b) OUTPUT MESSAGE AREA
      This area is used to store the output message to be inserted in the receiving terminal.
   c) DATABASE SEGMENT LAYOUTS
      These layouts are used in the DL/1 calls as input-output areas to store retrieved segment occurrence(s) or those occurrences to be updated or added. Database segment layouts are normally set up as "copybook" members to be copied to the message processing program.
   d) IMS CALL FUNCTIONS
      These are the DL/1 call functions used by the message processing program.
   e) SEGMENT SEARCH ARGUMENTS
      The database segment search arguments are used in DL/1 calls to qualify the calls. SSAs are normally set up as copybook members to be copied to the program.
   f) ATTRIBUTE VALUES
      Attribute values are used in dynamic attribute-byte modifications during construction of the output message. The most-used attribute values are normally set up in a copybook member to be copied to the program.
   g) INTERMEDIATE WORKING STORAGE AREAS
      Other intermediate working storage areas to be used by the PROCEDURE DIVISION are placed in this area.

   In the LINKAGE SECTION, we define the following:

   h) IO-PCB MASK
      The IO-PCB is referenced in DL/1 calls which are used to retrieve transactions from sending terminals and to transmit responses to the originating logical terminal.
   i) ALTERNATE PCB MASK
      This is referenced in DL/1 calls which transmit responses to the alternate logical terminal.

j) DATABASE PCB MASK
The database PCB is referenced in DL/1 calls which communicate with the databases and which retrieve the segment occurrences.

4. PROCEDURE DIVISION
In the PROCEDURE DIVISION, we have to perform the following functions (FIG. 4-1):

a) Issue an ENTRY statement using all PCBs and PSBs set up for the program.
The ENTRY statement is the first executable statement in an IMS application program. It provides the linkage of the PCB masks to the PCBs. IMS passes control to the application program and supplies the addresses of the PCBs to be used by the application program via the ENTRY statement.
b) Get next input message.
The GU call directs IMS to retrieve a transaction from the message queue and to place it in the INPUT MESSAGE AREA. The status code returned on the call is checked by the application program to see if there are no more input messages in the message queue; if the processing limit has been reached, issue a GOBACK statement to end the program.
c) Retrieve a segment.
The GU call directs IMS to retrieve from the database the qualified segment in the SSA.
d) Build the output message.
Move the appropriate values into the length field of the OUTPUT MESSAGE AREA and the data to the data fields of the OUTPUT MESSAGE AREA.
e) Send the message to the originating terminal.
The ISRT call directs IMS to transmit the contents of the OUTPUT MESSAGE AREA to the output message queue for display on the originating logical terminal.
f) Send the message to the alternate terminal.
The ISRT call directs IMS to transmit the contents of the OUTPUT MESSAGE AREA to the output message queue for the alternate logical terminal.
g) GOBACK to retrieve the next message.
After having completed processing the previous transaction, we should repeat issuing a GU call to retrieve the next input message for processing. If a status code ('QC') is returned for this call, meaning that there are no more input messages to process, a GOBACK statement should be issued to terminate the message processing program.

INTERFACING THE APPLICATION PROGRAM TO IMS

Now, let's summarize the mechanism that allows the application program to interface to IMS.

The components of DL/1 and the PCBs work together to provide a communication link between IMS and the application program. This link is made possible through DL/1 by the PCBs, along with the ENTRY statement in the application program, its PCB masks, its calls to DL/1, the I-O areas, and the GOBACK statement. The relationship among the ENTRY statement, the PCB Mask, and the PCB control blocks is illustrated in FIG. 4-2.

1. IMS passes control to the application program and supplies the addresses of the PCBs to be used by the application program via the ENTRY statement. This statement is the first executable statement in an IMS application program.

   To access information in a PCB for an IMS database, the application program must contain a definition of that PCB; this definition is called the PCB-MASK which provides the application program with a logical view of a PCB control block.
2. FIGURE 4-2 illustrates the relationship among the ENTRY statement, the PCB-MASK, and the PCB control blocks. For each PCB specified in the PSB, there must be a corresponding PCB Mask specified in the application program's LINKAGE section.
3. This box lists the PSB control statements that define the application program's view of the database.

CODING THE LINKAGE SECTION

In this section, you will learn how to code the LINKAGE SECTION for a message processing program.

First, we will examine processing of the data communication PCBs, the difference between the I-O and the alternate PCBs, and their corresponding formats. Then, we will cover the format of the database PCBs and its processing, and finally coding of the LINKAGE SECTION.

Data Communication PCB Processing

Online programs use teleprocessing program communication blocks (PCBs) to communicate with the logical terminals. Similar to database PCBs which give the application program a degree of data independence, data communication PCBs give the message processing program a degree of physical terminal independence.

In the IMS/VS data communication environment, there are two types of PCBs used by the application program:

- Input-output PCBs representing the originating terminal
- Alternate PCBs representing the alternate terminal

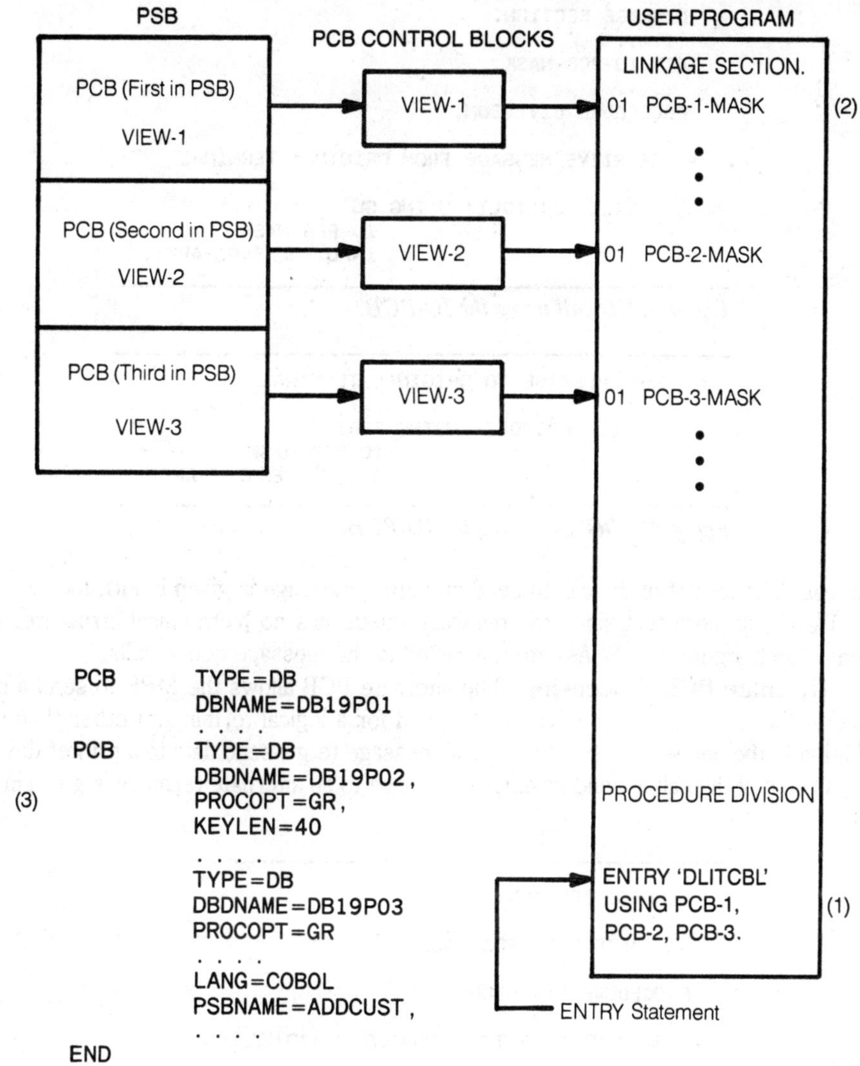

Fig. 4-2.

IO-PCB Processing. The IO-PCB allows the message processing program to retrieve input messages from and to transmit output messages to the message queue. There is one IO-PCB per message processing program.

To retrieve a message from the queue, the program issues a Get-Type call using the IO-PCB. The retrieved message is placed in the message I-O area defined in the call. The format of the call to retrieve an input message is given in FIG. 4-3.

To send a message to the message queue, the MPP program issues an ISRT call using the IO-PCB. The message is transmitted from the message I-O area referenced in

```
LINKAGE SECTION.
 .....
01  IO-PCB-MASK.
 .....
PROCEDURE DIVISION.
 .....
*  RETRIEVE MESSAGE FROM ORIGINAL TERMINAL

       CALL 'CBLTDLI' USING GU
                            IO-PCB-MASK
                            INPUT-MESSAGE-AREA.
```

Fig. 4-3. GU call using the IO-PCB.

```
*  SEND MESSAGE TO ORIGINAL TERMINAL

       CALL 'CBLTDLI' USING ISRT
                            IO-PCB-MASK
                            OUTPUT-MESSAGE-AREA.
```

Fig. 4-4. ISRT call using the IO-PCB.

that call. The format of the call to send an output message is given in FIG. 4-4..

We should note that since the message queue has no hierarchical structure, segment search arguments (SSAs) are not coded in the message queue calls.

Alternate PCB Processing. The alternate PCB allows the MPP to send a message to the message queue which is destined for a logical terminal(s) other than or in addition to the one which sent the original message (e.g., send data to a printer device). The format of the call to send an output message to an alternate terminal is given in FIG. 4-5.

```
LINKAGE SECTION.
 .....
01  ALTERNATE-PCB-MASK.
 .....
PROCEDURE DIVISION.
 .....
*  SEND MESSAGE TO ALTERNATE TERMINAL

       CALL 'CBLTDLI' USING ISRT
                            ALTERNATE-PCB-MASK
                            OUTPUT-MESSAGE-AREA.
```

Fig. 4-5. ISRT call using the alternate PCB.

Fixed and Modifiable Alternate PCBs. Fixed alternate PCBs contain the name of the logical terminal(s) with which they are interfacing. The name of the destination terminal assigned to the fixed alternate PCB cannot be changed. Whenever the MPP program issues a call with reference to that alternate PCB, the same destination will always be selected.

With a modifiable alternate PCB, a destination name is not assigned during PSBGEN. The MPP program will assign the destination name through the use of the CHNG call. FIGURE 4-6 shows an example of fixed alternate PCBs. The PSB lists two fixed alternate PCBs and one database PCB.

```
PCB     TYPE=TP,LTERM=LTERMA1                <=== ALTERNATE PCBS
PCB     TYPE=TP,LTERM=LTERMA2
PCB     TYPE=DB,DBDNAME=ACCOUNT....          <=== DATA BASE PCB
...     .....
...     .....
PSBGEN LANG=COBOL,PSBNAME=UPDATE
END
```

Fig. 4-6. Fixed alternate PCBs.

FIGURE 4-7 shows an example of a modifiable alternate PCB. For such PCBs, parameter MODIFY=YES is included in the PSB.

```
PCB     TYPE=TP,MODIFY=YES
PCB     TYPE=DB,DBDNAME=MASTER....
...     .....
...     .....
PSBGEN LANG=COBOL,PSBNAME=CHANGE
END
```

Fig. 4-7. Modifiable alternate PCB.

DATA COMMUNICATION PCB FORMATS

FIGURE 4-8 shows the formats of the I-O and alternate PCBs. The first three fields of the PCB are common to both the I-O and alternate PCB and the last four are unique to the IO-PCB.

1. Logical terminal name:
   Eight-bytes-long. For the IO-PCB, this field contains the logical terminal name of the originating terminal. For the alternate PCB, it contains the logical name of the destination terminal or the transaction code for a program-to-program message switch.
2. Reserved field:
   Two-bytes-long; reserved for IMS.
3. Status code:
   Two-bytes-long. This field indicates the result of a call. After each call to the message queue, IMS/VS places a status code in this area. If the call is successful, a blank status code is returned. If the call is unsuccessful, a nonblank status code is returned. This field should always be interrogated after each call by the application program.

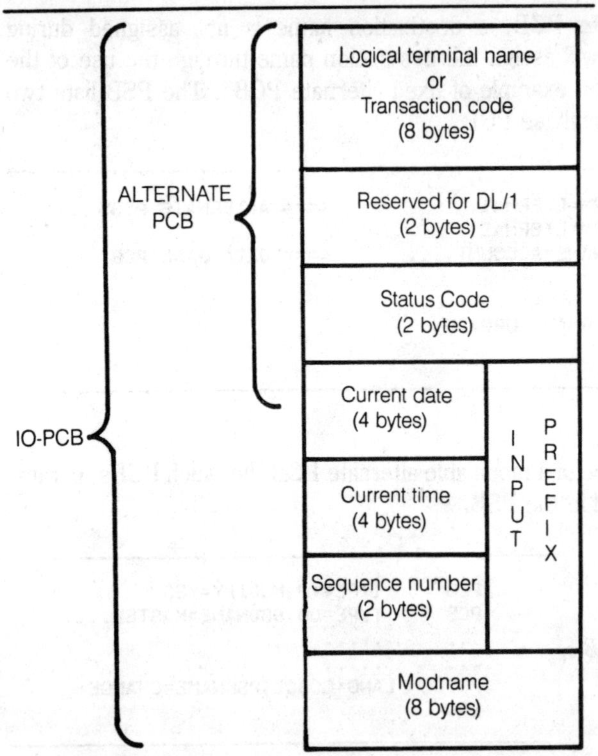

Fig. 4-8. Data communication PCB formats.

4. IO-PCB fields:
The next four fields are unique to the IO-PCB. The first three comprise the Input Prefix:

- Date: Julian date field (Format YYDDD) which indicates when a transaction is retrieved from the message queue. For example, if a message was received on the 365th day of 1986, then value '86365' is placed in this field.
- Time: Time at which the message was received (Format HHMMSS.S). For example, if the message was entered at 3:04:15.4 P.M., then value '150415.4' is placed in this field.
- Sequence Number: Automatically assigned by IMS.

The last field is used by the MFS.

- Message Output Descriptor field: Eight bytes long; contains the message output descriptor name (MODNAME) of the receiving terminal.

```
LINKAGE SECTION.

01  IO-PCB-MASK.
    05  ORIGIN-TERM-NAME              PIC X(8).
    05  IO-RESERVED                   PIC X(2).
    05  IO-STATUS-CODE                PIC X(2).
    05  IO-PREFIX.
        10 JULIAN-DATE                PIC S9(7) COMP-3.
        10 CURRENT-TIME               PIC S9(7) COMP-3.
        10 SEQUENCE-NO                PIC S9(7) COMP.
    05  IO-MODNAME                    PIC X(8).

01  ALTERNATE-PCB-MASK.
    05  ALT-TERM-NAME                 PIC X(8).
    05  ALT-RESERVED                  PIC X(2).
    05  ALT-STATUS-CODE               PIC X(2).
```

Fig. 4-9. Coding of data communication PCBs.

Coding of the I-O and alternate PCBs is given in FIG. 4-9. IO-PREFIX has been defined in terms of three fields: JULIAN-DATE, CURRENT-TIME, and SEQUENCE-NO. The SEQUENCE-NO is defined in binary format.

DATABASE PCB FORMAT

The database PCB is needed if it is referenced in the MPP program. One database PCB is required for each database referenced. For each database specified in the PSB, there must be a corresponding PCB mask specified in the LINKAGE SECTION.

FIGURE 4-10 shows the format of the database PCB.

The following fields comprise a PCB for a logical data structure from a database:

1. Name of database:
   First field in the PCB, and is eight-bytes long. It provides the DBD name from the library of database descriptions associated with a particular database.
2. Segment hierarchy level:
   DL/1 loads this area with the level number of the last segment encountered which satisfied a level of the call. This field is two-bytes long and is right-justified.
3. Status code:
   Two-bytes long; indicates the result of a call. After each call to the database, IMS places a status code in this call. If the call is successful, a blank status is returned. If the call is unsuccessful, a nonblank status is returned.
   This field should be interrogated after each call by the application program.
4. Processing options:
   This field is four-bytes long and is left-justified. It contains a character code which tells DL/1 the kinds of calls that can be used by the application program for processing data against this database. It gives the value coded in the PCB PROCOPT parameter.

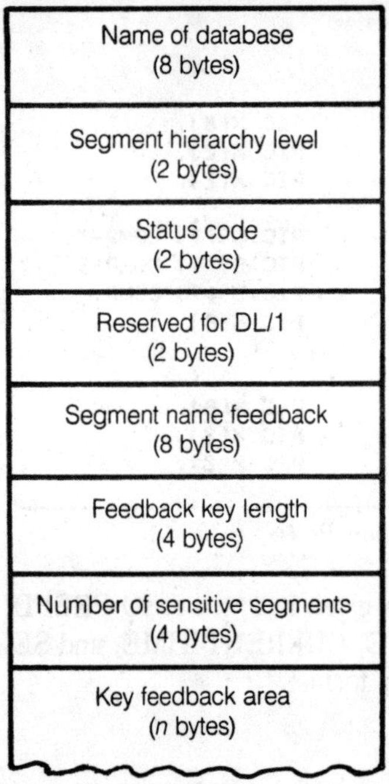

Fig. 4-10. Database PCB format.

The possible values for the processing are listed in FIG. 4-11.

5. Reserved for DL/1:
   This field is two-bytes long and is reserved for DL/1 for its own internal linkage related to an application program.
6. Segment name feedback area:
   This field is eight-bytes-long. It contains the name of the last segment encountered which satisfied a level of the call.
7. Length of key feedback area:
   This field is four-bytes long. It specifies the current active length of the key feedback area.
8. Number of sensitive segments:
   This field is four-bytes long. It specifies the number of segment types in the database to which the application program is sensitive. This would represent a count of the number of segments in the logical data structure viewed through this PCB.
9. Key feedback area:
   DL/1 places in this area the concatenated key of the last segment encountered which satisfied a level of the call. The key fields are positioned from left to right, beginning with the root segment key and following the hierarchical path. Keys for both key-sensitive and data-sensitive segments are placed in the key feedback area.

When a retrieve call is successful, the key of the requested segment and the key field of each segment along the path to the requested segment are concatenated and placed in this area. When a retrieve call is unsuccessful, the keys of all segments along the path to the requested segment for which the search was successful are concatenated and placed in this area (FIG. 4-12).

Processing Options	Description
G	Get Function
GO	Get Only (without integrity)
GOT	Get Only with retry
GON	Get Only; check for invalid pointers
I	Insert Function
R	Replace Function
D	Delete Function
A	All; includes G,I,R,D
P	Required when the D command code is used on a Get Type Call or Insert Call Function
E	Exclusive use of the database or segment; used in conjunction with G,I,R,D,A and L
L	Load Function for database loading (except HIDAM)
S	Segments in ascending sequence only; used in conjunction with G,I,R,D,A and L
GS	Get segments in ascending sequence only (HSAM only)
LS	Load segments in ascending sequence only (HIDAM,HDAM); required for HIDAM

Fig. 4-11. Processing options.

```
LINKAGE SECTION.
    .....
01  ACCOUNT-PCB-MASK.
    05  ACCT-DBD-NAME            PIC X(8).
    05  ACCT-SEG-LEVEL           PIC X(2).
    05  ACCT-STATUS-CODE         PIC X(2).
    05  ACCT-PROCESS-OPTIONS     PIC X(4).
    05  IMS-RESERVED             PIC S9(5) COMP.
    05  ACCT-SEG-NAME-FB         PIC X(8).
    05  ACCT-LENGTH-FB-KEY       PIC S9(5) COMP.
    05  ACCT-NBR-SENS-SEG        PIC S9(5) COMP.
    05  ACCT-KEY-FB-AREA         PIC X(8).
```

Fig. 4-12. Coding the data base PCB.

The application program contains a mask of the database PCB. All actual PCBs associated with the application program are contained in a program specification block (PSB) accessible only by IMS/VS. Normally, there is a one-to-one relationship between the PSBs and the application programs.

A PSB and the PCBs associated with it are created by a PSB generation-utility program. The result of a PSB generation is to place a compiled PSB in a library—the PSBLIB.

To access the DL/1 database, the MPP program issues a database call having the format of FIG. 4-13.

```
LINKAGE SECTION.
  .....
01  DATA-BASE-PCB-MASK.
  .....
PROCEDURE DIVISION.
  .....
*  CALL TO ACCESS DL/I DATA BASE

     CALL 'CBLTDLI' USING FUNCTION
                          DATA-BASE-PCB-MASK
                          SEGMENT-IO-AREA
                          SSA-1
                          SSA-2
                          .....
                          SSA-N.
```

Fig. 4-13. Call using database PCB.

Check the status code of each call. After each call is executed, IMS/VS loads the database PCBs with the results of the call. The MPP program should always interrogate the returned status code to see if the call was successful. A successful call always has a returned status code equal to spaces. (A sample coding of database calls is presented in FIG. 4-14).

```
WORKING-STORAGE SECTION.
  .....
01  ACCOUNT-SSA.
    03  ACCT-SEG-NAME              PIC X(8) VALUE 'ACCTMSTR'.
    03  ACCT-LEFT-PAREN            PIC X    VALUE '('.
    03  ACCT-KEY-NAME              PIC X(8) VALUE 'ACTNUMBR'.
    03  ACCT-OPRERATOR             PIC XX   VALUE ' ='.
    03  ACCT-KEY-VALUE             PIC X(8) VALUE SPACES.
    03  ACCT-RIGHT-PAREN           PIC X    VALUE ')'.

01  ACCOUNT-SSA-UNQUALIFIED        PIC X(9) VALUE 'ACCTMSTR '.

LINKAGE SECTION.
  .....
01  ACCOUNT-PCB-MASK.
    05  ACCT-DBD-NAME              PIC X(8).
    05  ACCT-SEG-LEVEL             PIC X(2).
    05  ACCT-STATUS-CODE           PIC X(2).
    05  ACCT-PROCESS-OPTIONS       PIC X(4).
    05  IMS-RESERVED               PIC S9(5) COMP.
```

Fig. 4-14. Sample coding of database calls.

Fig. 4-14. continued

```
           05  ACCT-SEG-NAME-FB         PIC X(8).
           05  ACCT-LENGTH-FB-KEY       PIC S9(5) COMP.
           05  ACCT-NBR-SENS-SEG        PIC S9(5) COMP.
           05  ACCT-KEY-FB-AREA         PIC X(8).

       PROCEDURE DIVISION.
        .....

      *  QUALIFY ACCOUNT SSA WITH ACCOUNT NUMBER FROM TERMINAL

           MOVE ACCOUNT-NUMBER TO ACCT-KEY-VALUE.
           CALL 'CBLTDLI' USING GU
                                ACCOUNT-PCB-MASK
                                ACCOUNT-IO-AREA
                                ACCOUNT-SSA.

           IF ACCT-STATUS-CODE EQUAL 'GE'
              PERFORM 900-ACCOUNT-NOT-FOUND.

           IF ACCT-STATUS-CODE NOT EQUAL SPACES
              PERFORM 2000-DB-ERROR-ROUTINE.
        .....
           CALL 'CBLTDLI' USING GHU
                                ACCOUNT-PCB-MASK
                                ACCOUNT-IO-AREA
                                ACCOUNT-SSA.
        .....

           CALL 'CBLTDLI' USING REPL
                                ACCOUNT-PCB-MASK
                                ACCOUNT-IO-AREA
                                ACCOUNT-SSA-UNQUALIFIED.
```

CODING THE LINKAGE SECTION

When coding the LINKAGE SECTION, there must be:

- One PCB-Mask for the IO-PCB
- One PCB-Mask for each alternate PCB
- One PCB-Mask for each database PCB

FIGURE 4-15 shows how to code the LINKAGE SECTION.

PCB-MASKS AND THE ENTRY STATEMENT

The ENTRY statement provides linkage between the PCB-Masks and the PCBs themselves. To provide proper linkage, the PCB-Masks must be listed in specific order:

- The IO-PCB-Mask must be listed first
- If there are more than one alternate PCB, these must be listed in the same order as listed in the PSB

```
LINKAGE SECTION.

01  IO-PCB-MASK.
    05  ORIGIN-TERM-NAME          PIC X(8).
    05  IO-RESERVED               PIC X(2).
    05  IO-STATUS-CODE            PIC X(2).
    05  IO-PREFIX.
        10 JULIAN-DATE            PIC S9(7) COMP-3.
        10 CURRENT-TIME           PIC S9(7) COMP-3.
        10 SEQUENCE-NO            PIC S9(7) COMP.
    05  IO-MODNAME                PIC X(8).

01  ALTERNATE-PCB-MASK.                               <=== REQUIRED IF THE
    05  ALT-TERM-NAME             PIC X(8).                MP PROGRAM SENDS
    05  ALT-RESERVED              PIC X(2).                RESPONSES TO
    05  ALT-STATUS-CODE           PIC X(2).                ALTERNATE TERMINALS

01  ACCOUNT-PCB-MASK.                                 <=== REQUIRED IF THE
    05  ACCT-DBD-NAME             PIC X(8).                MP PROGRAM
    05  ACCT-SEG-LEVEL            PIC X(2).                REFERENCES TO
    05  ACCT-STATUS-CODE          PIC X(2).                A DATA BASE.
    05  ACCT-PROCESS-OPTIONS      PIC X(4).
    05  IMS-RESERVED              PIC S9(5) COMP.
    05  ACCT-SEG-NAME-FB          PIC X(8).
    05  ACCT-LENGTH-FB-KEY        PIC S9(5) COMP.
    05  ACCT-NBR-SENS-SEG         PIC S9(5) COMP.
    05  ACCT-KEY-FB-AREA          PIC X(8).
```

Fig. 4-15. Coding the LINKAGE SECTION.

- If there are more than one database PCB, these must be listed in the same order as their PCBs are listed in the PSB

FIGURE 4-16 shows an example of a PSB (the PCBs are listed in the PSB). The PSB lists

- Two fixed alternate PCBs: LTERMA1 and LTERMA2
- One database PCB

Note that the IO-PCB is not listed in the PSB because it will be automatically included by IMS.

```
PCB      TYPE=TP,LTERM=LTERMA1                 <=== ALTERNATE PCBS
PCB      TYPE=TP,LTERM=LTERMA2
PCB      TYPE=DB,DBDNAME=ACCOUNT,PROCOPT=A,KEYLEN=125  <=== DATA BASE
SENSEG   NAME=ACCTMSTR,PARENT=0                             PCB
...      .....
PSBGEN LANG=COBOL,PSBNAME=UPDATE
END
```

Fig. 4-16. A sample PSB.

Each PCB-Mask defined in the LINKAGE SECTION must be listed in the ENTRY statement of the PROCEDURE DIVISION. FIGURE 4-17 shows how to code the ENTRY statement.

```
PROCEDURE DIVISION.

    ENTRY 'DLITCBL' USING IO-PCB-MASK
                          ALTERNATE-PCB-MASK
                          ACCOUNT-PCB-MASK.
```

Fig. 4-17. The ENTRY statement.

CODING INPUT AND OUTPUT MESSAGE AREAS

You learned in chapter 3 that the order and length of the input and output message segments depend on the message input descriptor (MID), the message output descriptor (MOD), and the formatting option that the message processing program (MPP) is using.

To learn how to code the input and output message areas, let's examine the data entry in FIG. 4-18. The input message definition of the screen format is given in FIG. 4-19.

```
                       CUSTOMER ADDRESS CHANGE
::::::::                                                  ACTION:_

ACCOUNT NO: ____________                   SOC SEC NO: :::::::::
LAST NAME: ::::::::::::::::::::            FIRST NAME: :::::::::::::::
        CURRENT ADDRESS:
              STREET: ::::::::::::::::::::
                      ::::::::::::::::::::
              CITY:   ::::::::::::::::::::
              STATE: :: ZIP CODE: :::::
        NEW ADDRESS:
              STREET:   ____________________
                        ____________________
              CITY:     ____________________
              STATE:    _____      ZIP CODE: _____
::::::::::::::::::::::::::::::::::::::::::::::::::::::::::::::::::
```

Fig. 4-18.

MFS may break a single-segment input message into a multisegment input message either to fit the message queue size or for programming convenience (FIG. 4-20).

So, we have given two input message definitions of the same screen format—the first has only one segment, and the second one has two segments.

Now, the operator would like to enter address changes for a customer holding Account No. 123456768. The number is given as input to the MPP which retrieves current customer data from the database and displays it on the terminal screen. New address fields are blanked out, ready for the operator to enter new data (FIG. 4-21). The operator reviews the displayed data and enters a new address and the letter "U" in the Action field (meaning to update) and presses the ENTER key (FIG. 4-22).

```
INPMESG  MSG    TYPE=INPUT,SOR=CUSTUP,NXT=OUTMESG,OPT=1
         SEG
         MFLD   TRANCD,LTH=09                         <==== SINGLE-SEGMENT
         MFLD   ACCTNO,LTH=08                               INPUT MESSAGE
         MFLD   ACTION,LTH=01
         MFLD   NEWSTR,LTH=20
         MFLD   NEWST2,LTH=20
         MFLD   NEWCTY,LTH=20
         MFLD   NEWSTA,LTH=02
         MFLD   NEWZIP,LTH=05,JUST=R,FILL=C'*'
         MSGEND
```

Fig. 4-19. Single-segment input message definition.

```
INPMESG  MSG    TYPE=INPUT,SOR=CUSTUP,NXT=OUTMESG,OPT=1
         SEG
         MFLD   TRANCD,LTH=09                         <==== SEGMENT 1
         MFLD   ACCTNO,LTH=08
         MFLD   ACTION,LTH=01
         SEG
         MFLD   NEWSTR,LTH=20                         <==== SEGMENT 2
         MFLD   NEWST2,LTH=20
         MFLD   NEWCTY,LTH=20
         MFLD   NEWSTA,LTH=02
         MFLD   NEWZIP,LTH=05,JUST=R,FILL=C'*'
         MSGEND
```

Fig. 4-20. Multisegment input message definition.

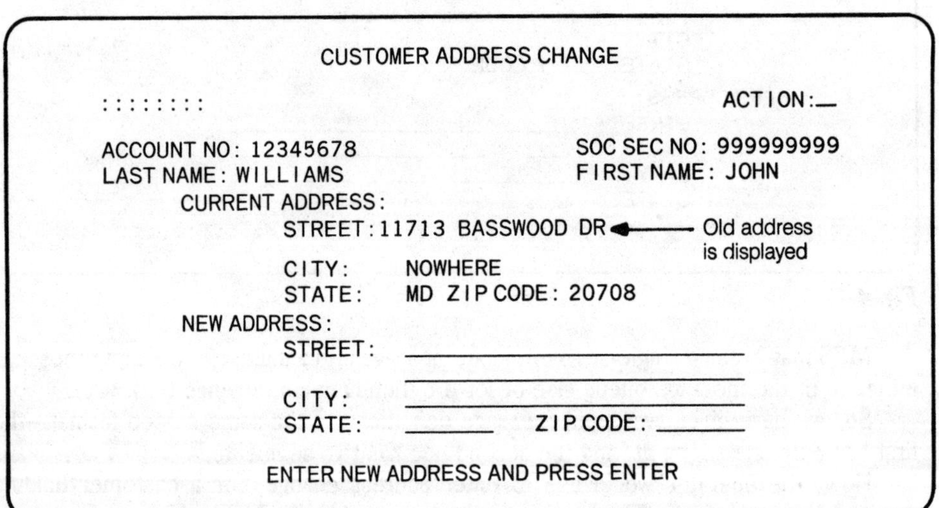

Fig. 4-21.

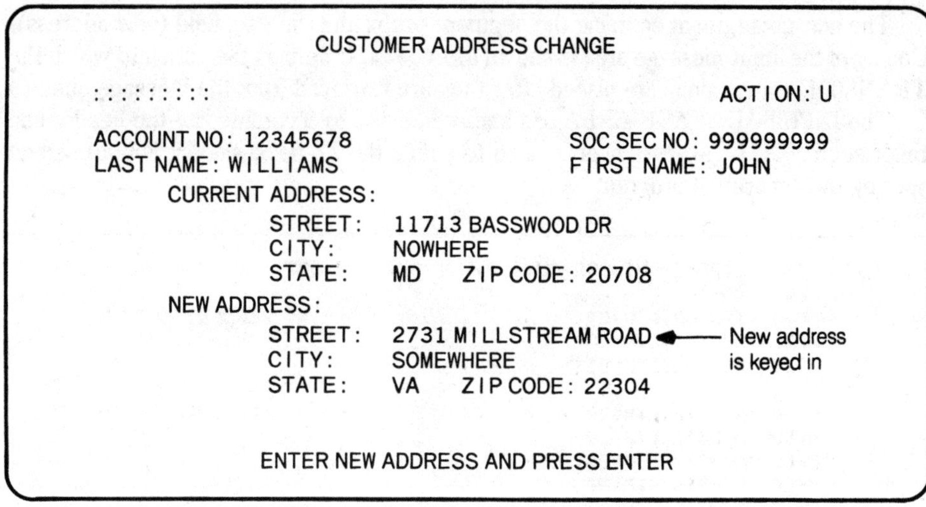

Fig. 4-22.

Based on the MID definition given in FIG. 4-23, the input message is segmented by MFS into two segments.

The header segment is appended with a message prefix—Transaction Code 'TRANS001'—the account number, and the action code.

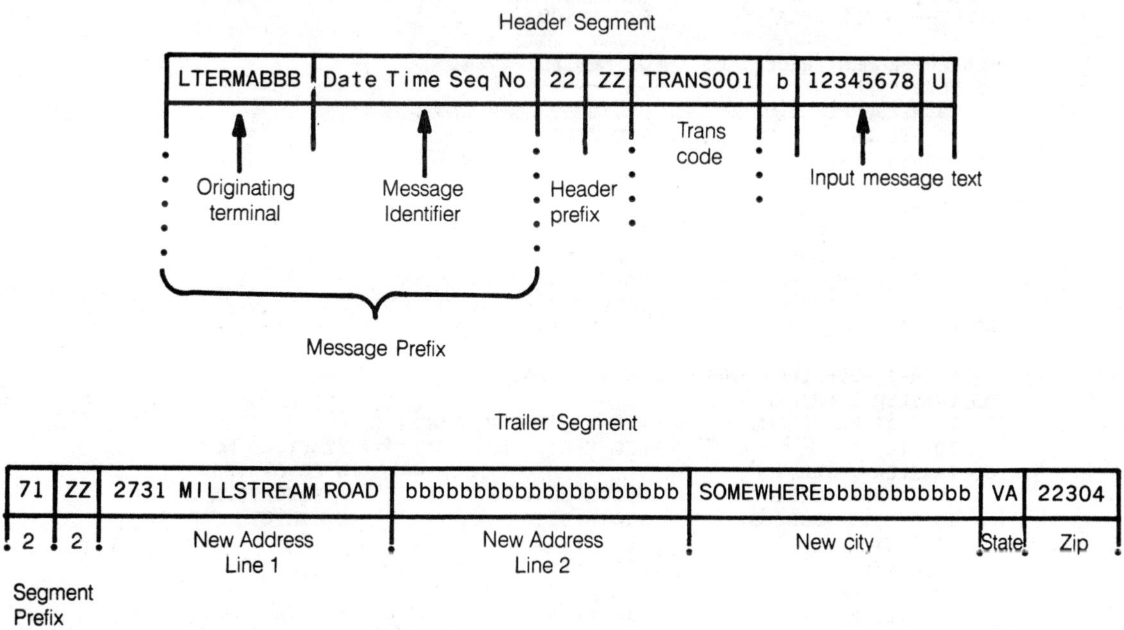

Fig. 4-23. Input data in message queue.

The second segment contains the segment prefix and the data field (new address). (Coding of the input message area is shown in FIG. 4-24. It defines the area into which the 'TRANS001' transactions are placed after they are retrieved from the message queue.)

The INPUT-MESSAGE-AREA has been redefined to accommodate the header and trailer segments. A two-byte filler is used to define the ZZ field, since it is not used on input by the application program.

```
INPMESG  MSG   TYPE=INPUT,SOR=CUSTUP,NXT=OUTMESG,OPT=1
         SEG
         MFLD  TRANCD,LTH=09                          <==== SEGMENT 1
         MFLD  ACCTNO,LTH=08
         MFLD  ACTION,LTH=01
         SEG
         MFLD  NEWSTR,LTH=20                          <==== SEGMENT 2
         MFLD  NEWST2,LTH=20
         MFLD  NEWCTY,LTH=20
         MFLD  NEWSTA,LTH=02
         MFLD  NEWZIP,LTH=05,JUST=R,FILL=C'*'
         MSGEND

      ----------

      WORKING-STORAGE SECTION.
       .....
      *
      *  INPUT MESSAGE AREA
      *
       01  INPUT-MESSAGE-AREA           PIC X(100).

       01  HEADER-SEGMENT REDEFINES INPUT-MESSAGE-AREA.
           05 HEADER-PREFIX.
              10 HEADER-LENGTH          PIC S999 COMP SYNC.
              10 FILLER                 PIC X(2).
           05 HEADER-TEXT.
              10 TRANS-CODE             PIC X(8).
              10 FILLER                 PIC X.
              10 ACCOUNT-NUMBER         PIC X(8).
              10 ACTION-CODE            PIC X.
                 88 ADDRESS-RETRIEVE    VALUE 'G'.
                 88 ADDRESS-UPDATE      VALUE 'U'.
           05 FILLER                    PIC X(48).

       01  TRAILER-1 REDEFINES INPUT-MESSAGE-AREA.
           05 TRAILER-1-PREFIX.
              10 TRAILER-1-LENGTH       PIC S999 COMP SYNC.
              10 FILLER                 PIC X(2).          <=== ZZ FIELD NOT
           05 TRAILER-1-TEXT.                                   USED BY THE
              10 STREET-ADDRESS1        PIC X(20).              APPLICATION
              10 STREET-ADDRESS2        PIC X(20).              ON INPUT
              10 CITY                   PIC X(20).
              10 STATE                  PIC X(2).
              10 ZIPCODE                PIC X(5).
              10 FILLER                 PIC X(29).
```

Fig. 4-24. Coding the input message area.

The LL and ZZ fields defined in the program I-O areas are not included in the message definitions in the format set; these are IMS control fields. For MFS, you have to define the data fields only, not the IMS control fields.

CODING THE OUTPUT MESSAGE AREA

Let's examine the request on FIG. 4-25 and the response on FIG. 4-26.

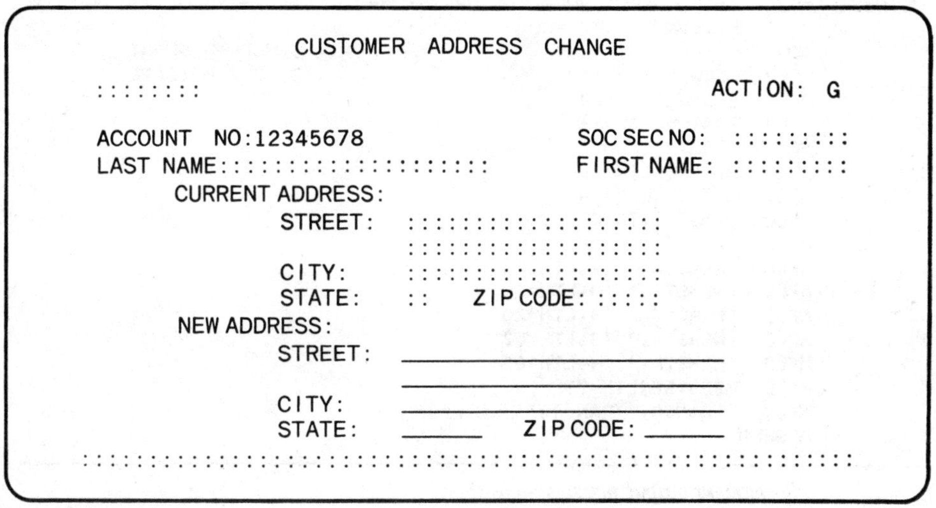

Fig. 4-25.

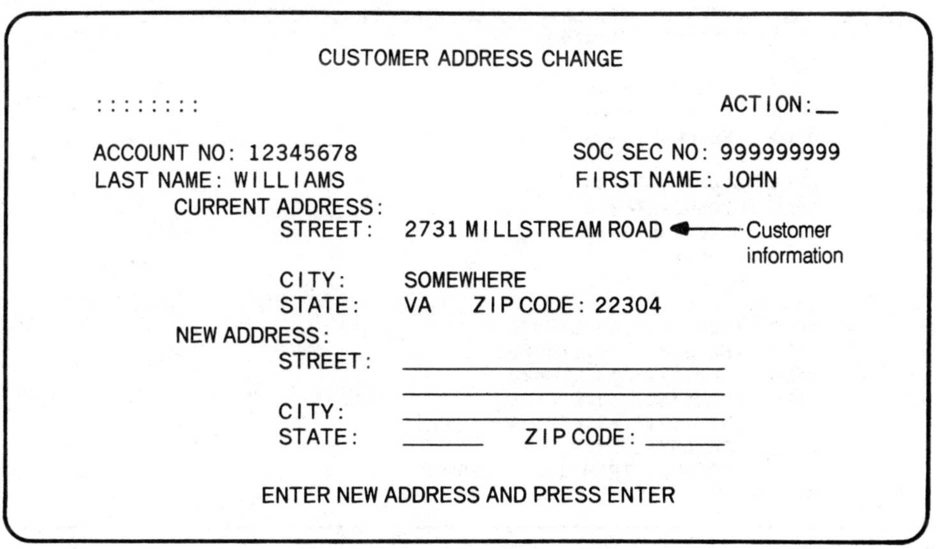

Fig. 4-26.

The operator enters the account number and a "G" (meaning to retrieve) in the Action field and presses ENTER. The account number is given as input to the MPP which retrieves current customer data from the database and displays it on the terminal screen.

The output message definitions are given in FIGS. 4-27 and 4-28. Note that Option I has been coded.

```
OUTMESG  MSG    TYPE=OUTPUT,SOR=(CUSTUP,IGNORE),NXT=INPMESG,OPT=1         *
                FILL=NULL,PAGE=NO
         SEG                                      <=== SINGLE-SEGMENT
         MFLD   SOCNUM,LTH=09                          OUTPUT MESSAGE
         MFLD   LASTNM,LTH=20
         MFLD   FRSTNM,LTH=15
         MFLD   OLDSTR,LTH=20
         MFLD   OLDST2,LTH=20
         MFLD   OLDCTY,LTH=20
         MFLD   OLDSTA,LTH=02
         MFLD   OLDZIP,LTH=05
         MFLD   (NEWSTR,' '),LTH=20
         MFLD   (NEWST2,' '),LTH=20
         MFLD   (NEWCTY,' '),LTH=20
         MFLD   (NEWSTA,' '),LTH=02
         MFLD   (NEWZIP,' '),LTH=05
         MFLD   MESSAGE,LTH=79
         MFLD   (TRANCD,'TRANS001'),LTH=08
         MSGEND
```

Fig. 4-27. Single-segment output message definition.

```
OUTMESG  MSG    TYPE=OUTPUT,SOR=(CUSTUP,IGNORE),NXT=INPMESG,OPT=1         *
                FILL=NULL,PAGE=NO
         SEG
         MFLD   SOCNUM,LTH=09
         MFLD   LASTNM,LTH=20
         MFLD   FRSTNM,LTH=15
         SEG
         MFLD   OLDSTR,LTH=20
         MFLD   OLDST2,LTH=20
         MFLD   OLDCTY,LTH=20
         MFLD   OLDSTA,LTH=02
         MFLD   OLDZIP,LTH=05
         SEG
         MFLD   (NEWSTR,' '),LTH=20
         MFLD   (NEWST2,' '),LTH=20
         MFLD   (NEWCTY,' '),LTH=20
         MFLD   (NEWSTA,' '),LTH=02
         MFLD   (NEWZIP,' '),LTH=05
         MFLD   MESSAGE,LTH=79
         MFLD   (TRANCD,'TRANS001'),LTH=08
         MSGEND
```

Fig. 4-28. Multisegment output message definition.

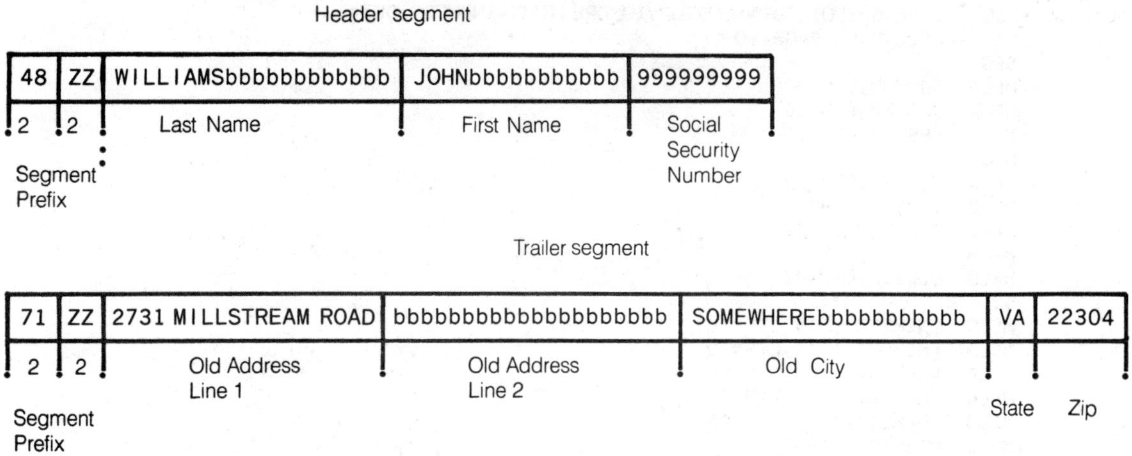

Fig. 4-29. Output data in message queue.

Based on the MOD definition given in FIG. 4-28, the output message is segmented by MFS into two segments as shown in FIG. 4-29.

Output messages do not contain the transaction code; therefore, there is no distinction between the Header and Trailer segments. Output-message segments—like input-message segments—contain a four-byte segment prefix and a variable-length segment text.

The coding in FIG. 4-30 defines the areas in which the output responses will be constructed before they are inserted to the message queue. Note that the ZZ field has been initialized to zero.

RETRIEVING INPUT MESSAGES

The message processing program uses two Get-Type calls to retrieve input messages from the message queue:

```
GU   GET UNIQUE
GN   GET NEXT
```

To retrieve transactions from the message queue, the application program must issue a sequence of GU and GN calls (FIG. 4-31). The retrieved message is placed in the input message I-O area defined in the call. The format of the call to retrieve an input message is shown in FIG. 4-32.

Retrieving the First Segment

The application program should always issue a GU call to the message queue as the first call.

```
OUTMESG  MSG    TYPE=OUTPUT,SOR=(CUSTUP,IGNORE),NXT=INPMESG,OPT=1          *
                FILL=NULL,PAGE=NO
         SEG
         MFLD   SOCNUM,LTH=09
         MFLD   LASTNM,LTH=20
         MFLD   FRSTNM,LTH=15
         SEG
         MFLD   OLDSTR,LTH=20
         MFLD   OLDST2,LTH=20
         MFLD   OLDCTY,LTH=20
         MFLD   OLDSTA,LTH=02
         MFLD   OLDZIP,LTH=05
         SEG
         MFLD   (NEWSTR,' '),LTH=20
         MFLD   (NEWST2,' '),LTH=20
         MFLD   (NEWCTY,' '),LTH=20
         MFLD   (NEWSTA,' '),LTH=02
         MFLD   (NEWZIP,' '),LTH=05
         MFLD   MESSAGE,LTH=79
         MFLD   (TRANCD,'TRANS001'),LTH=08
         MSGEND

      ----------
      WORKING-STORAGE SECTION.
        .....
      *
      *  OUTPUT MESSAGE AREA
      *
       01  OUTPUT-MESSAGE-AREA.
           05 PREFIX-1.
              10 RESP-1-LENGTH          PIC S999 COMP SYNC VALUE +0.
              10 RESP-1-ZZ              PIC S999 COMP SYNC VALUE +0. <== ZZ FIELD
           05 RESPONSE-1-TEXT.                                              IS
              10 RESP-1-LAST-NAME       PIC X(20).                   INITIALIZED
              10 RESP-1-FIRST-NAME      PIC X(15).                   TO ZEROES.
              10 RESP-1-SSN             PIC X(9).

       01  RESPONSE-2 REDEFINES OUTPUT-MESSAGE-AREA.
           05 RESP-2-PREFIX.
              10 RESP-2-LENGTH          PIC S999 COMP SYNC.
              10 RESP-2-ZZ              PIC S999 COMP SYNC.
           05 RESP-2-TEXT.
              10 RESP-2-ADDRESS-LINE1   PIC X(20).
              10 RESP-2-ADDRESS-LINE2   PIC X(20).
              10 RESP-2-CITY            PIC X(20).
              10 RESP-2-STATE           PIC X(2).
              10 RESP-2-ZIPCODE         PIC X(5).

       01  COMMON-MESSAGE REDEFINES OUTPUT-MESSAGE-AREA.
           05 COMM-PREFIX.
              10 COMM-LENGTH            PIC S999 COMP SYNC.
              10 COMM-ZZ                PIC S999 COMP SYNC.
           05 MESSAGE-TEXT              PIC X(40).
```

Fig. 4-30. Coding the output message area.

INPUT MESSAGE		CALL
MESSAGE A		
Segment 1	←	Get Unique
Segment 2	←	Get Next
Segment 3	←	Get Next
MESSAGE B		
Segment 1	←	Get Unique
Segment 2	←	Get Next

Fig. 4-31. Sequence of calls to retrieve input message.

```
 LINKAGE SECTION.
  .....
 01  IO-PCB-MASK.
  .....
 PROCEDURE DIVISION.
  .....
*  RETRIEVE MESSAGE FROM ORIGINAL TERMINAL

       CALL 'CBLTDLI' USING FUNCTION
                            IO-PCB-MASK
                            INPUT-MESSAGE-AREA.
```

Fig. 4-32. Call to retrieve input message.

Why? When IMS/VS schedules the MPP program, it transfers the first segment of the input message to the message processing region; thus, the message is already in waiting. If the MPP program does not issue a GU call as the first call, IMS/VS has to transfer the message again and the efficiency provided by message priming is lost (FIG. 4-33).

A status code is returned for this call:

- A blank status code means that the GU call was successful
- A 'QC' status code means that there are no more segments to process

Retrieving Subsequent Segments

If the input message has more than one segment, we have to issue GN calls to retrieve subsequent segments of the message. (FIG. 4-34). IMS/VS returns one segment at a time to the program I-O area each time we issue a GN call until we have retrieved all the segments of the message. (A 'QD' status code means that there are no more subsequent segments to process.)

```
*  GET THE FIRST MESSAGE SEGMENT
 200-GET-INPUT-MESSAGES.

      CALL 'CBLTDLI' USING GU
                              IO-PCB-MASK
                              INPUT-MESSAGE-AREA.

*  CHECK TO SEE IF MESSAGE QUEUE IS EMPTY
*  STATUS 'QC' MEANS THAT THERE ARE NO MORE MESSAGES.

      IF IO-STATUS-CODE EQUAL 'QC'
         MOVE 'Y' TO MESSAGE-SW
         GOBACK.

      IF IO-STATUS-CODE EQUAL SPACES
         NEXT SENTENCE
      ELSE
         MOVE NOTIFY-OPERATOR-MESSAGE TO MESSAGE-TEXT
         (NOTIFY OPERATOR OF ERROR)
         .....
         GOBACK.
```

Fig. 4-33. Coding to retrieve the first segment.

```
*  GET SUBSEQUENT MESSAGE SEGMENTS
 200-GET-NEXT-TRAILER.

      CALL 'CBLTDLI' USING GN
                              IO-PCB-MASK
                              INPUT-MESSAGE-AREA.

*  STATUS 'QD' MEAND THAT THERE ARE NO MORE SEGMENTS TO PROCESS.

      IF IO-STATUS-CODE EQUAL 'QD'
         NEXT SENTENCE
      ELSE
         MOVE NOTIFY-OPERATOR-MESSAGE TO MESSAGE-TEXT
         .....
         (NOTIFY OPERATOR OF ERROR)
```

Fig. 4-34. Coding to retrieve subsequent segments.

Sequence of Calls

The application program must issue the proper sequence of GU and GN calls to correctly retrieve the transactions (FIG. 4-35). If a GN call is erroneously issued in lieu of a GU call, a 'QE' status code is returned. If a GU call is erroneously issued in lieu of a GN call, trailer segments on the message queue will be bypassed.

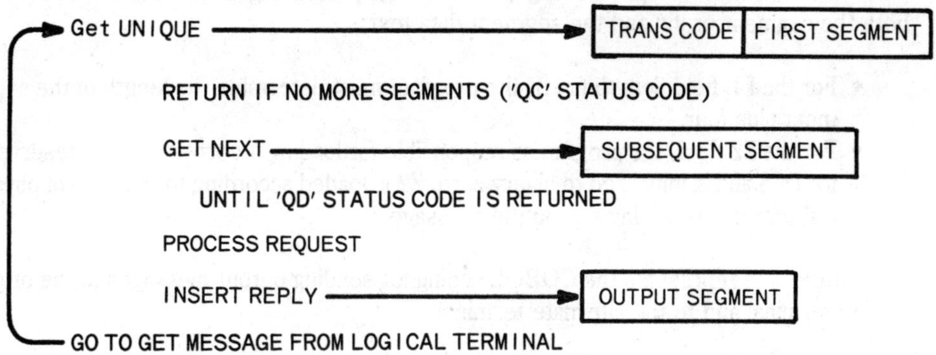

Fig. 4-35. Call sequence to retrieve input messages.

SENDING OUTPUT MESSAGES

When the MPP is ready to send a message, it will issue an ISRT call using the IO-PCB. The message is transmitted from the message I-O area referenced in that call. The format of the call to send an output message is shown in FIG. 4-36.

```
Send message to original terminal.
    CALL 'CBLTDLI' USING ISRT
                          IO-PCB-MASK
                          OUTPUT-MESSAGE-AREA.
```

Fig. 4-36. Call to send output message.

A single-segment response is placed on the message queue by an ISRT call. If a response consists of several segments, then the application program can be coded so that the segments are individually loaded into the message area and inserted on the message queue one at a time (FIG. 4-37). After each ISRT call, the related segment is loaded to the message queue. The next GU call will tell IMS/VS to take this response from the message queue and send it to the interfacing terminal.

Fig. 4-37. Sequence of calls to send output message.

OUTPUT MESSAGE	CALL
MESSAGE A	
Segment 1	Insert
Segment 2	Insert
Segment 3	Insert

When building an output message, the message processing program has to deal with both the segment prefix and the segment data text:

- For the LL field (length field), the program must determine the length of the segment plus four.
- For the ZZ field, the program is responsible for loading it correctly. Z1 is reserved for IMS and is initialized to binary zero. Z2 is loaded according to the type of physical terminal receiving the output message.

FIGURE 4-38 represents the COBOL coding for sending output messages to the originating terminal and to the alternate terminal.

BASIC RULES FOR MESSAGE PROCESSING PROGRAMMING

Following are the basic rules for message processing programming:

1. The program should be written to return and request another input message using a GU call.
2. GN calls to the IO-PCB for single-segment messages should be avoided.
3. The message segments GET and ISRT calls should be issued as consecutive calls whenever possible.
4. Never issue File OPEN and CLOSE operations.
5. Message processing programs should be used only for low-volume database accesses and updates.
6. Database PCBs should reflect accurate processing options selected by segment type.
7. Use large and single-segment responses whenever possible because this will result in fewer calls and less overhead.

Error-Handling

After each message processing call is executed by IMS, an associated status code is returned within the data communication PCB. The MPP should always interrogate this status code to determine if the call was successful. If the call was unsuccessful, the MPP must take some appropriate action. This may be the execution of an error routine. Coding the error routine varies from installation to installation; however, the following steps should be observed whenever the application program gets an I-O error condition that cannot be corrected:

1. Back out all database updates dynamically.
2. Abend the application program if necessary.

The purpose of backing out all database updates is to remove the invalid effects of the program's invalid processing and to maintain database integrity.

```
*     . BUILD OUTPUT MESSAGE
*     . DETERMINE LENGTH OF MESSAGE AND MOVE IT TO LENGTH FIELD
*     . INITIALIZE ZZ-FIELD TO ZEROES
*     . SEND OUTPUT MESSAGE TO ORIGINAL TERMINAL.
*     . THIS IS A TWO-SEGMENT OUTPUT MESSAGE

*  BUILD FIRST OUTPUT SEGMENT

        MOVE LAST-NAME           TO RESP-1-LAST-NAME
        MOVE FIRST-NAME          TO RESP-1-FIRST-NAME
        MOVE ACCT-SSN            TO RESP-1-SSN
        MOVE +48                 TO RESP-1-LENGTH     <=== EQUALS LENGTH OF
        MOVE +0                  TO RESP-1-ZZ              SEGMENT + 4
        PERFORM 600-SEND-MESSAGE-TO-ORIG-TERM.

*  BUILD SECOND OUTPUT SEGMENT

        MOVE ACCT-ADDRESS-LINE1 TO RESP-2-ADDRESS-LINE1
        MOVE ACCT-ADDRESS-LINE2 TO RESP-2-ADDRESS-LINE2
        MOVE ACCT-CITY           TO RESP-2-CITY
        MOVE ACCT-STATE          TO RESP-2-STATE
        MOVE ACCT-ZIPCODE        TO RESP-2-ZIPCODE
        MOVE +71                 TO RESP-2-LENGTH
        MOVE +0                  TO RESP-2-ZZ
        PERFORM 600-SEND-MESSAGE-TO-ORIG-TERM.
....
*  MOVE MODNAME OF MFS FORMAT TO MODNAME FIELD IN IO PCB

 600-SEND-MESSAGE-TO-ORIG-TERM.

        MOVE 'OUTMESG ' TO IO-MODNAME.

        CALL 'CBLTDLI' USING ISRT
                             IO-PCB-MASK
                             OUTPUT-MESSAGE-AREA.

     IF IO-STATUS-CODE NOT EQUAL SPACES
        PERFORM 1000-ERROR-ROUTINE.

*  SEND MESSAGE TO ALTERNATE TERMINAL USING ALTERNATE PCB

 700-SEND-MESSAGE-TO-ALT-TERM.

        CALL 'CBLTDLI' USING ISRT
                             ALTERNATE-PCB-MASK
                             OUTPUT-MESSAGE-AREA.

     IF ALT-STATUS-CODE NOT EQUAL SPACES
        PERFORM 1000-ERROR-ROUTINE.
```

Fig. 4-38. Coding to send output messages.

In this section, you will learn how to code some common error-handling techniques. Before doing that, let's look at the IMS/VS status codes.

IMS/VS Status Codes. IMS/VS status codes fall into four categories:

1. Those indicating valid conditions (the call is completed).
2. Those indicating warning or information-only status codes (the call is completed).
3. Those indicating a programming error (the call is not completed).
4. Those indicating system, I-O, or security-errors encountered during execution of the I-O requests (the call is not completed).

FIGURE 4-39 presents some of the status codes within these four categories. The most serious error situation involves an I-O error code; special IMS calls should be coded in the application program to deal with such situations so that database integrity can be maintained.

STATUS CODES

Indicative or Successful

bb Segment found
GE Segment not found
GB End of database
etc.

Warning

GA Crossing hierarchical boundary
GK Crossing segment boundary on same level
etc.

Program Errors

AB No I-O area specified
AC Hierarchical path error
AD Invalid function code
AJ SSA qualification format invalid
AK Invalid field name in call
etc.

Execution Time Errors

AI Open error
AO I-O Error
etc.

Fig. 4-39. IMS/VS status code categories.

MAINTAINING DATABASE INTEGRITY

Backing-Out Database Updates Dynamically: ROLL and ROLB Calls

Two calls make it possible for the application program to remove the invalid effects of its incorrect processing. These are the rollback calls ROLL and ROLB. ROLL and

ROLB are used to back-out database updates and messages in the message queue when errors have been encountered in the online program.

The main difference between ROLL and ROLB calls is that:

- ROLB returns control to the application program after backing out the database updates and cancelling the output messages; ROLL terminates the application program with a user abend code 0778.
- ROLB can return the last input message for the application program to reprocess; ROLL cannot.
- ROLB is valid only for single-mode programs; ROLL is valid for both single-mode and multiple-mode programs.

ROLL Function. The ROLL call is used by the MPP to back itself out. This call requests the user 0778 abnormal-abend code, but no dump is provided. All database and message activities (except EXPRESS) since the last synchronization point are backed out, and control is not returned to the application program.

The format of the ROLL call is:

```
CALL 'CBLTDLI' USING ROLL.
```

ROLB Function. The ROLB call requests that IMS/VS back-out all database updates and message activities (except EXPRESS) since the last synchronization point. No abnormal condition is reported, and the application program continues processing.

The format of the ROLB call is:

```
CALL 'CBLTDLI' USING ROLB
                     IO-PCB-MASK
                   [ IO-AREA ].
```

If the application program supplies the address of the I-O area as one of the ROLB parameters, the ROLB can act as a message retrieval call and represents the last input message segment that was being processed to the application program. FIGURE 4-40 illustrates a sample coding of a message processing error routine.

Reserving Segments for the Program's Exclusive Use

There are times when we want to reserve a segment to keep other programs from accessing it while we are processing it.

The Q Command. The Q command enables us to reserve segments for the program's exclusive use until it moves to another database record. It tells DL/1 that the application program needs to work with a segment and that no other task can be allowed to modify the segment until it has finished.

The Q command is particularly recommended in application programs that participate in IMS/VS data-sharing, and is coded in the same way as other command codes.

```
LINKAGE SECTION.

01  IO-PCB-MASK.
    05  ORIGIN-TERM-NAME         PIC X(8).
    05  IO-RESERVED              PIC X(2).
    05  IO-STATUS-CODE           PIC X(2).
    05  IO-PREFIX.
        10 JULIAN-DATE           PIC S9(7) COMP-3.
        10 CURRENT-TIME          PIC S9(7) COMP-3.
        10 SEQUENCE-NO           PIC S9(7) COMP.
    05  IO-MODNAME               PIC X(8).

.....
PROCEDURE DIVISION.
.....
800-REPLACE-ACCOUNT-INFO.

    CALL 'CBLTDLI' USING REPL
                         ACCOUNT-PCB-MASK
                         ACCOUNT-IO-AREA.

    IF ACCT-STATUS-CODE NOT EQUAL SPACES
       PERFORM 2000-DB-ERROR-ROUTINE
    ELSE
       MOVE UPDATE-COMPLETED-MESSAGE TO MESSAGE-TEXT
       MOVE +44 TO COMM-LENGTH
       PERFORM 600-SEND-MESSAGE-TO-ORIG-TERM.
 900-ACCOUNT-NOT-FOUND.

       MOVE ACCT-NOT-FOUND-MESSAGE TO MESSAGE-TEXT.
       MOVE +44 TO COMM-LENGTH.

       CALL 'CBLTDLI' USING ISRT
                            IO-PCB-MASK
                            OUTPUT-MESSAGE-AREA.

    IF IO-STATUS-CODE NOT EQUAL SPACES
       PERFORM 1000-ERROR-ROUTINE.

*  THE IO ERROR ROUTINE IS EXECUTED WHENEVER AN UNEXPECTED STATUS
*  CODE IS RETURNED. THIS ROUTINE VARIES FROM INSTALLATION TO
*  INSTALLATION. YOU SHOULD CHECK YOUR INSTALLATION'S STANDARDS ON
*  HOW TO CODE THIS ROUTINE.
*  IN THIS EXAMPLE, WE ISSUE A ROLB CALL TO DELETE THE CURRENT INPUT
*  MESSAGE AND TO LET THE PROGRAM CONTINUE WITH THE NEXT MESSAGE.
*  WE ONLY SPECIFY THE FUNCTION AND THE IO PCB MASK, NO IO AREA IS
*  SPECIFIED BECAUSE IT IS OPTIONAL.
*
 1000-ERROR-ROUTINE.

       CALL 'CBLTDLI' USING ROLB
                            IO-PCB-MASK.
```

Fig. 4-40. Sample coding of an MPP error routine.

When we use the Q command in the SSA, we will assign a queue class designated by one letter from A through J to the segment we are retrieving. This letter must immediately follow the Q command code (FIG. 4-41).

```
WORKING-STORAGE SECTION.
.....
01  ACCOUNT-SSA.
    03  ACCT-SEG-NAME           PIC X(8) VALUE 'ACCTMSTR'.
    03  ACCT-ASTERIX            PIC X    VALUE '*'.
    03  ACCT-COMMAND-1          PIC X    VALUE '-'.
    03  ACCT-COMMAND-2          PIC X    VALUE '-'.
    03  ACCT-LEFT-PAREN         PIC X    VALUE '('.
    03  ACCT-KEY-NAME           PIC X(8) VALUE 'ACTNUMBR'.
    03  ACCT-OPRERATOR          PIC XX   VALUE ' ='.
    03  ACCT-KEY-VALUE          PIC X(8) VALUE SPACES.
    03  ACCT-RIGHT-PAREN        PIC X    VALUE ')'.
.....
PROCEDURE DIVISION.
.....
900-BUILD-ACCOUNT-SSA.

    MOVE 'Q' TO ACCT-COMMAND-1.
    MOVE 'A' TO ACCT-COMMAND-2.
 .....
```

Fig. 4-41. Coding the Q command.

Using a Q command on a root segment, no other programs can access any of the segments in that database record. However, when using the Q command on a dependent segment, other programs may read the segment using a Get-type call.

Before using the Q command, the MAXQ parameter must be specified in the related PSB.

To release the segment reserved by the Q call, we issue the DEQ call.

DEQ Function. The DEQ releases resources previously reserved with a Q command code. When a segment occurrence is enqueued, no other tasks can update it. The DEQ call will release exclusive control of the segment.

When the DEQ call is issued, the resources will be automatically released at sync point. The DEQ call is used when sync points are infrequent.

The format of the DEQ call is:

```
CALL 'CBLTDLI' USING DEQ
                     IO-PCB-MASK
                     WORK-AREA.
```

The PCB used must be the IO-PCB; its only purpose is to return the status code.

WORK-AREA is a one-byte area with no LL and ZZ fields, and contains the identification of the queue class to be released. The range of allowed classes is A to J, which is the same range used by the Q command code.

The DEQ call releases all segments reserved by the Q call except:

- Segments required to keep our position in the database hierarchy, until the program moves to another database record.
- A queue class of a segment that has been locked again as another class.

If the application program does not issue a DEQ call, IMS/VS will release the reserved segments when the application program reaches the synchronization point, but by releasing them with a DEQ call before this point, we will make them available to other programs more quickly.

Database Error Routine. For debugging purposes, most installations require the execution of an error routine after each call to a database to handle an unexpected error code. This routine deals mainly with the application program's errors, and what it does is to display the type of DL/1 call to the database, the IMS status code returned, and the key value contained in the SSA at the time the bad status code occurred.

FIGURE 4-42 illustrates a sample coding of a database error routine.

```
WORKING-STORAGE SECTION.
 .....
*
*   ACCOUNT SSA
*
 01  ACCOUNT-SSA.
     03  ACCT-SEG-NAME           PIC X(8) VALUE 'ACCTMSTR'.
     03  ACCT-LEFT-PAREN         PIC X    VALUE '('.
     03  ACCT-KEY-NAME           PIC X(8) VALUE 'ACTNUMBR'.
     03  ACCT-OPRERATOR          PIC XX   VALUE ' ='.
     03  ACCT-KEY-VALUE          PIC X(8) VALUE SPACES.  <=== THIS KEY
     03  ACCT-RIGHT-PAREN        PIC X    VALUE ')'.          VALUE IS TO
                                                              BE DISPLAYED
                                                              WHEN A BAD
                                                              STATUS CODE
 LINKAGE SECTION.                                             IS RETURNED.
 .....
 01  ACCOUNT-PCB-MASK.
     05  ACCT-DBD-NAME           PIC X(8).
     05  ACCT-SEG-LEVEL          PIC X(2).
     05  ACCT-STATUS-CODE        PIC X(2).           <=== STATUS CODE TO
     05  ACCT-PROCESS-OPTIONS    PIC X(4).                BE DISPLAYED ALSO.
     05  IMS-RESERVED            PIC S9(5) COMP.
     05  ACCT-SEG-NAME-FB        PIC X(8).
     05  ACCT-LENGTH-FB-KEY      PIC S9(5) COMP.
     05  ACCT-NBR-SENS-SEG       PIC S9(5) COMP.
     05  ACCT-KEY-FB-AREA        PIC X(8).

 PROCEDURE DIVISION.
 .....
 400-RETRIEVE-DISPLAY-ACCOUNT.
```

Fig. 4-42. Sample coding of a database error routine.

Fig. 4-42. continued

```
 *  QUALIFY ACCOUNT SSA WITH ACCOUNT NUMBER FROM TERMINAL

        MOVE ACCOUNT-NUMBER TO ACCT-KEY-VALUE.
        CALL 'CBLTDLI' USING GU
                             ACCOUNT-PCB-MASK
                             ACCOUNT-IO-AREA
                             ACCOUNT-SSA.

        IF ACCT-STATUS-CODE EQUAL 'GE'
           PERFORM 900-ACCOUNT-NOT-FOUND.

        IF ACCT-STATUS-CODE NOT EQUAL SPACES
           PERFORM 2000-DB-ERROR-ROUTINE.
 *
 *  THE FOLLOWING ERROR ROUTINE IS EXECUTED WHENEVER A BAD STATUS
 *  CODE IS RETURNED FOR A DATA BASE CALL.
 *  MOST INSTALLATIONS REQUEST TO DISPLAY THE TYPE OF CALL, THE
 *  RETURNED STATUS CODE, THE KEY VALUE OF THE SSA AND THEN CALL
 *  A USER WRITTEN SUBROUTINE TO FORMAT A DUMP FOR DEBUGGING.
 *
  2000-DB-ERROR-ROUTINE.

           DISPLAY 'GET CALL ERROR TO ACCOUNT DATA BASE'.
           DISPLAY 'STATUS CODE: ' ACCT-STATUS-CODE.
           DISPLAY 'ACCOUNT NUMBER: ' ACCT-KEY-VALUE.
 *
 *         CALL 'ABENDPGM' TO PRINT DUMP
```

The examples we have provided in this section are the most common techniques to deal with error situations, but there are other techniques that your installation may use. Check your shop's standard manual to choose the most appropriate technique available.

PUTTING IT ALL TOGETHER: A SAMPLE MESSAGE PROCESSING PROGRAM

Now that you understand the elements of the message processing program required by IMS to support operation in a data communication environment, it is time to put these elements together into a complete program.

First, we will present the specifications for the program, and then we will look at the MFS control statements for the format used by the program.

This sample MPP will:

- Retrieve input messages from a terminal device
- Access a DL/1 database
- Update a DL/1 database
- Send output messages to the interfacing terminal

Program Specifications

A financial institution would like to enter address changes for its customers. The changes are to be done via the screen format illustrated by FIG. 4-43.

The sequence of events is as follows:

1. First, the operator calls up a format screen by entering

   ```
   /FORMAT OUTMESG
   ```

   and presses the ENTER key.
2. The resulting format is sent to the terminal screen (FIG. 4-44). The data fields are blank because no program has been scheduled and no I-O area has been used.
3. The operator enters the account number and "G" (meaning to retrieve) in the action field and presses ENTER (FIG. 4-45).
4. The account number is given as input to the MPP which retrieves current customer data from the database and displays it on the terminal screen (FIG. 4-46). The new address fields are blanked out, ready for the operator to enter new data.
5. The operator reviews the displayed data and enters a new address and the letter "U" in the action field (meaning to update) and presses ENTER (FIG. 4-47).
6. The MPP tests for a "U", then retrieves the new address, updates the database with the new address, displays the new address as being current, sends out the message "Transaction successfully completed," and erases the previous data on the screen (FIG. 4-48).
7. If the new address fails the edit tests in the program or access to the database is not successful, an error message will be sent back to the operator (FIG. 4-49).

Screen characteristics:

1. Reserved for transaction code which is always required but is not displayed for security reasons.
2. ACCOUNT NUMBER: This field is unprotected so that data may be entered.
3. Action to be taken by the program:
   - If "G" is entered, the account information will be displayed.
   - If "U" is entered, the old address will be updated with the new one.
4. Literal fields: "ACCOUNT NO", "SOC SEC NO", "LAST NAME", "FIRST NAME", etc. are protected and do not interface with the application program.
5. CURRENT ADDRESS: This area is protected and is displayed for the first time when the application program releases the information for the account.
6. NEW ADDRESS: This area is unprotected so that the operator may enter data.
7. ZIP CODE: This area is numeric, right-justified, and is filled with the "*" symbol if incomplete.
8. Area reserved for messages sent by the application program.

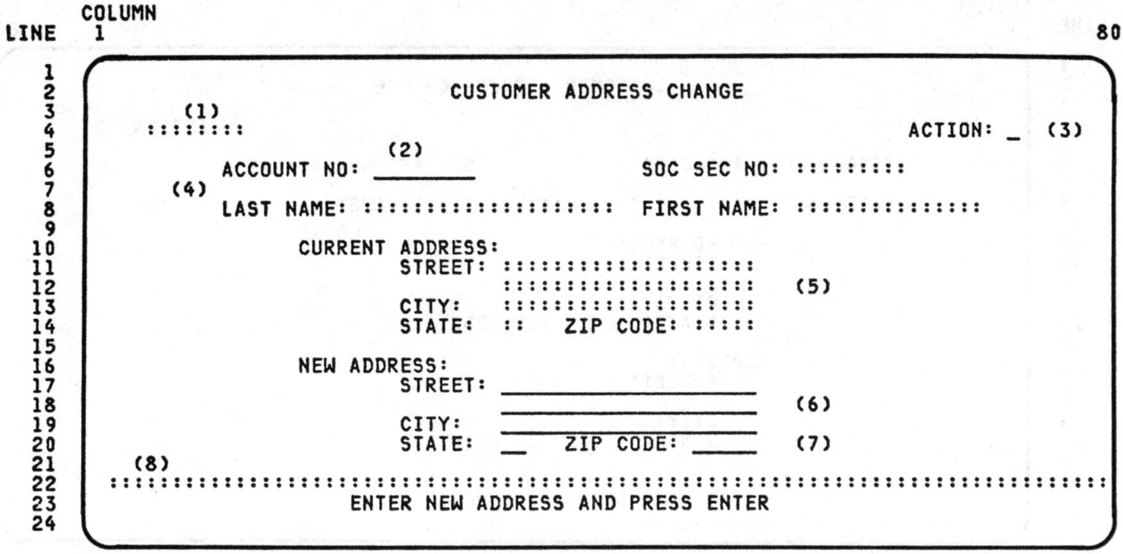

Fig. 4-43.

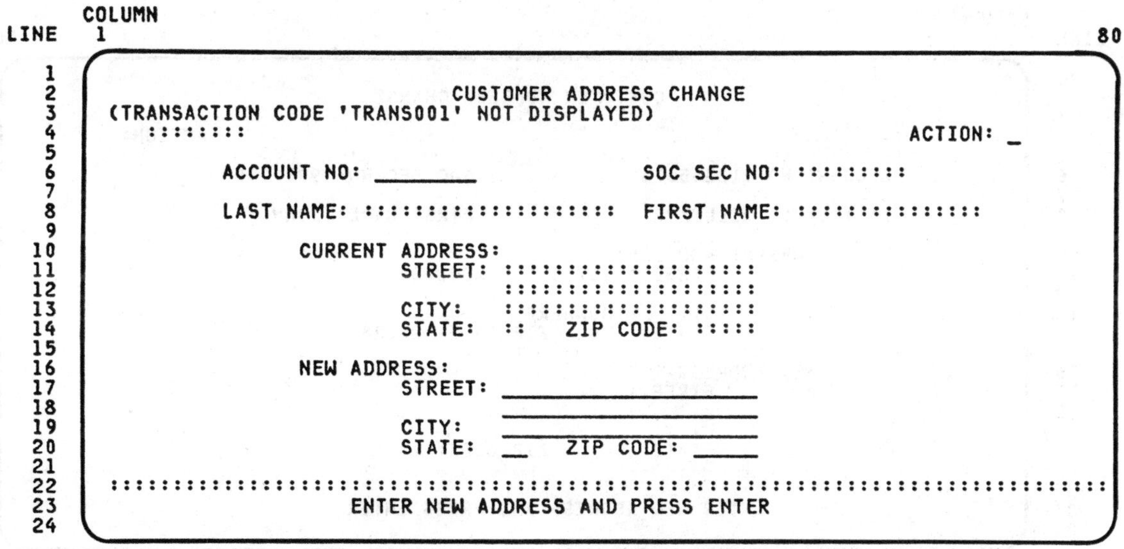

Fig. 4-44.

```
                                    CUSTOMER ADDRESS CHANGE

     ::::::::                                                              ACTION: G

          ACCOUNT NO: 12345678                SOC SEC NO: :::::::::

          LAST NAME: ::::::::::::::::::::     FIRST NAME: :::::::::::::::

               CURRENT ADDRESS:
                      STREET:

                      CITY:
                      STATE:      ZIP CODE:

               NEW ADDRESS:
                      STREET:

                      CITY:
                      STATE:      ZIP CODE:

                   ENTER NEW ADDRESS AND PRESS ENTER
```

Fig. 4-45.

```
                                    CUSTOMER ADDRESS CHANGE

     ::::::::                                                              ACTION:

          ACCOUNT NO: 12345678                SOC SEC NO: 999999999

          LAST NAME: WILLIAMS                 FIRST NAME: JOHN

               CURRENT ADDRESS:
                      STREET: 11713 BASSWOOD DR

                      CITY:   NOWHERE
                      STATE:  MD  ZIP CODE: 20708

               NEW ADDRESS:
                      STREET:

                      CITY:
                      STATE:      ZIP CODE:

                   ENTER NEW ADDRESS AND PRESS ENTER
```

Fig. 4-46

```
      COLUMN
LINE    1                                                                        80

                              CUSTOMER ADDRESS CHANGE

   ::::::::                                                           ACTION: U

          ACCOUNT NO: 12345678                SOC SEC NO: 999999999

          LAST NAME: WILLIAMS                 FIRST NAME: JOHN

                 CURRENT ADDRESS:
                         STREET: 11713 BASSWOOD DR

                         CITY:   NOWHERE
                         STATE:  MD    ZIP CODE: 20708

                 NEW ADDRESS:
                         STREET: 2731 MILLSTREAM ROAD

                         CITY:   SOMEWHERE
                         STATE:  VA    ZIP CODE: 22304


                      ENTER NEW ADDRESS AND PRESS ENTER
```

Fig. 4-47.

```
      COLUMN
LINE    1                                                                        80

                              CUSTOMER ADDRESS CHANGE

   ::::::::                                                           ACTION:

          ACCOUNT NO: 12345678                SOC SEC NO: 999999999

          LAST NAME: WILLIAMS                 FIRST NAME: JOHN

                 CURRENT ADDRESS:
                         STREET: 2731 MILLSTREAM ROAD

                         CITY:   SOMEWHERE
                         STATE:  VA    ZIP CODE: 22304

                 NEW ADDRESS:
                         STREET:

                         CITY:
                         STATE:        ZIP CODE:

  TRANSACTION SUCEESSFULLY COMPLETED
                      ENTER NEW ADDRESS AND PRESS ENTER
```

Fig. 4-48.

Coding MFS Control Statements

Before you start coding the COBOL MPP, you should have its screen format generated.

```
      COLUMN
LINE   1                                                                        80

                               CUSTOMER ADDRESS CHANGE

     ::::::::                                                         ACTION: G

            ACCOUNT NO: 99999999                SOC SEC NO:

            LAST NAME:                          FIRST NAME:

                  CURRENT ADDRESS:
                          STREET:

                          CITY:
                          STATE:       ZIP CODE:

                  NEW ADDRESS:
                          STREET:

                          CITY:
                          STATE:       ZIP CODE:

   ACCOUNT NOT FOUND
                       ENTER NEW ADDRESS AND PRESS ENTER
```

Fig. 4-49.

FIGURE 4-50 presents the MFS control statements for our sample program. These statements are compiled to generate the MFS format, and the DIF, DOF, MID, and MOD control blocks. These blocks will be used to format input and output messages to and from the terminal device during the online execution of the MPP.

Each message segment is defined by a SEG statement, and the message fields (MFLDs) are coded to identify separate individual fields within each message. There is a one-to-one relationship between the individual MFLDs and the fields defined in the I-O areas of the COBOL program. The layout of the input and output message areas in the MPP must be exactly in the same format as the input and output message definitions in the MFS format. If the device format has been changed, you must change your MPP accordingly.

Note that the LL and ZZ fields defined in the program I-O areas are not included in the message definitions in the format set; these are IMS control fields. For MFS, you have to define only the data fields, *not* the IMS control fields.

All literals to be displayed on the terminal are defined in the DIF/DOF; the application program does not have to be concerned with them.

Sample Message Processing Program

FIGURE 4-51 illustrates the complete message processing program with embedded IMS DB/DC calls.

```
1--------10----16-------------------------------------------------------72
         TITLE 'CUSTOMER NAME AND ADDRESS CHANGE'
         PRINT NOGEN
*
CUSTUP   FMT
         DEV   TYPE=(3270,2),FEAT=IGNORE,SYSMSG=MESSAGE
         DIV   TYPE=INOUT
         DPAGE CURSOR=((04,73))
         DFLD  'CUSTOMER ADDRESS CHANGE',POS=(02,29),LTH=23,           *
               ATTR=(PROT,HI)
TRANCD   DFLD  POS=(04,05),LTH=08,ATTR=(MOD,PROT,NODISP)
         DFLD  'ACTION:',POS=(04,65)
ACTION   DFLD  POS=(04,73),LTH=01,ATTR=MOD
         DFLD  'ACCOUNT NO:',POS=(06,11)
ACCTNO   DFLD  POS=(06,23),LTH=08,ATTR=MOD
         DFLD  'SOC SEC NO:',POS=(06,44)
SOCNUM   DFLD  POS=(06,56),LTH=09,ATTR=(MOD,PROT)
         DFLD  'LAST NAME:',POS=(08,11)
LASTNM   DFLD  POS=(08,22),LTH=20,ATTR=(MOD,PROT)
         DFLD  'FIRST NAME:',POS=(08,44)
FRSTNM   DFLD  POS=(08,56),LTH=15,ATTR=(MOD,PROT)
         DFLD  'CURRENT ADDRESS:',POS=(10,17)
         DFLD  'STREET:',POS=(11,25)
OLDSTR   DFLD  POS=(11,33),LTH=20,ATTR=PROT
OLDST2   DFLD  POS=(12,33),LTH=20,ATTR=PROT
         DFLD  'CITY:',POS=(13,25)
OLDCTY   DFLD  POS=(13,33),LTH=20,ATTR=PROT
         DFLD  'STATE:',POS=(14,25)
OLDSTA   DFLD  POS=(14,33),LTH=02,ATTR=PROT
         DFLD  'ZIP CODE:',POS=(14,38)
OLDZIP   DFLD  POS=(14,48),LTH=05,ATTR=PROT
         DFLD  'NEW ADDRESS:',POS=(16,17)
         DFLD  'STREET:',POS=(17,25)
NEWSTR   DFLD  POS=(17,33),LTH=20,ATTR=MOD
NEWST2   DFLD  POS=(18,33),LTH=20,ATTR=MOD
         DFLD  'CITY:',POS=(19,25)
NEWCTY   DFLD  POS=(19,33),LTH=20,ATTR=MOD
         DFLD  'STATE:',POS=(20,25)
NEWSTA   DFLD  POS=(20,33),LTH=02,ATTR=MOD
         DFLD  'ZIP CODE:',POS=(20,38)
NEWZIP   DFLD  POS=(20,48),LTH=05,ATTR=(MOD,NUM)
MESSAGE  DFLD  POS=(22,02),LTH=79,ATTR=(PROT,HI)
         DFLD  'ENTER NEW ADDRESS AND PRESS ENTER',POS=(23,21)
         FMTEND
*
INPMESG  MSG   TYPE=INPUT,SOR=CUSTUP,NXT=OUTMESG,OPT=1
         SEG
         MFLD  TRANCD,LTH=09                  TRANSACTION CODE + 1 FOR IMS
         MFLD  ACCTNO,LTH=08                  ACCOUNT NUMBER
         MFLD  ACTION,LTH=01                  ACTION TO BE TAKEN
         SEG
         MFLD  NEWSTR,LTH=20                  NEW STREET ADDRESS - FIRST LINE
         MFLD  NEWST2,LTH=20                  NEW STREET ADDRESS - SECOND LINE
         MFLD  NEWCTY,LTH=20                  NEW CITY
```

Fig. 4-50.

Fig. 4-50. continued

```
         MFLD   NEWSTA,LTH=02                          NEW STATE
         MFLD   NEWZIP,LTH=05,JUST=R,FILL=C'*'         NEW ZIP CODE
         MSGEND
*
OUTMESG  MSG    TYPE=OUTPUT,SOR=(CUSTUP,IGNORE),NXT=INPMESG,OPT=1,
                FILL=NULL,PAGE=NO
         SEG
         MFLD   SOCNUM,LTH=09
         MFLD   LASTNM,LTH=20
         MFLD   FRSTNM,LTH=15
         SEG
         MFLD   OLDSTR,LTH=20
         MFLD   OLDST2,LTH=20
         MFLD   OLDCTY,LTH=20
         MFLD   OLDSTA,LTH=02
         MFLD   OLDZIP,LTH=05
         SEG
         MFLD   (NEWSTR,' '),LTH=20
         MFLD   (NEWST2,' '),LTH=20
         MFLD   (NEWCTY,' '),LTH=20
         MFLD   (NEWSTA,' '),LTH=20
         MFLD   (NEWZIP,' '),LTH=20
         MFLD   MESSAGE,LTH=79
         MFLD   (TRANCD,'TRANS001'),LTH=08
         MSGEND
         END
```

```
IDENTIFICATION DIVISION.
PROGRAM-ID. PROGRAM1.
AUTHOR. ZIEP VUONG.
DATE-WRITTEN. AUGUST 1987.
REMARKS.
    ****************************************************
    *                                                  *
    *   PROGRAM FUNCTIONS:                             *
    *                                                  *
    *   . RETRIEVE INPUT MESSAGES FROM A TERMINAL DEVICE   *
    *   . ACCESS THE ACCOUNT DATA BASE                 *
    *   . UPDATE THE ACCOUT DATA BASE WITH NEW NAME AND    *
    *     ADDRESSES                                    *
    *   . SEND OUTPUT MESSAGES TO THE INTERFACING TERMINAL *
    *                                                  *
    ****************************************************

ENVIRONMENT DIVISION.
CONFIGURATION SECTION.
SOURCE-COMPUTER.  IBM-370.
OBJECT-COMPUTER.  IBM-370.

DATA DIVISION.
```

Fig. 4-51.

Fig. 4-51. continued

```
WORKING-STORAGE SECTION.

 01  FILLER                       PIC X(27)
         VALUE 'WORKING-STORAGE BEGINS HERE'.

 77  INVALID-ACTION-MESSAGE       PIC X(24)
         VALUE 'INVALID ACTION REQUESTED'.

 77  NOTIFY-OPERATOR-MESSAGE      PIC X(40)
         VALUE 'ERROR, OPERATOR MUST CORRECT AND REENTER'.

 77  ACCT-NOT-FOUND-MESSAGE       PIC X(19)
         VALUE 'ACCOUNT NOT FOUND'.

 77  UPDATE-COMPLETED-MESSAGE     PIC X(34)
         VALUE 'TRANSACTION SUCCESSFULLY COMPLETED'.

 01  MESSAGE-SW                   PIC X VALUE 'N'.
     88  END-OF-MESSAGE                 VALUE 'Y'.
*
*****************************************************************
*  THE LAYOUT OF THE INPUT AND OUPUT MESSAGE AREAS IN THE        *
*  PROGRAM MUST BE EXACTLY IN THE SAME FORMAT AS THE INPUT       *
*  AND OUTPUT DEFINITIONS IN THE MFS FORMAT.                     *
*  THERE IS A ONE-TO-ONE RELATIONSHIP BETWEEN THE INDIVIDUAL     *
*  INPUT AND OUTPUT FIELDS DEFINED IN THE FORMAT SET AND THOSE   *
*  DEFINED IN THE PROGRAM.                                       *
*  IN THIS PROGRAM THE INPUT AND OUTPUT MESSAGES ARE CODED AS    *
*  TWO SEGMENT MESSAGES.                                         *
*  THE ZZ FIELD ON INPUT IS DEFINED AS A FILLER BECAUSE IT IS    *
*  NOT USED.                                                     *
*  THE ZZ FIELD ON OUTPUT IS INITIALIZED TO ZEROES.              *
*****************************************************************
*
*  INPUT MESSAGE AREA
*
 01  INPUT-MESSAGE-AREA           PIC X(100).

 01  HEADER-SEGMENT REDEFINES INPUT-MESSAGE-AREA.
     05 HEADER-PREFIX.
        10 HEADER-LENGTH          PIC S999 COMP SYNC.
        10 FILLER                 PIC X(2).
     05 HEADER-TEXT.
        10 TRANS-CODE             PIC X(8).
        10 FILLER                 PIC X.
        10 ACCOUNT-NUMBER         PIC X(8).
        10 ACTION-CODE            PIC X.
           88 ADDRESS-RETRIEVE    VALUE 'G'.
           88 ADDRESS-UPDATE      VALUE 'U'.
     05 FILLER                    PIC X(48).

 01  TRAILER-1 REDEFINES INPUT-MESSAGE-AREA.
     05 TRAILER-1-PREFIX.
        10 TRAILER-1-LENGTH       PIC S999 COMP SYNC.
        10 FILLER                 PIC X(2).
     05 TRAILER-1-TEXT.
```

Fig. 4-51. continued

```
          10 STREET-ADDRESS1          PIC X(20).
          10 STREET-ADDRESS2          PIC X(20).
          10 CITY                     PIC X(20).
          10 STATE                    PIC X(2).
          10 ZIPCODE                  PIC X(5).
          10 FILLER                   PIC X(29).
*
*  OUTPUT MESSAGE AREA
*
 01   OUTPUT-MESSAGE-AREA.
      05 PREFIX-1.
          10 RESP-1-LENGTH            PIC S999 COMP SYNC VALUE +0.
          10 RESP-1-ZZ                PIC S999 COMP SYNC VALUE +0.
      05 RESPONSE-1-TEXT.
          10 RESP-1-LAST-NAME         PIC X(20).
          10 RESP-1-FIRST-NAME        PIC X(15).
          10 RESP-1-SSN               PIC X(9).
*
 01   RESPONSE-2 REDEFINES OUTPUT-MESSAGE-AREA.
      05 RESP-2-PREFIX.
          10 RESP-2-LENGTH            PIC S999 COMP SYNC.
          10 RESP-2-ZZ                PIC S999 COMP SYNC.
      05 RESP-2-TEXT.
          10 RESP-2-ADDRESS-LINE1     PIC X(20).
          10 RESP-2-ADDRESS-LINE2     PIC X(20).
          10 RESP-2-CITY              PIC X(20).
          10 RESP-2-STATE             PIC X(2).
          10 RESP-2-ZIPCODE           PIC X(5).
*
 01   COMMON-MESSAGE REDEFINES OUTPUT-MESSAGE-AREA.
      05 COMM-PREFIX.
          10 COMM-LENGTH              PIC S999 COMP SYNC.
          10 COMM-ZZ                  PIC S999 COMP SYNC.
      05 MESSAGE-TEXT                 PIC X(40).
*
*****************************************************************
*                                                               *
*                 DATA BASE SEGMENT LAYOUT                      *
*                                                               *
*****************************************************************
*
 01   ACCOUNT-IO-AREA.
      05 ACCT-NUMBER-KEY              PIC X(8).
      05 ACCT-NAME.
          10 LAST-NAME                PIC X(20).
          10 FIRST-NAME               PIC X(15).
      05 ACCT-SSN                     PIC X(9).
      05 ACCT-ADDRESS-LINE1           PIC X(20).
      05 ACCT-ADDRESS-LINE2           PIC X(20).
      05 ACCT-CITY                    PIC X(20).
      05 ACCT-STATE                   PIC X(2).
      05 ACCT-ZIPCODE                 PIC X(5).
*
```

Fig. 4-51. continued

```
*****************************************************************
*                                                               *
*                     DATA BASE SSA'S                           *
*                                                               *
*****************************************************************
*
 01  ACCOUNT-SSA.
     03  ACCT-SEG-NAME               PIC X(8) VALUE 'ACCTMSTR'.
     03  ACCT-LEFT-PAREN             PIC X    VALUE '('.
     03  ACCT-KEY-NAME               PIC X(8) VALUE 'ACTNUMBR'.
     03  ACCT-OPRERATOR              PIC XX   VALUE ' ='.
     03  ACCT-KEY-VALUE              PIC X(8) VALUE SPACES.
     03  ACCT-RIGHT-PAREN            PIC X    VALUE ')'.

 01  ACCOUNT-SSA-UNQUALIFIED         PIC X(9) VALUE 'ACCTMSTR '.
*
*****************************************************************
*                                                               *
*                   IMS CALL FUNCTION CODES                     *
*                                                               *
*****************************************************************
 01  IMS-CALL-FUNCTIONS.
     03  GU                          PIC X(4) VALUE 'GU  '.
     03  GN                          PIC X(4) VALUE 'GN  '.
     03  GNP                         PIC X(4) VALUE 'GNP '.
     03  GHU                         PIC X(4) VALUE 'GHU '.
     03  GHN                         PIC X(4) VALUE 'GHN '.
     03  GHNP                        PIC X(4) VALUE 'GHNP'.
     03  ISRT                        PIC X(4) VALUE 'ISRT'.
     03  DLET                        PIC X(4) VALUE 'DLET'.
     03  REPL                        PIC X(4) VALUE 'REPL'.
     03  CHKP                        PIC X(4) VALUE 'CHKP'.
     03  CHNG                        PIC X(4) VALUE 'CHNG'.
     03  PURG                        PIC X(4) VALUE 'PURG'.
     03  LOG                         PIC X(4) VALUE 'LOG '.
     03  XRST                        PIC X(4) VALUE 'XRST'.
     03  ROLB                        PIC X(4) VALUE 'ROLB'.
     03  FUNCTION                    PIC X(4) VALUE '    '.
*
 LINKAGE SECTION.
*
*  DATA COMMUNICATION PCB. THE IO PCB IS REQUIRED BECAUSE
*  THE PROGRAM SENDS RESPONSES TO THE INTERFACING TERMINAL
*
 01  IO-PCB-MASK.
     05  ORIGIN-TERM-NAME            PIC X(8).
     05  IO-RESERVED                 PIC X(2).
     05  IO-STATUS-CODE              PIC X(2).
     05  IO-PREFIX.
         10  JULIAN-DATE             PIC S9(7) COMP-3.
         10  CURRENT-TIME            PIC S9(7) COMP-3.
         10  SEQUENCE-NO             PIC S9(7) COMP.
     05  IO-MODNAME                  PIC X(8).

*
*  DATA BASE PCB - REQUIRED BECAUSE PROGRAM REFERENCES THE
```

Fig. 4-51. continued

```
*  ACCOUNT DATA BASE.
*
 01  ACCOUNT-PCB-MASK.
     05  ACCT-DBD-NAME             PIC X(8).
     05  ACCT-SEG-LEVEL            PIC X(2).
     05  ACCT-STATUS-CODE          PIC X(2).
     05  ACCT-PROCESS-OPTIONS      PIC X(4).
     05  IMS-RESERVED              PIC S9(5) COMP.
     05  ACCT-SEG-NAME-FB          PIC X(8).
     05  ACCT-LENGTH-FB-KEY        PIC S9(5) COMP.
     05  ACCT-NBR-SENS-SEG         PIC S9(5) COMP.
     05  ACCT-KEY-FB-AREA          PIC X(8).
PROCEDURE DIVISION.

    ENTRY 'DLITCBL' USING IO-PCB-MASK
                          ACCOUNT-PCB-MASK.

PROGRAM-ENTRY.

010-PROCESS-CUSTOMER-TRANS.

    MOVE 'N' TO MESSAGE-SW.
    PERFORM 100-PROCESS-INPUT-MESSAGES
       UNTIL END-OF-MESSAGE.

PROGRAM-EXIT.
    GOBACK.

100-PROCESS-INPUT-MESSAGES.

    PERFORM 200-GET-INPUT-MESSAGES.
    IF NOT END-OF-MESSAGE
    PERFORM 300-DETERMINE-ACTION-TAKEN.

*****************************************************************
*  GET THE FIRST MESSAGE SEGMENT,                               *
*  CHECK TO SEE IF MESSAGE QUEUE IS EMPTY,                      *
*  STATUS 'QC' MEANS THAT THERE ARE NO MORE MESSAGES.           *
*****************************************************************
 200-GET-INPUT-MESSAGES.

    CALL 'CBLTDLI' USING GU
                         IO-PCB-MASK
                         INPUT-MESSAGE-AREA.

    IF IO-STATUS-CODE EQUAL 'QC'
       MOVE 'Y' TO MESSAGE-SW
       GOBACK.

    IF IO-STATUS-CODE EQUAL SPACES
       NEXT SENTENCE
    ELSE
       MOVE NOTIFY-OPERATOR-MESSAGE TO MESSAGE-TEXT
       MOVE +44 TO COMM-LENGTH
       PERFORM 600-SEND-MESSAGE-TO-ORIG-TERM
       GOBACK.
```

Fig. 4-51. continued

```
           PERFORM 200-GET-NEXT-TRAILER.

      ****************************************************************
      *  GET SUBSEQUENT MESSAGE SEGMENTS,                            *
      *  CHECK TO SEE IF THERE ARE ANY MORE SEGMENTS,                *
      *  STATUS 'QD' MEANS THAT THERE ARE NO MORE SEGMENTS TO PROCESS. *
      ****************************************************************
       200-GET-NEXT-TRAILER.

           CALL 'CBLTDLI' USING GN
                                IO-PCB-MASK
                                INPUT-MESSAGE-AREA.

           IF IO-STATUS-CODE EQUAL 'QD'
              NEXT SENTENCE
           ELSE
              MOVE NOTIFY-OPERATOR-MESSAGE TO MESSAGE-TEXT
              MOVE +44 TO COMM-LENGTH
              PERFORM 600-SEND-MESSAGE-TO-ORIG-TERM.

           IF IO-STATUS-CODE EQUAL SPACES
              PERFORM 300-DETERMINE-ACTION-TAKEN.
      ****************************************************************
      *  ACTION CODE MUST BE EQUAL 'G' FOR RETRIEVE OR               *
      *                            'U' FOR UPDATE                    *
      *  OTHERWISE IT IS AN ERROR.                                   *
      ****************************************************************
       300-DETERMINE-ACTION-TAKEN.

           IF ACTION-CODE NOT EQUAL 'G' AND 'U'
              MOVE INVALID-ACTION-MESSAGE  TO MESSAGE-TEXT
              MOVE +44 TO COMM-LENGTH
              PERFORM 600-SEND-MESSAGE-TO-ORIG-TERM.

           IF ADDRESS-RETRIEVE
              PERFORM 400-RETRIEVE-DISPLAY-ACCOUNT.

           IF ADDRESS-UPDATE
              PERFORM 500-RETRIEVE-UPDATE-ACCOUNT.

      ****************************************************************
      *  QUALIFY ACCOUNT SSA WITH ACCOUNT NUMBER FROM TERMINAL,      *
      *  ACCESS ACCOUNT DATA BASE TO RETRIEVE ACCOUNT INFORMATION.   *
      *  IF ACCOUNT EXISTS                                           *
      *     . BUILD OUTPUT MESSAGE,                                  *
      *     . DETERMINE LENGTH OF MESSAGE AND MOVE IT TO LENGTH-FIELD *
      *     . MESSAGE LENGTH EQUALS LENGTH OF SEGMENT + 4,           *
      *     . INITIALIZE ZZ-FIELD TO ZEROES,                         *
      *     . SEND OUTPUT MESSAGE TO ORIGINAL TERMINAL.              *
      *                                                              *
      ****************************************************************
       400-RETRIEVE-DISPLAY-ACCOUNT.

           MOVE ACCOUNT-NUMBER TO ACCT-KEY-VALUE.
           CALL 'CBLTDLI' USING GU
```

Fig. 4-51. continued

```
                                  ACCOUNT-PCB-MASK
                                  ACCOUNT-IO-AREA
                                  ACCOUNT-SSA.

           IF ACCT-STATUS-CODE EQUAL 'GE'
              PERFORM 900-ACCOUNT-NOT-FOUND.

           IF ACCT-STATUS-CODE NOT EQUAL SPACES
              PERFORM 2000-DB-ERROR-ROUTINE.

      *  BUILD FIRST OUTPUT SEGMENT

              MOVE LAST-NAME           TO RESP-1-LAST-NAME
              MOVE FIRST-NAME          TO RESP-1-FIRST-NAME
              MOVE ACCT-SSN            TO RESP-1-SSN
              MOVE +48                 TO RESP-1-LENGTH
              MOVE +0                  TO RESP-1-ZZ
              PERFORM 600-SEND-MESSAGE-TO-ORIG-TERM.

      *  BUILD SECOND OUTPUT SEGMENT

              MOVE ACCT-ADDRESS-LINE1 TO RESP-2-ADDRESS-LINE1
              MOVE ACCT-ADDRESS-LINE2 TO RESP-2-ADDRESS-LINE2
              MOVE ACCT-CITY           TO RESP-2-CITY
              MOVE ACCT-STATE          TO RESP-2-STATE
              MOVE ACCT-ZIPCODE        TO RESP-2-ZIPCODE
              MOVE +71                 TO RESP-2-LENGTH
              MOVE +0                  TO RESP-2-ZZ
              PERFORM 600-SEND-MESSAGE-TO-ORIG-TERM.

        500-RETRIEVE-UPDATE-ACCOUNT.

           MOVE ACCOUNT-NUMBER TO ACCT-KEY-VALUE.
           CALL 'CBLTDLI' USING GHU
                                  ACCOUNT-PCB-MASK
                                  ACCOUNT-IO-AREA
                                  ACCOUNT-SSA.

           IF ACCT-STATUS-CODE EQUAL 'GE'
              PERFORM 900-ACCOUNT-NOT-FOUND.

           IF ACCT-STATUS-CODE NOT EQUAL SPACES
              PERFORM 2000-DB-ERROR-ROUTINE.

           IF ACCT-STATUS-CODE EQUAL SPACES
              MOVE STREET-ADDRESS1     TO ACCT-ADDRESS-LINE1
              MOVE STREET-ADDRESS2     TO ACCT-ADDRESS-LINE2
              MOVE CITY                TO ACCT-CITY
              MOVE STATE               TO ACCT-STATE
              MOVE ZIPCODE             TO ACCT-ZIPCODE
              PERFORM  800-REPLACE-ACCOUNT-INFO.
      *****************************************************************
      *  SEND MESSAGE TO INTERFACING TERMINAL USING IO-PCB            *
      *****************************************************************
       600-SEND-MESSAGE-TO-ORIG-TERM.
```

Fig. 4-51. continued

```
           CALL 'CBLTDLI' USING ISRT
                                IO-PCB-MASK
                                OUTPUT-MESSAGE-AREA.

      IF IO-STATUS-CODE NOT EQUAL SPACES
         PERFORM 1000-ERROR-ROUTINE.

*****************************************************************
*  UPDATE ACCOUNT SEGMENT,                                      *
*  SEND MESSAGE TO OPERATOR UPON COMPLETION OF UPDATE TRANSACTION*
*****************************************************************
 800-REPLACE-ACCOUNT-INFO.

      CALL 'CBLTDLI' USING REPL
                           ACCOUNT-PCB-MASK
                           ACCOUNT-IO-AREA.

      IF ACCT-STATUS-CODE NOT EQUAL SPACES
         PERFORM 2000-DB-ERROR-ROUTINE
      ELSE
         MOVE UPDATE-COMPLETED-MESSAGE TO MESSAGE-TEXT
         MOVE +44 TO COMM-LENGTH
         PERFORM 600-SEND-MESSAGE-TO-ORIG-TERM.

*****************************************************************
*  SEND NOT-FOUND-MESSAGE TO ORIGINAL TERMINAL USING IO-PCB     *
*****************************************************************
 900-ACCOUNT-NOT-FOUND.

         MOVE ACCT-NOT-FOUND-MESSAGE TO MESSAGE-TEXT
         MOVE +44 TO COMM-LENGTH

         CALL 'CBLTDLI' USING ISRT
                              IO-PCB-MASK
                              OUTPUT-MESSAGE-AREA.

      IF IO-STATUS-CODE NOT EQUAL SPACES
         PERFORM 1000-ERROR-ROUTINE.
*****************************************************************
*  THE IO ERROR ROUTINE IS EXECUTED WHENEVER AN UNEXPECTED STATUS*
*  CODE IS RETURNED. THIS ROUTINE VARIES FROM INSTALLATION TO   *
*  INSTALLATION. YOU SHOULD CHECK YOUR INSTALLATION'S STANDARDS *
*  ON HOW TO CODE THIS ROUTINE.                                 *
*  IN THIS EXAMPLE, WE ISSUE A ROLB CALL TO DELETE THE CURRENT  *
*  INPUT MESSAGE AND TO LET THE PROGRAM CONTINUE WITH THE NEXT  *
*  MESSAGE.                                                     *
*  WE ONLY SPECIFY THE FUNCTION AND THE IO PCB MASK, NO IO AREA *
*  IS SPECIFIED BECAUSE IT IS OPTIONAL.                         *
*****************************************************************
 1000-ERROR-ROUTINE.

         CALL 'CBLTDLI' USING ROLB
                              IO-PCB-MASK.
```

Fig. 4-51. continued

```
*****************************************************************
*  THE FOLLOWING ERROR ROUTINE IS EXECUTED WHENEVER A BAD STATUS *
*  CODE IS RETURNED FOR A DATA BASE CALL.                        *
*  MOST INSTALLATIONS REQUEST TO DISPLAY THE TYPE OF CALL, THE   *
*  RETURNED STATUS CODE, THE KEY VALUE OF THE SSA AND THEN CALL  *
*  A USER WRITTEN SUBROUTINE TO FORMAT A DUMP FOR DEBUGGING.     *
*****************************************************************
 2000-DB-ERROR-ROUTINE.

        DISPLAY 'GET CALL ERROR TO ACCOUNT DATA BASE'.
        DISPLAY 'STATUS CODE: ' ACCT-STATUS-CODE.
        DISPLAY 'ACCOUNT NUMBER: ' ACCT-KEY-VALUE.
*
*       CALL 'ABENDPGM' TO PRINT DUMP
```

Section II

MFS Programming Techniques

This section contains six chapters that expand the MFS background you acquired in the previous section. The chapters demonstrate how a well-designed MFS application improves communication efficiency by reducing the system resources that the application uses; ensuring data security and data integrity, improving operator convenience, and simplifying application programming.

This section presents several commonly-used techniques to consider when designing MFS applications. To assist you in making design goal trade-offs, the various MFS facilities and their efficiency considerations are discussed. Problems that can occur within an IMS/VS DB/DC environment are also pinpointed.

Some of the techniques may be efficient for one application but not for another. As a designer, you can determine which of the facilities best serves your design objectives. You can then make the best design decision based on the particular needs of your application and your installation's standards.

Each facility is presented with the available alternatives, followed by a discussion of the best alternative to use to achieve the desired result. COBOL programming samples related to the MFS techniques are provided whenever appropriate.

The following techniques are discussed:

- How to specify literals through MFS
- How to use the system message field
- How to use password protection
- How to specify device operations on output
- How to invoke logical and physical paging
- How to control multiple-screen flows
- How to specify special hardware features

After discussing these, we will discuss the design considerations of message format service.

5

MFS Literals, System Message Fields, and Password Protection

This chapter covers three separate techniques:

- How to specify literals through MFS
- How to use the system message field
- How to use password protection

These techniques are not related to each other and you can learn them in any order.

HOW TO SPECIFY LITERALS THROUGH MFS

MFS enables you to define literal fields that can be mapped as part of the input or output messages. First, we will see how to specify input literals, and then output literals. After that, we will consider the advantages and disadvantages of using literals.

Specifying Input Literals

Input message fields can be defined to contain literal data specified by the user during definition of the MID. There are two types of input literals—explicit literals and default literals. Explicit literals are always mapped by the MFS as part of the input message. Default literals are mapped as part of the input message when no data for the field is received from the terminal.

Let's see how these two types can be coded.

Explicit Literals. The following example shows how to specify an explicit literal for input messages:

```
INPMESG  MSG      TYPE=INPUT,SOR=(CUSTUP,IGNORE),NXT=OUTMESG,OPT=1
         SEG
         MFLD     '1'← MID literal
         ....
         MSGEND
```

In this example, the MFLD statement is used to provide fixed information which will be mapped into the message segment. The literal '1' number one is the actual data you want to place in the message segment. Since the literal is a positional parameter, it must be the first parameter coded.

The application program can examine the input message for the literal specified to determine the appropriate processing. An example is:

```
IF IN-FIELD = '1'
   PERFORM VALIDATE-DATA
ELSE
   PERFORM UPDATE-DATA.
```

The use of explicit literals is one of the most common uses of the MID literals.

Default Literals. The default literal is used to fill a field with a literal when the operator does not enter any data in that field. The application program can test if data has been entered or not. An example of specifying a default literal is:

```
INPMESG  MSG      TYPE=INPUT,SOR=(CUSTUP,IGNORE),NXT=OUTMESG,OPT=1
         SEG
         MFLD     (ORDERNO,'*****'),LTH=05
         ....
         MSGEND
```

If the user does not enter data into the ORDERNO field, its input message field will contain '*****'. Also, if no default literal is used as shown below, and the user does not enter data into this field, its input message field will contain blanks and the application program cannot determine if data has been entered or not.

```
MFLD ORDERNO,LTH=05
```

Another example with a default literal is:

```
MFLD (AMOUNT,'$$$$$$$'),LTH=07,JUST=R,FILL=C'0'
```

This is how it looks in the Program's I-O area:

```
Operator enters    Program I-O area
 1234               0001234
 0                  0000000
 Nothing            $$$$$$$
```

MID default literals can be used

- To inform the application program that no data has been entered in a device field. In this example, the literal '$$$$$$$' would be the default if no data is keyed in.
- To reduce the amount of data which must be entered and transmitted by requiring only exceptions to be keyed-in by the operator.

The default literal can be up to 256 characters. Defaults can be altered without changing the application program.

Input Justification and Fill

Input data fields can be left- or right-justified, and fill characters can be used to pad input message fields in the following situations:

- When the length of the data received from the device field is less than the length of the field specified in the MID.
- When no data is received and no default literal is specified in the MFLD statement.

The following fill characters are available:

- A blank (X'40')
- Any hexadecimal character (X'hh')
- Any graphic character (C'c')
- NULL, which will cause compression of the input message to the left by the amount of missing data

The input justification and fill are defined in the MID. JUST=L and X'40' are the defaults.

Following is an example that shows how to define input justification and fill characters:

```
INPMESG   MSG      TYPE=INPUT,SOR=(CUSTUP,IGNORE),NXT=OUTMESG,OPT1
          SEG
                                    ┌─Left-justify
          MFLD     CUSTNO,LTH=08,JUST=L,FILL=C'0'
          MFLD     (ORDERNO,'*****'),LTH=05
          ....                ↑
          MSGEND              │
                              Default literal
```

The example below shows how to define the FILL=NULL character:

```
INPMESG   MSG      TYPE=INPUT,SOR=(CUSTUP,IGNORE),NXT=OUTMESG,
                   OPT=n← OPT can be, 1, 2, or 3
```

```
          SEG
          MFLD      NAME,LTH=25,JUST=L,FILL=NULL
          ....
          MSGEND
```

The mapping of the input message fields depends on the OPT=n being used. The FILL=NULL character causes input data area to be potentially of variable length because the fields data is truncated to the length of the data entered.

When to Specify JUST and FILL. The default JUST=L and FILL=X'40' are used when input fields are of fixed length and when variable-length alphanumeric data is entered. The application program expects the data to be placed on the left side of the field, and any unused characters are filled with blanks.

The JUST= and FILL= parameters must be coded when variable-length numeric data is entered. For this situation, you should code

```
JUST=R, FILL=X'F0' or FILL=C'0'
```

This will cause the input data to be aligned to the rightmost position (low order) of the numeric field, causing leading zeroes to be inserted in the unused positions.

Now, let's look at field truncation.

Input Truncation

Truncation of an input field can be implied in the JUST= parameter. An example of a DFLD with its related MFLD appears below.

```
CUSTUP    FMT
          ....
          DIV       TYPE=INOUT
NAME      DFLD      POS=(05,10),LTH=25,ATTR=(MOD,PROT)

INPMESG   MSG       TYPE=INPUT,SOR=(CUSTUP,IGNORE),NXT=OUTMESG,      *
                    OPT=1
          SEG
          MFLD      NAME,LTH=20,JUST=R
          ....
          MSGEND
```

This instructs MFS to place the rightmost 20 characters of the device field 'NAME' into the message field 'NAME' and to drop the leftmost characters of device field 'NAME'.

Truncation—unlike JUST= and FILL= is not an MFLD parameter, but is implied and controlled by the JUST= parameter whenever the device field is larger than the associated input message field. The data truncation occurs opposite the direction of the justification; that is, if the field is to be right-justified in the message segment, then any truncation will be made to the left of the field.

Now, let's summarize the MFS justification and filling of input message fields.

MFS always justifies the data first, and then, depending on the situation for the input field,

- Fills the remaining positions of the input field if a FILL= a character is specified.
- Shortens the length of the field if FILL=NULL is specified.
- Truncates the field opposite the justification if the device field is larger than the associated input message field.

Specifying Output Literals

Output message fields can be defined to contain literal data specified by the user during definition of the MOD. There are two types of output literals: common MOD literals and system message literals. Let's see how each can be coded.

Common MOD Literals. The following example shows how to specify a common MOD literal for output messages.

```
DOF

CUSTUP      FMT
            DEV       TYPE=(3270,2),FEAT=IGNORE,SYSMSG=MESSAGE
            DIV       TYPE=INOUT
            DPAGE     CURSOR=((04,73))
HEADER      DFLD      POS=(02,29),LTH=23
            ....
            FMTEND
MOD
OUTMESG     MSG       TYPE=OUTPUT,SOR=(CUSTUP,IGNORE),NXT=INPMESG
            SEG
            MFLD      (HEADER'CUSTOMER ADDRESS CHANGE')<- MOD literal
            ....
            ....         (1)           (2)
            MSGEND
```

In this example, (1) is the label (DFLD name) of the DFLD statement that specifies where the literal information is to be mapped on the screen, and (2) is the literal you want to display on the screen. Note that neither the LTH= or JUST= parameters are coded.

The literal is used to display the heading of a screen to the operator. This is a common technique of using the MOD literal; it allows the use of a single general DOF to handle several different output messages. The screen heading can be changed depending on the MOD which processes the output message.

System Message Literals. The system message literal functions in the same manner as the common MOD literal, except that the information to be displayed is referred to by a system literal name. A system literal name is a keyword which allows MFS to furnish the desired information. Commonly-used literal names and their respective formats are listed in FIG. 5-1.

Name	Format of Value in DFLD	Length	Comments
TIME	HH.MM.SS	8	
DATE1	YY.DDD	6	
DATE2	MMDDYY	8	
DATE3	DDMMYY	8	
DATE4	YYMMDD	8	
LPAGENO	NNNN	4	Specifies the current the current logical page number relative to beginning of message, zero suppressed.
LTNAME	AAAAAAAA	8	Name of logical terminal for which the message is being formatted.
LTSEQ	NNNNN	5	Output message sequence number for the logical terminal. The value created is the logical terminal dequeue count plus 1. The first output message after IMS/VS coldstart or /NRESTART BUILDQ will have a sequence number of 00001.

Fig. 5-1.

See FIGS. 5-2 and 5-3 for an MFS example using system literals. Suppose we wish to display the time of day, the current date, and the name of the logical terminal on the screen. In this DOF, the system literal names TIME, DATE2 and LTNAME display the time of day, the current date, and the name of the logical terminal. These are the most-used system literals. (Remember, system literal names must be spelled correctly.)

```
10:15am                 18/27/86                 PAGE 1

TERMINAL:  IBM00270
```

Fig. 5-2.

MOD Literal Coding. Unlike DOF literals, MOD literals are transmitted to a terminal each time a message is formatted, and so they tend to affect response time. Unlike MID literals, MOD literals do not affect the location of any field in the output message. It is good practice to group all literals in a MOD either before or after the MFLDs which actually refer to the message segment. This will facilitate the application programming effort.

OUTPUT JUSTIFICATION AND FILL

Output formatting is accomplished through a combination of fill and justification for each data field contained in the output message.

```
       DOF:
       ---

FMT004    FMT
          DEV    TYPE=(3270,2),FEAT=IGNORE
          DIV    TYPE=INOUT
          DPAGE  CURSOR=((01,02,CURSOR)),FILL=NONE
          .....
          .....
TIMEY     DFLD   POS=(01,08),LTH=08,ATTR=(ALPHA,PROT)
DATEMDY   DFLD   POS=(01,60),LTH=08,ATTR=(ALPHA,PROT)
PAGEID    DFLD   POS=(01,70),LTH=10,ATTR=(ALPHA,PROT)
TERM      DFLD   POS=(02,08),LTH=08,ATTR=(ALPHA,PROT)
          .....
          .....
          MSGEND

       MOD:
       ---

INTDIS    MSG    TYPE=OUTPUT,SOR=(FMT004,IGNORE),OPT=1,NXT=INPUTA,         *
                 PAGE=YES,FILL=NULL
          SEG
          .....
          MFLD   (TIMEY,TIME),LTH=08
          MFLD   (DATEMDY,DATE2),LTH=08     <=== SYSTEM LITERAL NAMES
          MFLD   PAGEID,LTH=10
          MFLD   (TERM,LTNAME),LTH=08
          .....
          MSGEND
          END
```

Fig. 5-3.

Output Field Justification

Justification in an output message is controlled on a field-by-field basis with the JUST= parameter in the MFLD statement. For a 3270 device, all fields are left justified in the device field, and for the JUST= parameter to work, it must be accompanied with a character fill.

Output field justification is required in the following situations:

- When a character fill is used (X'hh' or C'c') and the DFLD is longer than the MFLD
- When the length of the message field is longer than the length of the device field specified in the MOD and you want the leftmost portion of the output message to be truncated rather than the right of the output message

Output Field Filling

Fill characters can be used to pad output message fields when the length of the data received from the application program is less than the length specified in the MOD, or when no data is received.

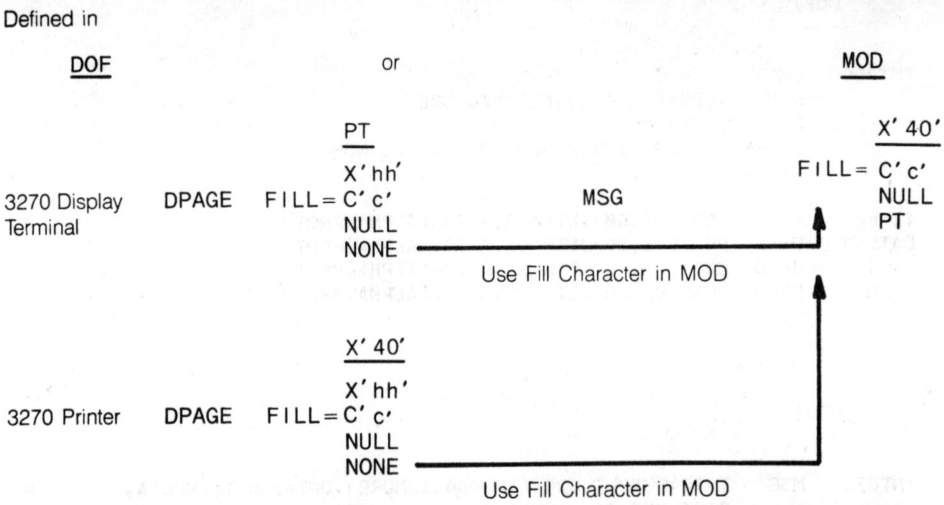

Fig. 5-4. Specifying output fill characters.

The fill character can be defined in the DPAGE statement of the DOF or in the MSG statement of the MOD. If specified in both, the fill character specified in the DPAGE statement will prevail.

If FILL=NONE is specified in the DPAGE statement, the fill character specified in the MSG statement will be used.

For 3270 terminals, the default is FILL=PT for the DPAGE statement and X'40' blanks for the MSG statement. For 3270 printers, the default is FILL=X'40' for the DPAGE statement.

Fill characters that may be specified for the DPAGE and MSG statements are given in FIG. 5-4.

Defining the Fill Character. The first example shows how to define a fill character in a DPAGE statement, and the second shows the definition of the character in an MSG statement.

```
         FOR 3270 DISPLAY TERMINAL
CUSTUP   FMT
         DEV   TYPE=(3270,2),FEAT=IGNORE
         DIV   TYPE=INOUT
         DPAGE CURSOR=((04,73),FILL=NONE     <===
         .....

         FOR 3270 PRINTER
CUSTUP   FMT
         .....
         DIV   TYPE=OUTPUT
         DPAGE FILL=X'40'                    <===
                            SPECIFYING FILL CHARACTER IN DPAGE STATEMENT
```

```
CUSTUP   FMT
         DEV   TYPE=(3270,2),FEAT=IGNORE
         DIV   TYPE=INOUT
         DPAGE CURSOR=((04,73),FILL=NONE      <===
         .....
OUTMESG  MSG   TYPE=OUTPUT,SOR=(CUSTUP,IGNORE),NXT=INPMESG,OPT=1,       *
               FILL=PT                        <===
         SEG
         ....
         MSGEND
```

SPECIFYING FILL CHARACTER IN MSG STATEMENT

Fill-Character Considerations. The selection of the fill character can affect the volume of data transmission and the data left in a field from the previous display.

- For the 3270 device, the character fill (X'hh' or C'c') should be avoided; it causes the transmission of the maximum number of characters to the terminal because all data fields are padded with the fill character.
- The FILL=NULL character minimizes the amount of characters to be transmitted and reduces response time as long as all unprotected fields are erased prior to display of the output message.
- The FILL=PT character causes a single character to be added to the data from the message field if it does not completely fill the device field. This program tab character—an X'05'—when detected by MFS, will cause the rest of the device field to be cleared to the 3270 device null character. For the 3270 device, this option is recommended when all unprotected fields cannot be erased by the display of the output message.

  Using the fill character tailored to the device should improve both message presentation and device performance.
- In addition to using the NULL and PT fill character, the application program can make a difference to the amount of data to be transmitted to the terminal device. In the message I-O area, the application program can place an X'3F' after the last character of data to be displayed, and MFS will recognize it as the end of the field and will fill the rest of the field after that point. This technique, used in conjunction with either NULL or PT fill, can minimize data transmission and response time.

Use of Literals

Before leaving the subject of specifying literals through MFS, let's see whether we should specify literals in the DOF, in the MOD, or in the message text. Each technique has its advantages and disadvantages.

In the DOF. Literals coded in the DOF are transmitted only when a full format write occurs. Full format write (or force format write) causes all fields on the screen to be reestablished and all DOF literals to be transmitted. On the average, 1100 bytes are transmitted when a full format write occurs, while only 700 bytes are transmitted when a Full Format Write is not required. You can minimize data transmission and response time by coding literals in the DOF and by avoiding the full format write option. Remember, DOF literals are not mapped on input.

One disadvantage of this technique is that literals coded in the DOF will customize the screen format to a particular application. This coding might make it necessary for you to create several screen formats. It also will have a negative impact on the message queue, MFS, and the format buffer pool.

In the MOD. Literals coded in the MOD can be mapped on input. They are always transmitted, and because of this, they tend to maximize data transmission and response time. As with DOF literals, MOD literals increase the size of the control blocks and thus have a negative impact on the message queue, on MFS, and the format buffer pool.

In the Message Text. Coding literals as part of the message text decreases the size of the control blocks and allows for more general formats. Message text literals are displayed on the screen only when they are transmitted; however, this may complicate programming.

Combining Fields. Combining DFLD literals will result in fewer DFLD definitions thereby reducing the size of the control blocks and reducing MFS processing time. However, combining fields may increase data transmission if there are many blank spaces between the fields to be combined.

Combining fields has the disadvantage of making the application device-dependent. It also complicates the programming effort; instead of having the fields mapped by the coding control blocks, the programmer has to remember how the data must be exactly formatted on the screen.

HOW TO USE THE SYSTEM MESSAGE FIELD

We recommend that you always define a message line in the device format to receive the system messages. When IMS/VS sends a system message to the terminal, and if no message field is allocated to receive it, the system message may erase the current display. The coding below shows how to define a system message field.

```
DIF

CUSTUP    FMT
          DEV     TYPE=(3270,2),FEAT=IGNORE,SYSMSG=MESSAGE,
                  DSCA=X'00A0'
          DIV     TYPE=INOUT
          ....       More DFLDs go here.
          ....
MESSAGE   DFLD    POS=(13,03),LTH=79,ATTR=(PROT,HI)← Line for display
          ....                                       of system messages
          FMTEND
```

In this coding, SYSMSG= specifies a label statement defining a field where IMS/VS system messages are to be displayed without destroying the current screen display. This field name will be defined in a DFLD statement. DFLDs for SYSMSG should be coded with LTH=79 to avoid the truncation of system messages. FIGURE 5-5 shows why there is a need for this parameter:

```
                CUSTOMER UPDATE

ACCOUNT NO: 12345678
LAST NAME: WILLIAMS
FIRST NAME: JOHN
SOC SEC NO: 999999999
CURRENT ADDRESS:
  STREET:     11713 BASSWOOD DR
  CITY:       NOWHERE
              ::::::::::::::::::::
  STATE:      MD    ZIP CODE: 20708
```

```
DFS256 PRINTER FOR COPY NOT AVAILABLE
```

Fig. 5-5.

```
                CUSTOMER UPDATE

ACCOUNT NO: 12345678
LAST NAME: WILLIAMS
FIRST NAME: JOHN
SOC SEC NO: 999999999
CURRENT ADDRESS:
  STREET:     11713 BASSWOOD DR
  CITY:       NOWHERE
              ::::::::::::::::::::
  STATE:      MD    ZIP CODE: 20708

DFS256 PRINTER FOR COPY NOT AVAILABLE
```

1. After having keyed-in the data (FIG. 5-5 SCREEN 5-1), the operator presses PRINT to print the screen image; however, the printer is not available.
2. The message is transmitted to IMS/VS which sends back the message

   DFS256 PRINTER FOR COPY NOT AVAILABLE

   and the entire screen has been erased (FIG. 5-5, SCREEN 5-2). The operator has to rekey.

3. To prevent the contents of the screen from being erased by the system message, we can specify a field in the SYSMSG= parameter of the DEV statement (FIG. 5-5, SCREEN 5-3).

Using a system message field or setting byte 1 bit 5 to binary '0' in the DSCA= specification will prevent IMS/VS messages from destroying the current display. The explanation of the bit setting is given in chapter 6.

HOW TO USE PASSWORD PROTECTION

Specifying NODISP for the password's attribute in the MFS coding will prevent the password from being seen and is a common technique for keeping passwords secure. However, two other methods are available for password protection: One is to let the application program check the password; the other is to use the IMS password assigned through the system either in the DIF/DOF or in the MID control blocks.

Let's cover the coding considerations involved for each of these techniques.

The Application Program Checks the Password

The password is coded as an MFLD data name in the MID. Once the message is received into the application program's input message I-O area, the program will validate this field before processing continues. Following is an example of coding the password in the MID.

```
        DIF:
        ___

         TITLE 'CUSTOMER NAME AND ADDRESS CHANGE'
         PRINT NOGEN
*
HISKIP   EQU   '(PROT,HI)'
CUSTUP   FMT
         DEV   TYPE=(3270,2),FEAT=IGNORE,SYSMSG=MESSAGE
         DIV   TYPE=INOUT
         DPAGE CURSOR=((04,73))
         DFLD  'PASSWORD',POS=(01,02),ATTR=(HI,PROT,NOMOD)
PSSWRD   DFLD  POS=(01,12),LTH=08,ATTR=(MOD,NODISP)
         DFLD  'CUSTOMER ADDRESS CHANGE',POS=(02,29),LTH=23,          *
               ATTR=HISKIP
TRANCD   DFLD  POS=(04,05),LTH=08,ATTR=(MOD,PROT,NODISP)
         .....
         FMTEND

        MID:
        ___

INPMESG  MSG   TYPE=INPUT,SOR=CUSTUP,NXT=OUTMESG
         SEG
         MFLD  PSSWRD,LTH=08,JUST=L,FILL=X'40'        <=== PASSWORD
         MFLD  TRANCD,LTH=09
         .....
         MSGEND
```

Use the IMS Password

Assignment in the DIF. Below is an example of specifying a password in the DFLD of the DIF/DOF to identify this field as the location of the IMS/VS password field for input messages.

```
DIF
          DFLD    'ENTER PASSWORD: ',POS=(01,02),ATTR=(HI,PROT,NOMOD)
          DFLD    PASSWORD,POS=(01,18),LTH=08,ATTR=(UNPROT,NODISP)
```

The label is not specified on the DFLD with the keyword PASSWORD, and thus no MFLD references the password DFLD. Also, the password is not presented to the application program; it is stripped by IMS/VS before it is placed on the message queue.

Assignment in the MID. In FIG. 5-6,

- The label PASSWD is specified for the DFLD statement.
- The keyword PASSWORD is specified in the MID. This is a signal to MFS that a password is being used.
- When used, the PASSWORD statement and its associated MFLD(s) must precede the first SEG statement in the MID.
- With the MID assignment, the password may be part of the input message. Up to eight MFLD statements may be specified after the PASSWORD statement, but the assembled password cannot exceed eight characters. Below is an example of an assembled password. Note that the fill character must be X'40'. USERIN and NUMBER are specified to create the IMS/VS password; their total length is eight characters.

```
INPMESG MSG      TYPE=INPUT,SOR=CUSTUP,NXT=OUTMESG
        PASSWORD
        MFLD     USERIN,LTH=03,FILL=X'40'
        MFLD     NUMBER,LTH=05,FILL=X'40'
        SEG
        ....
        MSGEND
```

Single and Multiple-Field Passwords

Now, let's look at the difference between a single-field password and an assembled password consisting of many fields (FIG. 5-7).

Remember, up to eight MFLD statements may be specified, but the cumulative length of the MFLDs cannot exceed eight bytes.

For Options I and II, the first eight characters of data after editing will be used for the IMS/VS password. For Option III, the data content of the first field after editing will be used for the IMS/VS password.

```
        DIF:
        ---

        ....
        DFLD   'ENTER PASSWORD: ',POS=(01,02),ATTR=(HI,PROT,NOMOD)
PASSWD  DFLD   POS=(01,18),LTH=08,ATTR=(UNPROT,NODISP)
  ^
  |
LABEL IS
SPECIFIED

        MID:
        ---
INPMESG  MSG    TYPE=INPUT,SOR=CUSTUP,NXT=OUTMESG
         PASSWORD                                      <=== PASSWORD KEYWORD
         MFLD   PASSWD,LTH=08
         SEG
         ....
         MSGEND
```

Fig. 5-6.

DIF

```
PSW     DFLD    PASSWORD,POS=(02,12),LTH=06,      *
                ATTR=(UNPROT,NODISP)
```

If the operator keys in YOSHUA, the password would be a single field.

MID

```
PASSWORD
MFLD      USERIN,LTH=3,FILL=X'40'
MFLD      NUMBER,LTH=5,FILL=X'40
```

The assembled password is C2798516.

Fig. 5-7.

We recommend the assignment of the password in the MID. This technique has more flexibility than assigning the password in the DIF since it allows a password to be made up of multiple fields. If the password is specified both in the DIF and the MID, the definition in the MID will prevail.

6

How to Specify Device Operations on Output

In this chapter, we will examine the specific device operations that may be requested when an output message is sent to the terminal. Device operations are typically used to alert the operator to data entry errors, such as highlighting a field and positioning the cursor to where the error needs correction, or to sound the device alarm when an error occurs. Other uses include producing hard copy of output messages or preventing the hard copy of sensitive information.

Device operations may be requested via the system control area (SCA), via its default DSCA, or from the application program.

In the first part of this chapter, we will show you how to use the SCA (or its default) to request various device operations. As we progress, you will learn the COBOL techniques for dynamically modifying field attributes through the application program.

HOW TO USE THE SYSTEM CONTROL AREA (SCA) OR DEFAULT SCA

Let's see how we can request specific device operations via the SCA or DSCA. Specific device operations requests are defined as half-word system control literals (either decimal or hexadecimal) and can be passed to the system.

- From the application program in the output message, or
- From the device output format as a default value

Control the SCA from the Application Program

For the application program to request a device operation, you have to code the SCA in the MOD. Here is an example:

```
MOD

OUTMESG  MSG      TYPE=OUTPUT,SOR=(FORMAT,IGNORE),NXT=INPUT
         SEG
         MFLD     (,SCA),LTH=2
```

The SCA is an optional field; if used, the MOD control block will contain an MFLD for it. The SCA is two-bytes-long. When an SCA is defined, it will appear in the first segment of the input message. The application program has to move the SCA=X value to its output message field before doing an ISRT call of the output message.

Control the Default DSCA in the DOF

To use the default system control area (SCA), you have to code a DSCA= value in the DOF. Here is an example:

```
DOF

FORMAT   FMT
         DEV      TYPE=(3270,2),FEAT=IGNORE,DSCA=X'VALUE'
```

The SCA values may be specified in both the MOD and the DOF, and a combination of values may be used.

System Control Area Options

There are four SCA options as listed in FIG. 6-1. The values reflect bit settings; to get multiple operations, we have to combine bit settings and use composite values.

Now, let's see how we can set the SCA values.

Setting the SCA Value. Each bit setting of the SCA value has a unique meaning. FIGURE 6-2 illustrates these settings.

OPTIONS	HEX VALUE	DECIMAL VALUE
1. FULL FORMAT WRITE	X'00C0'	+192
2. ERASE UNPROTECTED FIELDS BEFORE WRITE	X'00A0'	+160
3. SOUND DEVICE ALARM	X'0090'	+144
4. COPY OUTPUT TO CANDIDATE PRINTER (3270)	X'0088'	+136
THE DEFAULT IS	X'0000'	

Fig. 6-1.

BYTE	BIT	VALUES	FUNCTIONS
0	0 - 7	SET TO 0	
1	0	SET TO 0	
	1	SET TO 1	TO FORCE FULL FORMAT WRITE
	2	SET TO 1	TO ERASE UNPROTECTED FIELDS
	3	SET TO 1	TO SOUND DEVICE ALARM
	4	SET TO 1	TO COPY TO PRINTER
	5 - 7	SET TO 0	

Fig. 6-2. System control area bit settings.

The first byte of the SCA must have all bits set to zeroes. In byte one, the high-order bit must be set to 1; bits 5 through 7 must be set to zero. The remaining four bits can be used by the application program to request a particular action:

1. When bit 1 is set to 1, a full-format write will occur prior to transmission of the message segment.
2. When bit 2 is set to 1, all unprotected fields will be erased.
3. When bit 3 is set to 1, the device alarm will be sounded (if one is available).
4. When bit 4 is set to 1, the output message is copied to a printer.

If a nonzero value is specified for byte 0, or for bits 5, 6, 7 in byte 1, the MFS will override the specified value with zeroes.

You've learned how to set the SCA values to request specific device operations when an output message is sent to the terminal, and that there are four types of requests available:

1. Force-format write
2. Erase unprotected fields before write
3. Sound device alarm
4. Copy output to candidate printer

Now, let's find out when we should use the above options.

Force-format write. This option is used to cause full-formatting operation. Each time it is requested, the device buffer is erased, and all fields and literals are transmitted to the output device. The major disadvantages of this option are that full-formatting increases transmission time, and that each time we send an output message, we have to reconstruct the current display; for most applications, we want to preserve the current screen for subsequent displays.

This option is recommended only for building PFK screens.

Erase unprotected fields before write. This option is used when the application requires that all unprotected fields be cleared. It has a disadvantage—we have to reconstruct the contents of all the unprotected fields after they have been erased. This option is recommended for data entry applications when the current transaction has been processed and the user is ready to enter the next transaction.

There are situations when we want to preserve the contents on the current display for the user to make corrections before erasing them. This can be achieved by not specifying the DSCA= value. (When this default value is not specified, only those fields whose data or attributes were changed by the application program will be sent to the current display.)

To preserve the contents of the device fields on the current display, we need to move an X'3F' to the device field that we want to preserve.

FIGURE 6-3 illustrates the case of setting the DSCA= value for erasing unprotected fields.

Sound device alarm. This option is used when we want to draw the user's attention to an error.

MFS printer support. Three facilities are available for producing a hard copy facility of an output message. These are the DSCA method, the use of special terminal software, and the alternate PCB method.

1. The SCA method

   Use the SCA in the device output format as a default value, or let the application program manage the SCA value in the output message. Coding of the SCA in either way is:

   DOF

   ```
   FORMAT FMT
          DEV TYPE=(3270,2),FEAT=IGNORE,DSCA=X'0088'
   ```

   Each physical page is copied when displayed by the operator provided that a candidate printer is ready.

   Coding can also be managed by the MPP program in the output message:

   MOD

   ```
   OUTMESG MSG   TYPE=OUTPUT,SOR=(FORMAT,IGNORE),NXT=INPUT
           MFLD (,SCA),LTH=2
   ```

   The MPP program initiates the copy output message with a Hex X'0088'; each physical page will be printed in the same way as defined in the DOF.

   The SCA method has the disadvantage that it is controlled by your installation's network configuration. For the SCA method to work, the terminals and associated printers must be defined to IMS/VS in the SYSGEN. The printer must be defined within the same control unit cluster as the terminals. If, for some reason, the system configuration is redefined, you may find your print copy end up at another department or not get printed at all. This method should be avoided.

2. The special software method

   The 3270 terminals are available with the print function. The user may initiate a

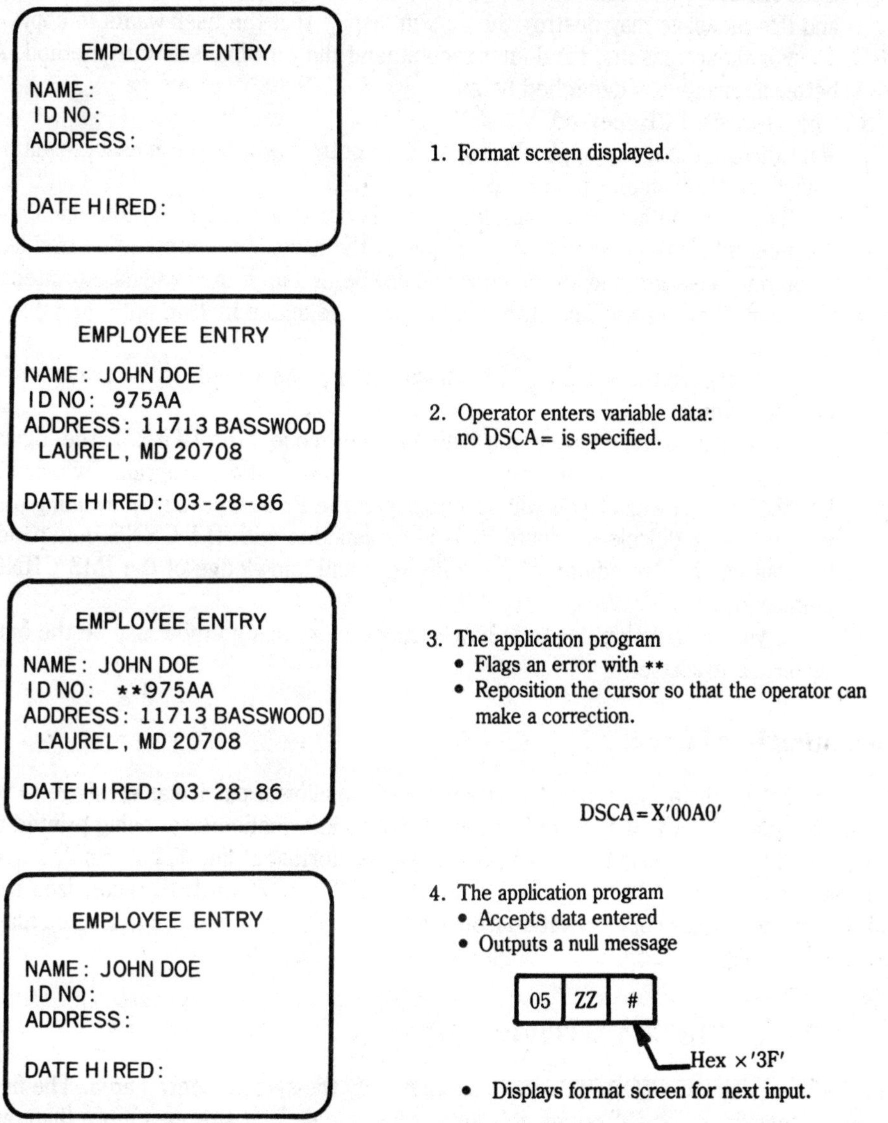

Fig. 6-3. Erasing unprotected fields.

copy of the screen display by using either the PA3 or PF2 key. Data on the screen is printed without application program intervention.

Like the SCA method, the special terminal software method also requires appropriate network configuration. Another disadvantage is that you will run into the situation where the terminal which initiated the print request to be "locked" if the candidate printer is not ready; an error message will be sent to the terminal and this message may destroy the screen display that the user wants to copy.

For these reasons, we do not recommend the terminal software method. A better alternative is described below.

3. The alternate PCB method
With this method, the application program controls where the message will be copied by using an alternate PCB.

This method has the advantage that it is not restricted to remote lines and does not affect the terminal which requests the copy. The output is treated like an output message; and so the copy will not be tied up if the candidate printer is not ready. The copy will be stored in the message queue by IMS until the printer is available.

This method is relatively free from restrictions based upon terminal and printer alignment.

One disadvantage is that you have to "hard code" the LTERM, the logical terminal name for the alternate PCB in the application program; whenever LTERMs are changed, you will have to regen the PSB. One way of avoiding this is to use a modifiable alternate PCB in conjunction with the CHNG command, but this will involve additional program logic and knowledge of the IMS CHNG command.

If your installation does not have remote lines, this method may be the only technique available.

Preventing Hard Copy

There will be instances where you do not want to allow a particular message to be printed (for example, you may want to prevent payroll information from being printed to hard copy). This can be done by coding on the screen format at line 1, column 2, a field with the attributes ALPHANUMERIC and PROTECTED. When IMS recognizes this field, it will prevent the copy operation from occurring. This protection can also be managed by the application program through the use of an alternate PCB.

MODIFYING THE SCA WITH COBOL

Now, let's examine two COBOL techniques to modify the system control area. The first technique specifies one SCA option at a time, while the second specifies more than one option at a time.

Specify One Option at a Time

We know that the first bit of the second byte must contain a 1, and that bits 5 through 7 must be set to zeroes. The binary presentation of the SCA is shown in FIG. 6-4. This is equivalent to X'0080' or character +128.

The other options values are listed in FIG. 6-5.

```
0000 0000   1000 0000

    |           |
    |           |
    |         BYTE 2
    |
  BYTE 1
```

Fig. 6-4. Binary presentation of the default SCA.

```
        OPTIONS                                HEX VALUE     DECIMAL VALUE
        -------                                ---------     -------------

 1. FULL FORMAT WRITE                          X'00C0'          +192
 2. ERASE UNPROTECTED FIELDS
    BEFORE WRITE                               X'00A0'          +160
 3. SOUND DEVICE ALARM                         X'0090'          +144
 4. COPY OUTPUT TO CANDIDATE PRINTER           X'0088'          +136
                                 (3270)
```

Fig. 6-5.

The output that follows illustrates the COBOL coding of the data constants we can use to set the SCA. Note that the operation requested already includes the basic pattern value of +128 of the SCA plus the value of the requested option. This example illustrates the instruction required to set the SCA to "sound the device alarm."

```
DATA DIVISION
.....
01  SCA-VALUES                    COMP SYNC.
    05 FULL-FORMAT-WRITE          PIC S9(04)          VALUE +192.
    05 ERASE-UNPROT               PIC S9(04)          VALUE +160.
    05 SOUND-DEVICE-ALARM         PIC S9(04)          VALUE +144.
    05 COPY-TO-PRINTER            PIC S9(04)          VALUE +136.
01  MESSAGE-IO-AREA.
    05 MESSAGE-LENGTH             PIC S9(04) COMP SYNC VALUE +88
    05 MESSAGE-ZZ                 PIC S9(04) COMP SYNC VALUE +0.
    05 SYSTEM-CONTROL-AREA        PIC S9(04) COMP.
PROCEDURE DIVISION
.....
    MOVE SOUND-DEVICE-ALARM TO SYSTEM-CONTROL AREA.
```

Specify More Than One Option at a Time

Now, let's use the values listed in FIG. 6-6. The following shows the COBOL coding of those values and illustrates the instruction required to set the SCA to specify "sound the device alarm and copy the message to a printer."

```
DATA DIVISION
.....
01  SCA-VALUES                    COMP SYNC.
```

How to Specify Device Operations on Output

```
         05 BASIC-SYSTEM-CONTROL     PIC S9(04)   VALUE +128
         05 FULL-FORMAT-WRITE        PIC S9(04)   VALUE +64.
         05 ERASE-UNPROT             PIC S9(04)   VALUE +32.
         05 SOUND-DEVICE-ALARM       PIC S9(04)   VALUE +16
         05 COPY-TO-PRINTER          PIC S9(04)   VALUE +08.
      01 MESSAGE-IO-AREA
         05 MESSAGE-LENGTH           PIC S9(04) COMP SYNC VALUE +88
         05 MESSAGE-ZZ               PIC S9(04) COMP SYNC VALUE +0.
         05 SYSTEM-CONTROL-AREA      PIC S9(04) COMP.
      PROCEDURE DIVISION.
      .....
         ADD BASIC-SYSTEM-CONTROL
             SOUND-DEVICE-ALARM
             COPY-TO-PRINTER
                  GIVING SYSTEM-CONTROL-AREA.
```

OPTIONS	HEX VALUE	DECIMAL VALUE
1. BASIC SYSTEM CONTROL AREA	X'0080'	+128
2. FULL FORMAT WRITE	X'0040'	+64
3. ERASE UNPROTECTED FIELDS BEFORE WRITE	X'0020'	+32
4. SOUND DEVICE ALARM	X'0010'	+16
5. COPY OUTPUT TO CANDIDATE PRINTER (3270)	X'0008'	+08

Fig. 6-6.

CURSOR POSITIONING

The cursor on a 3270 terminal can be initially set in three different ways.

1. By default (the default for the cursor is (1,2): line 1, column 2)
2. By control block coding (the cursor can be defined for the device output format)
3. Under application program control (by the application program through the use of a cursor field, or by dynamic attribute modification)

Default Cursor Positioning

When no cursor positioning is specified, MFS will automatically position the cursor in line 1, column 2. This is undesirable because it will create inconvenience for the operator.

Cursor Positioning by Control Block Coding

This method places the cursor in the same position on the screen each time the format is displayed. We can specify the cursor in the device output format via the DPAGE statement. An example is:

```
CUSTUP  FMT
        DEV     TYPE=(3270,2),FEAT=IGNORE,SYSMSG=MESSAGE
        DIV     TYPE=INOUT
        DPAGE   CURSOR=((04,73)) ← Specifies cursor on line 4, column 73
```

The CURSOR parameter allows you to specify where the cursor should be positioned for each physical page within the DPAGE. When a DPAGE consists of multiple pages, multiple cursor positions may be coded. CURSOR can also be used to specify a DFLD name which can be mapped to the application program, such as

```
DPAGE CURSOR=((04,73,DFLD))
```

The program can identify the cursor position on input, and, if the DFLD is linked to an MFLD, it can also specify the cursor position on output.

Cursor Positioning under Application Program Control

This method is used in situations where the application program determines the cursor location based on the result of processing a particular transaction. There are two ways by which the application program can specify the cursor position, and are described below.

Using a Cursor Field. The field that holds the cursor position must be composed of two half-word binary fields. The first field holds the line number, and the second holds the column number. If you are using a 3270 Model 2, the line number field varies from 1 to 24 and the column varies from 1 to 80.

Assume that we want to set the cursor at the position shown in FIG. 6-7. The DOF and MOD definitions are given below.

```
DOF

CUSTUP  FMT
        ....
        DPAGE   CURSOR=((04,73,CURSFLD))← Cursor field

MOD

INTDIS  MSG     TYPE=OUTPUT,SOR=(FMT004,IGNORE),NXT=INPUTA,OPT=1,  *
                PAGE=YES,FILL=NULL
        SEG
        MFLD    CURSFLD,LTH=04
        ....
        MSGEND
```

The application program will move the value specifying the cursor position (in the above example, Hex value '00040049') to the cursor field before doing the ISRT call to send the output message to the terminal.

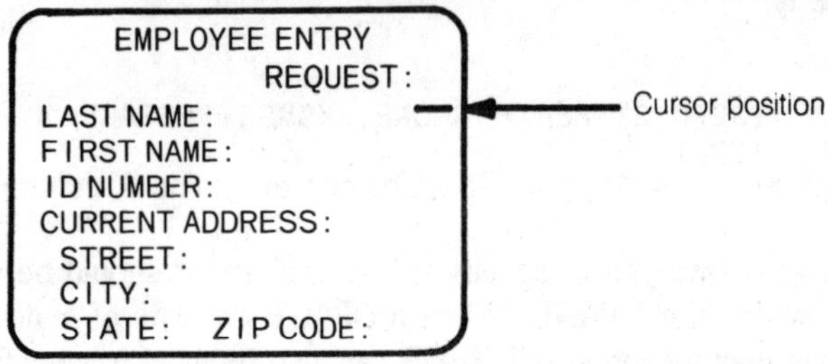

Fig. 6-7.

We do not recommend using this method of cursor positioning. This makes your application device- and format-dependent because the program must be conscious of line and column numbers, and these vary for different devices.

Under IMS/VS, there is another option for positioning the cursor—cursor positioning by the attribute byte.

Cursor Positioning by Attribute Byte. This method is done by allowing the application program to control the attribute byte for each field that requires cursor positioning. This technique changes the ATTR= parameter dynamically, that is, while the application program is running.

HOW TO MODIFY THE ATTRIBUTE BYTE DYNAMICALLY

MFS supports the Dynamic attribute modification feature to allow the application program to alter the attributes of the output message fields. To allow for dynamic attribute byte modification, we have to specify the output message field with ATTR=YES in the MFLD statement. MFS will reserve a two-byte area as the attribute field for the application program to move the desired value into it. MFS uses the first byte to determine whether or not to position the cursor in the field; the second is used to represent the field's actual attribute. These two bytes will immediately precede the field to which the dynamic attribute modification applies.

FIGURE 6-8 shows the bit settings for the dynamic system attribute. FIGURE 6-9 gives an example of dynamic attribute byte modification. The message processing program

- Moves "**" to the error flag field
- Moves an attribute value that is highlighted and updatable, with the numeric key lock turned on with the position of the cursor at the first position of the field in error
- Adds a protected attribute to other fields
- Performs an ISRT call to send the output message to the terminal

Here, field attribute cursor positioning is much more effective since it is field-oriented and not device-oriented; MFS determines where the field will be on the terminal screen.

MFS coding for FIG. 6-9 appears in FIG. 6-10, and the output layout appears in FIG. 6-11.

BYTE	BIT	VALUES	FUNCTIONS
0	0 - 1	SET TO 1	TO POSITION CURSOR TO THIS FIELD (FOR IMS/VS ONLY), OTHERWISE SET TO 0
	2 - 7	SET TO 0	
1	0	SET TO 0	
	1	SET TO 1	TO REPLACE ATTRIBUTES | (*)
		SET TO 0	TO ADD TO EXISTING ATTRIBUTES |
	2	SET TO 1	FOR PROTECTED FIELDS
	3	SET TO 1	FOR NUMERIC
	4	SET TO 1	FOR HI-INTENSITY
	5	SET TO 1	FOR NON-DISPLAYABLE
	6	SET TO 1	FOR DETECTABLE
	7	SET TO 1	FOR PREMODIFIED

Fig. 6-8. Dynamic attribute byte settings.

```
            EMPLOYEE ENTRY

LAST NAME:     DOE
FIRST NAME:  JOHN
ID NUMBER:    975AA
CURRENT ADDRESS:
   STREET:    11713 BASSWOOD DR
   CITY:      NOWHERE
   STATE:     MD  ZIP CODE 20708
DATE HIRED  10-27-86
```

Operator keys-in data into unprotected fields. An error is keyed into the ID number field.

```
            EMPLOYEE ENTRY

LAST NAME:    DOE
FIRST NAME:   JOHN
ID NUMBER:    **975AA
CURRENT ADDRESS:
  STREET:    11713 BASSWOOD DR
  CITY:      NOWHERE
  STATE:     MD  ZIP CODE: 20708
DATE HIRED: 10-27-86
```

The application program:

- Flags out the error with "**"
- Repositions the cursor
- Highlights the field in error
- Turns numeric key lock on
- Protects other fields

Fig. 6-9. Dynamic attribute modification.

COBOL TECHNIQUES FOR DYNAMIC ATTRIBUTE BYTE MODIFICATION

To change the attribute bytes dynamically, your COBOL program has to pass control information to MFS which formats the output message accordingly. To use this feature, you have to follow three steps:

- First, identify the fields that are eligible for dynamic attribute byte modification and specify the eligible fields with ATTR=YES.
- Second, define the content of the control bytes you want to pass to MFS to request dynamic attribute modification.
- Third, code the program logic to pass the control information to MFS.

```
         DIF/DIF:
         -------

FORMAT   FMT
         .....
         DFLD   'ID NUMBER:',POS=(05,02)....
ERRFLAG  DFLD   POS=(05,09),LTH=02
IDNO     DFLD   POS=(05,13),LTH=05
         .....
         FMTEND


         MOD:
         ---

OUTMESG  MSG    TYPE=OUTPUT,SOR=(FORMAT,IGNORE),NXT=INPUTA,OPT=1....
         .....
         SEG
         MFLD   ERRFLAG,LTH=02
         MFLD   IDNO,LTH=07,ATTR=YES        <=== LENGTH 05 + 02 FOR ATTRIBUTE
         .....
         MSGEND
```

Fig. 6-10.

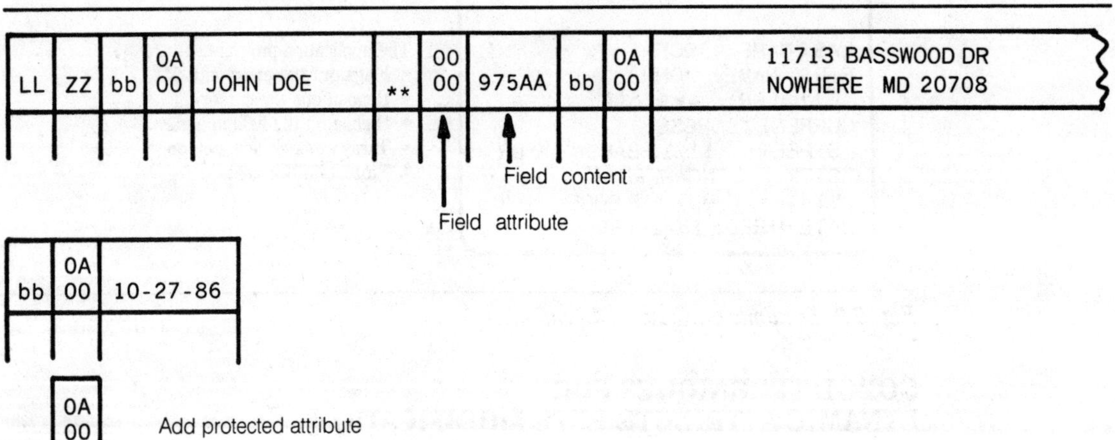

Fig. 6-11.

We will show you two COBOL techniques to modify the attribute byte dynamically. The first is to code attriute values for a group of attributes, and the second is to code attribute values for each attribute field.

Code Attribute Values for a Group of Attributes

The attributes can be coded in hexadecimal or decimal values. FIGURES 6-12 and 6-13 give sample codings for modifying the attribute byte of the example shown in FIG. 6-11.

The result is that if the ID number is invalid, we flag out "**" and the ID number will be highlighted and updatable, with the numeric key lock turned on and the cursor placed at the first position of the ID number.

```
WORKING-STORAGE SECTION.
    ......
01  THE-ATTRIBUTE-BYTES.
    05 ATTR-CUR-HI-NUM-MDT        PIC X(02)     VALUE ' R'.
*                                               HEX   COD9

01  OUTPUT-MESSAGE-AREA.
    05 OUTPUT-LL                  PIC S9(04)    COMP.
    05 OUTPUT-ZZ                  PIC X(02).
    05 NAME-ATTR                  PIC X(02).
    05 NAME                       PIC X(20).
    05 ERROR-FLAG                 PIC X(02).
    05 ID-NO-ATTR                 PIC X(02).     <=== DYNAMIC ATTRIBUTE
    05 ID-NO                      PIC 9(05).          MODIFICATION FIELD

    .....
PROCEDURE DIVISION.
    .....

*   VALIDATE ID NUMBER
    IF INVALID-ID-NO
       MOVE '**' TO ERROR-FLAG
       MOVE ATTR-CUR-HI-NUM-MDT TO ID-NO-ATTR
       CALL 'CBLTDLI' USING ISRT
                            IO-PCB-MASK
                            OUTPUT-MESSAGE-AREA
                            MODNAME.
```

Fig. 6-12. Using hexadecimal values for the attribute byte.

Code Attribute Values for Each Attribute Field

The alternative to the previous technique is to set up a field for each attribute, to add the individual values, and to move the result to the attribute bytes. This technique is illustrated in FIG. 6-14.

```
WORKING-STORAGE SECTION.
    .....
 01  THE-ATTRIBUTE-VARIABLES          COMP SYNC.
*    PREMODIFIED, NOT PROTECTED, NORMAL INTENSITY, ALPHANUMERIC
     05 ATTR-1                        PIC S9(04)    VALUE +193.
*    PREMODIFIED, NOT PROTECTED, NORMAL INTENSITY, NUMERIC
     05 ATTR-2                        PIC S9(04)    VALUE +209.
*    PREMODIFIED, NOT PROTECTED, HI-INTENSITY, ALPHANUMERIC
     05 ATTR-3                        PIC S9(04)    VALUE +201.
*    PREMODIFIED, NOT PROTECTED, HI-INTENSITY, NUMERIC
     05 ATTR-4                        PIC S9(04)    VALUE +217.
*    PREMODIFIED, NOT PROTECTED, HI-INTENSITY, ALPHANUMERIC, CURSOR
     05 ATTR-5                        PIC S9(04)    VALUE +49,353.
*    PREMODIFIED, NOT PROTECTED, HI-INTENSITY, NUMERIC, CURSOR
     05 ATTR-6                        PIC S9(04)    VALUE +49,369.

 01  OUTPUT-MESSAGE-AREA.
     05 OUTPUT-LL                     PIC S9(04)    COMP.
     05 OUTPUT-ZZ                     PIC X(02).
     05 NAME-ATTR                     PIC X(02).
     05 NAME                          PIC X(20).
     05 ERROR-FLAG                    PIC X(02).
     05 ID-NO-ATTR                    PIC X(02).     <=== DYNAMIC ATTRIBUTE
     05 ID-NO                         PIC 9(05).          MODIFICATION FIELD

     .....
 PROCEDURE DIVISION.
     .....

*   VALIDATE ID NUMBER
     IF INVALID-ID-NO
        MOVE '**' TO ERROR-FLAG
        MOVE ATTR-6                   TO ID-NO-ATTR

        CALL 'CBLTDLI' USING ISRT
                             IO-PCB-MASK
                             OUTPUT-MESSAGE-AREA
                             MODNAME.
```

Fig. 6-13. Using decimal values for the attribute byte. This coding will produce the same results as in FIG. 6-12.

SUMMARY OF DYNAMIC ATTRIBUTE BYTE MODIFICATION

FIGURE 6-15 summarizes the bit combinations that you can use to format the content of the attribute byte that you want the application program to pass to the MFS. Note the following points:

- If a field is defined to receive simulated attribute data but none is provided by the application program, the first byte will be blank.
- If used in combination, some options may be in conflict, i.e., (HI,NODISP). In such cases, the earlier bit takes precedence.
- Attributes can be dynamically modified by the application program if the MFLD for that field specifies ATTR=YES. However, any error on the screen that

```
DATA DIVISION.
     ......
01   THE-ATTRIBUTE-BYTES           COMP SYNC.
     05 LOCATE-CURSOR              PIC S9(04)   VALUE +49152.
     05 REPLACE-ATTRIBUTES         PIC S9(04)   VALUE +192.
     05 ADD-TO-ATTRIBUTES          PIC S9(04)   VALUE +128.
     05 PROTECT-FIELD              PIC S9(04)   VALUE +32.
     05 NUMERIC-FIELD              PIC S9(04)   VALUE +16.
     05 HIGH-INTENSITY             PIC S9(04)   VALUE +8.
     05 NON-DISPLAY                PIC S9(04)   VALUE +4.
     05 DETECT-FIELD               PIC S9(04)   VALUE +2.
     05 PRE-MODIFIED               PIC S9(04)   VALUE +1.

01   OUTPUT-MESSAGE-AREA.
     05 OUTPUT-LL                  PIC S9(04)   COMP.
     05 OUTPUT-ZZ                  PIC X(02).
     05 NAME-ATTR                  PIC X(02).
     05 NAME                       PIC X(20).
     05 ERROR-FLAG                 PIC X(02).
     05 ID-NO-ATTR                 PIC X(02).    <=== DYNAMIC ATTRIBUTE
     05 ID-NO                      PIC 9(05).         MODIFICATION FIELD
     .....
PROCEDURE DIVISION.
     .....

*    VALIDATE ID NUMBER
     IF INVALID-ID-NO
        MOVE '**' TO ERROR-FLAG
        ADD HIGH-INTENSITY
            ADD-TO-ATTRIBUTES
            NUMERIC-FIELD
            LOCATE-CURSOR
               GIVING ID-NO-ATTR.

        CALL 'CBLTDLI' USING ISRT
                             IO-PCB-MASK
                             OUTPUT-MESSAGE-AREA
                             MODNAME.
```

Fig. 6-14.

caused the screen to be reformatted will lose all attributes modified previously and will revert to the original definition of the DFLD definition. Therefore this facility should be limited to highlighting desired fields on the screens.

- The attribute byte values are commonly set up in a copy book table for handy use of the dynamic field attribute modification.

USE OF MODIFIED DATA TAG

Another feature of the attribute byte is the modified data tag (MDT). This is part of the attribute byte and is used to indicate whether or not data in a field has been changed by the operator since the last screen was displayed.

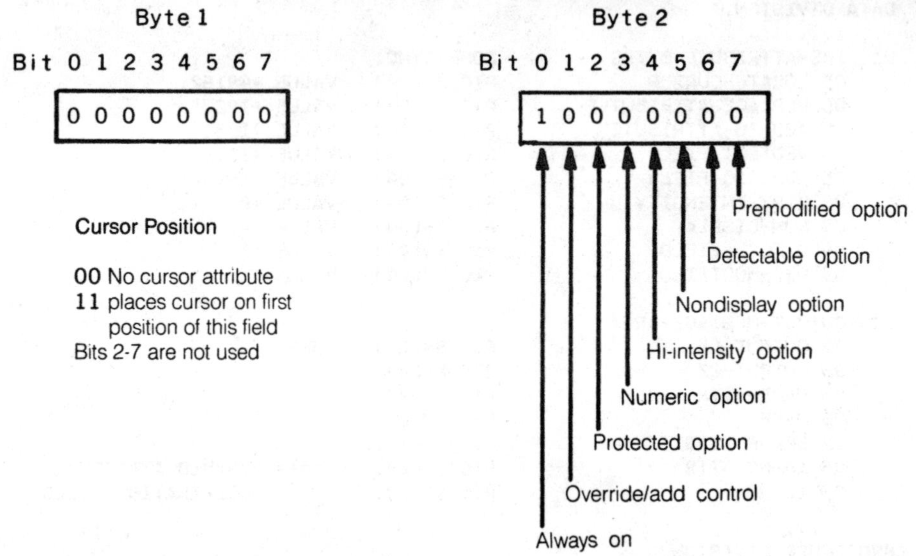

Fig. 6-15. Dynamic attribute values.

There are situations in which you want a field to be transmitted to the application program whether or not the operator has keyed-in data. In the course of an exchange between the operator and the application program, the program may display some information on the terminal, but also wants this data to be sent back with other data entered by the operator. By describing the field attribute as MOD, the field will automatically be transmitted again as input.

Specifying ATTR=MOD for a device field will allow you to artificially turn the MDT on, and so the content of the field will be made available to the application program.

The example that follows and FIG. 6-16 illustrate use of the modified data tag. Note that ATTR=MOD is ignored for literal fields.

```
         DIF/DOF

CUSTUP   FMT
         DEV      TYPE=(3270,2),FEAT=IGNORE
         ....
         DFLD     'NAME:',POS=(03,02)
NAME     DFLD     POS=(03,08),LTH=20,ATTR=MOD ← Modified data tag
         DFLD     'SOC SEC NO:',POS=(04,02)
SOCNUM   DFLD     POS=(04,14),LTH=09
         ....
         FMTEND
```

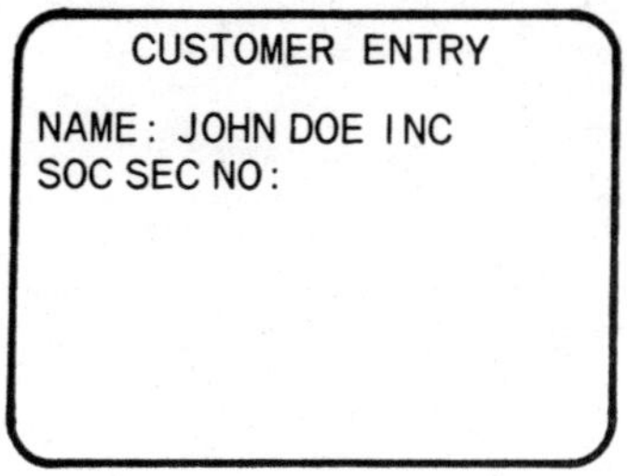

Data is entered. Modified fields are transmitted as the input message to the application program:

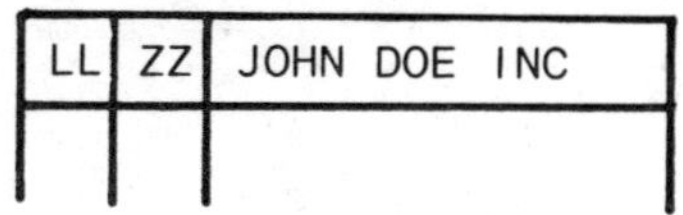

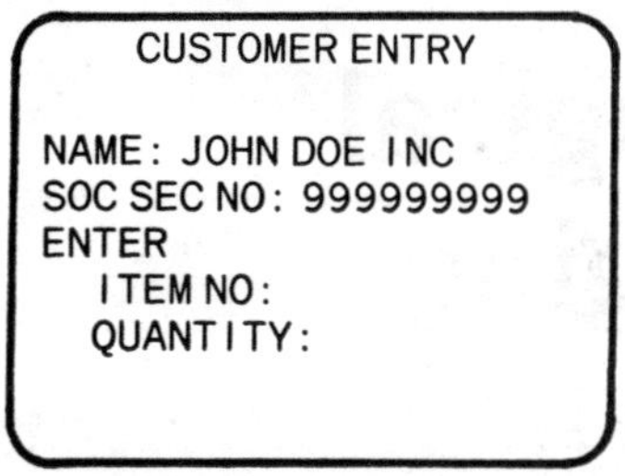

The application program sends back the customer's name and his Social Security number:

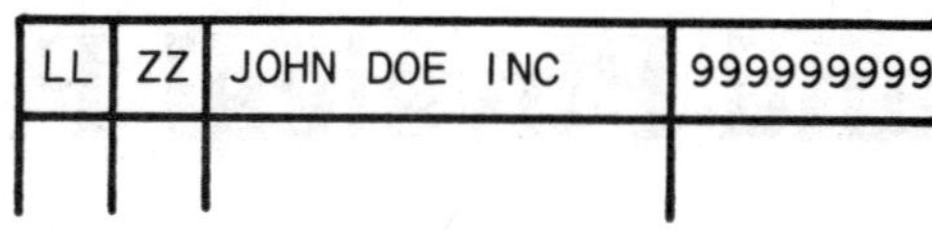

Now, the item number and the quantity ordered are entered. The input message looks like this:

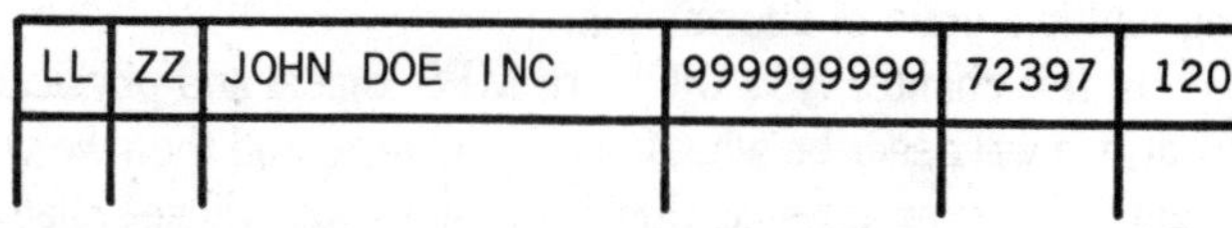

The name field is transmitted again, even though the operator does not rekey it because it has been defined as modified.

Fig. 6-16.

In summary, the MDT of a device field can be turned on in three ways:

1. The operator enters the data on the field.
2. The device field is specified with ATTR=MOD. This will force the MDT to be turned on.
3. The application program moves an attribute value to the attribute byte of the device field in the output message to turn the MDT on.

The MDT is commonly used in instances where the same value from the previous screen is to be used for the next transmission. By describing the field attribute as MOD, the field will automatically be transmitted again as input and the operator does not have to make more keystrokes than necessary.

Selective use of the modified data tag improves operator convenience and minimizes data entry error.

7

How to Invoke Logical and Physical Paging

Up to now, we've covered only messages containing one unit of information and which are mapped by MFS as a single unit. By single unit we mean one page of information. Let's now expand the concept of a single unit of information to include situations involving multiple units of information.

In this chapter, you will learn MFS logical and physical paging of output messages. First, we will describe what logical paging is, and then we will discuss the types of logical paging. As we progress in this discussion, you will see that a logical page can map to one or more physical pages, and you will also see that one output message can produce multiple logical pages. We will also cover the process of mapping the same output message to different devices (physical paging).

PHYSICAL AND LOGICAL PAGES

The output message may need to be displayed on more than one screen. Each screen of information that is displayed as part of a single message is called a page. MFS distinguishes between a physical page and a logical page.

- The physical page is device-oriented and is determined by the physical characteristics of the terminal devices. For example, the IBM 3270 terminal, Model 1 contains 480 characters to a physical page, while Model 2 contains 1,920 characters to a page. Data that would fit into Model 2 would require multiple pages on Model 1. Refer to chapter 9 for different device characteristics of the IBM 3270 terminals.
- The logical page is program-oriented. A series of one or more message segments may be mapped to one or more physical pages. Logical paging is a function of the MOD definition and application design.

LOGICAL PAGING OF OUTPUT MESSAGES

When the application program transmits multiple pages, the process is called logical paging. This facility allows the grouping of output message segments for formatting. FIGURE 7-1 illustrates the mapping of the logical page. Note that the program message is divided into several units of information called logical pages.

The segment or segments that comprise each logical page are defined in the MOD under an LPAGE statement. Each page may be formatted differently by having the LPAGE statement reference a different DPAGE statement in the DOF, but they can also be formatted the same by having all the LPAGE statements point to the same DPAGE statement.

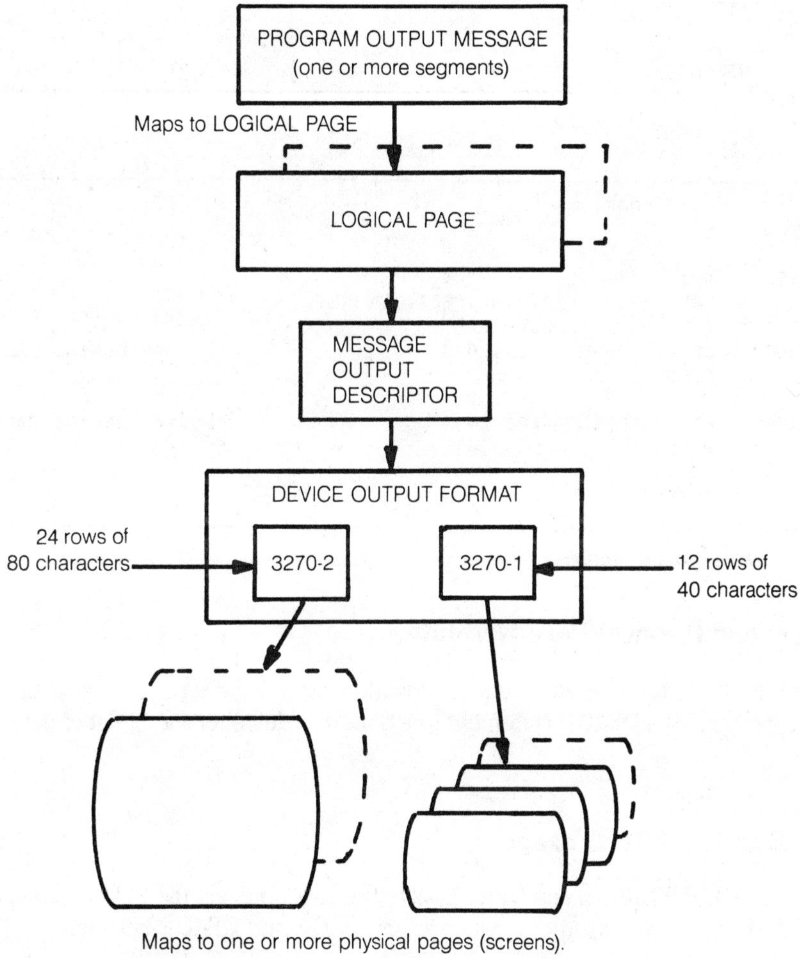

Fig. 7-1. Mapping of logical page.

```
                 MOD:
                 ---

INQ2      MSG    TYPE=OUTPUT,SOR=(FMT2,IGNORE)

          LPAGE                              <=== LOGICAL PAGE 1 HAS ONE SEGMENT
          SEG
          MFLD
          .....
          LPAGE                              <=== LOGICAL PAGE 2 HAS THREE SEGMENTS
          SEG
          MFLD
          .....
          SEG
          MFLD
          .....
          SEG
          .....
          MSGEND
```

Fig. 7-2. Logical page delimiter.

```
                 DOF:
                 ---

   FMT2      FMT
             DEV    TYPE=(3270,2),FEAT=IGNORE
             DIV    TYPE=INOUT
   DPAGE1    DPAGE  CURSOR=((04,20))                  <=== DEVICE PAGE 1
             DFLD
             .....
   DPAGE2    DPAGE  CURSOR=((02,14))                  <=== DEVICE PAGE 2
             DFLD
             .....
             FMTEND
```

Fig. 7-3. Device page delimiter.

Logical and Physical Page Delimiters

In the MOD, the LPAGE statement functions as a delimiter for a logical page (FIG. 7-2). In the DOF, the DPAGE statement functions as a delimiter for a related device page (FIG. 7-3).

LPAGE and DPAGE Linkage

Linkage of the LPAGE and DPAGE statements is done via the SOR= parameter in the LPAGE statement. FIGURE 7-4 shows the LPAGE and DPAGE linkage.

```
MOD                                                 DOF
INQ2 MSG    TYPE=OUTPUT,SOR=(FMT2,IGNORE)           FMT2    FMT
                                                            DEV     TYPE=(3270,1),FEAT=..
     LPAGE  COND=(IND.='1'),SOR=DPAGE1 ----------> DPAGE1  DPAGE   CURSOR=((04,20))
     SEG     (3)                  (2)               (1)     ....
IND  MFLD   LTH=1                                           DFLD    'ORDERS RECEIVED',POS
     MFLD   ORDERS,LTH=04                           ORDERS  DFLD    POS=(04,20),LTH=04
     ....                                                   ....
     LPAGE COND=(IND.='2'),SOR=DPAGE2 ----------> DPAGE2  DPAGE   CURSOR=((02,14))
     ....    (3)                 (2)                (1)     ....
     SEG                                                    DFLD    'PAGE',POS=(01,21)
IND  MFLD   LTH=1                                   PAGE    DFLD    POS=(01,26),LTH=01
     MFLD   PAGE,LTH=01                                     ....
     ....                                                   ....
     SEG                                                    DFLD    'QTY DECR VALUE',
     MFLD   QTY,LTH=04                              QTY     DFLD    POS=(06,04),LTH=04
     ....                                                   ....
     MSGEND                                                 FMTEND
```

Fig. 7-4. LPAGE and DPAGE linkage.

Take note of these points:

1. For this linkage to function, DPAGE statement must have a label. The label for the first DPAGE is DPAGE1. The label for the second DPAGE is DPAGE 2.
2. The DPAGE names referenced by the LPAGE statements via the SOR= operand must exist in the DOF.
3. There is no one-to-one relationship between the LPAGE and DPAGE statements. One or more LPAGEs can reference the same DPAGE. Selection of the LPAGE to be mapped to the related DPAGE is performed by the application program. (This will be discussed later in the section entitled "Explicit Logical Paging.")

In summary:

- Logical paging is accomplished by defining the output message with one or more logical pages via the LPAGE statement in the MOD.
- Each LPAGE description with one or a series of segments is mapped to its related DPAGE via the SOR= operand.
- Each DFLD can specify in the POS= operand which physical page to map data to:

  `POS=(Line,Column,Page)`

  Here, the default page number is 1.

FIGURE 7-5 shows how the MFS maps output to more than one physical page via the POS= parameter.

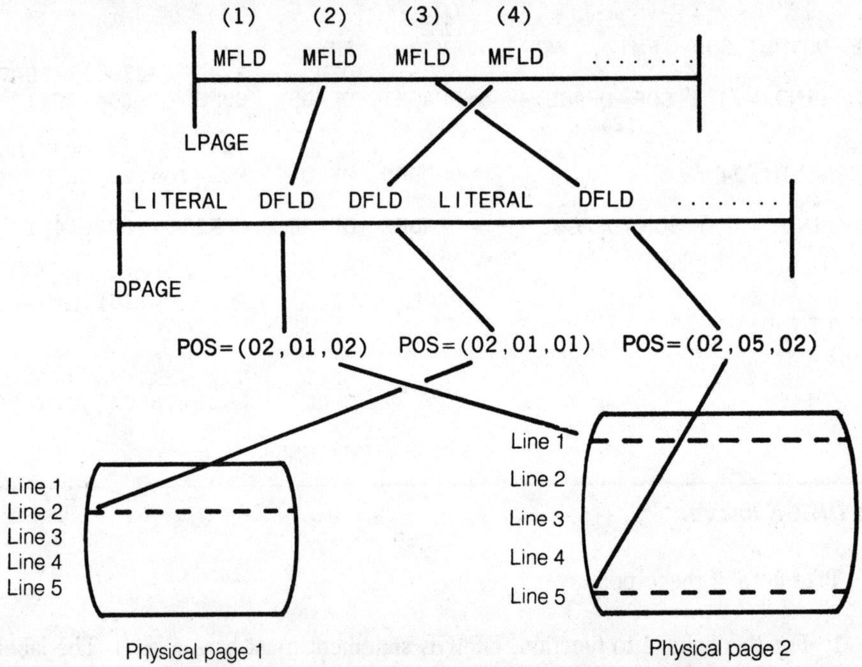

- MFLD (2) is mapped to DFLD with POS=(02,01,02) on physical page 2.
- MFLD (3) is mapped to DFLD with POS=(02,05,02) on physical page 2.
- MFLD (4) is mapped to DFLD with POS=(02,02,01) on physical page 1.

Fig. 7-5.

TYPES OF LOGICAL PAGING

There are two types of logical paging:

- Implicit logical paging
- Explicit logical paging

Implicit Logical Paging

The process of using the same logical page to produce more than one physical page is called implicit logical paging. "Implicit" means that the application program does not have to indicate to MFS that it is transmitting more than one physical page. One or many pages of data can be transmitted, and the application program can vary this number each time it transmits the message.

Implicit logical paging is totally controlled by the application program, and may be used when we want to display multiple occurrences of the same screen. However, there are restrictions:

1. The segments of the output message have to be transmitted in order.
2. Since the segment are mapped according to their relative positions, they cannot be omitted.
3. NULL segments can be transmitted for lines that the application program wants to omit. (You learned how to use this feature in chapter 3.)

Next, we will study three cases of implicit logical paging:

1. One logical page with one segment mapped to one physical page.
2. One logical page with one segment mapped to two physical pages.
3. One logical page consisting of a series of segments mapped to one physical page.

As we progress, you will see that the coding logic for each of the above cases will become more and more complicated.

One Logical Page Maps to One Physical Page. The simplest form of implicit logical paging consists of one logical page (LPAGE) and one output segment. FIGURE 7-6 shows the logical paging of an output message consisting of one segment to be mapped to one physical page (screen format).

Take note of the following:

1. In the MOD, the LPAGE statement is not coded; the entire output message is taken by MFS as one LPAGE which has one segment containing all the fields in the output message. SOR=FMT1 in the MSG statement refers to the format name of the DOF.
2. One LPAGE maps to one DPAGE which has one screen format.
3. In the DOF, there is one DPAGE. DFLDs are defined as POS=(Line,Column) only; thus, the default is to the first physical page.

```
MOD                                                   DOF
OUTA     MSG      TYPE=OUTPUT,SOR=(FMT1,IGNORE)       FMT1     FMT
                                   (1)                         DEV      TYPE=(3270,2),FEAT=..
                                                      (2)      DIV      TYPE=INOUT
         SEG  ---------------------------------------------->  DPAGE    CURSOR=((04,73))
         ....                                                  ....
         ....                                         TRANCD   DFLD     POS=(04,05),LTH=08..
         MFLD     LASTNM,LTH=20                                DFLD     'LAST NAME:',POS=(06.
         ....                                         LASTNM   DFLD     POS=(06,22),LTH=20,..
         MDLD     (TRANCD,'TRANS001'),LTH=08                   ....     (3)
         ....                                                  ....
         MSGEND                                                FMTEND
```

Fig. 7-6.

4. The application issues only one ISRT call in response to an input transaction:

```
MOVE 'OUTA     ' TO MODNAME
CALL 'CBLTDLI' USING ISRT
                     IO-PCB
                     OUTPUT-MESSAGE
                     MODNAME.
```

One Logical Page Maps to Two Physical Pages. FIGURE 7-7 is an example of paging a single LPAGE using one DPAGE but having a different physical page assignment.

Take note of the following:

1. One LPAGE maps to one DPAGE which has two screen formats.
2. We have set the same INQUIRY DATE on both physical pages by positioning DATE on two DFLDs with POS=(2,30,1) and POS=(2,30,2); the third digit on the POS= operand refers to pages 1 and 2.
3. The cursor is located on both physical pages at position (6,3) on page 1 and at position (9,3) on page 2.
4. Data LINE1 is to be displayed on page 1, LINE2, LINE3, and LINE4 are to be displayed on page 2.

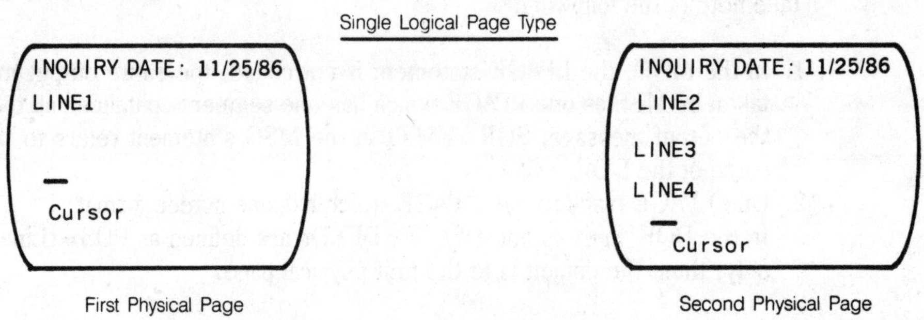


```
MOD                                                   DOF

OUTB    MSG      TYPE=OUTPUT,SOR=(FMT2,IGNORE)       FMT2      FMT
                                                               DEV       TYPE=(3270,1),FEAT=..
        (1)                                                    DIV       TYPE=INOUT
        LPAGE    SOR-DPAGE1 ----------------------> DPAGE1    DPAGE     CURSOR=((06,3),(9,3))
        SEG                                                    ....      (3)
        ....                                          (2)       DFLD      'INQUIRY DATE:' ,POS=.
        MFLD     DATE,LTH=08                          DATE      DFLD      POS=(2,30,1),LTH=08
        MFLD     LINE1,LTH=10                         LINE1     DFLD      POS=(3,2,1)...
        MFLD     LINE2,LTH=10                         DATE      DFLD      POS=(2,30,2),LTH=08
        MFLD     LINE3,LTH=10                         LINE2     DFLD      POS=(3,2,2)...
        MFLD     LTH4,LTH=10                          LINE3     DFLD      POS=(4,2,2)...
        ....                                          LINE4     DFLD      POS=(5,2,2)...
        ....                                                    ....      (4)
        MSGEND                                                  FMTEND
```

Fig. 7-7.

Multiple LPAGE Segments. The next level of complexity is that of one output message defined with a single LPAGE consisting of a series of segments. FIGURE 7-8 shows the logical paging of an output message consisting of a series of segments to be mapped to one physical page (screen format). An inquiry for information on two employees is displayed in FIGS. 7-9 and 7-10.

```
                EMPLOYEE INQUIRY
:::::::::
SKILL: :::::
LEVEL: :
NAME: ::::::::::::::::
EMPLOYEE ID: :::::
DATE HIRED: ::::::::::
EXPERIENCE: ::::::::::::::::::::::::::
            ::::::::::::::::::::::::::
            ::::::::::::::::::::::::::
```

Fig. 7-8.

```
                EMPLOYEE INQUIRY
:::::::::

SKILL: PROG
LEVEL: 5
NAME: JOHN DOE
EMPLOYEE ID: 67432
DATED HIRED: MAR 1984
EXPERIENCE: COBOL PROGRAMMING, 5 YRS
            ALC PROGRAMMING, 2 YRS
```

Fig. 7-9.

```
                EMPLOYEE INQUIRY
:::::::::

SKILL: PROG
LEVEL: 3
NAME: WILLIAMS SMITH
EMPLOYEE ID: 92133
DATE HIRED: DEC 1985
EXPERIENCE: COBOL PROGRAMMING, 2 YRS
```

Fig. 7-10.

The message output definition for this message is shown in FIG. 7-11. Here, the MOD (on the left) maps to one physical page (on the right).

Take note of the following:

1. One LPAGE maps to one DPAGE which has one screen format.
2. The LPAGE has been defined to have four segments (by four SEG statements). The output message layout will look as shown in FIG. 7-12.

```
MOD                                                          DOF
OUTC    MSG      TYPE=OUTPUT,SOR=(FMT3,IGNORE)  FMT3         FMT
        (1)                                                  DEV     TYPE=(3270,1),FEAT=..
                                                             DIV     TYPE=INOUT
        LPAGE    SOR=DPAGE1 ------------------> DPAGE1       DPAGE   CURSOR=((02,72))
        SEG                         (2)                      ....
        ....                                                 DFLD    'SKILL:',POS=(3,4)
        MFLD     SKILL,LTH=04                   SKILL        DFLD    POS=(3,10),LTH=04
        MFLD     LEVEL,LTH=01                                DFLD    'LEVEL:',POS=(4,4)
        MFLD     NAME,LTH=15                    LEVEL        DFLD    POS=(4,10),LTH=01
        MFLD     EMPNO,LTH=05                                ....
        MFLD     HIRED,LTH=10                                ....
        SEG                         (2)                      DFLD    'EXPERIENCE:',POS=(5,4)
        MFLD     EXPER1,LTH=25                  EXPER1       DFLD    POS=(5,15),LTH=25
        SEG                         (2)         EXPER2       DFLD    POS=(6,15),LTH=25
        MFLD     EXPER2,LTH=25                  EXPER3       DFLD    POS=(7,15),LTH=25
        SEG                         (2)                      ....
        SEG      EXPER3.LTH=25                               ....
        ....                                                 ....
        MSGEND                                               FMTEND
```

Fig. 7-11.

In this figure, the LPAGE has been defined to have four segments, but Message 1 has only three segments, and Message 2 has only two segments.

Now, how does the application program map a full page with missing segments? When multiple series of output segments are presented and some are omitted, the application program will move a Hex X'40' to the second byte of the ZZ field to indicate a new page.

Explicit Logical Paging (Multiple Logical Page Types)

The process of using more than one logical page per message is called explicit logical paging. "Explicit" means that the application has to notify IMS which logical pages it wishes to transmit.

We may use multiple logical page types when

- The output message is larger than the screen
- We wish to give the application program a choice of format at run time
- We wish to make multiple screens available for reference

Coding Considerations

1. When we use explicit logical paging, we have to include a test field (FIG. 7-13) to indicate which logical page we want to use. The test field must be included in the first segment of each transmitted page.

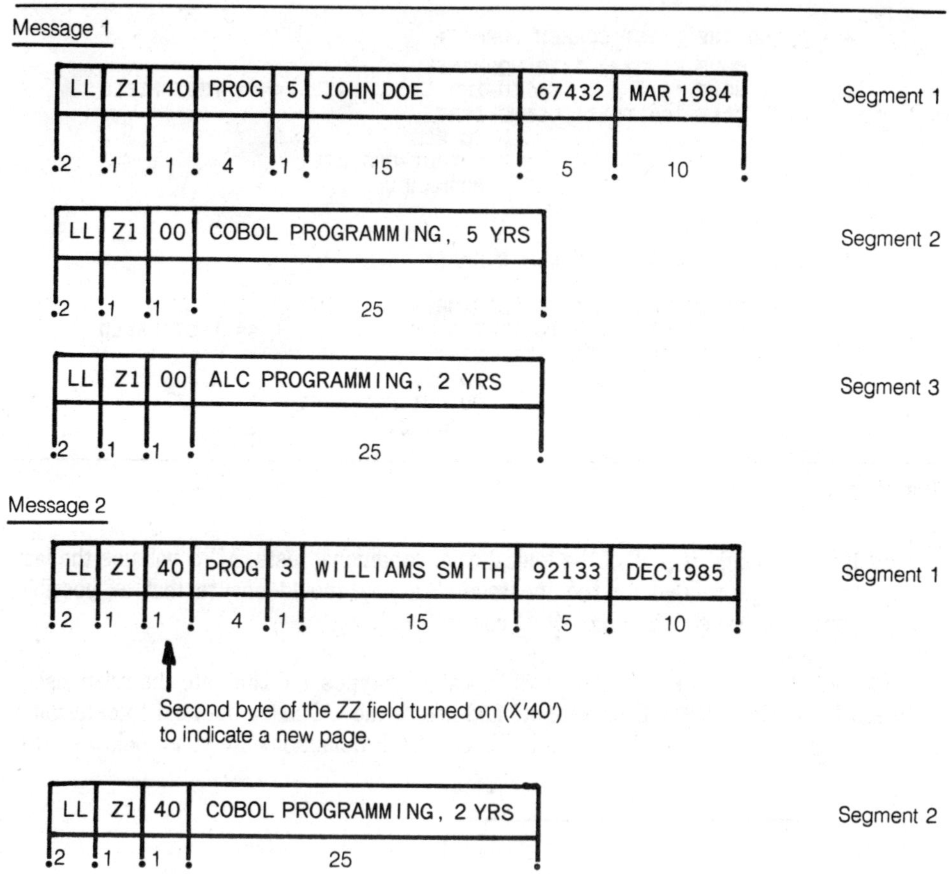

Fig. 7-12. Segmented output message.

Fig. 7-13. Position of test field.

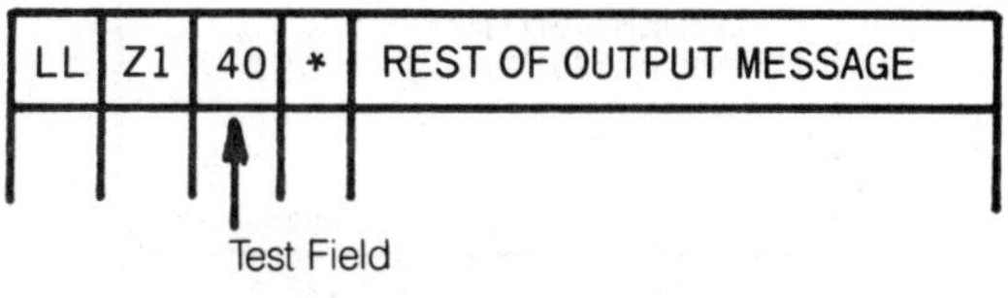

2. In the MOD, define multiple LPAGE descriptions and use the COND= parameter to describe a conditional test. If successful, the segments following the LPAGE statement will be used for output editing.
3. The COND= operand is not required for the last LPAGE in the MOD.
4. The application program will determine which DPAGE to be used. To do this, set the content of the test field described in the LPAGE statement to the value desired, and then do an ISRT call (FIG. 7-14).

```
*     SEND THE FIRST SCREEN FORMAT:
          MOVE 'INQ2    ' TO MODNAME
          MOVE '1'        TO IO-IND                 <=== TEST FIELD
          CALL 'CBLTDLI' USING ISRT
                               IO-PCB
                               OUTPUT-MESSAGE1
                               MODNAME.

*     SEND THE SECOND SCREEN FORMAT:

          MOVE 'INQ2    ' TO MODNAME
          MOVE '2'        TO IO-IND                 <=== TEST FIELD
          CALL 'CBLTDLI' USING ISRT
                               IO-PCB
                               OUTPUT-MESSAGE2
                               MODNAME.
```

Fig. 7-14.

5. If the test field fails all of the logical page conditional tests, MFS will use the last logical page defined for the message. So, you should ensure that all possible conditions are coded in the MOD control block.

FIGURES 7-15, 7-16, and 7-17 show two logical page types and illustrate the relationship between LPAGE and DPAGE statements and use of the COND= operand to determine which page layout maps the data. The MOD and DOF definitions are given below in FIG. 7-18.

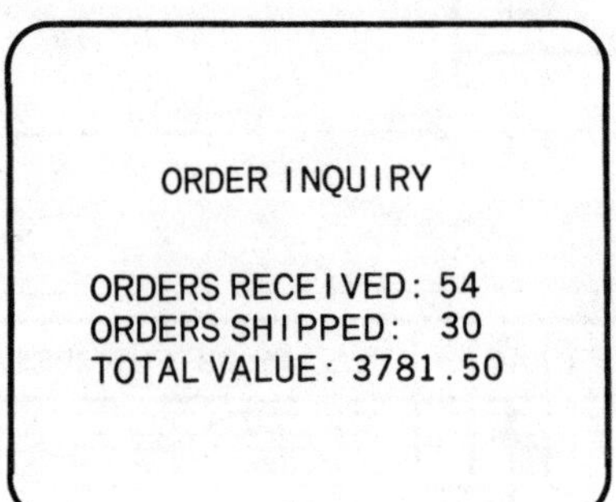

Fig. 7-15. First logical page.

Take note of the following:

1. The DIF/DOF contains two DPAGEs whose labels are DPAGE1 and DPAGE2.
2. Logical page 1 is defined to contain a "1" in the first byte of the segment text. Logical page 2 is defined to contain a "2" in the first byte of the segment.
3. The MFLD of the test field must have a label.

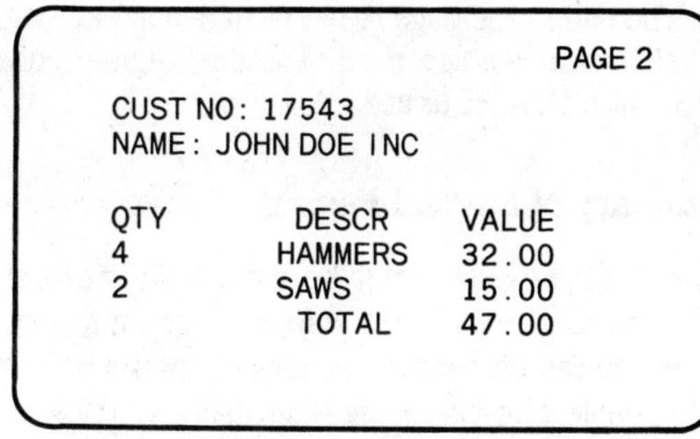

Fig. 7-16. Second logical page.

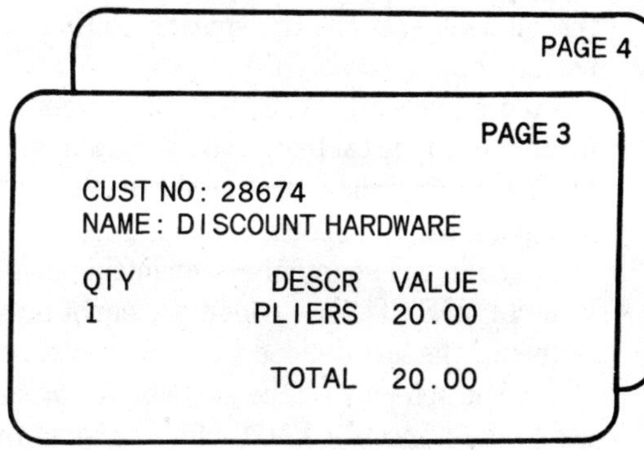

Fig. 7-17. Subsequent page(s).

```
MOD                                                     DOF
INQ2 MSG    TYPE=OUTPUT,SOR=(FMT2,IGNORE)   FMT2       FMT
                                                       DEV     TYPE=(3270,1),FEAT=..
     LPAGE  COND=(IND.='1'),SOR=DPAGE1 ---> DPAGE1     DPAGE   CURSOR=((04,20))
     SEG                                           (1) DFLD    'ORDER INQUIRY',POS..
IND  MFLD   LTH=1            (2)                       DFLD    'ORDERS RECEIVED',POS
 (3) MFLD   ORDERS,LTH=04                   ORDERS     DFLD    POS=(04,20),LTH=04
     MFLD   SHIPPED,LTH=04                  SHIPPED    DFLD    POS=(05,20),LTH=04
     ....                                              ....
     LPAGE  COND=(IND.='2'),SOR=DPAGE2 ---> DPAGE2     DPAGE   CURSOR=((02,14))
     SEG                                           (1) DFLD    'PAGE',POS=(01,21)
IND  MFLD   LTH=1                           PAGE       DFLD    POS=(01,26),LTH=01
 (3) MFLD   PAGE,LTH=01                                DFLD    'CUST NO:',POS=....
     MFLD   CUSTNO,LTH=08                   CUSTNO     DFLD    POS=(02,14),LTH=08
     ....                                              ....
     SEG                                               DFLD    'QTY DECR VALUE',
     MFLD   QTY,LTH=04                      QTY        DFLD    POS=(06,04),LTH=04
     ....                                              ....
     SEG                                               DFLD    'TOTAL',POS=(08,13)
     ....                                              ....
     MSGEND                                            FMTEND
```

Fig. 7-18. Multiple logical page types.

How to Invoke Logical and Physical Paging

The output message layout is shown in FIG. 7-19. Hex X'40' in the second byte of the ZZ field indicates a new page. The first segment of each page includes an indicator telling MFS which DPAGE to use.

Summary of Logical Paging

- Program output may be divided into several logical pages; each within an output message may have a different screen format.
- You can use implicit or explicit logical paging.
- Implicit logical paging is normally used if you have only one logical page defined for an output message. When you use implicit logical paging, you have to make sure that all segments are transmitted so that the MFS can map them to the proper position on the screen display.
- If you use explicit LPAGE, the application must include a test field in the first segment in each logical page. The program must move a X'40' to the Z2 field of the first segment of the page to tell IMS that a new logical page is being transmitted.
- If segments in the middle of an LPAGE are to be omitted, the application program has to code null segments to maintain position within the LPAGE.
- If the LPAGE COND= condition cannot be satisfied with the data in the message segment, the last-defined LPAGE will be used. This last LPAGE is also used to format the screen with the /FORMAT command. Therefore, it is advantageous to define the principal LPAGE of a format as the last LPAGE.
- Each change in the DPAGE will cause the screen to be reformatted. Therefore, all LPAGEs should reference the same DPAGE to avoid reformatting unless the application program requires a new screen.
- To avoid device-dependence, you should not allow the size of the smallest device to limit the size of the logical page.

PHYSICAL PAGING OF OUTPUT MESSAGES (DEVICE-RELATED)

We have learned that an application can use multiple logical pages to produce different screens of the same output message. This is accomplished by defining multiple logical pages (LPAGEs) in the MOD, but up to now, we have used only one device type. MFS allows us to use multiple device types for the same output message

The process of mapping the same output message to different devices is called physical paging. Multiple physical pages per logical page are used whenever the logical page is designed for a large screen (3270, Model 2) but is also displayed on a smaller screen device (3270, Model 1).

Coding Considerations

Unlike logical paging which is controlled by the application program, physical paging is controlled by the MFS based on the physical page assignments made in the DOF.

Physical Paging of Output Mesages (Device-related)

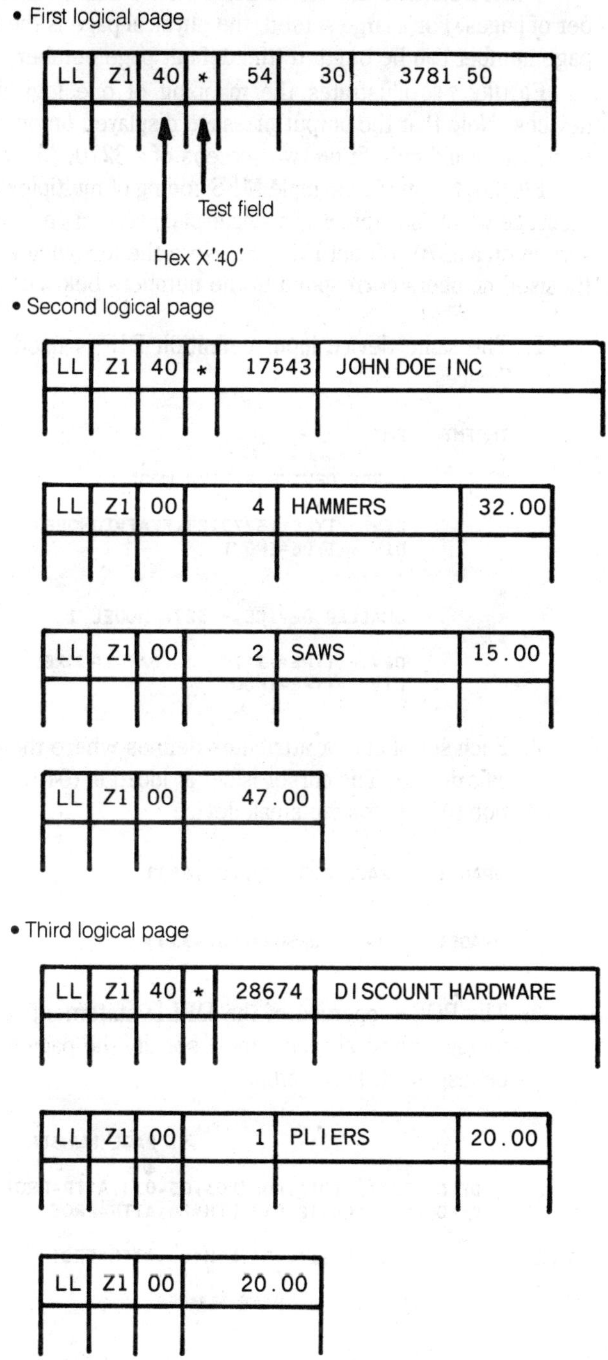

Fig. 7-19. Output message layout.

How to Invoke Logical and Physical Paging

When we define the device fields for a smaller screen, we need to specify the number of pages. For a large screen, the physical page *is* the logical page, and so the physical page number can be omitted (the default page number is 1).

FIGURE 7-20 illustrates the mapping of one logical page to two different output devices. Note that the output message displayed on one physical page (a 3270, Model 2 terminal) would only fit on two screens of a 3270, Model 1 terminal.

FIGURE 7-21 gives a sample MFS coding of multiple device types for the same output message which is mapped as a single-page screen on a 3270, Model 2, and as a two-page screen on a 3270, Model 1 device. Note the following key points in FIG. 7-21 (the parenthesized numbers correspond to the numbers below):

1. The same device input definition DIF is used for both Model 1 and Model 2 devices:

```
INQFMT   FMT
*
*        LARGE DEVICE - 3270 MODEL 2
*
         DEV    TYPE=(3270,2),FEAT=IGNORE
         DIV    TYPE=INOUT
         ....
*
*        SMALLER DEVICE - 3270 MODEL 1
*
         DEV    TYPE=(3270,1),FEAT=IGNORE
         DIV    TYPE=INOUT
```

2. Each set of cursor attributes defines where the cursor will be located for a specific device. The cursor is set at location (04,66) for the large device and at location (02,31) for the small device:

```
DPAGE1   DPAGE CURSOR=((04,66))             <=== CURSOR ON LARGE DEVICE
         ....
DPAGE1   DPAGE CURSOR=((02,31))             <=== CURSOR ON SMALL DEVICE
```

3. The POS= operand of the DFLD statement of the small device (which allows multiple physical pages) must specify the page number on which the fields are to be displayed. For example:

```
                                  PAGE NUMBER
                                       ↓
         DFLD  'BILL TO:',POS=(03,03,01),ATTR=PROT <=== THIS FIELD IS DISPLAYED
BILLTO   DFLD  POS=(03,12,01),LTH=20,ATTR=PROT          ON PAGE 1
         ....
UNIT3    DFLD  POS=(08,17,02),LTH=06,ATTR=PROT     <=== THIS FIELD IS DISPLAYED
                          ↑                             ON PAGE 2
                      PAGE NUMBER
```

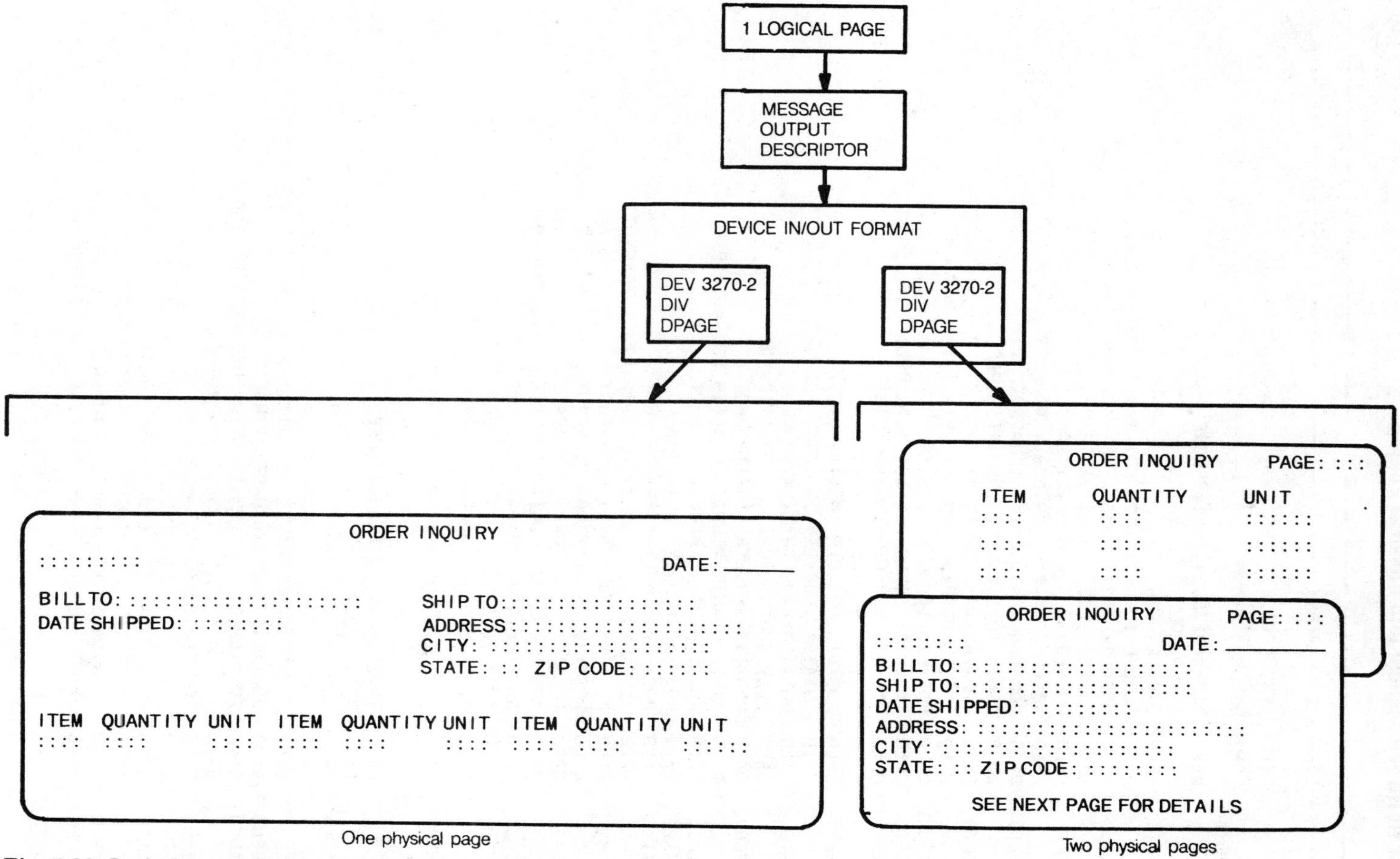

Fig. 7-20. Logical page mapped to different output devices.

```
1--------10----16------------------------------------------------------7-*

         TITLE 'TWO DEVICE TYPES'
         PRINT NOGEN
INQFMT   FMT
         DEV   TYPE=(3270,2),FEAT=IGNORE                                  (1)
         DIV   TYPE=INOUT
DPAGE1   DPAGE CURSOR=((04,66))                                           (2)
         DFLD  'ORDER INQUIRY',POS=(02,32),ATTR=(PROT,HI)
TRANCD   DFLD  POS=(04,03),LTH=08,ATTR=(MOD,PROT,NODISP)
         DFLD  'DATE:',POS=(04,60),ATTR=PROT
DATEIN   DFLD  POS=(04,66),LTH=06,ATTR=MOD
         DFLD  'BILL TO:',POS=(08,03),ATTR=PROT
BILLTO   DFLD  POS=(08,12),LTH=20,ATTR=PROT
         DFLD  'SHIP TO:',POS=(08,35),ATTR=PROT
SHIPTO   DFLD  POS=(08,44),LTH=15,ATTR=PROT
         DFLD  'DATE SHIPPED:',POS=(10,03),ATTR=PROT
DATESHIP DFLD  POS=(10,17),LTH=08,ATTR=PROT
         DFLD  'ADDRESS:',POS=(10,35),ATTR=PROT
STREET   DFLD  POS=(10,44),LTH=20,ATTR=PROT
         DFLD  'CITY:',POS=(12,35),ATTR=PROT
CITY     DFLD  POS=(12,41),LTH=20,ATTR=PROT
         DFLD  'STATE:',POS=(13,35),ATTR=PROT
STATE    DFLD  POS=(13,42),LTH=02,ATTR=PROT
         DFLD  'ZIP CODE:',POS=(13,46),ATTR=PROT
ZIPCODE  DFLD  POS=(13,56),LTH=05,ATTR=PROT
         DFLD  'ITEM QUANTITY UNIT',POS=(16,03),ATTR=PROT
ITEM1    DFLD  POS=(18,03),LTH=04,ATTR=PROT
QTY1     DFLD  POS=(18,09),LTH=04,ATTR=PROT
UNIT1    DFLD  POS=(18,17),LTH=06,ATTR=PROT
         DFLD  'ITEM QUANTITY UNIT',POS=(16,27),ATTR=PROT
ITEM2    DFLD  POS=(18,27),LTH=04,ATTR=PROT
QTY2     DFLD  POS=(18,33),LTH=04,ATTR=PROT
UNIT2    DFLD  POS=(18,41),LTH=06,ATTR=PROT
         DFLD  'ITEM QUANTITY UNIT',POS=(16,49),ATTR=PROT
ITEM3    DFLD  POS=(18,49),LTH=04,ATTR=PROT
QTY3     DFLD  POS=(18,55),LTH=04,ATTR=PROT
UNIT3    DFLD  POS=(18,63),LTH=06,ATTR=PROT
*
*        SMALLER DEVICE
*
         DEV   TYPE=(3270,1),FEAT=IGNORE                                  (1)
         DIV   TYPE=INOUT
DPAGE1   DPAGE CURSOR=((02,31))                                           (2)
         DFLD  'ORDER INQUIRY',POS=(01,12,01),ATTR=(PROT,HI)
         DFLD  'PAGE:',POS=(01,31,01),ATTR=PROT
PAGENO   DFLD  POS=(01,37,01),LTH=03,ATTR=PROT
TRANCD   DFLD  POS=(02,03,01),LTH=08,ATTR=(MOD,PROT,NODISP)
         DFLD  'DATE:',POS=(02,25,01),ATTR=PROT
DATEIN   DFLD  POS=(02,31,01),LTH=06,ATTR=MOD
         DFLD  'BILL TO:',POS=(03,03,01),ATTR=PROT                        (3)
BILLTO   DFLD  POS=(03,12,01),LTH=20,ATTR=PROT
         DFLD  'SHIP TO:',POS=(04,03,01),ATTR=PROT
SHIPTO   DFLD  POS=(04,12,01),LTH=15,ATTR=PROT
         DFLD  'DATE SHIPPED:',POS=(05,03,01),ATTR=PROT
```

Fig. 7-21.

Fig. 7-21 continued

```
DATESHIP DFLD  POS=(05,17,01),LTH=08,ATTR=PROT
         DFLD  'ADDRESS:',POS=(06,03,01),ATTR=PROT
STREET   DFLD  POS=(06,12,01),LTH=20,ATTR=PROT
         DFLD  'CITY:',POS=(07,03,01),ATTR=PROT
CITY     DFLD  POS=(07,09,01),LTH=20,ATTR=PROT
         DFLD  'STATE:',POS=(08,03,01),ATTR=PROT
STATE    DFLD  POS=(08,10,01),LTH=02,ATTR=PROT
         DFLD  'ZIP CODE:',POS=(08,14,01),ATTR=PROT
ZIPCODE  DFLD  POS=(08,24,01),LTH=05,ATTR=PROT
         DFLD  'SEE NEXT PAGE FOR DETAILS',                           *
               POS=(12,05,01),ATTR=PROT
                    |_________________________PAGE NUMBER          (3)
*
*        LAYOUT OF SECOND PAGE
*
         DFLD  'ORDER INQUIRY',POS=(01,12,02),ATTR=(PROT,HI)
         DFLD  'PAGE:',POS=(01,31,02),ATTR=PROT
PAGENO   DFLD  POS=(01,37,02),LTH=03,ATTR=PROT
         DFLD  'ITEM QUANTITY UNIT',POS=(03,03,02),ATTR=PROT
ITEM1    DFLD  POS=(04,03,02),LTH=04,ATTR=PROT
QTY1     DFLD  POS=(04,09,02),LTH=04,ATTR=PROT
UNIT1    DFLD  POS=(04,17,02),LTH=06,ATTR=PROT
ITEM2    DFLD  POS=(06,03,02),LTH=04,ATTR=PROT
QTY2     DFLD  POS=(06,09,02),LTH=04,ATTR=PROT
UNIT2    DFLD  POS=(06,17,02),LTH=06,ATTR=PROT
ITEM3    DFLD  POS=(08,03,02),LTH=04,ATTR=PROT
QTY3     DFLD  POS=(08,09,02),LTH=04,ATTR=PROT
UNIT3    DFLD  POS=(08,17,02),LTH=06,ATTR=PROT
                    |_________________________ PAGE NUMBER         (3)
         FMTEND
*
INQUIRY  MSG   TYPE=INPUT,SOR=INQFMT,NXT=ORDEROUT,OPT=1
         SEG
         MFLD  TRANCD,LTH=09
         MFLD  DATEIN,LTH=06
         MSGEND
*
ORDEROUT MSG   TYPE=OUTPUT,SOR=(INQFMT,IGNORE),NXT=INQUIRY,OPT=1      *
               FILL=NULL
         LPAGE SOR=DPAGE1
         SEG
         MFLD  (TRANCD,'TRANS007'),LTH=08
         MFLD  (PAGENO,LPAGENO)              <=== LOGICAL PAGE NUMBER
         MFLD  BILLTO,LTH=20
         MFLD  SHIPTO,LTH=15
         MFLD  DATESHIP,LTH=08
         MFLD  STREET,LTH=20
         MFLD  CITY,LTH=20
         MFLD  STATE,LTH=02
         MFLD  ZIPCODE,LTH=05
         MFLD  ITEM1,LTH=04
         MFLD  QTY1,LTH=04
         MFLD  UNIT1,LTH=06
         MFLD  ITEM2,LTH=04
         MFLD  QTY2,LTH=04
```

Fig. 7-21 continued

```
MFLD   UNIT2,LTH=06
MFLD   ITEM3,LTH=04
MFLD   QTY3,LTH=04
MFLD   UNIT3,LTH=06
MSGEND
END
```

Physical paging allows the use of multiple-device types for the same output message. This feature is controlled by the MFS based on physical page assignments in the DOF.

So far, we have covered the logical and physical paging of output messages. Now, let's turn to paging input messages. In the following section, you will learn input logical paging and how to create identical input messages for a transaction regardless of the physical capacity of the device being used.

INPUT LOGICAL PAGING

An input message may consist of more than one logical page. A logical page is initiated and defined by the LPAGE control statement.

On input, if LPAGE is not defined, MFS considers the entire input message as one logical page. An input LPAGE identified by an LPAGE statement may refer to one or more DPAGEs (input device pages).

An input DPAGE is defined by a DPAGE statement. When no DPAGE statement is defined, all device field definitions following the DIV statement are treated as a single page. If multiple DPAGEs are defined, each DPAGE statement must be labeled, and each labeled DPAGE must be referenced by an LPAGE statement.

Multiple Physical Page Input

This facility for 3270 terminal devices allows the creation of identical input messages for a transaction regardless of the physical capacity of the device being used.

Let's look at an example where the same input can be entered on one physical page of Model 2 but would only fit on two screens of Model 1 (FIG. 7-22). The Order Entry and Order Detail input is done via one physical page (screen) of Model 2. For Model 1, the Order Entry input fits only on one physical page and the order detail input requires another physical page.

FIGURE 7-23 presents a sample MFS coding of our Order Entry format set using the physical page input. Note the following key points in this example:

1. The same device input definition DIF is used for both Model 1 and Model 2 devices:

```
FMTIN     FMT
*              Large Device = 3270 Model 2
```

```
MAINPAGE  DEV  TYPE=(3270,2),FEAT=IGNORE,                          *
               SYSMSG=MESSAGE
          DIV  TYPE=INOUT
               .....
*
*              Model 1
*
SMALL     DEV  TYPE=(3270,1),FEAT=IGNORE,                          *
               SYSMSG=MESSAGE
          DIV  TYPE=INOUT
```

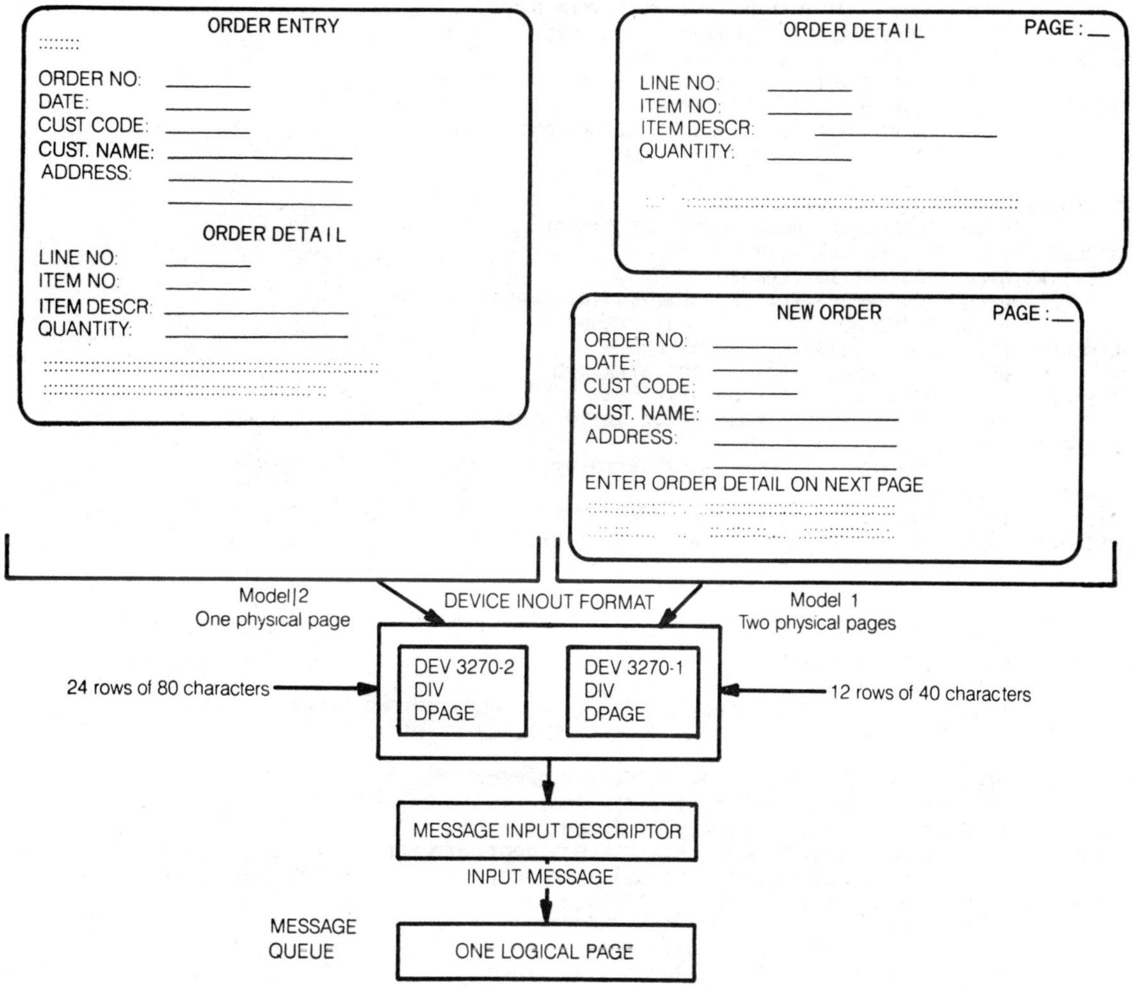

Fig. 7-22. Multiple physical page input.

```
1--------10----16---------------------------------------------------7-*

         TITLE 'MULTIPLE PHYSICAL PAGES INPUT'
         PRINT NOGEN
FMTIN    FMT
*
*              LARGE DEVICE - 3270 MODEL 2
*
MAINPAGE DEV   TYPE=(3270,2),FEAT=IGNORE,                           * (1)
               SYSMSG=MESSAGE                                         (5)
         DIV   TYPE=INOUT
         DPAGE CURSOR=((04,13))
TRANCD   DFLD  POS=(02,02),LTH=08,ATTR=(MOD,PROT,NODISP)
         DFLD  'ORDER ENTRY:',POS=(02,30),ATTR=PROT
         DFLD  'ORDER NO:',POS=(04,02),ATTR=PROT
ORDERNUM DFLD  POS=(04,13),LTH=08,ATTR=NUM
         DFLD  'DATE:',POS=(05,02),ATTR=PROT
DATE     DFLD  POS=(05,13),LTH=08,ATTR=NUM
         DFLD  'CUST CODE:',POS=(06,02),ATTR=PROT
CUSTNUBR DFLD  POS=(06,13),LTH=08,ATTR=NUM
         DFLD  'CUST NAME:',POS=(07,02),ATTR=PROT
CUSTNAME DFLD  POS=(07,13),LTH=20
         DFLD  'ADDRESS:',POS=(08,02),ATTR=PROT
STREET   DFLD  POS=(08,13),LTH=20
CITYSTAT DFLD  POS=(09,13),LTH=20
         DFLD  'ORDER DETAIL:',POS=(11,30),ATTR=PROT
         DFLD  'LINE NO:',POS=(12,02),ATTR=PROT
LINENUM  DFLD  POS=(12,13),LTH=04,ATTR=NUM
         DFLD  'ITEM NO:',POS=(13,02),ATTR=PROT
ITEMNUM  DFLD  POS=(13,13),LTH=08,ATTR=NUM
         DFLD  'ITEM DESCR:',POS=(14,02),ATTR=PROT
ITEMDESC DFLD  POS=(14,14),LTH=25
         DFLD  'QUANTITY:',POS=(15,02),ATTR=PROT
QUANTITY DFLD  POS=(15,14),LTH=05,ATTR=NUM
REPLY    DFLD  POS=(17,02),LTH=31,ATTR=(PROT,HI)
MESSAGE  DFLD  POS=(18,02),LTH=37,ATTR=(PROT,HI)
*
*              SMALLER DEVICE - 3270 MODEL 1
*
SMALL    DEV   TYPE=(3270,1),FEAT=IGNORE,                           * (1)
               SYSMSG=MESSAGE                                         (5)
         DIV   TYPE=INOUT
         DPAGE CURSOR=((04,13),(05,13))   <=== CURSOR ON TWO PAGES    (3)
               MULT=YES                 <=== MUTIPLE PHYSICAL PAGES   (2)
*
         DFLD  'NEW ORDER:',POS=(02,12,01),ATTR=PROT
         DFLD  'PAGE:',POS=(01,31,01),ATTR=PROT
PAGENO   DFLD  POS=(01,37,01),LTH=02,ATTR=NUM
TRANCD   DFLD  POS=(01,04,01),LTH=08,ATTR=(MOD,PROT,NODISP)
         DFLD  'ORDER NO:',POS=(04,02,01),ATTR=PROT
ORDERNUM DFLD  POS=(04,13,01),LTH=08,ATTR=NUM
         DFLD  'DATE:',POS=(05,02,01),ATTR=PROT
DATE     DFLD  POS=(05,13,01),LTH=08,ATTR=NUM
         DFLD  'CUST CODE:',POS=(06,02,01),ATTR=PROT
CUSTNUBR DFLD  POS=(06,13,01),LTH=08,ATTR=NUM
         DFLD  'CUST NAME:',POS=(07,02,01),ATTR=PROT
```

Fig. 7-23.

Fig. 7-23 continued

```
CUSTNAME DFLD  POS=(07,13,01),LTH=20
         DFLD  'ADDRESS:',POS=(08,02,01),ATTR=PROT
STREET   DFLD  POS=(08,13,01),LTH=20
CITYSTAT DFLD  POS=(09,13,01),LTH=20
         DFLD  'ENTER ORDER DETAIL ON NEXT PAGE',POS=(10,02,01),ATTR=PROT
REPLY    DFLD  POS=(11,02,01),LTH=31,ATTR=(PROT,HI)
MESSAGE  DFLD  POS=(12,02,01),LTH=37,ATTR=(PROT,HI)
                               |________________________PAGE NUMBER   (4)
*
*        LAYOUT OF SECOND PAGE
*
         DFLD  'ORDER DETAIL:',POS=(02,12,02),ATTR=PROT
         DFLD  'PAGE:',POS=(01,31,02),ATTR=PROT
PAGENO   DFLD  POS=(01,37,02),LTH=02,ATTR=NUM
         DFLD  'LINE NO:',POS=(05,02,02),ATTR=PROT
LINENUM  DFLD  POS=(05,13,02),LTH=04,ATTR=NUM
         DFLD  'ITEM NO:',POS=(06,02,02),ATTR=PROT
ITEMNUM  DFLD  POS=(06,13,02),LTH=08,ATTR=NUM
         DFLD  'ITEM DESCR:',POS=(07,02,02),ATTR=PROT
ITEMDESC DFLD  POS=(07,14,02),LTH=25
         DFLD  'QUANTITY:',POS=(08,02,02),ATTR=PROT
QUANTITY DFLD  POS=(08,14,02),LTH=05,ATTR=NUM
MESSAGE  DFLD  POS=(12,02,02),LTH=37,ATTR=(PROT,HI)
                               |________________________PAGE NUMBER   (4)
         FMTEND
*
*        MID FOR ORDERS
*
NEWMID   MSG   TYPE=INPUT,SOR=FMTIN,NXT=ORDEROUT,                      *
               OPT=1      |
*                         |_____   DO NOT USE 'IGNORE' IN SOR PARAMETER
         SEG
         MFLD  TRANCD,LTH=09
         MFLD  ORDERNUM,LTH=08
         MFLD  DATE,LTH=08
         MFLD  CUSTNUBR,LTH=08
         MFLD  CUSTNAME,LTH=20
         MFLD  STREET,LTH=20
         MFLD  CITYSTAT,LTH=20
         MFLD  LINENUM,LTH=04
         MFLD  ITEMNUM,LTH=08
         MFLD  ITEMDESC,LTH=25
         MFLD  QUANTITY,LTH=05
         MSGEND
*
*        MOD
*
ORDEROUT MSG   TYPE=OUTPUT,SOR=(FMTIN,IGNORE),NXT=MEWMID,              *
               OPT=1
         SEG
         MFLD  (PAGENO,LPAGENO)
         MFLD  (TRANCD,'ORDERTRN'),LTH=08
         MFLD  ORDERNUM,LTH=10,ATTR=YES
         MFLD  (DATE,DATE2)
         MFLD  CUSTNUBR,LTH=10,ATTR=YES
```

Fig. 7-23 continued

```
MFLD  CUSTNAME,LTH=22,ATTR=YES
MFLD  STREET,LTH=22,ATTR=YES
MFLD  CITYSTAT,LTH=22,ATTR=YES
MFLD  LINENUM,LTH=06,ATTR=YES
MFLD  ITEMNUM,LTH=10,ATTR=YES
MFLD  ITEMDESC,LTH=25
MFLD  QUANTITY,LTH=07,ATTR=YES
MFLD  REPLY,LTH=33,ATTR=YES
MFLD  MESSAGE,LTH=37
MSGEND
END
```

2. The request to allow multiple-page input is specified in the DPAGE statement with MULT=YES:

```
DPAGE    CURSOR=((04,13),(05,13)),
         MULT=YES
```

3. For multiple physical page input, each set of cursor attributes defines where the cursor will be located for a specific page. Above, the cursor is set at location (04,13) for Page 1 and at location (05,13) for Page 2.
4. The POS= operand of the DFLD statements of the device (which allows multiple physical pages) must specify the page number on which the fields are to be displayed. As an example:

```
                                          Page number
                                               ↓
          DFLD  'ORDER NO:',POS=(04,02,01) ← This field is displayed
                                              on Page 1
ORDERNUM  DFLD  POS=(04,13,01),LTH=08,ATTR=NUM
                ....
          DFLD  'LINE NO:',POS=(05,02,02)
LINENUM   DFLD  POS=(05,13,02),LTH=04,ATTR=NUM ← This field is displayed
                                 ↑                  on Page 2
                            Page number
```

5. Since there are multiple physical pages, SYSMSG DFLD must be included for each physical page. If omitted, a warning message will be issued, and compilation of the control blocks will thus be terminated:

```
FMTIN      FMT
*                Large Device-3270 Model 2                    *
MAINPAGE   DEV   TYPE=(3270,2),FEAT=IGNORE,
*                SYSMSG=MESSAGE
           DIV   TYPE=INOUT
*
```

```
*                  Smaller Device-3270 Model 1
*
SMALL      DEV     TYPE=(3270,1),FEAT=IGNORE,
+                  SYSMSG=MESSAGE
           DIV     TYPE=INOUT
```

6. To enter the multiple physical page input on the last screen, we have to enter the control function ENDMPPI (end multiple physical page input). This function will be discussed later in the section "Operator Control of MFS."

Summary of Input Logical Paging

- Input logical paging allows the mapping of multiple physical pages into a logical page regardless of the capacity of the device used.
- The request to allow multiple pages is specified in the DPAGE statement with MULT=YES.
- You must specify the page number on which the fields are to be displayed via the POS= operand.
- SYSMSG DFLD must be included in each physical page to ensure successful compilation of the control blocks.

OPERATOR CONTROL OF MFS

Next, we will turn to operator control of the display. MFS supports three facilities to enhance flexibility in viewing output messages:

1. Operator logical paging
2. Operator control table
3. 3270 function keys

Each will be discussed individually.

Operator Logical Paging (OLP)

Operator logical paging allows the operator to request a specific logical page of an output message. The operator can view any page of a multiscreen format in any order desired.

Without operator logical paging, pages may be viewed only once in sequential order by pressing the PA1 key. FIGURE 7-24 shows that to retrieve page 2 of Message 1, the operator has to press the PA1 key and then press it again to go to page 3. To get the next output message, he would would have to press the PA2 key.

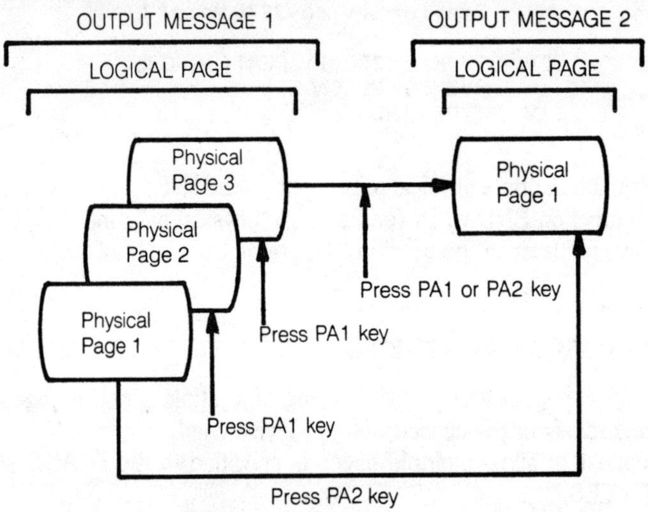

Fig. 7-24. Physical paging without OLP.

In contrast, OLP allows a greater degree of flexibility for viewing output messages. FIGURE 7-25 shows how to request the OLP facility in the MSG statement.

1. Operator logical paging is defined via the PAGE statement in the MSG statement of the MOD:

```
PAGE=YES
```

2. In the MID, the logical page request must be mapped to the beginning of the input message. After the input message is mapped to the MID, IMS checks for a "=" sign in the first byte which signifies a logical page request.
3. For this MID to function, the corresponding DFLD in the DIF/DOF must exist.

Available OLP Functions

You have seen that for a Logical page request to work, you must code in the MID, a field to request this facility. This field must be mapped to the beginning of the input message and has a "=" sign. The "=" sign in the first position of the IO-Area signifies Logical page request and the operator can enter a value on the sign to move forward and backward within one output message. For example, if the operator is viewing page one and wishes to view logical page 3, he or she can enter "=3" or "+2".

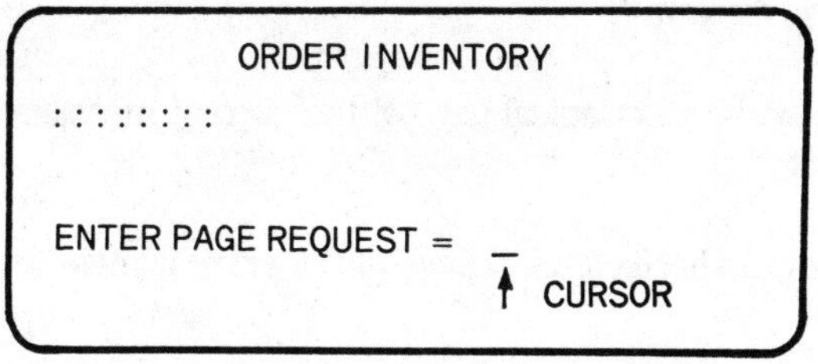

First position of the I-O area of input page

```
     DIF/DOF:
     -------

FORMAT    FMT
          DEV    TYPE=(3270,2),FEAT=IGNORE
          DIV    TYPE=INOUT
DPAGE1    DPAGE  CURSOR=((10,22))                            <=== CURSOR POSITION
          .....
          DFLD   'ENTER PAGE REQUEST',POS=(10,02)
ISTFLD    DFLD   POS=(10,21),LTH=04           <=== FIRST FIELD OF INPUT MESSAGE
          .....                                                             (3)
          FMTEND

     MID:
     ----

INPUT     MSG    TYPE=INPUT,SOR=(FORMAT,IGNORE),NXT=OUTMESG
          SEG
          MFLD   ISTFLD,LTH=04,FILL=NULL
          .....                                                             (2)
          MSGEND

     MOD:
     ----

OUTMESG   MSG    TYPE=OUTPUT,SOR=(FORMAT,IGNORE),NXT=INPUT,                 *
                 PAGE=YES                                  <===             (1)
          SEG
          LAPGE  SOR=DPAGE1
          .....
          MFLD   (ISTFLD,'=')             <=== INDICATES LOGICAL PAGE REQUEST
          .....
          MSGEND
          END
```

Fig. 7-25. OLP definition.

How to Invoke Logical and Physical Paging

The following functions are available to the operator after the first physical page of the output message is displayed:

'=' To display the next logical page of the current message

'=n '<br>'=nn ' To display a specific logical page of the current message
'=nnn '

'=+n '<br>'=+nn ' To display the nth logical page past the current logical page
'=+nnn '

'=−n '<br>'=−nn ' To display the nth logical page before the current logical page
'=−nnn '

'=L ' To display the first physical page of the last logical page of the current message

FIGURE 7-26 summarizes the various options the operator might have to handle with multiple logical page types.

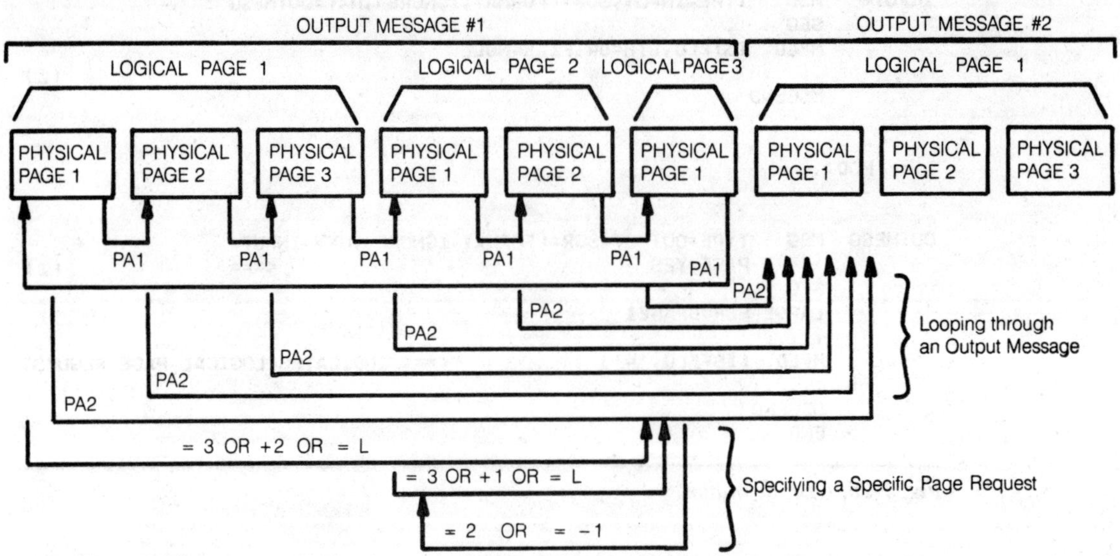

Fig. 7-26. Operator logical paging.

Operator Control Table

The input data entered on a device field can be defined to invoke MFS control functions when either the *data* or the *length* satisfies any of the conditions set in the operator control table. The purpose of the table is to define control functions to be performed based on operator-keyed values in a DFLD statement associated with that particular table.

In the device input format, we can set a DFLD to refer to an operator control table via the OPCTL= operand. The operator control table is a named control block defined as a separate macro set outside of the DIF definition. It resides on the MFS format library much the same as do other control blocks. OPTCL= specifies the name of the operator control table, defined by a table statement that is checked for operator control request when this device field is received.

Here are some coding considerations:

- Three source statement types are required to create an OPCTL—TABLE, IF, and TABLEEND.
- We must associate the OPCTL with a specific input via a DFLD statement.
- Use DATA and LENGTH keywords to specify the nature of the test to be performed. DATA means that the test is to be performed on the data entered in the field associated with the OPCTL. LENGTH means that the test is to be performed on the number of characters entered into the OPCTL field.

FIGURE 7-27 shows how to define an operator control table. In this figure, the data and length are used to invoke MFS control functions. If the length of the input message is equal to 1, the conditional testing will branch to the next IF statement bearing the label LABELA to continue the testing.

```
      DIF/DOF:
      -------

FORMAT   FMT
         DEV   TYPE=(3270,2),FEAT=IGNORE
         DIV   TYPE=INOUT
         .....
         DFLD  POS=(09,10),LTH=05,OPTCL=MYTABLE  <===  ASSOCIATE INPUT VIA DFLD

MYTABLE  TABLE
         IF DATA,=,'P',NEXTPP                    <===  DATA TEST
         IF LENGTH,=,1,LABELA                    <===  LENGTH TEST
         IF DATA,=,'MP',NEXTMSGP
LABELA   IF DATA,=,'M',NEXTMSG
         TABLEEND
```

Fig. 7-27. Operator control table coding.

How to Invoke Logical and Physical Paging

Available Operator Control Table Functions. Six control functions are available through the use of operator control tables:

1. NEXTPP (page advance)
   Display the next physical page of the current message. This function can be used to browse the entire output message.
2. NEXTLP (next logical page)
   Display the next logical page of a current message.
3. NEXTMSG (message advance)
   Dequeue the current message and send the next output message from the queue.
4. NEXTMSGP (message advance protect)
   Dequeue the output message in progress (if any) and send the next output message or return an information message indicating that no next message exists.
5. ENDMPPI (end multiple page request)
   Terminate a multiple physical page input message.
6. PAGEREQ (logical page request)
   Provide the operator logical paging specified by the second through last characters of input data entered on the device field with the OPTCL= operand. The first character is a page request trigger character defined by the user; the remaining characters must be:

   `n, +n[nn], -n[nn], or L.`

   No "=" sign is allowed.

FIGURE 7-28 shows how to request the PAGEREQ control function through the use of the operator control table. Here, the trigger character is P. If the operator enters P2 on the PAGEREQ device field, the second page of the current message will be displayed. If he enters P5, the fifth logical page of the current output message will be displayed (if any).

```
     DIF/DOF:
     -------

FORMAT   FMT
         DEV    TYPE=(3270,2),FEAT=IGNORE
         DIV    TYPE=INOUT
         .....
         DFLD   POS=(09,10),LTH=05,OPTCL=OPCTBLE   <===  ASSOCIATE INPUT VIA DFLD

OPCTBLE  TABLE
         IF DATA,=,'P',PAGEREQ                     <===  TRIGGER CHARACTER
         TABLEEND
```

Fig. 7-28. PAGEREQ control table coding.

3270 Function Keys

For 3270, Model 2 terminal devices, MFS control functions can be invoked via the use of program function keys. The PA1 key is equivalent and reserved for the NEXTPP function, and the PA2 key is equivalent to the NEXTMSG function.

Using PA1 and PA2 keys is the most efficient way of invoking the NEXTPP and NEXTMSG functions. The PF12 key causes a copy of the current displayed physical page to be printed, and the PA3 key is equivalent to the NEXTMSGP function.

Summary of Operator Control of MFS. The MFS control functions can be specified via three facilities:

1. Operator logical paging
2. Operator control table
3. 3270 function keys

These facilities are designed to allow flexibility in viewing selective output pages.

Invoking the operator control functions via 3270 program access keys is the most effective technique. The PA1 key provides the NEXTPP function, the PA2 key provides the NEXTMSG function, and PA3 provides the NEXTMSGP function. Program access keys should be used in lieu of a logical page request. This facility requires less operator action and communication line time and does not require input editing before page-request processing.

However, for the remaining functions which are not available by the 3270 program access keys, we have to use either the operator logical technique or the operator control table. Coding the operator logical technique is simpler than coding the operator control table.

Before leaving this chapter, let's look at the last feature related to logical paging, the PROMPT facility.

THE PROMPT FACILITY

You can use PROMPT to automatically notify the operator that the current logical page is the last page. The notification text is defined as a literal which MFS will insert into a specific device field when it formats the last logical page of the output message. The prompting message is defined in the LPAGE statement of MOD (FIG. 7-29). Here the literals 'THIS IS THE LAST LOGICAL PAGE' will be inserted into the device field MESSAGE when MFS formats the last logical page.

The notification text of the PROMPT facility should be displayed as the last line on the screen. This feature should be used when logical paging is involved to improve operator convenience.

```
          MOD:
          ----

ORDERMOD MSG     TYPE=OUTPUT,SOR=(FMT009,IGNORE),OPT=1,
                 FILL=PT
*
         LPAGE   SOR=DPAGE2,COND=(IND,=,'2'),
                 PROMPT=(MESSAGE,'THIS THE LAST LOGICAL PAGE')
         .....                             |
         SEG                               |
         MFLD    MESSAGE,LTH=79   <============
         MSGEND
```

Fig. 7-29. The prompt facility.

8

How to Control Multiple Screen Flows

All the application examples you have seen so far in this book have been limited to single-screen formats; they have one thing in common: The output message transmitted to the terminal device determines what the next input message will be, and one screen format is used for the entire application.

In this chapter, you will learn how to develop applications that use a series of two or more different screen displays. You will see that the control of multiple screen flows can be done entirely within MFS or from the application programs. We will begin with a discussion of the program function key feature available with the 3270 device, and then we will present a sample menu application that illustrates the use of the program function keys to invoke multiple-screen flows. After that, you will see how to control screen flows from the application program.

USING THE PROGRAM FUNCTION KEYS

The program function keys on the terminal may be defined to have special meanings which are received and interpreted by the application program. This feature is specified in the DEV statement via the PFK= parameter.

If the PF key that the operator presses is defined in advance in the DEV statement, MFS moves literal data that you have specified for that key to a field in the input message before passing it to IMS for queuing. This literal data field is commonly coded at the beginning of a message and is used to specify the destination of the message. The destination can be an IMS command, a terminal, or a transaction code.

The PFK key can be used as a substitute for keyed input or as a means of entering MFS page and message control functions.

How to Control Multiple Screen Flows

For each format, we can use PFKs to provide up to 11 unique items of predetermined input. The maximum length of each input item is 256 characters. This feature can be used to

- Enter a transaction code instead of keying it in
- Enter an MFS command
- Enter predefined data to be processed by the application program. This would save keying and would prevent possible data entry errors.

MFS Page and Message Control Functions

PFKs can be used to assist the operator in entering the request for MFS page and message control functions. The MFS page and message control functions (which are keywords) which can be defined as PFK functions are:

1. NEXTPP — Display the next physical page of the current message. This function can be used to browse the entire output message.
2. NEXTLP — Display the next logical page of a current message.
3. NEXTMSG — Dequeue the current message and send the next output message from the queue.
4. NEXTMSGP — Same as NEXTMSG, except return a message indicating that no more messages exist if the queue is empty.
5. ENDMPPI — Terminate a multiple physical page input message.

Coding the PFK Keys

The PFK can be defined as positional from left to right or in the keyword form.

Positional Method. Here's an example of defining each PFK positionally.

```
     DIF
     ---

FMTC     FMT
         DEV    TYPE=(3270,2),FEAT=IGNORE,                                  *
                PFK=(PFKA,'/FOR DDAINQ.','/FOR SVGINQ.',                    *
                '/FOR ADDCUS.','/FOR OUTMSG.','/FOR INTDIS.')
                DSCA=X'00A0'
         DIV    TYPE=INOUT

     MID
     ---

INPUT    MSG    TYPE=INPUT,SOR=FMTC,NXT=INDEXC,OPT=1
         SEG
         MFLD   PFKA,LTH=14,FILL=NULL
         MSGEND
```

In this example, five literals are associated with particular PF keys:

- The transaction code 'DDAINQ' is associated with PKK1

- The transaction code 'SVGINQ' is associated with PKK2
- The transaction code 'ADDCUS' is associated with PKK3
- The transaction code 'OUTMSG' is associated with PKK4
- The transaction code 'INTDIS' is associated with PKK5

It is possible to have up to 36 PK keys.

When using the positional method, any intervening PF key not being used must be represented by a comma.

Keyword Method. Here's an example of defining the PFK with keywords.

```
     DIF
     ---

CUSTUP    FMT
          DEV     TYPE=(3270,2),FEAT=IGNORE,                            *
                  PFK=(PFKIN,1='/FOR NEWCUSTM',2='/FOR PAYROLL',        *
                      5=NEXTLP)
                  DSCA=X'00A0'
          DIV     TYPE=INOUT

     MID
     ---

INPMESG   MSG     TYPE=INPUT,SOR=CUSTUP,NXT=OUTMESG,OPT=1
          SEG
          MFLD    PFKIN,LTH=14,FILL=NULL
          MSGEND
```

No intervening commas are required by this method, and literals may be up to 256 characters.

Note that PFKA in the first example and PFKIN in the second example are pseudo-DFLD names. The pseudo-DFLD name does not refer to any field on the screen; it provides a label which will be referenced by an MFLD statement in the associated MID if the PFK is defined to transmit a literal value to the application program. The pseudo-DFLD name must be unique within the device format, and its length is the length of the longest literal.

Coding PFK Keys for Page and Message Control Functions

Now, let's see how to define the PFK key for entering MFS page and message control functions, as in the following example:

```
     DIF
     ---

FMTD      FMT
          DEV     TYPE=(3270,2),FEAT=IGNORE,                            *
                  PFK=(DUMFLD,NEXTLP,NEXTMSG,ENDMPPI)

                         (1)     (2)     (3)      (4)
```

The DFLD name DUMFLD is provided to satisfy compiler syntax requirements, and

- PFK1 will request the next logical page of the current output message.
- PFK2 will request the first physical page of the next output message.
- PFK3 will end physical page input.

These actions are purely MFS-interpreted control functions and do not involve the application program.

Combination of PFKs for Keyed Input and MFS Control Functions

The following example shows how to define a combination of PFKs to substitute keyed input and to enter MFS control functions:

```
     DIF

FMTD      FMT
          DEV   TYPE=(3270,2),FEAT=IGNORE,                          *
                PFK=(PFKIN,'NEWCUSTM','PAYROLL',ENDMPPI)
```

In this coding, PFK3 is defined to terminate a multiple physical page. PFK1 will prompt transaction NEWCUSTM, PFK2 will prompt transaction PAYROLL, and PFK3 is defined to terminate multiple physical page input.

The PFK= parameter is commonly used to set up a main-menu facility controlled within MFS (FIG. 8-1). With this menu, the operator can invoke a specified format by pressing the associated PF key. For example, to bring up DDA STATEMENT SUMMARY, the operator presses the PF key 1 to bring up SAVINGS ACCOUNT INQUIRY, then PF 2, etc.; there is no need to enter a /FORMAT command to invoke these screens.

```
                              MENU C PFK INDEX

 PFK KEY   DESCRIPTION                                  FORMAT

     1     DDA STATEMENT SUMMARY                        DDAINQ
     2     SAVINGS ACCOUNT INQUIRY                      SVGINQ
     3     ADD A NEW CUSTOMER                           ADDCUS
     4     CUSTOMER NAME AND ADDRESS CHANGE             OUTMSG
     5     INTEREST RATE DISPLAY                        INTDIS
     6     EMPLOYEE CHECKING ACCOUNTS                   EMPLOY
     7     PAYROLL DISPLAY                              PAYROL
     8     INDEX FOR MENU F                             INDEXF
     9     INDEX FOR MENU D                             INDEXD
    10     INDEX FOR MENU A                             INDEXA
    11     INDEX FOR MENU B                             INDEXB

                                                              INDEX C
```

Fig. 8-1.

The control-statements coding for this menu is presented in FIG. 8-2. Note the following points:

1. The IGNORE operand is coded in the DEV statement because differentiation by features in this format is not necessary. All screens to be invoked from this main menu have the PF key feature.
2. The positional method is used, and associated screen formats are prompted by DFLD literals of the available transaction codes.
3. The pseudo-DFLD name PFKEY is used to map PFK action to the application program's input message.

```
COLUMN
1--------10----16-------------------------------------------------------72

         TITLE 'USING PFK TO FORMAT INDEX SCREEN'
         PRINT NOGEN
FMTC     FMT
         DEV   TYPE=(3270,2),FEAT=IGNORE,                                * (1)
PSEUDO ===>    PFK=(PFKEY,'/FOR DDAINQ.','/FOR SVGINQ.',                  *
DFLDNAME       '/FOR ADDCUS.','/FOR OUTMSG.','/FOR INTDIS.',              *
 (3)           '/FOR EMPLOY.','/FOR PAYROL.','/FOR INDEXF.',              * (2)
               '/FOR INDEXD.','/FOR INDEXA.','/FOR INDEXB.'),             *
               DSCA=X'00A0'
         DIV   TYPE=INOUT
         DPAGE CURSOR=((01,02)),FILL=NONE
DUMMY    DFLD  POS=(01,02),LTH=79,ATTR=(NUM,PROT)
         DFLD  'MENU C PFK INDEX',POS=(04,31)
         DFLD  'PFK KEY',POS=(07,11)
         DFLD  'DESCRIPTION',POS=(06,23)
         DFLD  'FORMAT',POS=(06,60)
         DFLD  '1',POS=(08,14)
         DFLD  'DDA STATEMENT SUMMARY',POS=(08,23)
         DFLD  'DDAINQ',POS=(08,60)
         DFLD  '2',POS=(09,14)
         DFLD  'SAVINGS ACCOUNT INQUIRY',POS=(09,23)
         DFLD  'SVGINQ',POS=(09,60)
         DFLD  '3',POS=(10,14)
         DFLD  'ADD A NEW CUSTOMER',POS=(10,23)
         DFLD  'ADDCUS',POS=(10,60)
         DFLD  '4',POS=(11,14)
         DFLD  'CUSTOMER NAME AND ADDRESS CHANGE',POS=(11,23)
         DFLD  'OUTMSG',POS=(11,60)
         DFLD  '5',POS=(12,14)
         DFLD  'INTEREST RATE DISPLAY',POS=(12,23)
         DFLD  'INTDIS',POS=(12,60)
         DFLD  '6',POS=(13,14)
         DFLD  'EMPLOYEE CHECKING ACCOUNTS',POS=(13,23)
         DFLD  'EMPLOY',POS=(13,60)
         DFLD  '7',POS=(14,14)
         DFLD  'PAYROLL DISPLAY',POS=(14,23)
         DFLD  'PAYROL',POS=(14,60)
         DFLD  '8',POS=(15,14)
         DFLD  'INDEX FOR MENU F',POS=(15,23)
```

Fig. 8-2.

Fig. 8-2. continued

```
         DFLD  'INDEXF',POS=(15,60)
         DFLD  '9',POS=(16,14)
         DFLD  'INDEX FOR MENU D',POS=(16,23)
         DFLD  'INDEXD',POS=(16,60)
         DFLD  '10',POS=(17,13)
         DFLD  'INDEX FOR MENU A',POS=(17,23)
         DFLD  'INDEXA',POS=(17,60)
         DFLD  '11',POS=(18,13)
         DFLD  'INDEX FOR MENU B',POS=(18,23)
         DFLD  'INDEXB',POS=(18,60)
         DFLD  'INDEX C',POS=(24,72)
         FMTEND
*
INPUT    MSG   TYPE=INPUT,SOR=FMTC,NXT=INDEXC,OPT=1
         SEG
         MFLD  PFKEY,LTH=14,FILL=NULL                                (3)
         MSGEND
*
INDEXC   MSG   TYPE=OUTPUT,SOR=(FMTC,IGNORE),NXT=INPUT,OPT=1,        *
               PAGE=NO,FILL=NULL
         SEG
         MFLD  DUMMY,LTH=79
         MSGEND
         END
```

INVOKING MULTIPLE-SCREEN FLOWS (MFS CONTROL)

Using PF Keys for Operator Logical Paging

Let's look at the order processing application using the order database with the hierarchy (FIG. 8-3). This system can update or add a new order and the order details.

- In the inquiry mode, the operator can page forward and backward among the line item segments comprising an order.
- In the update mode, the operator can update or add new orders and their associated line items.
- The operator can return to the main selection menu via PF keys.
- There is also provision for remaining in the formatted mode, allowing entry of requests for other formatted screens, transaction codes or IMS/VS commands.

To accomplish the above, we have utilized the following MFS features:

- Use of program function keys as substitutes for keyed input
- Use of logical operator paging
- Use of logical page selection
- Use of LPAGE NXT chaining

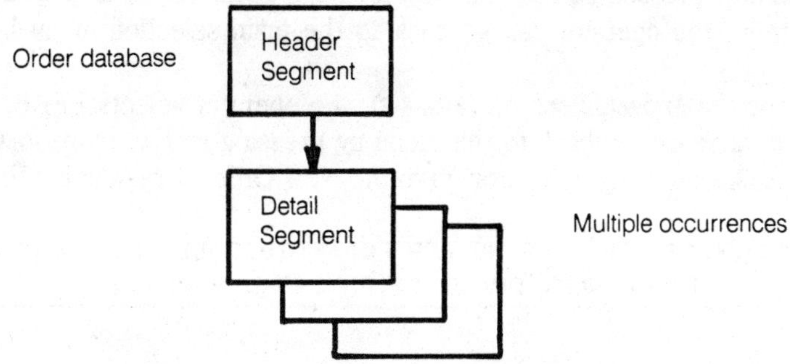

Fig. 8-3.

Some other features are also used. These include:

- Use of system message
- Use of prompt facility
- Use of system control area
- Use of system literals

To enter the application, the operator keys in:

/FORMAT ORDERMOD

and presses Enter. The main selection menu is displayed (FIG. 8-4). Two PF keys are enabled from this screen, and each is associated with one function: PFK4 for New Order, PFK5 for Order Detail. To use these functions, the operator does not have to clear the screen and enter another /FORMAT command. The menu format will generate the appropriate /FORMAT command based on the PF key selected by the operator.

```
DFS1040I DEVICE MAPPING FOR FMT=FMT009 DEVICE=3270 = 1
         TYPE=INOUT DPAGE=01 PHYSICAL PAGE=01

                       MAIN SELECTION MENU
   FOR                                          PLEASE DEPRESS:
 NEW ORDER                                           PFK4
 ORDER DETAIL                                        PFK5



  OTHER FORMAT OR COMMAND: ____________


 :::::::::::::::::::::::::::::::::::::::::::::::::::::::::::
```

Fig. 8-4.

If the operator presses PFK5, the New Order screen will be displayed (FIG. 8-5). From this screen, the operator can go back to the main selection menu by pressing PFK1.

To go to the Order Detail screen (FIG. 8-6), the operator selects PFK6. From this screen, the operator can go back to the menu by pressing PFK1, move forward using PFK2, move backward using PFK3, or go to the New Order screen using PFK4.

```
DFS1040I DEVICE MAPPING FOR FMT=FMT009 DEVICE=3270 = 1
           TYPE=INOUT DPAGE=02 PHYSICAL PAGE=01

 ::::::                                                PAGE:__
                 NEW ORDER

 ORDER NO:       __________
 DATE:           __________
 CUST CODE:      __________
 CUST NAME:      ____________________
 ADDRESS:        ____________________
                 ____________________

 PF1 = MAINMENU
 :::::::::::::::::::::::::::::::::::
 ::::::::::::::::::::::::::::::::::::::::::
```

Fig. 8-5.

FIGURE 8-7 presents the MFS control blocks coding for this format set. Note the following key points in this example (the parenthesized numbers refer to the numbers below):

1. Only one format (FMT009) is used for three different screens:
   - Main menu selection screen
   - New Order screen
   - Order Detail screen
2. There are three different MID definitions:
   - MENUMID
   - NEWMID
   - DETLMID

   These MIDs point to the same MOD ORDERMOD via the NXT= parameter and to the same format FMT009 via the SOR= parameter.

   ```
   MENUMID MSG TYPE=INPUT,SOR=(FMT009,IGNORE),NXT=ORDERMOD

   NEWMID  MSG TYPE=INPUT,SOR=(FMT009,IGNORE),NXT=ORDERMOD

   DETLMID MSG TYPE=INPUT,SOR=(FMT009,IGNORE),NXT=ORDERMOD
   ```

   This establishes control blocks linkage.

```
DFS1040I DEVICE MAPPING FOR FMT=FMT009 DEVICE=3270 = 1
         TYPE=INOUT DPAGE=03 PHYSICAL PAGE=01

                                                    PAGE:_
                   ORDER DETAIL

 ORDER NO:         __________
 LINE NO:          __________
 ITEM NO:          __________
 ITEM DESCR.       _____________________________
 QUANTITY:         __________
 PF1 = MAINMENU        PF2 = FORWARD
 PF3 = BACKWARD        PF4 = NEW ORDER
 :::::::::::::::::::::::::::::::::
 ::::::::::::::::::::::::::::::::::::::::
```

Fig. 8-6

```
COLUMN
1--------10----16-----------------------------------------------------72


         TITLE 'USING PF KEYS FOR OPERATOR LOGICAL PAGING'
         PRINT NOGEN
FMT009   FMT
 (1)     DEV   TYPE=(3270,1),FEAT=IGNORE,                              *
               SYSMSG=MESSAGE,                                         * (4)
               PFK=(PFKEY,                                             *
               '1          ',      PF1 RETURN TO SELECTION MENU        *
               '=          ',      PF2 PAGE FORWARD                    *
               '=-1        ',      PF3 PAGE BACKWARD                   * (3)
               '/FOR ADDOR',       PF4 NEW ORDER SCREEN                *
               '/FOR ORDET')       PF5 ORDER DETAIL SCREEN
         DIV   TYPE=INOUT
*
*        MAIN SELECTION SCREEN
*
MENU     DPAGE CURSOR=((09,27)),FILL=NONE                                (5)
         DFLD  'MAIN SELECTION MENU',POS=(02,12),ATTR=PROT
         DFLD  'FOR ',POS=(03,06),ATTR=PROT
         DFLD  'PLEASE DEPRESS:',POS=(03,22),ATTR=PROT
         DFLD  'NEW ORDER',POS=(04,02),ATTR=PROT
         DFLD  'PFK4',POS=(04,30),ATTR=PROT
         DFLD  'ORDER DETAIL',POS=(05,02),ATTR=PROT
         DFLD  'PFK5',POS=(05,30),ATTR=PROT
         DFLD  'OTHER FORMAT OR COMMAND:',POS=(09,02),ATTR=PROT
COMMAND  DFLD  POS=(09,27),LTH=10,ATTR=(ALPHA,MOD)
MESSAGE  DFLD  POS=(12,02),LTH=37,ATTR=(PROT,HI)                         (4).
*
*        NEW ORDER SCREEN
*
```

Fig. 8-7.

Fig. 8-7. continued

```
NEWORD   DPAGE CURSOR=((04,13)),FILL=NONE                                    (5)
TRANCD   DFLD  POS=(01,04),LTH=08,ATTR=(MOD,PROT,NODISP)
         DFLD  'PAGE:',POS=(01,31),ATTR=PROT
PAGE     DFLD  POS=(01,37),LTH=02,ATTR=NUM
         DFLD  'NEW ORDER:',POS=(02,12),ATTR=PROT
         DFLD  'ORDER NO:',POS=(04,02),ATTR=PROT
ORDERNUM DFLD  POS=(04,13),LTH=08,ATTR=NUM
         DFLD  'DATE:',POS=(05,02),ATTR=PROT
DATE     DFLD  POS=(05,13),LTH=08,ATTR=NUM
         DFLD  'CUST CODE:',POS=(06,02),ATTR=PROT
CUSTNUBR DFLD  POS=(06,13),LTH=08,ATTR=NUM
         DFLD  'CUST NAME:',POS=(07,02),ATTR=PROT
CUSTNAME DFLD  POS=(07,13),LTH=20
         DFLD  'ADDRESS:',POS=(08,02),ATTR=PROT
STREET   DFLD  POS=(08,13),LTH=20
CITYSTAT DFLD  POS=(09,13),LTH=20
         DFLD  'PF1 - MAINMENU',POS=(10,02),ATTR=PROT
REPLY    DFLD  POS=(11,02),LTH=31,ATTR=(PROT,HI)
MESSAGE  DFLD  POS=(12,02),LTH=37,ATTR=(PROT,HI)                             (4)
*
*        ORDER DETAIL SCREEN
*
DETAIL   DPAGE CURSOR=((04,13)),FILL=NONE                                    (5)
         DFLD  'PAGE:',POS=(01,31),ATTR=PROT
PAGE     DFLD  POS=(01,37),LTH=02,ATTR=NUM
         DFLD  'ORDER DETAIL:',POS=(02,12),ATTR=PROT
         DFLD  'ORDER NO:',POS=(04,02),ATTR=PROT
ORDERNUM DFLD  POS=(04,13),LTH=08,ATTR=NUM
         DFLD  'LINE NO:',POS=(05,02),ATTR=PROT
LINENUM  DFLD  POS=(05,13),LTH=04,ATTR=NUM
         DFLD  'ITEM NO:',POS=(06,02),ATTR=PROT
ITEMNUM  DFLD  POS=(06,13),LTH=08,ATTR=NUM
         DFLD  'ITEM DESCR:',POS=(07,02),ATTR=PROT
ITEMDESC DFLD  POS=(07,14),LTH=25
         DFLD  'QUANTITY:',POS=(08,02),ATTR=PROT
QUANTITY DFLD  POS=(08,14),LTH=05,ATTR=NUM
         DFLD  'PF1 - MAINMENU   PF2 - FORWARD',POS=(09,02),ATTR=PROT
         DFLD  'PF3 - BACKWARD   PF4 - NEW ORDER',POS=(10,02),ATTR=PROT
REPLY    DFLD  POS=(11,02),LTH=31,ATTR=(PROT,HI)
MESSAGE  DFLD  POS=(12,02),LTH=37,ATTR=(PROT,HI)                             (4)
         FMTEND
*
*        MID
*
MENUMID  MSG   TYPE=INPUT,SOR=(FMT009,IGNORE),NXT=ORDERMOD,                * (2)
               OPT=1
         SEG
         MFLD  PFKEY,LTH=10,FILL=NULL                                        (3)
         MFLD  COMMAND,LTH=10
         MSGEND
*
*        MID FOR HEADER ORDER
*
MEWMID   MSG   TYPE=INPUT,SOR=(FMT009,IGNORE),NXT=ORDERMOD,                * (2)
               OPT=1
         SEG
```

Fig. 8-7. continued

```
         MFLD  PFKEY,LTH=10,FILL=NULL                                       (3)
         MFLD  TRANCD,LTH=09
         MFLD  ORDERNUM,LTH=08
         MFLD  DATE,LTH=08
         MFLD  CUSTNUBR,LTH=08
         MFLD  CUSTNAME,LTH=20
         MFLD  STREET,LTH=20
         MFLD  CITYSTAT,LTH=20
         MSGEND
*
*        MID FOR DETAIL LINE
*
DETLMID  MSG   TYPE=INPUT,SOR=(FMT009,IGNORE),NXT=ORDERMOD,               * (2)
               OPT=1
         SEG
         MFLD  PFKEY,LTH=10,FILL=NULL                                       (3)
         MFLD  ORDERNUM,LTH=08
         MFLD  LINENUM,LTH=04
         MFLD  ITEMNUM,LTH=08
         MFLD  ITEMDESC,LTH=25
         MFLD  QUANTITY,LTH=05
         MSGEND
*
*        MOD - USING EXPLICIT LOGICAL PAGING
*
ORDERMOD MSG   TYPE=OUTPUT,SOR=(FMT009,IGNORE),                             *
               OPT=1,FILL=PT,PAGE=YES     <=== OPERATOR LOGICAL PAGING      (6)
*
LPAGE1   LPAGE SOR=MENU,                                                    *
               COND=(PAGE1,=,'1')           <=== USE OF COND KEYWORD      * (7)
               NEXT=MENUMID
         SEG
PAGE1    MFLD  LTH=1
*
LPAGE2   LPAGE SOR=NEWORD,                                                  *
               COND=(PAGE2,=,'2')                                         * (7)
               NEXT=NEWMID
         SEG
PAGE2    MFLD  LTH=1                                                        *
         MFLD  (,SCA),LTH=02           <=== SYSTEM CONTROL AREA DEFINED   (9)
         MFLD  PAGE,LTH=02
         MFLD  (TRANCD,'NEWTRAN '),LTH=08
         MFLD  ORDERNUM,LTH=10,ATTR=YES
         MFLD  (DATE,DATE2)             <=== USE OF SYSTEM LITERAL          (10)
         MFLD  CUSTNUBR,LTH=10,ATTR=YES      <=== LENGTH INCREASED          (11)
         MFLD  CUSTNAME,LTH=22,ATTR=YES           BY 2 FOR ATTRIBUTE
         MFLD  STREET,LTH=22,ATTR=YES             BYTE MODIFICATION
         MFLD  CITYSTAT,LTH=22,ATTR=YES
*
LPAGE3   LPAGE SOR=DETAIL,                                                  *
               COND=(PAGE3,=,'3')                                         * (7)
               NEXT=DETLMID,                                                *
               PROMPT=(MESSAGE,'LAST ORDER OF LINE ITEM')                   (8)
                           |_____  USE OF PROMPT FACILITY
         SEG
```

Fig. 8-7. continued

```
PAGE3     MFLD  LTH=1                                                  *
          MFLD  (,SCA),LTH=02                                        (9)
          MFLD  PAGE,LTH=02
          MFLD  ORDERNUM,LTH=10,ATTR=YES                            (11)
          MFLD  LINENUM,LTH=06,ATTR=YES
          MFLD  ITEMNUM,LTH=10,ATTR=YES
          MFLD  ITEMDESC,LTH=25
          MFLD  QUANTITY,LTH=07,ATTR=YES
          MFLD  REPLY,LTH=33,ATTR=YES
          MSGEND
          END
```

3. The PF keys are defined using the positional method:

```
PFK=(PFKEY,
'1            ',
'=            ',
'=-1          ',
'/FOR ADDOR   ',
'/FOR ORDET   ',
```

The pseudo-DFLD name is PFKEY (you can use any other name for this) and is referenced by an MFLD in each associated MID:

```
MFLD PFKEY,LTH=10,FILL=NULL
```

This MFLD is coded as the first field of the input message. When the operator selects a predefined PF key, the literal associated with it by the PFK parameter in the DEV statement will be moved to this message field. Because this field is at the beginning of the message and because the literal begins with a /FOR (the abbreviation of /FORMAT), it will be interpreted as an IMS command that invokes the application provided in the main menu selection screen.

The literal value is handled completely within MFS; it is not passed to the application program.

4. The system message is used by coding.

```
FMT009     FMT
           DEV       TYPE=(3270,1),FEAT=IGNORE,
                     SYSMSG=MESSAGE
           ....
MESSAGE    DFLD      POS=(12,02),LTH=37,ATTR=(PROT,HI)
```

5. The three device pages are delimited by three DPAGE statements. Each has a different location for the cursor:

```
MENU      DPAGE CURSOR=((09,27)),FILL=NONE
          ....
```

```
NEWORD     DPAGE CURSOR=((04,13)),FILL=NONE
           ....
DETAIL     DPAGE CURSOR=((04,13)),FILL=NONE
           ....
```

6. Explicit logical paging is defined with PAGE=YES:

```
ORDERMOD MSG        TYPE=OUTPUT,SOR=(FMT009,IGNORE),*
                    OPT=1,FILL=PT,PAGE=YES
```

7. The three logical pages are delimited by three LPAGE statements:

```
LPAGE1     LPAGE     SOR=MENU,                 *
                     COND=(PAGE1,=,'1'),       *
                     NXT=MENUMID
           SEG
PAGE1      MFLD      LTH=1
           .....
LPAGE2     LPAGE     SOR=NEWORD,               *
                     COND=(PAGE2,=,'2'),       *
                     NXT=NEWMID
           SEG
PAGE2      MFLD      LTH=1
           .....
LPAGE3     LPAGE     SOR=DETAIL,               *
                     COND=(PAGE3,=,'3'),       *
                     NXT=DETLMID,     *

           ....
           SEG
PAGE3      MFLD      LTH=1
           .....
```

The corresponding test fields are PAGE1, PAGE2, and PAGE3.

8. The PROMPT facility is used on the third logical page.

```
LPAGE3     LPAGE     SOR=DETAIL,               *
           ....
                     PROMPT=(MESSAGE,'LAST ORDER OF LINE ITEM')
```

9. The system control area is defined in the MOD for logical pages 2 and 3:

```
           SEG
PAGE2      MFLD      LTH=1
           MFLD      (,SCA),LTH=02
           ....
           SEG
PAGE3      MFLD      LTH=1
           MFLD      (,SCA),LTH=02
```

The SCA is defined as two-bytes-long and appears in the first segment of the logical page.

The application program has to move the desired SCA=X value to its output message field before doing the ISRT call of the output message.

10. The date is provided by using the system literal; it has the format MM/DD/YY.

```
MFLD (DATE,DATE2)
```

11. The fields with dynamic attribute byte modification are increased by 2 for the attribute:

```
*    MID
          MFLD CUSTNUBR,LTH=08
          MFLD CUSTNAME,LTH=20
          ....
*    MOD
          MFLD CUSTNUBR,LTH=10,ATTR=YES
          MFLD CUSTNAME,LTH=22,ATTR=YES
```

HOW TO INVOKE MULTIPLE SCREEN FLOWS FROM THE APPLICATION PROGRAM

You've learned how to control multiple screen flows entirely within MFS. Now, let's see how you can control screen flows from the application program. Our order processing system can be modified to illustrate this second technique.

You can redefine the PF keys as follows:

```
PFK=(PFKEY,
'1              ',
'=              ',
'=-1            ',
'ADDORDER       ',
'ORDERDET       ',
```

Each PF key is referenced by an MFLD in each MID associated with it:

```
MFLD PFKEY,LTH=10,FILL=NULL
```

Note that we no longer use the literal /FOR.

When the operator presses PFK4 or PFK5, the result is a transaction code ADDORDER or ORDERDET which is passed to the application program. The program examines the transaction, and, on the basis of this transaction code, will determine which of the three screen formats it should display. If the transaction is ADDORDER, the New Order screen will be invoked, and if the transaction is ORDERDET, the Order Detail screen will be invoked.

You also have to code two separate MOD definitions, one for the New Order Screen and the other for the Order Detail screen. Depending on the transaction received, the application will specify the appropriate MOD name before issuing an ISRT call to display the requested screen.

The COBOL source code for this processing is:

```
WORKING-STORAGE SECTION.
....
```

```
 01 INPUT-MESSAGE-IO-AREA.
    05 INPUT-LENGTH             PIC S999 COMP SYNC.
    05 FILLER                   PIC X(02).       <=== ZZ FIELD IS
    05 IN-TRANSACTION-CODE      PIC X(08).            NOT USED BY
    05 FILLER                   PIX X.                PROGRAM ON INPUT
    05 IN-DATA-FIELDS           PIC .....
    .....
 01 OUTPUT-MESSAGE-IO-AREA.
    05 OUTPUT-LENGTH             PIC S999 COMP SYNC.
    05 OUTPUT-ZZ                 PIC S999 COMP SYNC.
    05 OUTPUT-MESSAGE-TEXT       PIC .....
    .....
 01 MOD-NAME                     PIC X(8).
    .....
 PROCEDURE DIVISION.
  .....
 100-PROCESS-INPUT-MESSAGES.
  ....
     IF IN-TRANSACTION-CODE EQUAL 'ADDORDER'
  .....
* BUILD NEW ORDER OUTPUT MESSAGE
  .....
     MOVE 'ADDORDER' TO MOD-NAME
     ELSE
     IF IN-TRANSACTION-CODE EQUAL 'ORDERDET'
  .....
* BUILD ORDER DETAIL OUTPUT MESSAGE
  .....
     MOVE 'ORDERDET' TO MOD-NAME.

 600-SEND-OUTPUT-MESSAGES.
     CALL 'CBLTDLI' USING ISRT,
                          IO-PCB-MASK,
                          OUTPUT-MESSAGE-IO-AREA,
                          MOD-NAME.
```

MULTIPLE SCREEN FLOW VERSUS PERFORMANCE

The application which uses multiple screen flow techniques needs to store data from one screen to the next for its processing. For that reason, the multiple screen technique is most suitable for conversational applications.

This technique can present some performance problems. When the MOD is changed either by pressing the PF keys or by the application program, IMS "fetches" for the new MOD. MFS then has to perform a full-formatting operation which affects performance because MFS has to send all variable data and screen literals to the terminal.

The program-supplied MOD name has a disadvantage in that it makes the application program dependent on control blocks. If the MOD names are changed, you have to recompile the program so that it can process the new names.

Due to the inefficiencies involved in full-formatting operations, you should limit your application to single-screen formats by using the same device format for many applications whenever possible.

9

How to Specify Special Hardware Features

In this chapter, we will examine some special hardware features available with the 3270 device. These features have not been covered earlier in this book. If you work in a large computer installation which uses several different 3270 terminals, you may need to know some of the features presented in this chapter.

First, we will discuss the coding requirements involved in specifying the special device features, and then we will see how MFS selects the appropriate device format for the associated terminal. The coding techniques that we will discuss will include the control of the printed-page format, the use of the selector light pen, and the magnetic card reader.

SPECIFYING SPECIAL DEVICE FEATURES

You can specify the use of different device types within one generated MFS format. This is done by specifying multiple DEV statements for each device type within the FMT statement.

You can use the 3270 CRT, Model 2, the 3270 CRT, Model 1, and the 3270 printer. To specify their use, you have to code them within the device format control block as follows:

```
DEV TYPE=(3270,2) signifies a 3270 CRT device, model 2.
DEV TYPE=(3270,1) signifies a 3270 CRT device, model 1.
DEV TYPE=(3270P)  signifies a printer such as the 3284 or 3286.
```

Along with the DEV statement you can use the FEAT= parameter to specify the special features for the device specified in the DEV statement. As an example:

```
INQFMT    FMT
          DEV     TYPE=(3270,2),FEAT=IGNORE            Model 2
          DIV     TYPE=INOUT
DPAGE1    DPAGE   CURSOR=((04,66))
          .....
*
          DEV     TYPE=(3270,1),FEAT=IGNORE            Model 1
          DIV     TYPE=INOUT
DPAGE1    DPAGE   CURSOR=((02,31))
          ....
*
PRINTER   DEV     TYPE=(3270P,2),FEAT=IGNORE,PAGE=(24,FLOAT) Printer
*
          DIV     TYPE=OUTPUT                           Output only
          ....
```

The DEV statement defines device characteristics for a particular device type. The DFLD statements following this statement are mapped using these characteristics until the next DEV or FMTEND statement is encountered.

FEAT= specifies special features for this device, such as the type of card reader and keyboard. For 3270 display units, FEAT=IGNORE is usually coded. For 3270 printer units, we may code:

- FEAT=120 or
- FEAT=126 or
- FEAT=132

specifying the number of characters allowed on a print line (the default is 120).

IGNORE specifies that device features are to be ignored for this device. When FEAT=IGNORE is specified for 3270 devices, the operands CARD=, PEN=, PFK=, may still be specified.

The following shows how to code specific features in the DEV statement:

```
DEV  TYPE=(3270,2),FEAT=(CARD,NOPFK,NOPEN)   ← For card reader
DEV  TYPE=(3270,2),FEAT=(NOCD,PFK,NOPEN)     ← For program function keys
DEV  TYPE=(3270,2),FEAT=(NOCD,NOPFK,PEN)     ← For light pen
```

- CARD specifies that the device has a magnetic card reader.
- NOCD specifies the absence of the CARD feature.
- PEN= specifies the selector light pen detect feature.
- NOPEN specifies the absence of the PEN feature.

- PFK= specifies the device has program function keys.
- NOPFK specifies the absence of the PFK feature

How to Specify Special Hardware Features

The special features can be coded separately or may be combined. When the special features are coded in the DEV statement, then the SOR= operand in the MID/MOD must not specify IGNORE:

```
   DIF/DOF

INQFMT      FMT
            DEV   TYPE=(3270,2),FEAT=(CARD,NOPFK,PEN)
            DIV   TYPE=INOUT
   MOD

ORDEROUT    MSG   TYPE=OUTPUT,SOR=INQFMT.NXT=INQUIRY
            ....
            SEG                        ↑_IGNORE operand is not specified
```

The MOD tells MFS whether it should look for a precise set of specific features in the DOF or whether to ignore them.

Control Block Selection Process

You may wonder how to handle the environment of a large computer installation which has a variety of 3270 terminals of different device characteristics. The two methods for handling this situation are discussed below.

Specify Individual Feature. In this method, code the individual device control blocks for each hardware configuration (FIG. 9-3). Up to nine hardware configurations may be coded for each single format. Thus up to nine DIFs and nine DOFs will be generated for each format.

Specify FEAT=IGNORE. The second method is to code the device control blocks with the FEAT=IGNORE parameter and to make use of the special features available at the time of operation.

In the above instances, we have multiple DIFs and DOFs associated with one format name. How does MFS select the appropriate DIF/DOF for the related device? For each control block, MFS develops a unique eight-character name by adding a two-position prefix to the FMT label name for every DIF and/or DOF that is generated. This two-position prefix represents the particular device and the special features on the device for which the format control block is coded.

FIGURE 9-1 explains how the eight-character name is built by the MFS compiler. Characters 3 through 8 represent the label of the FMT statement. For DOF, character position 3 is specified as uppercase, and for DIF as lowercase. Character 1 (byte 1) of the name contains a hexadecimal value indicating the device this format is associated with, such as:

- X'00'—3270, Model 1
- X'02'—3270, Model 2

The device type is specified in the TYPE= parameter.

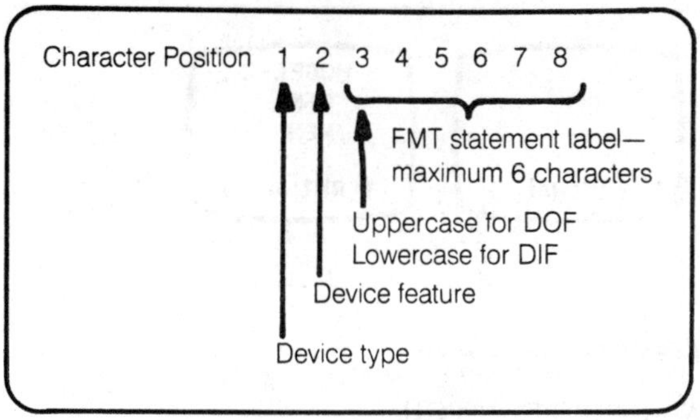

Fig. 9-1. Building FMT label names.

Character 2 (byte 2) contains a hexadecimal value indicating device features necessary for this format to be used. The device feature is specified in the FEAT= parameter. For the IGNORE feature, it has a value of X'7F'.

Device format control block selection is based on the device which is *active* at the time of operation without regard to the message descriptor coding.

When FEAT=IGNORE is coded in the DEV statement and

```
SOR=(DOF name, IGNORE)
```

is coded in the MSG statement of the MOD, MFS will select the DOF without regard to the special hardware features of the active terminal device. However, if SOR=(DOF-name) is coded in the MSG statement of the MOD without the IGNORE= parameter, MFS will select only the appropriate device format where the FEAT= operand specifies the exact set of hardware features of the active device to which the message is being sent.

FIGURE 9-2 illustrates the selection of control blocks.

Let's find out which DOF will be used to map the output of MOD OUTMESG to terminals 1, 2, 3, and 4.

- DOF 3 will be used to map the output message to terminal 1 because it specifies Model 1 and PFK only.
- DOF 4 will be used to map the output message to terminal 2 because it specifies Model 2, CARD and PEN.
- DOF 2 will be used to map the output message to terminal 3 because it specifies Model 2 and PFK only.
- No message is sent to terminal 4 because there is no DOF which specifies Model 2, PFK and PEN.

We recommend that you always code FEAT=IGNORE unless you are given specifications that explicitly specify the wanted features. This will give you flexibility in using the devices which are actually active at the time of operation without regard to the message descriptor coding.

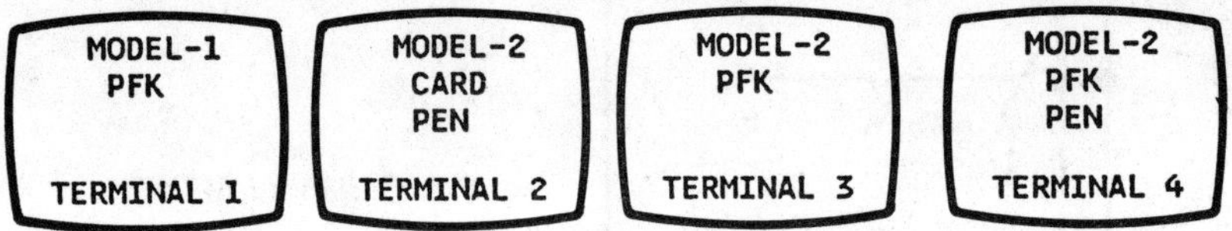


```
CUSTUP    FMT
          .....
 (1)      DEV    TYPE=(3270,2),FEAT=(NOCD,NOPFK,PEN)

 (2)      DEV    TYPE=(3270,2),FEAT=(NOCD,PFK,NOPEN)

 (3)      DEV    TYPE=(3270,1),FEAT=(NOCD,PFK,NOPEN)

 (4)      DEV    TYPE=(3270,2),FEAT=(CD,NOPFK,PEN)

          DIV    TYPE=INOUT
          .....
          FMTEND
OUTMESG   MSG    TYPE=OUTPUT,SOR=CUSTUP,NXT=INPMESG          <=== MOD DEFINITION
          SEG
          .....

                      IGNORE OPERAND IS NOT CODED
```

Fig. 9-2.

HOW TO CONTROL PRINTED PAGE FORMAT

Now, let's learn how to control the printed page format on a remote printer.

MOD Coding

In the MOD coding, the NXT= parameter in the MSG statement is not coded because the 3270 printer is strictly an output device:

```
PRTOUT MSG TYPE=OUTPUT,SOR=(FORMAT,IGNORE) ← NXT= is not coded
```

MFS provides several specifications to control the format of the messages to 3270 printer devices. The control options that we can specify are:

- Print mode
- Page depth
- Line width
- Additional or deletion of print lines on the output listing.

The PAGE= keyword of the DEV statement is used to determine the format of output messages sent to the printer:

```
PRINTER  DEV  TYPE=(3270P,2),FEAT=IGNORE,PAGE=(24,FLOAT)
         DIV  TYPE=OUTPUT
```

The options that may be specified for the DEV statement are given in FIG. 9-3.

Defining Format Options

FIGURE 9-4 shows how to define format control options for a 3270 printer, Model 2. Here, the output listing is printed with 60 lines per page, 120 print characters per line (default). Lines with no data (all blank or null) are not printed.

Defined in the DOF;	Function
DEV TYPE=(3270P) .FEAT=<u>120</u> 126 132	For 3270 printer units we may code: FEAT=120 or FEAT=126 or FEAT=132 specifying the number of characters allowed on a print line. The default is 120.
IGNORE	IGNORE specifies that device features are to be ignored for this device.
1 2 3 4 5 6 7 8 9 10	Values 1, 2, 3, 4, 5, 6, 7, 8, 9, and 10 are valid values for 3270P printers. The FEAT= specification of 1 to 10 can be used to group devices with specific features or hardware data stream dependencies. For example, value 1 group devices with a maximum of 80 print positions; value 2 group devices with a maximum of 132 print positions. When WIDTH= is specified, FEAT=(1,. . .10) must be also specified. If FEAT= is specified but WIDTH= is not specified, WIDTH= defaults to 120.
.WIDTH=<u>120</u>	Specifies the maximum line width for this DEV type.
Number	Number of print positions per line of input or output data. Default value is 120.
.PAGE=<u>55</u>	Specifies the number of print lines on a printed page.
Number	Must be greater than 1 and less than 256. Default value is 55.
DEFN	Specifies that lines are to be printed for each line as defined by the DFLD statements. No lines are to be moved or added to output page.
SPACE	Specifies that each output page will contain the exact number of lines specified in the 'number' parameter. Blank lines are inserted at the bottom of the page to make the total lines printed equal the maximum number of lines per page as specified by the 'number' parameter.
FLOAT	Specifies that lines with no data (all blanks or NULL) after formatting are to be deleted.

Fig. 9-3. Specifying printer options.

```
| LL | ZZ | 1 |

| LL | ZZ | PRINT LINE4 |               No NXT=  parameter is coded
| XXXXXXXXXXXXXXXXXX      |     MOD:          |
                                ---           v

PRTOUT   MSG    TYPE=OUTPUT,SOR=(FORMAT,IGNORE),      <=== NXT=  PARAMETER IS
                FILL=PT                                          NOT CODED
         SEG
         MFLD   (TITLE,'END OF MONTH REPORT')               <=== HEADING
         MFLD   PAGENO,LTH=2                                <=== PAGE NUMBER
         SEG
         MFLD   LINE4,LTH=113
         .....

                DOF:
                ---

FORMAT   FMT
         DEV    TYPE=(3270P,2),FEAT=IGNORE,
                PAGE=(60,FLOAT)                             <=== PRINT OPTIONS
         DIV    TYPE=OUTPUT
TITLE    DFLD   POS=(02,06),LTH=19
         DFLD   'PAGE',POS=(02,105)
PAGENO   DFLD   POS=(02,110),LTH=02
LINE4    DFLD   POS=(04,6),LTH=113
         .....

   END OF MONTH REPORT                                     PAGE 1

   PRINT LINE 4 XXXXXXXXXXXXXXXXXX
```

Fig. 9-4. 3270 printer flow.

Note that the NXT= parameter is not coded in the MSG statement of the MOD because the 3270 printer is strictly an output device.

In the DOF, we have specified FEAT=IGNORE, PAGE=(60,FLOAT) requesting that blank lines are to be deleted.

Defining Page Options

FIGURE 9-5 shows how to define page control options. Note that in the MOD and DOF definitions, we have specified eight line segments. The application program's output contains only four lines of data. How the output listing will appear depends on the options specified in the PAGE parameter.

Now, refer to FIG. 9-6 for the PAGE options.

- For PAGE=(10,DEFN), we have four lines of data plus four blank lines. Altogether, we have eight lines of print. No lines are to be moved or added to the output message.

Program Output

Segment 1

LL	ZZ	LINE1 XXXXXXXXXX

Segment 2

LL	ZZ	LINE2 XXXXXXXXXX

Segment 3

LL	ZZ	LINE3 XXXXXXXXXX

Segment 4

LL	ZZ	LINE4 XXXXXXXXXX

```
                MOD:
                ---
PRTOUT   MSG    TYPE=OUTPUT,SOR=(FORMAT,IGNORE),....
         SEG
         MFLD   LINE1
         SEG
         MFLD   LINE2
         SEG
         MFLD   LINE3
         SEG
         MFLD   LINE4
         SEG
         MFLD   LINE5
         SEG
         MFLD   LINE6
         SEG
         MFLD   LINE7
         SEG
         MFLD   LINE8
         .....

                DOF:
                ---
FORMAT   FMT
         .....
LINE1    DFLD   POS=(01,04),LTH=16
LINE2    DFLD   POS=(02,04),LTH=16
LINE3    DFLD   POS=(03,04),LTH=16
LINE4    DFLD   POS=(04,04),LTH=16
LINE5    DFLD   POS=(05,04),LTH=16
LINE6    DFLD   POS=(06,04),LTH=16
LINE7    DFLD   POS=(07,04),LTH=16
LINE8    DFLD   POS=(08,04),LTH=16
```

Fig. 9-5. MOD and DOF definitions.

- For PAGE=(10,SPACE), we have four lines of data plus six blank lines. Altogether, we have 10 lines of print, the exact number of print lines specified in the PAGE parameter.
- For PAGE=(10,FLOAT) we have only four lines of data. No blank lines are added.

SELECTOR LIGHT PEN

The selector light pen is a light-sensitive pen that can detect the light emitted from characters displayed on the device screen. It can be used to create data. The pen is attached to the 3270 terminal device by a cable. When the operator presses the tip of the pen against the screen, the circuitry in the 3270 identifies which field has been selected for presentation to the application program.

PAGE=(10,DEFN)

```
LINE 1 XXXXXXXXXX
LINE 2 XXXXXXXXXX
LINE 3 XXXXXXXXXX
LINE 4 XXXXXXXXXX
   B
   B      FOUR BLANK LINES
   B
   B
```

PAGE=(10,SPACE)

```
LINE 1 XXXXXXXXXX
LINE 2 XXXXXXXXXX
LINE 3 XXXXXXXXXX
LINE 4 XXXXXXXXXX
   B
   B
   B      SIX BLANK LINES
   B
   B
   B
```

PAGE=(10,FLOAT)

```
LINE 1 XXXXXXXXXX
LINE 2 XXXXXXXXXX
LINE 3 XXXXXXXXXX
LINE 4 XXXXXXXXXX
          NO BLANK LINES
```

Fig. 9-6. PAGE options.

There are two types of pen-detectable fields:

- Deferred detectable field
- Immediately detectable field

Deferred Detectable Fields

Deferred detectable fields do not cause data to be transmitted until the entire message is entered. If the operator selects this field, he must press the ENTER key or select an immediately detectable field for data to be transmitted. A deferred detectable field is identified to the operator by the designator |?| (X‘6F’). When it is selected,

- The ? is changed to > (X‘6E’)
- The modified data tag is turned on to transmit the field contents

We can delete this field by a second selection:

- The > is changed back to ?
- The modified data tag is turned off

Immediately Detectable Fields

Immediately detectable fields cause data to be transmitted as soon as they are selected. This field is identified by a designator character of blank (X'40'). When selected, the addresses of all fields with the modified data tag on are read by MFS.

Pen-Detectable Field Format

Both types of pen detectable fields have the format shown in FIG. 9-7.

1. The attribute byte defines the fields as being pen-detectable. This is done by specifying (ATTR=.....) on the DFLD statement.
2. The field including the attribute byte is preceded by three blanks or NULL characters.
3. The first character of the field following the attribute byte is a detectable-field designator character.
4. The last character displayed in the detectable field must be followed by three blanks or NULL characters.

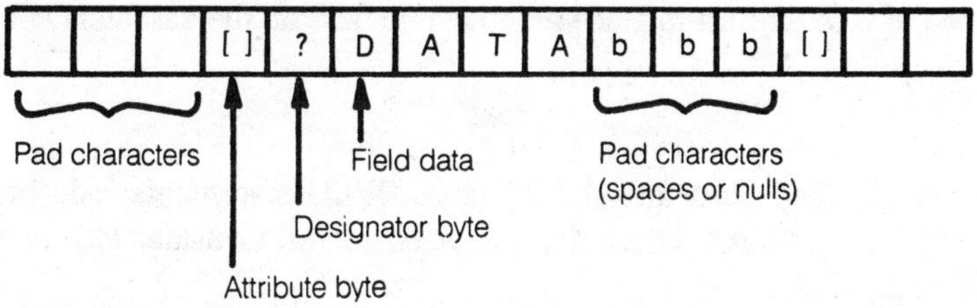

Fig. 9-7. Pen-detectable field format.

The attribute byte can have the following values:

NODET Identifies that a field can be selected with the light pen operations.
DET Specifies a deferred detectable field.
IDET Indicates an immediately detectable field.
STRIP Specifies whether or not the pen detects designator byte
NOSTRIP Preceding the input field should be stripped (STRIP) before presentation to the program.

NODET and STRIP are the defaults.

MFS CODING OF PEN-DETECTABLE FIELDS

Coding Deferred Detectable Fields

<u>DOF</u>

In the DEV statement, we can code as follows:

```
DEV TYPE=(3270,2),FEAT=(NOCD,NOPFK,PEN)
```

We can also code FEAT=IGNORE (unless the mixture of different hardware features requires specialized DIF/DOFs to handle the same message from different device types):

```
DEV TYPE=(3270,2),FEAT=IGNORE
```

For a DFLD statement:

- Code ATTR=DET for deferred detectable fields.
- Allow at least three blanks or null characters preceding and trailing the detectable field.
- The use of DOF literals to place a detectable field on the screen is not feasible.

<u>MID</u>

If NOSTRIP is specified on deferred detectable DFLD statements, add one byte to LTH= of MID MFLDs to handle the designator character. Consider FIG. 9-8 with eight deferred detectable fields.

```
                    AIRLINE RESERVATIONS

 ::::::::                                       DATE:______

NAME: ________________________
DESTINATION: _____________

FARES:                   ?FIRST CLASS      ?ECONOMY
SEAT SELECTION:          ?WINDOW           ?AISLE
                         ?SMOKING          ?NON-SMOKING
MEALS:                   ?MIXED            ?VEGETARIAN
```

Fig. 9-8.

<u>DOF/DIF</u>

```
AIRRES   FMT
         DEV      TYPE=(3270,2),FEAT=IGNORE
         ....
         DFLD     'FARES:',POS(08,02)
```

```
FISRTCL   DFLD     POS=(08,23),LTH=15,ATTR=(PROT,DET,STRIP)
ECONOMY   DFLD     POS=(08,41),LTH=15,ATTR=(PROT,DET,STRIP)
          DFLD     'SEAT SELECTION',POS=(09,02)
WINDOW    DFLD     POS=(09,23),LTH=15,ATTR=(PROT,DET,STRIP)   Deferred
AISLE     DFLD     POS=(09,41),LTH=15,ATTR=(PROT,DET,STRIP)   detectable
SMOKNG    DFLD     POS=(10,23),LTH=15,ATTR=(PROT,DET,STRIP)   fields
NONSMOK   DFLD     POS=(10,41),LTH=15,ATTR=(PROT,DET,STRIP)
          DFLD     'MEALS:',POS=(11,02)
MIXED     DFLD     POS=(10,23),LTH=15,ATTR=(PROT,DET,STRIP)
VEGETAR   DFLD     POS=(10,41),LTH=15,ATTR=(PROT,DET,STRIP)
          FMTEND
```

For the above note the following:

- LTH= includes three trailing blanks or null characters for detectable fields.
- PROT is coded to prevent the operator from accidentally modifying the field.
- DET specifies the deferred detectable field.
- STRIP is the default, but is coded here for illustration; the designator character will not be mapped to the input message.

<u>MOD</u>

```
DESTINA   MSG      TYPE=OUTPUT,SOR=(AIRRES,IGNORE),NXT=RESERVN
          SEG
          MFLD     (FIRSTCL,'?FIRST CLASS'),LTH=12
          MFLD     (ECONOMY,'?ECONOMY'),LTH=12
          MFLD     (WINDOW,'?WINDOW'),LTH=12
          MFLD     (AISLE,'?AISLE'),LTH=12
          MFLD     (SMOKING,'?SMOKING'),LTH=12
          MFLD     (NONSMOK,'?NON-SMOKING'),LTH=12
          MFLD     (MIXED,'?MIXED'),LTH=12
          MFLD     (VEGETAR,'?VEGETARIAN'),LTH=12
          MSGEND
```

For the above, note the following:

- Literals are provided along with the designator character |?|.
- The lengths in the MOD are shorter than the lengths in the DOF DFLDs (by three characters).

Next, see what will happen when the operator selects the deferred detectable fields in FIG. 9-9. The designator character ? is changed to > for each field selected. The operator keys in the customer's name and selects four items in deferred detectable fields.

<u>MID</u>

```
RESERVN   MSG      TYPE=INPUT,SOR=AIRRES,NXT=DESTINA
          SEG
          MFLD     'AIRBOOKG',LTH=09
          MFLD     NAME,LTH=20
```

```
                  AIRLINE RESERVATIONS
 ::::::::                                DATE:_______

 NAME: JOHN DOE
 DESTINATION: BALTIMORE

 FARES:             >FIRST CLASS   ?ECONOMY
 SEAT SELECTION:    >WINDOW        ?AISLE
                    ?SMOKING       >NON-SMOKING
 MEALS:             >MIXED         ?VEGETARIAN
```

Fig. 9-9.

```
MFLD     DESTIN,LTH=10
MFLD     FIRSTCL,LTH=11,FILL=NULL
MFLD     ECONOMY,LTH=07,FILL=NULL
MFLD     WINDOW,LTH=06,FILL=NULL
MFLD     AISLE,LTH=05,FILL=NULL
MFLD     SMOKNG,LTH=07,FILL=NULL
MFLD     NONSMOK,LTH=11,FILL=NULL
MFLD     MIXED,LTH=05,FILL=NULL
MFLD     VEGETAR,LTH=10,FILL=NULL
MSGEND
```

Note the following for the above:

- Transaction code 'AIRBOOKG' is a MID literal.
- The coded lengths reflect the true length of the literals.

With ATTR=(.....,STRIP), the designator character is stripped from the input by MFS.

The input message presented to the application program will appear as in FIG. 9-10. If we specify NOSTRIP in the ATTR= operand, each MFLD length specification of deferred detectable fields is increased by 1.

<u>MID</u>

```
RESERVN  MSG      TYPE=INPUT,SOR=AIRRES,NXT=DESTINA
         SEG
         MFLD     'AIRBOOKG',LTH=09
         MFLD     NAME,LTH=20
         MFLD     DESTIN,LTH=10
         MFLD     FIRSTCL,LTH=12,FILL=NULL    }
         MFLD     ECONOMY,LTH=08,FILL=NULL    }
         MFLD     WINDOW,LTH=07,FILL=NULL     }
         MFLD     AISLE,LTH=06,FILL=NULL      }
         MFLD     SMOKNG,LTH=08,FILL=NULL     } Deferred detectable fields
         MFLD     NONSMOK,LTH=12,FILL=NULL    }
         MFLD     MIXED,LTH=06,FILL=NULL      }
         MFLD     VEGETAR,LTH=11,FILL=NULL    }
         MSGEND
```

LL	ZZ	AIRBOOKG	JOHN DOE	BALTIMORE	FIRST CLASS	WINDOW	NON-SMOKING	MIXED
		9	20	10	11	6	11	5

Fig. 9-10.

LL	ZZ	AIRBOOKG	JOHN DOE	BALTIMORE	>FIRST CLASS	>WINDOW	>NON-SMOKING	>MIXED
		9	20	10	12	7	12	6

Fig. 9-11.

For the above, note that the lengths of deferred detectable fields are increased by 1. The resulting input message will appear as in FIG. 9-11. With ATTR=(.....,NOSTRIP), the selected fields are now preceded by character |>|.

Coding Immediately Detectable Fields

Immediately detectable fields are used:

- To enter the final information to terminate input in a mixed input mode.
- In a situation where only one option is allowed.
- To provide MFS page and message control function requests.

<u>DOF</u>

In the DEV statement, we can code as follows:

```
DEV TYPE=(3270,2),FEAT=(NOCD,NOPFK,PEN)
```
← For pen

We can also code FEAT=IGNORE unless the mixture of different hardware features requires specialized DIF/DOFs to handle the same message from different device types.

In addition to the above, we must code:

```
DEV TYPE=(3270,2),FEAT=IGNORE,PEN=DFLDNAME
```
← Pseudo-DFLDNAME

This parameter provides a pseudo-DFLD name which an MFLD can reference. The DFLD coding for an immediately detectable field requires the IDET subparameter of the ATTR= as follows:

ATTR=IDET

It also requires a new parameter called PEN= . The options of PEN= are:

```
        'Literal'
        NEXTPP
PEN=    NEXTLP
        NEXTMSG
        NEXTMSGP
        ENDMPPI
```

We also must provide for the designator character and three leading and trailing separation characters (blanks or null).

Now, consider FIG. 9-12 with three immediately detectable fields.

DOF/DIF

```
AIRRES    FMT                                                          ← Pseudo-
          DEV      TYPE=(3270,2),FEAT=IGNORE,PEN=PENFIELD                 DFLDNAME
          ....
          DFLD     'MODE OF PAYMT:',POS=(13,02)
CASHER    DFLD     POS=(14,11),LTH=08,PEN='C',ATTR=(PROT,IDET)         ← Immediately
CHARGIT   DFLD     POS=(14,23),LTH=09,PEN='H',ATTR=(PROT,IDET)            Detectable
BILLING   DFLD     POS=(14,38),LTH=10,PEN='B',ATTR=(PROT,IDET)            fields
          FMTEND
```

Where:

LTH= includes 3 trailing blanks or null characters for detectable fields
PROT is coded to prevent the operator from accidentally modifying the field.
IDET specifies Immediately Detectable field.
PEN=PENFIELD is coded in the DEV statement. The PEN parameter provides PENFIELD as pseudo-Dfldname which is referred to by an MFLD name in the MID shown in on the following page.

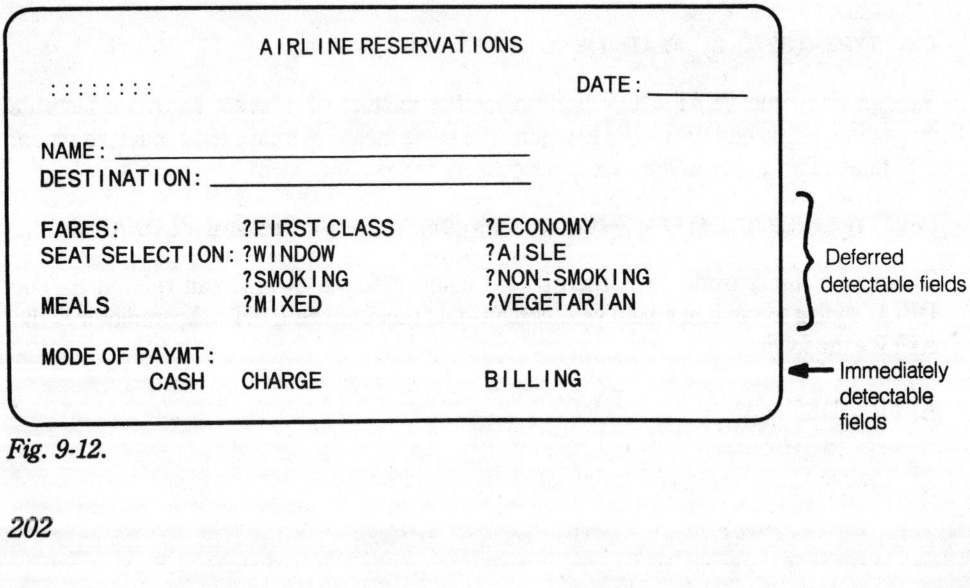

Fig. 9-12.

<u>MOD</u>

```
DESTINA  MSG      TYPE=OUTPUT,SOR=(AIRRES,IGNORE),NEXT=RESERVN
         SEG
         ....
         MFLD     (CASHER,'CASH'),LTH=05
         MFLD     (CHARGIT,'CHARGE'),LTH=07
         MFLD     (BILLING,'BILLING'),LTH=08
         MSGEND
```

<u>MID</u>

```
RESERVN  MSG     TYPE=INPUT,SOR=AIRRES,NXT=DESTINA
         SEG
         ....
         MFLD    PENFIELD,LTH=01       ← Literal 'C' is mapped to this field
         MFLD    CASHER,LTH=05
         MFLD    CHARGIT,LTH=07
         MFLD    BILLING,LTH=08
         MSGEND
```

Next, see how a literal is mapped to the Pseudo-Dfldname when the operator selects an Immediately detectable field. The selection of an Immediately detectable field can be performed in two modes:

1. Single mode operation, when only one Immediately detectable field is selected
2. Mixed mode operation, when other fields are selected prior to an Immediately detectable field

SINGLE MODE OPERATION

If the operator selects only CASH and no other field has been selected, the literal C defined in the DFLD,

```
CASHER DFLD POS=(14,11),LTH=08,PEN='C',ATTR=(PROT,IDET)
```

will be mapped to PENFIELD, the pseudo-DFLD name defined in the DEV statement. The input message will appear as in FIG. 9-13.

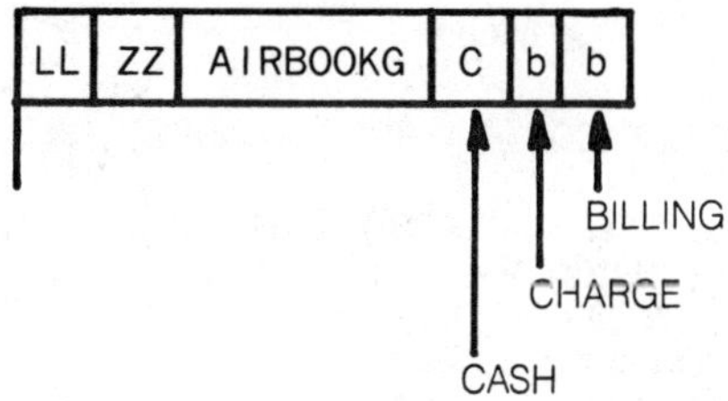

Fig. 9-13.

The application program "knows" that CASH was selected by checking the field PENFIELD and finds a literal C in that field. It also recognizes that, by finding a C in PENFIELD, no other data has been selected.

If we do not code a literal for a selected immediately detectable field, MFS will transmit a |?| as a default.

MIXED-MODE OPERATIONS

When other fields are selected prior to selecting an immediately detectable field, the operation is called a mixed mode operation. Within a mixed mode operation MFS transmits a |?| to indicate its occurrence.

Now refer to the AIRLINE RESERVATIONS example of FIG. 9-12. This screen lists eight Deferred detectable fields and three Immediately detectable fields.

The DOF/DIF for a mixed mode operation are defined in the next display.

DOF/DIF

```
AIRRES   FMT
         DEV     TYPE=(3270,2),FEAT=IGNORE,PEN=PENFIELD           ← Pseudo-Dfldname
         ....
         DFLD    'FARES:',(POS=(08,02)
FISRTCL  DFLD    POS=(08,23),LTH=15,ATTR=(PROT,DET,STRIP)
ECONOMY  DFLD    POS=(08,41),LTH=15,ATTR=(PROT,DET,STRIP)         Deferred
         DFLD    'SEAT SELECTION',POS=(09,02)                     Detectable
WINDOW   DFLD    POS=(09,23),LTH=15,ATTR=(PROT,DET,STRIP)         Fields
AISLE    DFLD    POS=(09,41),LTH=15,ATTR=(PROT,DET,STRIP)
SMOKNG   DFLD    POS=(10,23),LTH=15,ATTR=(PROT,DET,STRIP)
NONSMOK  DFLD    POS=(10,41),LTH=15,ATTR=(PROT,DET,STRIP)
         DFLD    'MEALS:',POS=(11,02)
MIXED    DFLD    POS=(10,23),LTH=15,ATTR=(PROT,DET,STRIP)
VEGETAR  DFLD    POS=(10,41),LTH=15,ATTR=(PROT,DET,STRIP)
*
         DFLD    'MODE OF PAYMT:',POS=(13,02)
CASHER   DFLD    POS=(14,11),LTH=08,PEN='C',ATTR=(PROT,IDET)      Immediately
CHARGIT  DFLD    POS=(14,23),LTH=09,PEN='H',ATTR=(PROT,IDET)      Detectable
BILLING  DFLD    POS=(14,38),LTH=10,PEN='B',ATTR=(PROT,IDET)      Fields
         FMTEND
```

The next display illustrates the MOD and MID of our example.

MOD

```
DESTINA  MSG     TYPE=OUTPUT,SOR=(AIRRES,IGNORE),NXT=RESERVN
         SEG
         MFLD    (FIRSTCL,'?FIRST CLASS'),LTH=12
         MFLD    (ECONOMY,'?ECONOMY'),LTH=12
         MFLD    (WINDOW,'?WINDOW'),LTH=12
         MFLD    (AISLE,'?AISLE'),LTH=12
         MFLD    (SMOKNG,'?SMOKING'),LTH=12
         MFLD    (NONSMOK,'?NON-SMOKING'),LTH=12
         MFLD    (MIXED,'?MIXED'),LTH=12
```

```
         MFLD     (VEGETAR,'?VEGETARIAN'),LTH=12
*
         MFLD     (CASHER,'CASH'),LTH=05
         MFLD     (CHARGIT,'CHARGE'),LTH=07
         MFLD     (BILLING,'BILLING'),LTH=08
         MSGEND
```

<u>MID</u>

```
RESERVN  MSG      TYPE=INOUT,SOR=AIRRES,NXT=DESTINA
         SEG
         MFLD     'AIRBOOKG',LTH=09
         MFLD     NAME,LTH=20
         MFLD     DESTIN,LTH=10
         MFLD     FIRSTCL,LTH=11,FILL=NULL
         MFLD     ECONOMY,LTH=07,FILL=NULL
         MFLD     WINDOW,LTH=06,FILL=NULL
         MFLD     AISLE,LTH=05,FILL=NULL
         MFLD     SMOKNG,LTH=07,FILL=NULL
         MFLD     NONSMOK,LTH=11,FILL=NULL
         MFLD     MIXED,LTH=05,FILL=NULL
         MFLD     VEGETAR,LTH=10,FILL=NULL
*
         MFLD     PENFIELD,LTH=01      ← The |?| is mapped to this field
         MFLD     CASHER,LTH=05        ← Literal CASH is mapped to this field'
         MFLD     CHARGIT,LTH=07
         MFLD     BILLING,LTH=08
         MSGEND
```

Next, see what will happen when other fields are selected in conjunction with the Immediately detectable field (Mixed mode operation). If the operator selects some other deferred detectable fields: First Class, Window, Non-Smoking and Mixed and then selects CASH, the result is that a |?| will be mapped to the PENFIELD pseudo-DFLDname and the literals ' CASH' will be mapped to the MFLD which references the DFLD labeled CASHER.

The resulting input message appears in FIG. 9-14.

CODING PEN-DETECTABLE FIELDS IN COBOL

The following illustrates a possible COBOL coding of our AIRLINE RESERVATIONS example.

```
WORKING-STORAGE SECTION.
.....
01   RESERVATION-SCREEN.
```

LL	ZZ	AIRBOOKG	?	JOHN DOE	BALTIMORE	FIRST CLASS	WINDOW	NON-SMOKING	MIXED	CASH	b	b
		9	1	20	10	11	6	11	5	5	1	1

Fig. 9-14.

```
05 SCREEN-PREFIX.
    10 SCREEN-LENGTH              PIC S999 COMP SYNC.
    10 SCREEN-ZZ                  PIC S999 COMP SYNC.
05 SCREEN-TEXT.
    10 SCREEN-DETECT-FIELD        PIC X.                 (1)
    .....
    10 FARES                      PIC X(12).             (2)
    10 SEAT-SELECT                PIC X(12).             (3)
    10 MEALS                      PIC X(12).             (4)
    10 CASH                       PIC X(05).             (5)
    10 CHARGE                     PIC X(07).             (6)
    10 BILLING                    PIC X(08).             (7)
```

Field (1) is used to contain the pen-detectable designator. In our example, this field may contain

- A C for CASH or
- AN H for CHARGE or
- A B for BILLING

The input message for immediately detectable fields would depend upon whether or not other fields are selected. If no other fields are selected, a predefined literal is transmitted to the application program. In the case of FIG. 9-13 when only CASH is selected, a C is transmitted to the application program.

If other fields are selected in conjunction with immediately detectable fields (mixed-mode operation), MFS transmits a "?" to indicate its occurrence.

See the input message of FIG. 9-14 where some fields are selected in conjunction with the immediately detectable field CASH.

USING THE SELECTOR PEN TO REQUEST CONTROL FUNCTIONS FROM MFS

The selector pen can be used to request five operator control functions from MFS. These functions are: NEXTPP, NEXTLP, NEXTMSG, NEXTMSGP and ENDMPPI. The meanings of each of these functions are explained in chapter 7. Here is an example using the selector pen to request two operator control functions. The next code is required in the DOF.

In the DEV statement, we can code as follows:

```
DEV TYPE=(3270,2),FEAT=IGNORE,PEN=ABCDE
```

In this code, PEN-ABCDE or any other name can be assigned. The parameter PEN= is required for the pen functions to work.

For a DFLD statement, we can provide a literal for prompting and also define the desired function:

```
DFLD 'BGET NEXT PAGEBBB',POS=(15,02),PEN=NEXTLP,ATTR=(PROT,IDET)
DFLD 'BEND OF INPUTBBB',POS=(15,40),PEN=ENDMPPI,ATTR=(PROT,IDET)

       (2)      (3)                           (4)                  (1)
```

In the above:

1. IDET specifies an Immediately detectable field.
2. The leading blank is the designator character for an immediately detectable field.
3. Literal used for prompting. The selection of this field by the operator will cause an immediate request for the IMS control function specified in (4). However, if no other data has been selected, this function will not be performed.

WHEN TO USE DETECTABLE FIELDS

Special attention should be given to the use of detectable fields. This is especially true when the application program is allowed to make a field *dynamically detectable*. If the application program makes a field *deferred detectable*, the designator byte is not stripped on the subsequent input of the field. Detectable fields also require padding characters, subsequent input may be difficult for the program to handle. This compromises input data integrity.

Because the designator byte is device related, if you allow a program to make a field dynamically detectable, you make the program device-dependent.

A similar problem occurs when a program is allowed to make a field *immediately detectable*. MFS transmits a predefined literal for each immediately detectable field that can be selected. MFS uses the MID to determine which literal should be transmitted for each field. When the program makes a field immediately detectable, MFS does not know which literal should be used. In this situation MFS transmits the default '?'. This will certainly confuse what actually occurred on the screen.

MAGNETIC CARD OPERATIONS

The magnetic card reader is a hardware device that allows for user identification via insertion of a card. The device has a slot for the plastic card which is similar to a credit card. The card carries up to 37 characters representing a password, badge number, secret code, etc.

To use the reader, the screen must contain an unprotected field which is large enough to accept all the characters on the card plus an attribute byte. As with immediately detectable fields, the magnetic card causes an immediate transmission of data. When the card is inserted, data is read into the designated field and the attributes of this field are changed into

```
ALPHA,MOD,PROT,NODISP
```

This causes a transmission of data to the MFS, but the operator's identification is not displayed. The cursor—which is originally positioned at the field prior to insertion of the card—will automatically advance to the next field on the screen.

Coding Considerations

DIF/DOF

In the DEV statement, we must assign a pseudo-DFLD name which is associated with the input data from the card reader. (The numbers in parentheses refer to the numbered list below.)

```
MAGNET   FMT
         DEV     TYPE=(3270,2),FEAT=IGNORE,CARD=MCARD (1)← Pseudo-
         ....                                            DFL name
         DFLD    'INSERT MAG CARD',POS=(02,02)
FIELDIN  DFLD    POS=(03,14),LTH=37
         ....
         FMTEND
```

MID

The MID would look like this:

```
CARDIN   MSG     TYPE=INPUT
         SEG
         ....
         MFLD    MCARD,LTH=12      (2)
         MFLD    FIELDIN,LTH=37    (3)
         MSGEND
```

1. The card input is associated with the pseudo-DFLD name MCARD.
2. When the magnetic card is inserted, the operator's identification is read into the field of the input message associated with MCARD.
3. If other data is entered into the screen location—here, (03,14)—the keyed data will be presented to the application program via the field associated with FIELDIN.

AN MFS APPLICATION WITH MULTIPLE PHYSICAL DEVICES

Before leaving this chapter, let's examine a sample application to show how to code MFS control statement for multiple types of physical devices. The devices include Models 1 and 2 display terminals and a 3270P, Model 2 printer. The device mapping of the screens and printed report are presented in FIGS. 9-15 and 9-16 and 9-17. You may have noted that the input and output data which fit into one physical page of Model 2 FIG. 9-15 would fit into two physical pages of Model 1 (FIG. 9-16).

The report format (FIG. 9-17) can be produced with either the SPACE or FLOAT option.

DFS1040I DEVICE MAPPING FOR FMT=INQFMT DEVICE=3270 = 2
TYPE=INOUT DPAGE=01 PHYSICAL PAGE=01

```
                              ORDER INQUIRY
 :::::::::                                                       DATE:______

BILL TO: ::::::::::::::::::::::              SHIP TO: :::::::::::::::::
DATE SHIPPED: :::::::::                      ADDRESS: ::::::::::::::::::::::

                                             CITY: ::::::::::::::::::::::
                                             STATE: ::    ZIP CODE: :::::

ITEM QUANTITY UNIT    ITEM  QUANTITY UNIT    ITEM  QUANTITY  UNIT
:::: ::::      :::::: ::::  ::::      :::::: ::::  ::::       ::::::
```

Fig. 9-15. Model 2 physical page.

DFS1040I DEVICE MAPPING FOR FMT=INQFMT DEVICE=3270 = 1
TYPE=INOUT DPAGE=01 PHYSICAL PAGE=01

```
                   ORDER INQUIRY      PAGE: :::
 :::::::::                        DATE:______
BILL TO: ::::::::::::::::::::::
SHIP TO: :::::::::::::::::
DATE SHIPPED: :::::::::
ADDRESS: ::::::::::::::::::::::
CITY: ::::::::::::::::::::
STATE: ::     ZIP CODE: :::::
              SEE NEXT PAGE FOR DETAILS
```

Physical page 1

DFS1040I DEVICE MAPPING FOR FMT=INQFMT DEVICE=3270 =1
TYPE=INOUT DPAGE=01 PHYSICAL PAGE=02

```
                   ORDER INQUIRY      PAGE: :::

 ITEM  QUANTITY  UNIT
 ::::  ::::::::::  ::::
 ::::  ::::::::::  ::::

 ::::  ::::::::::  ::::
 ::::  ::::::::::  ::::

 ::::  ::::::::::  ::::
 ::::  ::::::::::  ::::
```

Physical page 2

Fig. 9-16. Model 1 physical pages.

```
DFS1040I DEVICE MAPPING FOR FMT=INQFMT DEVICE=3270P-2
TYPE=OUTPUT DPAGE=01 PHYSICAL PAGE=01 (DEFINED 01)
______________________________________________________________________

                    PRINTED REPORT OF ORDER INQUIRY
                                                    DATE: ________

BILL TO: ____________________            SHIP TO: __________________
DATE SHIPPED: ________                   ADDRESS: __________________
                                         CITY: _____________________
                                         STATE: _____   ZIP CODE: ______
ITEM  QUANTITY  UNIT  ITEM  QUANTITY  UNIT  ITEM  QUANTITY  UNIT
____  ________  ____  ____  ________  ____  ____  ________  ____
```

Fig. 9-17. A 3270P, Model 2 printer format.

The next display presents the MFS control statements of our sample application. Note the following key points (the numbers in the list below refer to parenthesized numbers in the display):

1. The same DIF device definition DIF is used for the three devices:

```
INQFMT     FMT
           DEV   TYPE=(3270,2),FEAT=IGNORE
           ....
           DEV   TYPE=(3270,1),FEAT=IGNORE
           ....
PRINTER    DEV   TYPE=(3270P,2),FEAT=IGNORE,PAGE=(24,FLOAT)
```

2. FEAT=IGNORE is coded in the DEV statements for the three devices, and SOR=(INQFMT,IGNORE) is coded in the MSG statement of the MOD. Coding the IGNORE feature gives you flexibility in using the devices which are active at the time of operation without regard to the message descriptor definition.
3. The label DPAGE1 is used for all three devices.
4. Since the message data fit on two physical pages of Model 1, each device field of this model has to specify the page number on which each field is to be displayed. This is done via the POS= parameter. For example, the ITEM1 field with the definition

```
ITEM1 DFLD POS=(04,03,02),LTH=4,ATTR=PROT
```

   is displayed on page 2 of the display. Page specification is not necessary for Model 2.
5. Since the printer is an output device only, TYPE=OUTPUT is coded.
6. No ATTR keyword is coded for the printer device fields.
7. No cursor specification is coded for the printer.

8. The option FLOAT is used for the printer report format; there are 24 lines of print per page, but FLOAT specifies that blank lines are to be deleted.

```
PRINTER DEV TYPE=(3270P,2),FEAT=IGNORE,PAGE=(24,FLOAT)
```

FIGURE 9-18 illustrates the difference between the FLOAT and SPACE options.

Report format using FLOAT keyword

```
PRINTER  DEV   TYPE=(3270P,2),FEAT=IGNORE,PAGE=(24,FLOAT)   ← Keyword
         DIV   TYPE=OUTPUT                                   ← Output Only
```

The report layout will look like this:

```
------------------------------------------------------------------------
                 PRINTED REPORT OF ORDER INQUIRY
                                              DATE:________
BILL TO:_________________________       SHIP TO: ______________
DATE SHIPPED: __________                ADDRESS:
                                        CITY: _________________
                                        STATE: ______ZIP CODE: _____
ITEM  QUANTITY  UNIT   ITEM  QUANTITY  UNIT  ITEM   QUANTITY  UNIT
____  ________  _____  ____  ________  ____  _____  ________  _____
------------------------------------------------------------------------
```

There are 24 lines of print per page, but FLOAT specifies that blank lines are to be deleted and only the lines with print characters are shown.

Report format using SPACE keyword

```
PRINTER  DEV  TYPE=(3270P,2),FEAT=IGNORE,PAGE=(24,SPACE)   ← Keyword
         DIV  TYPE=OUTPUT                                   ← Output Only
```

The report layout will look like this:

```
                 PRINTED REPORT OF ORDER INQUIRY

                                              DATE:________

BILL TO: ______________________        SHIP TO: ________________
DATE SHIPPED: _________________        ADDRESS: ________________
                                       CITY: ___________________
                                       STATE: _______ZIP CODE: _______

ITEM  QUANTITY  UNIT  ITEM  QUANTITY  UNIT  ITEM  QUANTITY  UNIT
____  ________  ____  ____  ________  ____  ____  ________  ____
```

Fig. 9-18. FLOAT and SPACE page definition options. SPACE specifies that each output page will contain the exact number of lines specified in the "number" parameter. The blank lines are not omitted and are printed on the above report.

Fig. 9-19.

```
1--------10----16----------------------------------------------------7-*
         TITLE 'USE MULTIPLE PHYSICAL DEVICES AND PRINTER'
         PRINT NOGEN
INQFMT   FMT
 (1)     DEV   TYPE=(3270,2),FEAT=IGNORE                                 (2)
         DIV   TYPE=INOUT
DPAGE1   DPAGE CURSOR=((04,66))                                          (3)
         DFLD  'ORDER INQUIRY',POS=(02,32),ATTR=(PROT,HI)
TRANCD   DFLD  POS=(04,03),LTH=08,ATTR=(MOD,PROT,NODISP)
         DFLD  'DATE:',POS=(04,60),ATTR=PROT
DATEIN   DFLD  POS=(04,66),LTH=06,ATTR=MOD
         DFLD  'BILL TO:',POS=(08,03),ATTR=PROT
BILLTO   DFLD  POS=(08,12),LTH=20,ATTR=PROT
         DFLD  'SHIP TO:',POS=(08,35),ATTR=PROT
SHIPTO   DFLD  POS=(08,44),LTH=15,ATTR=PROT
         DFLD  'DATE SHIPPED:',POS=(10,03),ATTR=PROT
DATESHIP DFLD  POS=(10,17),LTH=08,ATTR=PROT
         DFLD  'ADDRESS:',POS=(10,35),ATTR=PROT
STREET   DFLD  POS=(10,44),LTH=20,ATTR=PROT
         DFLD  'CITY:',POS=(12,35),ATTR=PROT
CITY     DFLD  POS=(12,41),LTH=20,ATTR=PROT
         DFLD  'STATE:',POS=(13,35),ATTR=PROT
STATE    DFLD  POS=(13,42),LTH=02,ATTR=PROT
         DFLD  'ZIP CODE:',POS=(13,46),ATTR=PROT
ZIPCODE  DFLD  POS=(13,56),LTH=05,ATTR=PROT
         DFLD  'ITEM QUANTITY UNIT',POS=(16,03),ATTR=PROT
ITEM1    DFLD  POS=(18,03),LTH=04,ATTR=PROT
QTY1     DFLD  POS=(18,09),LTH=04,ATTR=PROT
UNIT1    DFLD  POS=(18,17),LTH=06,ATTR=PROT
         DFLD  'ITEM QUANTITY UNIT',POS=(16,27),ATTR=PROT
ITEM2    DFLD  POS=(18,27),LTH=04,ATTR=PROT
QTY2     DFLD  POS=(18,33),LTH=04,ATTR=PROT
UNIT2    DFLD  POS=(18,41),LTH=06,ATTR=PROT
         DFLD  'ITEM QUANTITY UNIT',POS=(16,49),ATTR=PROT
ITEM3    DFLD  POS=(18,49),LTH=04,ATTR=PROT
QTY3     DFLD  POS=(18,55),LTH=04,ATTR=PROT
UNIT3    DFLD  POS=(18,63),LTH=06,ATTR=PROT
*
*        SMALLER DEVICE - MODEL 1
*
         DEV   TYPE=(3270,1),FEAT=IGNORE                                 (2)
         DIV   TYPE=INOUT
DPAGE1   DPAGE CURSOR=((02,31))                                          (3)
         DFLD  'ORDER INQUIRY',POS=(01,12,01),ATTR=(PROT,HI)
         DFLD  'PAGE:',POS=(01,31,01),ATTR=PROT
PAGENO   DFLD  POS=(01,37,01),LTH=03,ATTR=PROT
TRANCD   DFLD  POS=(02,03,01),LTH=08,ATTR=(MOD,PROT,NODISP)
         DFLD  'DATE:',POS=(02,25,01),ATTR=PROT
DATEIN   DFLD  POS=(02,31,01),LTH=06,ATTR=MOD
         DFLD  'BILL TO:',POS=(03,03,01),ATTR=PROT
BILLTO   DFLD  POS=(03,12,01),LTH=20,ATTR=PROT
         DFLD  'SHIP TO:',POS=(04,03,01),ATTR=PROT
SHIPTO   DFLD  POS=(04,12,01),LTH=15,ATTR=PROT
         DFLD  'DATE SHIPPED:',POS=(05,03,01),ATTR=PROT
```

Fig. 9-19. continued

```
DATESHIP DFLD   POS=(05,17,01),LTH=08,ATTR=PROT
         DFLD   'ADDRESS:',POS=(06,03,01),ATTR=PROT
STREET   DFLD   POS=(06,12,01),LTH=20,ATTR=PROT
         DFLD   'CITY:',POS=(07,03,01),ATTR=PROT
CITY     DFLD   POS=(07,09,01),LTH=20,ATTR=PROT
         DFLD   'STATE:',POS=(08,03,01),ATTR=PROT
STATE    DFLD   POS=(08,10,01),LTH=02,ATTR=PROT
         DFLD   'ZIP CODE:',POS=(08,14,01),ATTR=PROT
ZIPCODE  DFLD   POS=(08,24,01),LTH=05,ATTR=PROT
         DFLD   'SEE NEXT PAGE FOR DETAILS',
                POS=(12,05,01),ATTR=PROT
*
*        LAYOUT OF SECOND PAGE PHYSICAL PAGE
*
         DFLD   'ORDER INQUIRY',POS=(01,12,02),ATTR=(PROT,HI)
         DFLD   'PAGE:',POS=(01,31,02),ATTR=PROT
PAGENO   DFLD   POS=(01,37,02),LTH=03,ATTR=PROT
         DFLD   'ITEM QUANTITY UNIT',POS=(03,03,02),ATTR=PROT
ITEM1    DFLD   POS=(04,03,02),LTH=04,ATTR=PROT                      (4)
QTY1     DFLD   POS=(04,09,02),LTH=04,ATTR=PROT
UNIT1    DFLD   POS=(04,17,02),LTH=06,ATTR=PROT
ITEM2    DFLD   POS=(06,03,02),LTH=04,ATTR=PROT
QTY2     DFLD   POS=(06,09,02),LTH=04,ATTR=PROT
UNIT2    DFLD   POS=(06,17,02),LTH=06,ATTR=PROT
ITEM3    DFLD   POS=(08,03,02),LTH=04,ATTR=PROT
QTY3     DFLD   POS=(08,09,02),LTH=04,ATTR=PROT
UNIT3    DFLD   POS=(08,17,02),LTH=06,ATTR=PROT
*
*        LAYOUT OF REPORT LISTING
*
PRINTER  DEV    TYPE=(3270P,2),FEAT=IGNORE,PAGE=(24,FLOAT)           (8)
*                                          USING 'FLOAT' KEYWORD
         DIV    TYPE=OUTPUT             <=== OUTPUT ONLY             (5)
DPAGE1   DPAGE (7)
 (3)                          <=== LABEL DPAGE1 MUST MATCH WITH THAT
*                                  SPECIFIED EARLIER
         DFLD   'PRINTED REPORT OF ORDER INQUIRY',                  *
                 POS=(02,30)            <=== DO NOT USE ATTR KEYWORD (6)
*                                            FOR PRINTER FORMAT
         DFLD   'DATE:',POS=(04,60)
DATEIN   DFLD   POS=(04,66),LTH=06
         DFLD   'BILL TO:',POS=(08,03)
BILLTO   DFLD   POS=(08,12),LTH=20
         DFLD   'SHIP TO:',POS=(08,35)
SHIPTO   DFLD   POS=(08,44),LTH=15
         DFLD   'DATE SHIPPED:',POS=(10,03)
DATESHIP DFLD   POS=(10,17),LTH=08
         DFLD   'ADDRESS:',POS=(10,35)
STREET   DFLD   POS=(10,44),LTH=20
         DFLD   'CITY:',POS=(12,35)
CITY     DFLD   POS=(12,41),LTH=20
         DFLD   'STATE:',POS=(13,35)
STATE    DFLD   POS=(13,42),LTH=02
         DFLD   'ZIP CODE:',POS=(13,46)
ZIPCODE  DFLD   POS=(13,56),LTH=05
         DFLD   'ITEM QUANTITY UNIT',POS=(16,03)
```

Fig. 9-19. continued

```
ITEM1     DFLD  POS=(18,03),LTH=04
QTY1      DFLD  POS=(18,09),LTH=04
UNIT1     DFLD  POS=(18,17),LTH=06
          DFLD  'ITEM QUANTITY UNIT',POS=(16,27)
ITEM2     DFLD  POS=(18,27),LTH=04
QTY2      DFLD  POS=(18,33),LTH=04
UNIT2     DFLD  POS=(18,41),LTH=06
          DFLD  'ITEM QUANTITY UNIT',POS=(16,49)
ITEM3     DFLD  POS=(18,49),LTH=04
QTY3      DFLD  POS=(18,55),LTH=04
UNIT3     DFLD  POS=(18,63),LTH=06
          FMTEND
*
INQUIRY   MSG   TYPE=INPUT,SOR=INQFMT,NXT=ORDEROUT,OPT=1
          SEG
          MFLD  TRANCD,LTH=09
          MFLD  DATEIN,LTH=06
          MSGEND
*
ORDEROUT  MSG   TYPE=OUTPUT,SOR=(INQFMT,IGNORE),NXT=INQUIRY,OPT=1,       *
                FILL=NULL
          LPAGE SOR=DPAGE1
          SEG
          MFLD  (TRANCD,'TRANS007'),LTH=08
          MFLD  (PAGENO,LPAGENO)                   <=== LOGICAL PAGE NUMBER
          MFLD  BILLTO,LTH=20
          MFLD  SHIPTO,LTH=15
          MFLD  DATESHIP,LTH=08
          MFLD  STREET,LTH=20
          MFLD  CITY,LTH=20
          MFLD  STATE,LTH=02
          MFLD  ZIPCODE,LTH=05
          MFLD  ITEM1,LTH=04
          MFLD  QTY1,LTH=04
          MFLD  UNIT1,LTH=06
          MFLD  ITEM2,LTH=04
          MFLD  QTY2,LTH=04
          MFLD  UNIT2,LTH=06
          MFLD  ITEM3,LTH=04
          MFLD  QTY3,LTH=04
          MFLD  UNIT3,LTH=06
          MSGEND
          END
```

10

MFS Screen Design Considerations

In previous chapters, we studied several commonly-used facilities in designing MFS applications. Each facility was presented with the available alternatives, followed by a discussion as to which technique best serves to achieve a given end. We pointed out that each alternative has its advantages and disadvantages in relation to each objective, and when you attempt to achieve one objective, you may adversely affect another.

The aim of this chapter is to examine the MFS design objectives and to review the techniques which are likely to benefit most of the design objectives. You should bear in mind that there are no techniques that apply to all designs, so you will have to weigh the effects of each technique and then determine which will best satisfy your application requirements while complying with your installation's standards.

First, let's list the main MFS screen design objectives, and then we'll see how each one of these objectives can be attained. Finally, we'll briefly summarize the techniques which will best optimize your MFS applications.

MFS APPLICATION DESIGN OBJECTIVES

The design of MFS application should address the following objectives:

1. Ensure data security
2. Ensure data integrity
3. Minimize data transmission and response times
4. Minimize impact on message queues
5. Minimize impact on message format service
6. Minimize impact on format buffer pool
7. Maximize device independence
8. Improve operator convenience
9. Simplify application programming

Ensure Data Security

There are three methods available through MFS for securing data—password protection, hardcopy protection, and the use of the alphanumeric protected attribute.

Whenever your application deals with sensitive data, you should use password protection techniques to restrict processing to authorized uses only. Also, if the hardcopy facility is available at your installation, you should be concerned with sensitive data. You should ask whether you should restrict the hardcopy copy of a message altogether, or to allow the hardcopy to selected terminals.

If you want to suppress printing of a message, make sure that the first field on the screen format is defined as alphanumeric and protected. To restrict hardcopy to some selected terminals, you should consider using the alternate PCB method.

Ensure Data Integrity

The second design objective is to ensure data integrity. First, we will focus on what you have to do to ensure data integrity on input, and then we'll discuss how to ensure data integrity on output.

On Input.

Use of the FILL= Character. You may recall from chapter 3 that the use of the FILL= character affects input and output data. When the FILL=NULL character is specified, fields on the right of a missing field will shift to the left and the segment length is adjusted. With this specification, the operator can inadvertently enter invalid data. This problem is eliminated when the missing data is filled with spaces (when you do not specify FILL=NULL). By not specifying this FILL=NULL character, however, you will increase the volume of data transmission.

Existing data. When entering data, if the operator does not use the space bar to blank-out unwanted characters on the screen, these may be transmitted to the application's I-O area. You can eliminate this problem by specifying the Erase Unprotected option field before Write or by specifying a Force Format Write. Here again, this increases data transmission and response times.

Use of high-intensity attribute. When the application program dynamically makes a field high-intensity, the field may automatically become detectable, and this may cause a problem. The operator can enter a space (X'40') in the first byte of the field which will be transmitted to the program. You should consider the possibility of this problem when using the high-intensity attribute.

Use of numeric attribute. Specifying the numeric attribute for a field will ensure that numeric data is entered, and if an invalid numeric is entered, the keyboard will lock itself until the operator presses the RESET key. You should not assume that all numeric data entered is valid, because the numeric attribute allows the use of the decimal point and the plus and minus signs, and the unwanted entry of the sign or decimal point will affect your data. We recommend that when you use the numeric attribute, always let the application program edit the numeric data.

What follows is a summary of what you should do to ensure data integrity on input:

1. Do not specify use of the FILL=NULL character.
2. Specify Erase Unprotected or Force Format Write.
3. Limit the use of the high-intensity attribute.
4. Use the numeric attribute wherever appropriate.
5. Let the application edit the numeric data.

On Output.

Invalid data from previous transmission. Data left from the previous display may affect output data integrity. The following situations may leave data from the previous transmission:

- Use of FILL=NULL character
- Absence of Force Format Write request
- The application program transmits short fields or omits fields

To eliminate this problem, you can use the following techniques:

- Use output FILL-character other than NULL
- Specify a Force Format Write prior to output transmission
- Avoid omitted fields
- Ensure that the application program clears all short fields before display

Lost screens. A lost screen may accidentally be caused by the operator hitting the CLEAR key. You can use Operator Logical Paging to recover a lost screen; the operator can specify the value = +0 to recover the current screen.

What follows is a summary of what you should do to ensure data integrity on output:

1. Use an output FILL= character other than NULL.
2. Specify a Force Format Write prior to output transmission.
3. Avoid omitted fields.
4. Let the application program clear all short fields before display.
5. Use Operator Logical Paging.

You will see in the next section that the techniques used to attain data integrity adversely affect the objective of minimizing data transmission and response time.

Minimize Data Transmission and Response Times

The techniques which have an impact on this objective include:

- Force format write request
- Output FILL= character

- Input options
- Dynamic attribute byte modification
- Input segmentation
- Paging request
- Use of CLEAR key
- Use of DFLD literals

Let's consider each of these factors individually.

Force Format Write Request. A force format write causes the entire screen to be retransmitted; the device buffer is erased and all fields and literals are transmitted to the output device. The following situations will cause MFS to perform a full-formatting operation:

- A change in the device output format (DOF)
- A change in the logical page
- A change in DPAGE within a DOF
- A change in the Physical page number within a DPAGE
- A DOF request via the DSCA operand
- An application program request via the SCA
- Use of the magnetic card reader
- Operator using the CLEAR key
- The terminal has been stopped because of a permanent I-O error

On the average, a force format write causes 1,100 bytes of data to be transmitted, while only 700 bytes are transmitted if it is not requested. This option should be avoided to minimize response time.

Output FILL = Character. The use of FILL=NULL or PT can reduce transmission time to the output device tremendously. During the format transmission:

- PT or NULL are identical and result in a minimum amount of transmitted data. The Format command is an ERASE/WRITE, so the screen is cleared to nulls (X'00'), and then all data are written to the screen.
- IF FILL=NULL or PT are used, only the fields sent from the application program I-O area and literals will be transmitted.
- IF FILL=blank (default) is used, every field defined on the screen (DOF) must be transmitted. This can double or triple transmission time.

On subsequent transmissions to an already formatted screen:

- If FILL=NULL is used, no "padding" will be sent, and data already within the associated field on the screen will be undisturbed.
- If FILL=PT is used, one byte of padding will be appended to the application program's data to clear the rest of the field to nulls. This is more efficient than having

the application program sending a field padded with all blanks to clear the remainder of the field.

- In the FILL=NULL and PT modes, the screen acts as an overlay device. New data that is transmitted merely adds to or overlays existing data on the screen. In the case of FILL=blank, all fields except literals are retransmitted each time.

Input Options. Option III message segments require more processing time by the application programs since they are of variable lengths. Some space is saved in the queue buffer pool by this technique, especially if many fields are defined in the message segment but few fields are received on input. When most of the fields are received on input, then Option III performance is not as good as that of Options I or II, in terms of time or space.

The use of Option II with FILL=X'40' (blank) will accomplish a similar effect. This gives the application program a fixed-length segment and fixed-length fields, unless the entire segment was not entered, in which case a single NULL character (X'3F') will be presented to the application program.

Dynamic Attribute Byte Modification. Attributes can be dynamically modified by the application program if the MFLD for that field specifies ATTR=YES. However, any error on the screen that caused the screen to be reformatted will lose all attributes modified previously and will revert to the original definition of the DFLD definition. Therefore, this facility should be limited to highlighting desired fields on the screen.

Input Segmentation. Messages should be be segmented for application program convenience or to meet segment-size restrictions. So, minimize the number of input message segments. Segment processing in MFS and DL/1 requires a considerable number of CPU cycles. Multiple GET calls must be used to retrieve multiple input messages. Therefore, do not segment unnecessarily.

Paging Request. The program access key PA1 page advance facility should be used in lieu of operator entry of a logical page request. The PA1 facility requires less operator action and communication line time and does not require input editing before page request processing.

Use of CLEAR Key. Avoid use of the CLEAR key as much as possible. This key gets the operator out of the MFS mode, and he must enter the format command again.

Minimizing use of the CLEAR key will result in improved response time and more effective utilization of communication lines.

Use of DFLD Literals. When multiple DFLD literals are positioned at nearly adjacent device field locations (not more than five bytes apart), combine them. For example, instead of

```
HEADER1: DataXXXX HEADER2: DataXXXX
HEADER3: DataXXXX HEADER4: DataXXXX
```

use

```
HEADER1    HEADER2    HEADER3    HEADER4
DataXXX    DataXXX    DataXXX    DataXXX
```

Combining DFLD literals will result in fewer DFLD definitions, thereby reducing block sizes, and MFS processing and transmission times.

Also consider defining the length of the DFLD literal which is followed by a nonliteral DFLD to include the space between the end of the DFLD literal and the position immediately preceding the attribute byte of the adjacent nonliteral DFLD. This action will reduce the block size and character transmission. However, the separating space should only be from two to five bytes long.

Summary. The importance of this design objective depends upon your installation's network configuration. The volume of data to be transmitted is relatively unimportant if you are working with local lines and if you are dealing with a small number of terminal devices. On the other hand, if you are using remote communication lines connected to a large number of terminals, then the volume of data to be transmitted can have a large impact on response time.

Following is a summary of what you should do to minimize the volume of data transmission and response time:

1. Avoid the force format write.
2. Use the same format on input and output.
3. Use an output FILL=NULL or PT.
4. Minimize input segmentation.
5. Define literals in the DOF.
6. Combine DFLD literals.
7. Minimize changes in the DPAGE.
8. Minimize the need to clear the screen.
9. Avoid mixed-mode operations.
10. Minimize the use of the magnetic card.

Minimize Impact on Message Queues

The fourth objective is to minimize the impact of the application on the IMS message queue.

Logical Record Length. You have learned that message queues are defined during the IMS/VS system definition. The buffers making up the message queues are defined to be 48-bytes-long plus the size of the largest segment to be processed. The larger the logical record length, the more you affect the message queues, and this will limit the number of buffers available in the message queues.

Operator Logical Paging. Operator logical paging also impacts the message queues because output messages remain longer on the queues.

Following is a list of what you should do to minimize impact on the message queues:

1. Use short segments wherever possible.
2. Use single messages if possible.
3. Avoid using the /FORMAT command.

4. Select formatting Option II if there are multiple segments but many may be omitted.
5. Select formatting Option III if there are multiple segments but very few can be omitted.
6. Avoid operator logical paging.

Minimize Impact on MFS

The fifth design objective is to minimize the impact that the application program has on MFS. This is to minimize the amount of processing MFS has to do in mapping data to and from your application, and to use MFS effectively.

Following are techniques for satisfying this objective:

- On input

  1. Avoid message segmentation.
  2. Use single segments.
  3. Select formatting Option II if there are multiple segments but many may be omitted.
  4. Select formatting Option III if there are multiple segments but very few can be omitted.
  5. Use program access keys instead of Operator paging.

- On output

  1. Avoid Force Format Write wherever possible.
  2. Use FILL=NULL or PT.

Minimize Impact on Format Buffer Pool

If the buffer pool is not managed efficiently, response time will suffer due to increased I-O required to read the MFS control blocks.

Following are techniques for satisfying this objective:

1. Chain the control blocks to make use of the prefetch facility.
2. Reduce the number of control blocks used by

   - Using common formats
   - Using the same format on input and output
   - Avoiding device feature specifications

3. Reduce the size of control blocks by

   - Combining DFLD literals
   - Reducing the number of fields
   - Minimizing changes in the DPAGEs and LPAGEs

Maximize Device Independence

The importance of this objective depends on your installation's hardware configuration. In a large installation, where different terminal types are used and your application is required to support them, device independence carries great importance. However, if only a single device type will be used, this objective will become a minor concern.

As a general rule, consider making your applications device-independent when first designed. These applications can, of course, be changed in the future to accommodate special device features.

Following is a list of what you have to do to achieve device independence:

1. Avoid using the system control area (SCA) and the default DSCA.
2. Avoid cursor positioning by control block coding.
3. Avoid using formatting Option III.
4. Avoid using literals.
5. Do not allow the size of the smallest device to limit the size of the logical page.
6. Avoid using immediately detectable fields.
7. Always strip the designator byte for detectable fields.

Improve Operator Convenience

Improving operator convenience makes your application user-friendly, minimizes the possibility of the user entering invalid data, and of course relieves the operator's frustration when working with applications over long periods of time. We recommend the following techniques to improve operator convenience:

1. Use numeric and protected attributes for auto-skip literals. The auto-skip feature simplifies the operator's procedure since the cursor rests at the position where the operator is expected to enter data.
2. Provide for both input and output on the common device format to simplify the amount of work the operator has to do.
3. Provide operator logical paging to allow a greater degree of flexibility for viewing output messages.
4. Designate usage for PFK keys as a substitute for keyed input or as a means of entering MFS page and message control functions.
5. Minimize the need to clear the screen each time the user wants to enter data.

Simplify Application Programming

Simplifying application programming reduces development costs and makes the applications easy to maintain. Following is a summary of what you can do in this regard:

1. Use MFS formatting Options I and II. The segments are fixed-format, making them easier to handle and thus making programming straight-forward.

2. Avoid the FILL = NULL character with both Options on input because NULL fill makes input segments free form, and this makes them difficult to handle.
3. Avoid immediately detectable fields because they make the program's input dependent upon whether or not a mixed mode operation took place.
4. Use control block chaining to allow the application program to take advantage of the prefetching of MFS control blocks.

CONSIDERATIONS FOR EFFICIENT SCREEN DESIGN

In reviewing the MFS design objectives, we have seen that, frequently, when you attempt to achieve one objective, you may adversely affect another. In this section, we will summarize the techniques that will best benefit all the design objectives that we addressed. For efficient screen design, we recommend the following:

1. Use a common device format for as many applications as possible. This will reduce the number of full formatting operations, format block pool requirements, and format pool I-O activity, and will improve operator's convenience.
2. Use the NXT= linkage specification on MSG and LPAGE statements to allow the application to take advantage of the prefetching of MFS control blocks.
3. Use auto-skip over literals for operator convenience.
4. Use password protection to insure data security.
5. If hardcopies are to be prevented, specify an alphanumeric and protected attribute for the first field in the message.
6. Provide standard usage for PFK keys to standardize user procedures and to reduce the possibility of the user entering invalid data.
7. Specify the ATTR = NUM operand to force the operator to enter only numeric data into specified numeric input fields.
8. Specify the ATTR = NOMOD. This will cause MFS to transmit only the fields which have been modified by the operator. This command will reduce the amount of data transmission and improve the performance.
9. Place common data into DFLDs so that it is transmitted just once when the format is invoked.
10. In the conversational mode, pass all data through the feature prior to edit processing. The application stores data in the SPA which passes the edit and continues to update the SPA throughout the conversation with data that are corrected and retransmitted.
11. Segment the output messages and use multiple message output descriptors to avoid sending all of the output data all the time.
12. Use FILL characters for input message fields to attain field padding and zero fill input fields wherever appropriate.
13. Use Options I and II.
14. Use FILL = PT on output to ensure that fields on the output device receive only data from the application program's output message.
15. Be selective in full-formatting.

16. Use the Erase All Unprotected option via the SCA or DSCA operand if the application program requires that unprotected fields are to be cleared.
17. In regard to data integrity vs. response time, techniques used to attain data integrity adversely affect the objective of minimizing data transmission and response times. To prevent the problem created by compressed or omitted fields, you can specify a force format write on input and output and avoid using an output FILL=NULL or PT to ensure data integrity.

There is an attractive technique which will help you eliminate adverse effects—use the output FILL=PT and let the application program supply all fields. To omit a field, the program transmits a one-character space followed by X'3F'. When MFS encounters X'3F' it blanks-out the rest of the field. However, this technique has the disadvantage of complicating the programming effort.

In the design process, you will have to weigh the effects of each technique and determine which will be best for your application based upon your established design goal(s) and priorities. You also have to comply with your installation's standards. The best approach is to make tentative design trade-off decisions and to analyze their impact on certain parts of the design, and then make changes to improve the design process.

Section III
Advanced DC Programming Techniques

This section goes over the more challenging topics of IMS DC functions. You will learn

- How to send output messages to alternate terminals
- Conversational processing programming
- Batch message processing programming
- How to invoke the checkpoint/restart facility via OS JCL

11

Sending Output Messages to Alternate Terminals

So far, all of the examples presented in this book have one feature in common: When an output message is sent by the application program, it is routed to the originating terminal. Now, we will expand this concept to allow for sending output messages to *alternate* destinations. An alternate destination can be a printer, a display terminal, or an IMS transaction. The alternate destination feature of IMS gives you flexibility to go beyond the originating terminal by sending output messages to multiple destinations.

We'll start with a review of the difference between the fixed alternate PCB and the modifiable alternate PCB. Then, we'll present the techniques to send output messages via these two types of PCBs. After that, we'll examine the program-to-program message switching technique.

SENDING MESSAGES TO AN ALTERNATE DESTINATION

FIGURE 11-1 illustrates message routing to an alternate terminal. A transaction message is sent via terminal LTERMA1 or an IO-PCB. The transaction requests information from the database. The message processing program then accesses the database using DL/1 and the database PCB to retrieve the segment containing the information requested by the transaction. Normally, a response is sent back to the original terminal, which is LTERMA1.

However, if a bad status code is returned from the database call, the MPP program sends the error condition message to the printer which issued the transaction. In this case, by using an alternate terminal PCB, the program will send the response to logical terminal LTERMA2.

To send an output message to an alternate destination, the application issues an ISRT call using ALTERNATE PCB instead of IO-PCB. The IO-PCB specifies the originating terminal from which all messages are received and to which all messages are sent.

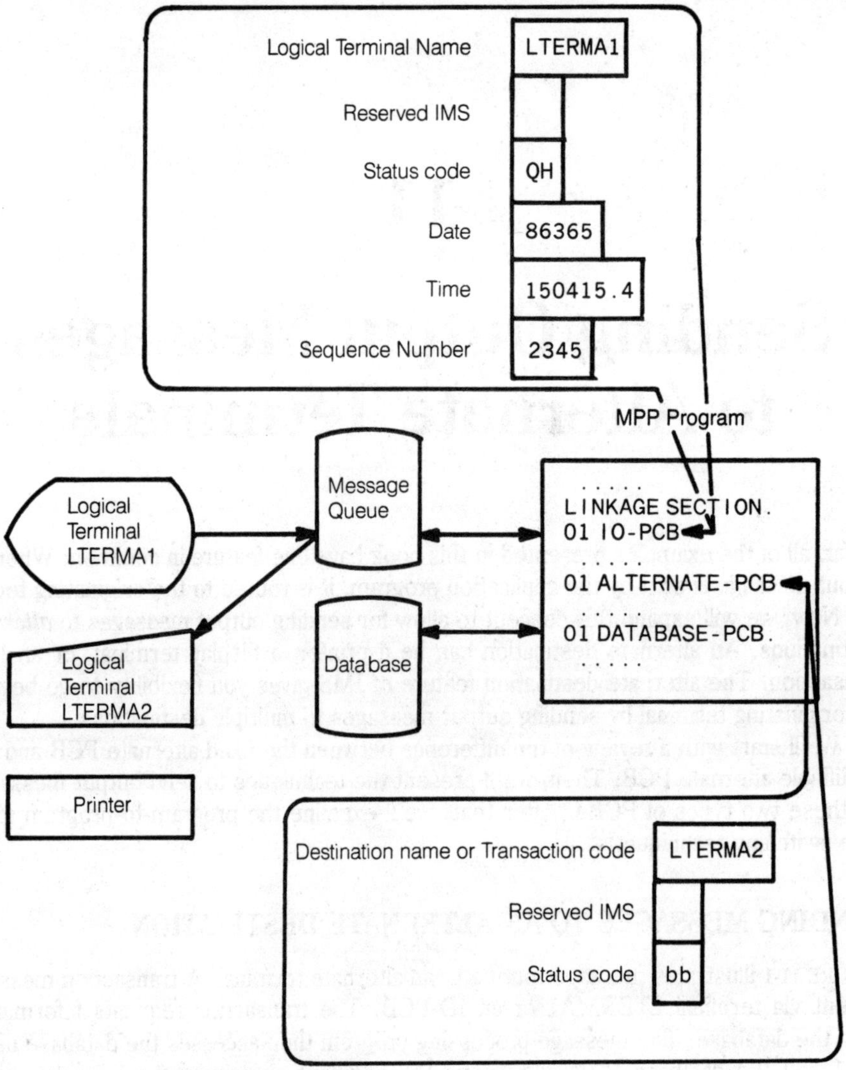

Fig. 11-1. I-O and alternate PCBs.

The alternate PCB names other terminals or transactions to which the application can route messages.

The COBOL source coding for sending an output message to an alternate terminal is given in FIG. 11-2. Note that the alternate PCB Mask must be listed in the ENTRY statement after the IO-PCB, and in the same sequence as it is coded in the PSBGEN job.

```
WORKING-STORAGE SECTION.
  ......
01  OUTPUT-MESSAGE-AREA.
  ......
LINKAGE SECTION.

01  IO-PCB-MASK.
    05  ORIGIN-TERM-NAME            PIC X(8).
    05  IO-RESERVED                 PIC X(2).
    05  IO-STATUS-CODE              PIC X(2).
    05  IO-PREFIX.
        10 JULIAN-DATE              PIC S9(7) COMP-3.
        10 CURRENT-TIME             PIC S9(7) COMP-3.
        10 SEQUENCE-NO              PIC S9(7) COMP.
    05  IO-MODNAME                  PIC X(8).

01  ALTERNATE-PCB-MASK.
    05  ALT-TERM-NAME               PIC X(8).
    05  ALT-RESERVED                PIC X(2).
    05  ALT-STATUS-CODE             PIC X(2).
  .....
PROCEDURE DIVISION.

    ENTRY 'DLITCBL' USING IO-PCB-MASK
                          ALTERNATE-PCB-MASK
                          .....
  ......
700-SEND-MESSAGE-TO-ALT-TERM.

       CALL 'CBLTDLI' USING ISRT
                            ALTERNATE-PCB-MASK
                            OUTPUT-MESSAGE-AREA.

    IF ALT-STATUS-CODE NOT EQUAL SPACES
       PERFORM 1000-ERROR-ROUTINE.
```

Fig. 11-2. Sending messages to alternate terminals.

FIXED AND MODIFIABLE ALTERNATE PCBs

As you may remember from chapter 4, fixed alternate PCBs contain the name of the logical terminal(s) with which they are interfacing. The name of the destination terminal assigned to the fixed alternate PCB is specified during PSBGEN and cannot be changed. When the application program issues an ISRT call referencing the alternate PCB, the same destination will always be selected.

With a modifiable alternate PCB, a destination name is not assigned during PSBGEN. The application program will assign a destination name through the use of the CHNG call.

SENDING MESSAGES TO MODIFIABLE ALTERNATE DESTINATIONS

There is a slight difference in coding output messages to be sent via the modifiable alternate PCB. Before you issue the ISRT call, you have to ensure that the alternate PCB specifies the destination that you want.

Sending Output Messages to Alternate Terminals

To do that, you have to issue a CHNG call which is used to set the destination of an alternate PCB to any valid logical terminal or transaction code in the system. When you issue a CHNG call, IMS will store the name of the destination you supply in the modifiable alternate PCB so that you can issue an ISRT call and have the output message routed to the proper destination.

How to Use the CHNG Call

To use the CHNG call, the alternate PCB must be defined as being modifiable during PSBGEN:

```
PCB TYPE=TP,MODIFY=YES
```

FIGURE 11-3 presents the format of the CHNG call.

```
WORKING-STORAGE SECTION.
  ......
01  DEST-NAME                        PIC X(8) VALUE SPACES.
        .
  ......
PROCEDURE DIVISION.
* CHANGE DESTINATION TO LTERMBB
        MOVE 'LTERMBB' TO DEST-NAME.
        CALL 'CBLTDLI' USING CHNG
                             ALTERNATE-PCB-MASK <=== MODIFIABLE ALT.
                             DEST-NAME.              ALTERNATE PCB OR
                                                     TRANSACTION
                                                     CODE
```

Fig. 11-3. Issuing a CHNG call.

The result of the CHNG call is illustrated in FIG. 11-4. The logical terminal (LTERM) name or transaction code placed in the modifiable alternate PCB by a CHNG call remains unchanged until the application program

1. Issues a GU call using the alternate PCB or
2. Terminates by a GOBACK statement or
3. Issues another CHNG call to the alternate PCB (this CHNG call must be preceded by a PURG call).

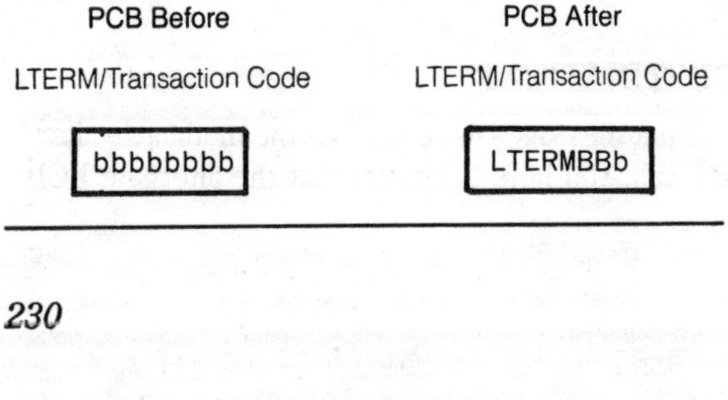

Fig. 11-4. Result of a CHNG call.

In the first and second instances, the LTERM name or transaction code is reset to blanks.

How to Use the PURG Call

Most applications that use a modifiable alternate PCB send only one output message to one alternate destination. Sometimes, though, you may need to send several output messages to different alternate destinations, all via one alternate modifiable PCB. How does IMS know that you are done with one alternate destination before it sends the next output message to another destination? You can use the PURG call to signal IMS that routing the output message through the alternate PCB is complete and that you want to send another message to another destination.

The following paragraph presents the sequence of calls to place multiple terminal names into a modifiable alternate PCB. Here, the application issues a CHNG call to place 'LTERMBB' into the alternate PCB, and then issues an ISRT call to send the message. After that, the program issues a PURG call (call 3) to signal IMS to reuse the alternate PCB for another destination.

Modifiable Alternate PCB Call Sequence

When you use a single modifiable alternate PCB for several destinations, you should issue the following sequence of calls to reuse the same alternate PCB:

```
CHNG
ISRT (segments)
PURG
CHNG
ISRT (segments)
PURG
```

PROGRAM-TO-PROGRAM MESSAGE SWITCH

Another use of the alternate PCB is to pass control to another application program by using a transaction code instead of a logical terminal name in the alternate terminal PCB. A message can be placed in the message queue that will schedule another program to receive the message. This is called a program-to-program message switch.

FIGURE 11-6 describes the data flow associated with a program-to-program message switch. In this cycle, the programs Customer Edit and Customer Update communicate with each other (the numbers in the list below refer to the parenthesized numbers in the figure):

1. Terminal LTERMA1 sends a message.
2.,3. Program Customer Edit retrieves the message and processes it.
4. After having edited the message, Customer Edit sends a message.

```
         WORKING-STORAGE SECTION.
          ......
         01  RESPONSE-A.
          ......
         01  IMS-CALL-FUNCTIONS.
             05 CHNG                      PIC X(4) VALUE 'CHNG'.
          ......
         01  DEST-NAME                    PIC X(8) VALUE SPACES.
         LINKAGE SECTION.
         01  IO-PCB-MASK.
          .....
         01  ALTERNATE-PCB-MASK.
             05  ALT-TERM-NAME            PIC X(8).
             05  ALT-RESERVED             PIC X(2).
             05  ALT-STATUS-CODE          PIC X(2).
          .....
         PROCEDURE DIVISION.
CALL 1    * CHANGE DESTINATION TO LTERMBB
                MOVE 'LTERMBB' TO DEST-NAME.
                CALL 'CBLTDLI' USING CHNG
                                  ALTERNATE-PCB-MASK <=== MODIFIABLE
                                  DEST-NAME.              ALTERNATE PCB
                                                          OR TRANSACTION
                                                          CODE.
          .....
CALL 2    * INSERT RESPONSE TO LTERMBB
                CALL 'CBLTDLI' USING ISRT
                                  ALTERNATE-PCB-MASK
                                  RESPONE-A.
             IF ALT-STATUS-CODE NOT EQUAL SPACES
                PERFORM 1000-ERROR-ROUTINE.
          .....
CALL 3    * FREE RESPONSE TO LTERMBB
                CALL 'CBLTDLI' USING PURG
                                  ALTERNATE-PCB-MASK.
          .....
CALL 4    * CHANGE DESTINATION TO LTERMCC
                MOVE 'LTERMCC' TO DEST-NAME.
                CALL 'CBLTDLI' USING CHNG
                                  ALTERNATE-PCB-MASK <=== MODIFIABLE
                                  DEST-NAME.              ALTERNATE PCB.
          .....
CALL 5    * INSERT RESPONSE TO LTERMCC
                CALL 'CBLTDLI' USING ISRT
                                  ALTERNATE-PCB-MASK
                                  RESPONE-A.
             IF ALT-STATUS-CODE NOT EQUAL SPACES
                PERFORM 1000-ERROR-ROUTINE.
```

Fig. 11-5. Placing terminal names into a modifiable PCB.

5.,6. The message is loaded to the message queue and retrieved by the Customer Update program.
7.,8. This second program updates the customer database and responds to terminal LTERMA1 which sent the original message.
9. Terminal LTERMA1 receives the response.

To pass control to the Customer Update program, Customer Edit has to issue a CHNG call indicating the destination of the message; in this case, the destination is the transaction CUSTUPDT and not the LTERM name. The program then issues an ISRT call using the alternate PCB to place the message on the message queue.

The format of the message on the message queue is given in FIG. 11-7. It contains a message prefix, a segment prefix, a transaction code, and the message text. Although this message does not originate from a terminal, the message prefix contains the logical terminal name LTERMA1 from which the original input message was received.

Now, control is passed to Customer Update. This program retrieves the message sent by the Customer Edit program by issuing a GU call via the IO-PCB. This same GU call initializes the IO-PCB with the LTERMA1 name placed in the message prefix by the first program.

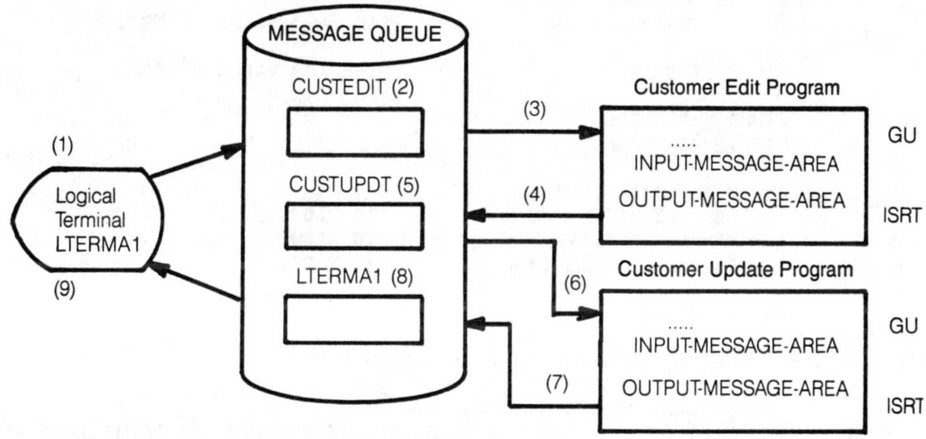

Fig. 11-6. Program-to-program messge switch.

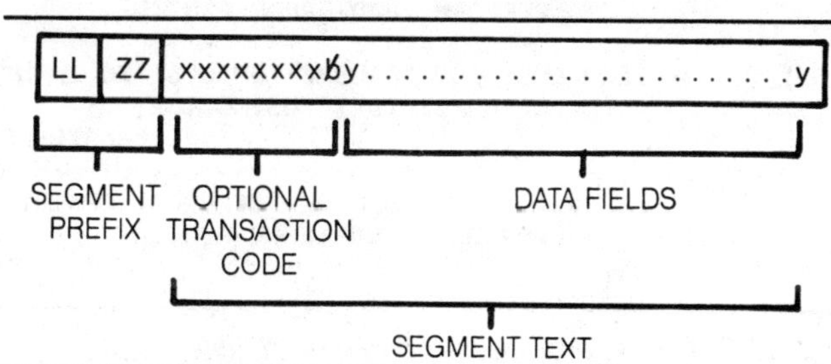

Fig. 11-7. Message switch format.

Sending Output Messages to Alternate Terminals

After having processed the transaction received, Customer Update issues an ISRT call to the IO-PCB to load the response to the message queue; the message will then be sent to the originating terminal. The COBOL coding to place a transaction into a modifiable alternate PCB is presented in FIG. 11-8.

SENDING MESSAGES TO ALTERNATE DESTINATIONS

Now that you have seen how to send output messages to alternate destinations using either the fixed alternate PCB or modifiable alternate PCB, we will present a simple application to send data to an alternate printer device.

```
          WORKING-STORAGE SECTION.
             .....
          01  OUTPUT-MESSAGE-AREA.
              05 FILLER                        PIC X(8) VALUE 'CUSTUPDT'.
              05 FILLER                        PIC X    VALUE SPACES.
              05 TRANS-TEXT.
                 10 TRANS-TEXT-1
                 10 .....
             .....
          01  IMS-CALL-FUNCTIONS.
              05 CHNG                          PIC X(4) VALUE 'CHNG'.
             .....
          01  DEST-NAME                        PIC X(8) VALUE SPACES.

          LINKAGE SECTION.
          01  IO-PCB-MASK.
              .....
          01  ALTERNATE-PCB-MASK.
              05  ALT-TERM-NAME                PIC X(8).
              05  ALT-RESERVED                 PIC X(2).
              05  ALT-STATUS-CODE              PIC X(2).

          PROCEDURE DIVISION.
              .....
CALL 1    * CHANGE DESTINATION TO TRANSACTION CODE
                 MOVE 'CUSTUPDT' TO DEST-NAME.
                 CALL 'CBLTDLI' USING CHNG
                                   ALTERNATE-PCB-MASK <= MODIFIABLE ALT PCB
                                   DEST-NAME.         <= TRANSACTION
                                                         CODE.
              IF ALT-STATUS-CODE NOT EQUAL SPACES
                 PERFORM 1000-ERROR-ROUTINE.
              .....
CALL 2    * SEND CUSTUPDT TRANSACTION CODE TO INPUT QUEUE
                 CALL 'CDLTDLI' USING ISRT
                                   ALTERNATE-PCB-MASK
                                   OUTPUT-MESSAGE-AREA. <== NEW TRANSACTION
              IF ALT-STATUS-CODE NOT EQUAL SPACES
                 PERFORM 1000-ERROR-ROUTINE.
              .....
```

Fig. 11-8. Placing a transaction into a modifiable PCB.

Program Specification

Modify the Customer Address Change program in chapter 4 to perform the following additional function: After successfully updating the customer's database with the new name and address, send the updated information to an alternate display terminal and print a report on an active printer device. The format of the printed report is given in FIG. 11-9; refer to SCREEN 4.43 for the required screen format.

Before you modify the COBOL source, you have to change the MFS control statement and generate a new MFS format for the message processing program. The changes to the control statement are presented in FIG. 11-10.

The COBOL Program

FIGURE 11-11 presents the modified program to print the updated report. Note the boxed areas of the program. To send data to the printer device, the program

- Moves printer ID 'PRINTERA' to WS-DESTINATION.
- Issues a CHNG call using ALTERNATE-PCB-MASK and WS-DESTINATION to specify the logical printer as the new destination.
- Issues an ISRT call to send the report to the printer.

Note the following key points:

- Since the printer is an output device only, TYPE=OUTPUT is coded.
- No ATTR keyword is coded for the printer device fields.
- No cursor specification is coded for the printer.
- The option SPACE is used for the printer report format. SPACE specifies that each output page will contain the exact number of lines specified in the PAGE definition.

```
DEVICE MAPPING FOR FMT=CUSTUP DEVICE=3270P- 2 TYPE=OUTPUT DPAGE=01 PHYSICAL PAGE=01

            PRINTED REPORT OF CUSTOMER NAME AND ADDRESS CHANGE

   ACCOUNT NO: __________                  SOC SEC NO: ____________
   LAST NAME: ______________________       FIRST NAME: _______________
         CURRENT ADDRESS:
                 STREET:      ____________________
                              ____________________
                 CITY:        ____________________
                 STATE:       _____   ZIP CODE: ______
         NEW ADDRESS:
                 STREET:      ____________________
                              ____________________
                 CITY:        ____________________
                 STATE:       _____   ZIP CODE: ______
```

Fig. 11-9. Printed report format.

```
1--------10----16-----------------------------------------------------72
         TITLE 'MFS CODING OF REPORT FORMAT'
         PRINT NOGEN
*
CUSTUP   FMT
         DEV   TYPE=(3270,2),FEAT=IGNORE,SYSMSG=MESSAGE
         DIV   TYPE=INOUT
         DPAGE CURSOR=((04,73))
         DFLD  'CUSTOMER ADDRESS CHANGE',POS=(02,29),LTH=23,          *
               ATTR=(PROT,HI)
TRANCD   DFLD  POS=(04,05),LTH=08,ATTR=(MOD,PROT,NODISP)
         .....
         .....  MORE DFLDS TO DEFINE SCREEN FORMAT
         .....  SAME AS FIGURE 4.42
*
*        LAYOUT OF REPORT LISTING
*
PRINTER  DEV   TYPE=(3270P,2),FEAT=IGNORE,PAGE=(24,SPACE)
         DIV   TYPE=OUTPUT                  <==== OUTPUT ONLY
DPAGE1   DPAGE
*
         DFLD  'PRINTED REPORT OF CUSTOMER NAME AND ADDRESS CHANGE',  *
               POS=(02,30)
         DFLD  'ACCOUNT NO:',POS=(06,11)
ACCTNO   DFLD  POS=(06,23),LTH=08
         DFLD  'SOC SEC NO:',POS=(06,44)
SOCNUM   DFLD  POS=(06,56),LTH=09
         DFLD  'LAST NAME:',POS=(08,11)
LASTNM   DFLD  POS=(08,22),LTH=20
         DFLD  'FIRST NAME:',POS=(08,44)
FRSTNM   DFLD  POS=(08,56),LTH=15
         DFLD  'CURRENT ADDRESS:',POS=(10,17)
         DFLD  'STREET:',POS=(11,25)
OLDSTR   DFLD  POS=(11,33),LTH=20
OLDST2   DFLD  POS=(12,33),LTH=20
         DFLD  'CITY:',POS=(13,25)
OLDCTY   DFLD  POS=(13,33),LTH=20
         DFLD  'STATE:',POS=(14,25)
OLDSTA   DFLD  POS=(14,33),LTH=02
         DFLD  'ZIP CODE:',POS=(14,38)
OLDZIP   DFLD  POS=(14,48),LTH=05
         DFLD  'NEW ADDRESS:',POS=(16,17)
         DFLD  'STREET:',POS=(17,25)
NEWSTR   DFLD  POS=(17,33),LTH=20
NEWST2   DFLD  POS=(18,33),LTH=20
         DFLD  'CITY:',POS=(19,25)
NEWCTY   DFLD  POS=(19,33),LTH=20
         DFLD  'STATE:',POS=(20,25)
NEWSTA   DFLD  POS=(20,33),LTH=02
         DFLD  'ZIP CODE:',POS=(20,38)
NEWZIP   DFLD  POS=(20,48),LTH=05
         FMTEND
*
```

Fig. 11-10.

Fig. 11-10. continued

```
INPMESG  MSG    TYPE=INPUT,SOR=CUSTUP,NXT=OUTMESG,OPT=1
         SEG
         MFLD   TRANCD,LTH=09
         .....
         .....   MORE MFLDS
         .....   SAME AS FIGURE 4.42
         MSGEND
*
OUTMESG  MSG    TYPE=OUTPUT,SOR=(CUSTUP,IGNORE),NXT=INPMESG,OPT=1,        *
                FILL=NULL,PAGE=NO
         SEG
         MFLD   SOCNUM,LTH=09
         .....
         .....   MORE MFLDS
         .....   SAME AS FIGURE 4.42
         MSGEND
         END
```

```
       IDENTIFICATION DIVISION.
       PROGRAM-ID. PROGRAM2.
       AUTHOR. ZIEP VUONG.
       DATE-WRITTEN. AUGUST 1987.
       REMARKS.
           *********************************************************
           *                                                       *
           *    PROGRAM FUNCTIONS:                                 *
           *                                                       *
           *    . RETRIEVE INPUT MESSAGES FROM A TERMINAL DEVICE   *
           *    . ACCESS THE ACCOUNT DATA BASE                     *
           *    . UPDATE THE ACCOUT DATA BASE WITH NEW NAME AND    *
           *      ADDRESSES                                        *
           *    . SEND OUTPUT MESSAGES TO THE INTERFACING TERMINAL *
           *    . SEND OUTPUT MESSAGES TO AN ALTERNATE TERMINAL    *
           *    . PRINT THE UPDATED REPORT ON AN ACTIVE PRINTER    *
           *                                                       *
           *********************************************************

       ENVIRONMENT DIVISION.
       CONFIGURATION SECTION.
       SOURCE-COMPUTER.  IBM-370.
       OBJECT-COMPUTER.  IBM-370.

       DATA DIVISION.

       WORKING-STORAGE SECTION.

       01  FILLER                          PIC X(27)
               VALUE 'WORKING-STORAGE BEGINS HERE'.

       77  INVALID-ACTION-MESSAGE          PIC X(24)
               VALUE 'INVALID ACTION REQUESTED'.
```

Fig. 11-11.

Fig. 11-11. continued

```
 77  NOTIFY-OPERATOR-MESSAGE         PIC X(40)
         VALUE 'ERROR, OPERATOR MUST CORRECT AND REENTER'.

 77  ACCT-NOT-FOUND-MESSAGE          PIC X(19)
         VALUE 'ACCOUNT NOT FOUND'.

 77  UPDATE-COMPLETED-MESSAGE        PIC X(34)
         VALUE 'TRANSACTION SUCCESSFULLY COMPLETED'.

 01  MESSAGE-SW                      PIC X VALUE 'N'.
     88  END-OF-MESSAGE                    VALUE 'Y'.

 01  WS-DESTINATION                  PIC X(8).

 01  WS-MODNAME                      PIC X(8).
*
*****************************************************************
*  THE LAYOUT OF THE INPUT AND OUPUT MESSAGE AREAS IN THE       *
*  PROGRAM MUST BE EXACTLY IN THE SAME FORMAT AS THE INPUT      *
*  AND OUTPUT DEFINITIONS IN THE MFS FORMAT.                    *
*  THERE IS A ONE-TO-ONE RELATIONSHIP BETWEEN THE INDIVIDUAL    *
*  INPUT AND OUTPUT FIELDS DEFINED IN THE FORMAT SET AND THOSE  *
*  DEFINED IN THE PROGRAM.                                      *
*  IN THIS PROGRAM THE INPUT AND OUTPUT MESSAGES ARE CODED AS   *
*  TWO SEGMENT MESSAGES.                                        *
*  THE ZZ FIELD ON INPUT IS DEFINED AS A FILLER BECAUSE IT IS   *
*  NOT USED.                                                    *
*  THE ZZ FIELD ON OUTPUT IS INITIALIZED TO ZEROES.             *
*****************************************************************
*
*  INPUT MESSAGE AREA
*
  01  INPUT-MESSAGE-AREA             PIC X(100).

  01  HEADER-SEGMENT REDEFINES INPUT-MESSAGE-AREA.
      05 HEADER-PREFIX.
         10 HEADER-LENGTH            PIC S999 COMP SYNC.
         10 FILLER                   PIC X(2).
      05 HEADER-TEXT.
         10 TRANS-CODE               PIC X(8).
         10 FILLER                   PIC X.
         10 ACCOUNT-NUMBER           PIC X(8).
         10 ACTION-CODE              PIC X.
            88 ADDRESS-RETRIEVE      VALUE 'G'.
            88 ADDRESS-UPDATE        VALUE 'U'.
      05 FILLER                      PIC X(48).

  01  TRAILER-1 REDEFINES INPUT-MESSAGE-AREA.
      05 TRAILER-1-PREFIX.
         10 TRAILER-1-LENGTH         PIC S999 COMP SYNC.
         10 FILLER                   PIC X(2).
      05 TRAILER-1-TEXT.
         10 STREET-ADDRESS1          PIC X(20).
         10 STREET-ADDRESS2          PIC X(20).
         10 CITY                     PIC X(20).
         10 STATE                    PIC X(2).
```

Fig. 11-11. continued

```
          10 ZIPCODE                 PIC X(5).
          10 FILLER                  PIC X(29).
*
*   OUTPUT MESSAGE AREA
*
 01   OUTPUT-MESSAGE-AREA.
      05 PREFIX-1.
          10 RESP-1-LENGTH           PIC S999 COMP SYNC VALUE +0.
          10 RESP-1-ZZ               PIC S999 COMP SYNC VALUE +0.
      05 RESPONSE-1-TEXT.
          10 RESP-1-LAST-NAME        PIC X(20).
          10 RESP-1-FIRST-NAME       PIC X(15).
          10 RESP-1-SSN              PIC X(9).
*
 01   RESPONSE-2 REDEFINES OUTPUT-MESSAGE-AREA.
      05 RESP-2-PREFIX.
          10 RESP-2-LENGTH           PIC S999 COMP SYNC.
          10 RESP-2-ZZ               PIC S999 COMP SYNC.
      05 RESP-2-TEXT.
          10 RESP-2-ADDRESS-LINE1    PIC X(20).
          10 RESP-2-ADDRESS-LINE2    PIC X(20).
          10 RESP-2-CITY             PIC X(20).
          10 RESP-2-STATE            PIC X(2).
          10 RESP-2-ZIPCODE          PIC X(5).
*
 01   COMMON-MESSAGE REDEFINES OUTPUT-MESSAGE-AREA.
      05 COMM-PREFIX.
          10 COMM-LENGTH             PIC S999 COMP SYNC.
          10 COMM-ZZ                 PIC S999 COMP SYNC.
      05 MESSAGE-TEXT                PIC X(40).
*
****************************************************************
*                                                              *
*                  DATA BASE SEGMENT LAYOUT                    *
*                                                              *
****************************************************************
*
 01   ACCOUNT-IO-AREA.
      05 ACCT-NUMBER-KEY             PIC X(8).
      05 ACCT-NAME.
          10 LAST-NAME               PIC X(20).
          10 FIRST-NAME              PIC X(15).
      05 ACCT-SSN                    PIC X(9).
      05 ACCT-ADDRESS-LINE1          PIC X(20).
      05 ACCT-ADDRESS-LINE2          PIC X(20).
      05 ACCT-CITY                   PIC X(20).
      05 ACCT-STATE                  PIC X(2).
      05 ACCT-ZIPCODE                PIC X(5).
*
****************************************************************
*                                                              *
*                      DATA BASE SSA'S                         *
*                                                              *
****************************************************************
*
 01   ACCOUNT-SSA.
```

Fig. 11-11. continued

```
       03  ACCT-SEG-NAME           PIC X(8) VALUE 'ACCTMSTR'.
       03  ACCT-LEFT-PAREN         PIC X    VALUE '('.
       03  ACCT-KEY-NAME           PIC X(8) VALUE 'ACTNUMBR'.
       03  ACCT-OPRERATOR          PIC XX   VALUE ' ='.
       03  ACCT-KEY-VALUE          PIC X(8) VALUE SPACES.
       03  ACCT-RIGHT-PAREN        PIC X    VALUE ')'.

   01  ACCOUNT-SSA-UNQUALIFIED     PIC X(9) VALUE 'ACCTMSTR '.
  *
  ************************************************************
  *                                                          *
  *                 IMS CALL FUNCTION CODES                  *
  *                                                          *
  ************************************************************
   01  IMS-CALL-FUNCTIONS.
       03  GU                      PIC X(4) VALUE 'GU  '.
       03  GN                      PIC X(4) VALUE 'GN  '.
       03  GNP                     PIC X(4) VALUE 'GNP '.
       03  GHU                     PIC X(4) VALUE 'GHU '.
       03  GHN                     PIC X(4) VALUE 'GHN '.
       03  GHNP                    PIC X(4) VALUE 'GHNP'.
       03  ISRT                    PIC X(4) VALUE 'ISRT'.
       03  DLET                    PIC X(4) VALUE 'DLET'.
       03  REPL                    PIC X(4) VALUE 'REPL'.
       03  CHKP                    PIC X(4) VALUE 'CHKP'.
       03  CHNG                    PIC X(4) VALUE 'CHNG'.
       03  PURG                    PIC X(4) VALUE 'PURG'.
       03  LOG                     PIC X(4) VALUE 'LOG '.
       03  XRST                    PIC X(4) VALUE 'XRST'.
       03  ROLB                    PIC X(4) VALUE 'ROLB'.
       03  FUNCTION                PIC X(4) VALUE '    '.
      *
       LINKAGE SECTION.
      *
      *  DATA COMMUNICATION PCB'S - BOTH IO PCB AND ALTERNATE PCB
      *  ARE REQUIRED BECAUSE PROGRAM SENDS RESPONSES TO THE
      *  ORIGINATING AND TO THE ALTERNATE TERMINALS.
      *
       01  IO-PCB-MASK.
           05  ORIGIN-TERM-NAME        PIC X(8).
           05  IO-RESERVED             PIC X(2).
           05  IO-STATUS-CODE          PIC X(2).
           05  IO-PREFIX.
               10 JULIAN-DATE          PIC S9(7) COMP-3.
               10 CURRENT-TIME         PIC S9(7) COMP-3.
               10 SEQUENCE-NO          PIC S9(7) COMP.
           05  IO-MODNAME              PIC X(8).

       01  ALTERNATE-PCB-MASK.
           05  ALT-TERM-NAME           PIC X(8).
           05  ALT-RESERVED            PIC X(2).
           05  ALT-STATUS-CODE         PIC X(2).
      *
      *  DATA BASE PCB - REQUIRED BECAUSE PROGRAM REFERENCES THE
      *  ACCOUNT DATA BASE.
      *
```

Fig. 11-11. continued

```
    01  ACCOUNT-PCB-MASK.
        05  ACCT-DBD-NAME               PIC X(8).
        05  ACCT-SEG-LEVEL              PIC X(2).
        05  ACCT-STATUS-CODE            PIC X(2).
        05  ACCT-PROCESS-OPTIONS        PIC X(4).
        05  IMS-RESERVED                PIC S9(5) COMP.
        05  ACCT-SEG-NAME-FB            PIC X(8).
        05  ACCT-LENGTH-FB-KEY          PIC S9(5) COMP.
        05  ACCT-NBR-SENS-SEG           PIC S9(5) COMP.
        05  ACCT-KEY-FB-AREA            PIC X(8).
 PROCEDURE DIVISION.

     ENTRY 'DLITCBL' USING IO-PCB-MASK
                           ALTERNATE-PCB-MASK
                           ACCOUNT-PCB-MASK.

 PROGRAM-ENTRY.

 010-PROCESS-CUSTOMER-TRANS.

     MOVE 'N' TO MESSAGE-SW.
     PERFORM 100-PROCESS-INPUT-MESSAGES
        UNTIL END-OF-MESSAGE.

 PROGRAM-EXIT.
     GOBACK.

 100-PROCESS-INPUT-MESSAGES.

     PERFORM 200-GET-INPUT-MESSAGES.
     IF NOT END-OF-MESSAGE
     PERFORM 300-DETERMINE-ACTION-TAKEN.

*****************************************************************
*  GET THE FIRST MESSAGE SEGMENT,                               *
*  CHECK TO SEE IF MESSAGE QUEUE IS EMPTY,                      *
*  STATUS 'QC' MEANS THAT THERE ARE NO MORE MESSAGES.           *
*****************************************************************
 200-GET-INPUT-MESSAGES.

     CALL 'CBLTDLI' USING GU
                          IO-PCB-MASK
                          INPUT-MESSAGE-AREA.

     IF IO-STATUS-CODE EQUAL 'QC'
        MOVE 'Y' TO MESSAGE-SW
        GOBACK.

     IF IO-STATUS-CODE EQUAL SPACES
        NEXT SENTENCE
     ELSE
        MOVE NOTIFY-OPERATOR-MESSAGE TO MESSAGE-TEXT
        MOVE +44 TO COMM-LENGTH
        PERFORM 600-SEND-MESSAGE-TO-ORIG-TERM
        GOBACK.
```

Fig. 11-11. continued

```
       PERFORM 200-GET-NEXT-TRAILER.

*****************************************************************
*  GET SUBSEQUENT MESSAGE SEGMENTS,                             *
*  CHECK TO SEE IF THERE ARE ANY MORE SEGMENTS,                 *
*  STATUS 'QD' MEANS THAT THERE ARE NO MORE SEGMENTS TO PROCESS. *
*****************************************************************
 200-GET-NEXT-TRAILER.

       CALL 'CBLTDLI' USING GN
                            IO-PCB-MASK
                            INPUT-MESSAGE-AREA.
       IF IO-STATUS-CODE EQUAL 'QD'
          NEXT SENTENCE
       ELSE
          MOVE NOTIFY-OPERATOR-MESSAGE TO MESSAGE-TEXT
          MOVE +44 TO COMM-LENGTH
          PERFORM 600-SEND-MESSAGE-TO-ORIG-TERM.

       IF IO-STATUS-CODE EQUAL SPACES
          PERFORM 300-DETERMINE-ACTION-TAKEN.
*****************************************************************
*  ACTION CODE MUST BE EQUAL 'G' FOR RETRIEVE OR                *
*                            'U' FOR UPDATE                     *
*  OTHERWISE IT IS AN ERROR.                                    *
*****************************************************************
 300-DETERMINE-ACTION-TAKEN.

       IF ACTION-CODE NOT EQUAL 'G' AND 'U'
          MOVE INVALID-ACTION-MESSAGE  TO MESSAGE-TEXT
          MOVE +44 TO COMM-LENGTH
          PERFORM 600-SEND-MESSAGE-TO-ORIG-TERM.

       IF ADDRESS-RETRIEVE
          PERFORM 400-RETRIEVE-DISPLAY-ACCOUNT.

       IF ADDRESS-UPDATE
          PERFORM 500-RETRIEVE-UPDATE-ACCOUNT
          PERFORM 750-PRINT-UPDATE-REPORT.

*****************************************************************
*  QUALIFY ACCOUNT SSA WITH ACCOUNT NUMBER FROM TERMINAL,       *
*  ACCESS ACCOUNT DATA BASE TO RETRIEVE ACCOUNT INFORMATION.    *
*  IF ACCOUNT EXISTS                                            *
*     . BUILD OUTPUT MESSAGE,                                   *
*     . DETERMINE LENGTH OF MESSAGE AND MOVE IT TO LENGTH-FIELD *
*     . MESSAGE LENGTH EQUALS LENGTH OF SEGMENT + 4,            *
*     . INITIALIZE ZZ-FIELD TO ZEROES,                          *
*     . SEND OUTPUT MESSAGE TO ORIGINAL TERMINAL.               *
*                                                               *
*****************************************************************
 400-RETRIEVE-DISPLAY-ACCOUNT.

       MOVE ACCOUNT-NUMBER TO ACCT-KEY-VALUE.
       CALL 'CBLTDLI' USING GU
                            ACCOUNT-PCB-MASK
```

Fig. 11-11. continued

```
                                ACCOUNT-IO-AREA
                                ACCOUNT-SSA.

           IF ACCT-STATUS-CODE EQUAL 'GE'
              PERFORM 900-ACCOUNT-NOT-FOUND.

           IF ACCT-STATUS-CODE NOT EQUAL SPACES
              PERFORM 2000-DB-ERROR-ROUTINE.

      *  BUILD FIRST OUTPUT SEGMENT

              MOVE LAST-NAME             TO RESP-1-LAST-NAME
              MOVE FIRST-NAME            TO RESP-1-FIRST-NAME
              MOVE ACCT-SSN              TO RESP-1-SSN
              MOVE +48                   TO RESP-1-LENGTH
              MOVE +0                    TO RESP-1-ZZ
              PERFORM 600-SEND-MESSAGE-TO-ORIG-TERM.

      *  BUILD SECOND OUTPUT SEGMENT

              MOVE ACCT-ADDRESS-LINE1 TO RESP-2-ADDRESS-LINE1
              MOVE ACCT-ADDRESS-LINE2 TO RESP-2-ADDRESS-LINE2
              MOVE ACCT-CITY             TO RESP-2-CITY
              MOVE ACCT-STATE            TO RESP-2-STATE
              MOVE ACCT-ZIPCODE          TO RESP-2-ZIPCODE
              MOVE +71                   TO RESP-2-LENGTH
              MOVE +0                    TO RESP-2-ZZ
              PERFORM 600-SEND-MESSAGE-TO-ORIG-TERM.
       500-RETRIEVE-UPDATE-ACCOUNT.

           MOVE ACCOUNT-NUMBER TO ACCT-KEY-VALUE.
           CALL 'CBLTDLI' USING GHU
                                ACCOUNT-PCB-MASK
                                ACCOUNT-IO-AREA
                                ACCOUNT-SSA.

           IF ACCT-STATUS-CODE EQUAL 'GE'
              PERFORM 900-ACCOUNT-NOT-FOUND.

           IF ACCT-STATUS-CODE NOT EQUAL SPACES
              PERFORM 2000-DB-ERROR-ROUTINE.

           IF ACCT-STATUS-CODE EQUAL SPACES
              MOVE STREET-ADDRESS1       TO ACCT-ADDRESS-LINE1
              MOVE STREET-ADDRESS2       TO ACCT-ADDRESS-LINE2
              MOVE CITY                  TO ACCT-CITY
              MOVE STATE                 TO ACCT-STATE
              MOVE ZIPCODE               TO ACCT-ZIPCODE
              PERFORM  800-REPLACE-ACCOUNT-INFO.

      *****************************************************************
      *  MOVE MOD NAME OF MFS FORMAT TO MODNAME FIELD IN IO-PCB,      *
      *  SEND MESSAGE TO ORIGINAL TERMINAL USING IO-PCB.              *
      *****************************************************************
       600-SEND-MESSAGE-TO-ORIG-TERM.
```

Fig. 11-11. continued

```
           MOVE 'OUTMESG ' TO IO-MODNAME.

           CALL 'CBLTDLI' USING ISRT
                                IO-PCB-MASK
                                OUTPUT-MESSAGE-AREA.

       IF IO-STATUS-CODE NOT EQUAL SPACES
           PERFORM 1000-ERROR-ROUTINE.
```

```
***************************************************************
*  SEND MESSAGE TO ALTERNATE TERMINAL USING ALTERNATE PCB.    *
***************************************************************
 700-SEND-MESSAGE-TO-ALT-TERM.

           CALL 'CBLTDLI' USING ISRT
                                ALTERNATE-PCB-MASK
                                OUTPUT-MESSAGE-AREA.

       IF ALT-STATUS-CODE NOT EQUAL SPACES
           PERFORM 1000-ERROR-ROUTINE.
***************************************************************
*  MOVE PRINTER ID TO DESTINATION OF MESSAGE,                 *
*  ISSUE A CHNG CALL TO SET THE DESTINATION OF THE ALTERNATE PCB *
*  TO THE LOGICAL PRINTER ID,                                 *
*  BUILD PRINT AREA,                                          *
*  DETERMINE LENGTH OF MESSAGE AND MOVE IT TO LENGTH-FIELD    *
*  MESSAGE LENGTH EQUALS LENGTH OF SEGMENT + 4,               *
*  INITIALIZE ZZ-FIELD TO ZEROES,                             *
*  SEND OUTPUT MESSAGE TO PRINTER.                            *
*                                                             *
***************************************************************
 750-PRINT-UPDATE-REPORT.

           MOVE 'PRINTERA' TO WS-DESTINATION.

           CALL 'CBLTDLI' USING CHNG
                                ALTERNATE-PCB-MASK
                                WS-DESTINATION.

* BUILD FIRST PRINT MESSAGE AREA

           MOVE LAST-NAME           TO RESP-1-LAST-NAME
           MOVE FIRST-NAME          TO RESP-1-FIRST-NAME
           MOVE ACCT-SSN            TO RESP-1-SSN
           MOVE +48                 TO RESP-1-LENGTH
           MOVE +0                  TO RESP-1-ZZ.

* SEND MESSAGE TO PRINTER

           MOVE 'OUTMESG ' TO WS-MODNAME.

           CALL 'CBLTDLI' USING ISRT
                                ALTERNATE-PCB-MASK
                                OUTPUT-MESSAGE-AREA
                                WS-MODNAME.
```

Fig. 11-11. continued

```
    IF ALT-STATUS-CODE NOT EQUAL SPACES
       PERFORM 1000-ERROR-ROUTINE.

 * BUILD SECOND PRINT MESSAGE AREA

       MOVE ACCT-ADDRESS-LINE1 TO RESP-2-ADDRESS-LINE1
       MOVE ACCT-ADDRESS-LINE2 TO RESP-2-ADDRESS-LINE2
       MOVE ACCT-CITY          TO RESP-2-CITY
       MOVE ACCT-STATE         TO RESP-2-STATE
       MOVE ACCT-ZIPCODE       TO RESP-2-ZIPCODE
       MOVE +71                TO RESP-2-LENGTH
       MOVE +0                 TO RESP-2-ZZ

 * SEND MESSAGE TO PRINTER

       CALL 'CBLTDLI' USING ISRT
                           ALTERNATE-PCB-MASK
                           OUTPUT-MESSAGE-AREA
                           WS-MODNAME.

    IF ALT-STATUS-CODE NOT EQUAL SPACES
       PERFORM 1000-ERROR-ROUTINE.
*****************************************************************
*  UPDATE ACCOUNT SEGMENT,                                      *
*  SEND MESSAGE TO OPERATOR UPON COMPLETION OF UPDATE TRANSACTION*
*****************************************************************
 800-REPLACE-ACCOUNT-INFO.

     CALL 'CBLTDLI' USING REPL
                         ACCOUNT-PCB-MASK
                         ACCOUNT-IO-AREA.

     IF ACCT-STATUS-CODE NOT EQUAL SPACES
        PERFORM 2000-DB-ERROR-ROUTINE
     ELSE
        MOVE UPDATE-COMPLETED-MESSAGE TO MESSAGE-TEXT
        MOVE +44 TO COMM-LENGTH
        PERFORM 600-SEND-MESSAGE-TO-ORIG-TERM
        PERFORM 700-SEND-MESSAGE-TO-ALT-TERM.

*****************************************************************
*  SEND NOT-FOUND-MESSAGE TO ORIGINAL TERMINAL USING IO-PCB     *
*****************************************************************
 900-ACCOUNT-NOT-FOUND.

        MOVE ACCT-NOT-FOUND-MESSAGE TO MESSAGE-TEXT
        MOVE +44 TO COMM-LENGTH

        CALL 'CBLTDLI' USING ISRT
                            IO-PCB-MASK
                            OUTPUT-MESSAGE-AREA.

     IF IO-STATUS-CODE NOT EQUAL SPACES
        PERFORM 1000-ERROR-ROUTINE.
```

Fig. 11-11. continued

```
*****************************************************************
*  THE IO ERROR ROUTINE IS EXECUTED WHENEVER AN UNEXPECTED STATUS*
*  CODE IS RETURNED. THIS ROUTINE VARIES FROM INSTALLATION TO    *
*  INSTALLATION. YOU SHOULD CHECK YOUR INSTALLATION'S STANDARDS  *
*  ON HOW TO CODE THIS ROUTINE.                                  *
*  IN THIS EXAMPLE, WE ISSUE A ROLB CALL TO DELETE THE CURRENT   *
*  INPUT MESSAGE AND TO LET THE PROGRAM CONTINUE WITH THE NEXT   *
*  MESSAGE.                                                      *
*  WE ONLY SPECIFY THE FUNCTION AND THE IO PCB MASK, NO IO AREA  *
*  IS SPECIFIED BECAUSE IT IS OPTIONAL.                          *
*****************************************************************
 1000-ERROR-ROUTINE.

        CALL 'CBLTDLI' USING ROLB
                             IO-PCB-MASK.

*****************************************************************
*  THE FOLLOWING ERROR ROUTINE IS EXECUTED WHENEVER A BAD STATUS *
*  CODE IS RETURNED FOR A DATA BASE CALL.                        *
*  MOST INSTALLATIONS REQUEST TO DISPLAY THE TYPE OF CALL, THE   *
*  RETURNED STATUS CODE, THE KEY VALUE OF THE SSA AND THEN CALL  *
*  A USER WRITTEN SUBROUTINE TO FORMAT A DUMP FOR DEBUGGING.     *
*****************************************************************
 2000-DB-ERROR-ROUTINE.

        DISPLAY 'GET CALL ERROR TO ACCOUNT DATA BASE'.
        DISPLAY 'STATUS CODE: ' ACCT-STATUS-CODE.
        DISPLAY 'ACCOUNT NUMBER: ' ACCT-KEY-VALUE.
*
*       CALL 'ABENDPGM' TO PRINT DUMP
```

12

Conversational Processing

This chapter describes the conversational programming technique. Conversational programming uses special IMS/VS facilities to provide a mechanism for storing data between terminal interactions before processing. First, we'll explain what conversational processing is, and then we'll cover the scratch pad area—a special work area provided by IMS to store information between terminal exchanges—and the type of DL/1 calls you need to know to code a conversational program. After that, we'll cover the program switching technique in conversational programs.

WHAT IS CONVERSATIONAL PROCESSING?

Conversational processing is an optional IMS/VS feature which allows the operator to interface with an application program more than once during the execution of a single transaction. A conversation is a series of exchanges of input messages and responses between a logical terminal and application program. Each input message and associated response constitute an *interaction* of the conversation.

A conversational program does not process the entire transaction at once. It divides processing into a series of terminal-to-program-to-terminal cycles.

Conversational processing is used in situations where an input message contains many segments. When such a message is processed in a normal mode, an edit error can only be detected after the last segment of the message has been entered. In a conversational mode, each segment is edited separately, and if an error is detected, a response will be sent to the terminal indicating which part of the message needs correction. To initiate a conversation, the terminal operator sends a message which contains a transaction code defined as being conversational. This will engage the logical terminal into an interactive exchange with the application program.

The application program saves all information essential to continuing the conversation in a special work area and sends a response to the terminal.

The operator enters additional information and sends another message to continue the conversation. The program is scheduled once again. The second message is processed, the new data is saved, and the program sends another response.

This interchange continues until either the application program or the operator terminates the conversation.

THE SCRATCH PAD AREA

In conversational processing, a special work area is provided by IMS/VS to store information between terminal exchanges. This data storage area is called the *scratch pad area* (SPA) which can exist on disk or in main storage; however, it is best to have small SPAs in main storage.

The maximum number and size of SPAs to be maintained by IMS are defined at system definition time.

When a conversation is initiated from a terminal, a SPA is assigned by IMS to that terminal to be used for the duration of the conversation. The SPA is provided for the application program so that is can save information about the current conversation, and provides the link between two interactions of a conversation.

FIGURE 12-1 illustrates the format of the SPA.

- LL is two-bytes-long and contains a half-word binary number which specifies the total number of bytes in the entire SPA. This field is loaded by IMS and cannot be modified by the application program.
- ZZ is two-bytes-long and is reserved for use by IMS. This field should not be modified by the application program.
- CI is two-bytes-long and is reserved for use by IMS. This is a conversational identification to connect the proper SPA with the proper conversation. This field should not be modified by the application program.
- TRAN CODE is eight-bytes-long and contains the actual transaction code that caused the associated program to be scheduled. This field is left-justified and may be changed to spaces by the application program to terminate the conversation, or to another transaction code to pass control to another program.
- USER WORK AREA is a variable-length area and is 14 bytes less than that defined at IMS/VS system definition time for each conversational transaction code. This area is cleared to binary zeroes on initial entry to the program for this conversation. Information essential to continuity of the conversation is saved in this area.

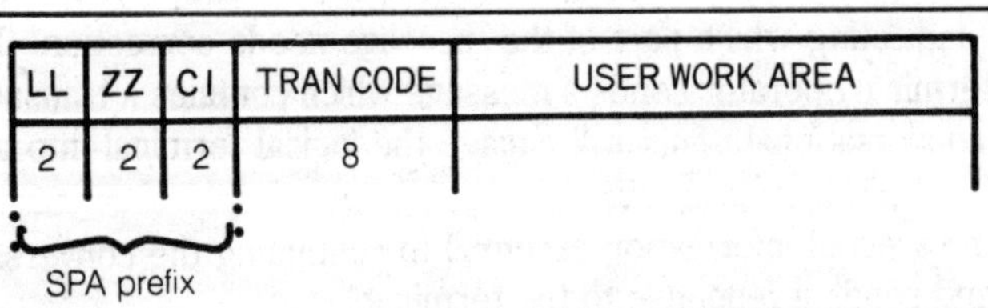

Fig. 12-1. SPA format.

Coding the SPA-IO Area

To develop conversational applications, you need to know how to define and reference the SPA in your program.

The SPA-IO area is defined in the application program's WORKING STORAGE. Whenever the SPA is used by the application program, it is placed in the program's SPA-IO area, and any information that the program provides for the SPA is moved into the SPA-IO area before it is placed in the SPA. The coding of this area is given below:

```
01     SPA-IO-AREA.
       05 SPA-LENGTH                 PIC S9(4) COMP.
       05 SPA-CONTROL                PIC X(4).
       05 SPA-TRANCODE               PIC X(8).
       05 SPA-WORK-AREA              PIC X(100).
```

Conversational Program Sequence

During each conversational cycle (interaction), follow these steps:

1. Retrieve the SPA using the GU call.
2. Retrieve the message text using the GN call.
3. Process the message, including any necessary database calls.
4. Move information essential to continuing the conversation to SPA-IO-AREA. Return the SPA to IMS using an ISRT call to IO-PCB.
5. Send a response to the originating terminal using another ISRT call to IO-PCB.

Retrieving the SPA

You must retrieve the SPA before you retrieve any message segments. To retrieve the SPA, issue a GU call against IO-PCB and store it in SPA-IO-AREA. The format of this call is presented in FIG. 12-2. The SPA can be seen as the first segment of the input message.

Retrieving Input Messages

After retrieving the SPA, issue a GN call to retrieve the first segment of the input message. This segment does not contain the transaction code because IMS removes the code and stores it in the SPA. In subsequent messages of the conversation, the transaction is not removed.

Saving the SPA

To save the SPA, you must issue an ISRT call against the IO-PCB. You must save the SPA *before* you issue subsequent ISRT calls to send messages to the terminal. You can save the SPA only once during a cycle of the conversation. The SPA-IO-AREA used for output is the same as for input. The application should not modify the SPA prefix

```
       WORKING-STORAGE SECTION.
         .....
*               SCRATCH PAD AREA
*      THE SPA-SWITCH IS INCREMENTED BY '1' DURING EACH CYCLE OF
*      THE CONVERSATION.
*
 01    SPA-IO-AREA.
       05 SPA-LENGTH              PIC S9(4) COMP.
       05 SPA-CONTROL             PIC X(4).
       05 SPA-TRANCODE            PIC X(8).
       05 SPA-CUST-NO             PIC X(8).
       05 SPA-ITEM                PIC X(5).
       05 SPA-QTY                 PIC X(2).
       05 FILLER                  PIC X(10).
       05 SPA-SWITCH              PIC S9(3) COMP.
          88 FIRST-CYCLE                VALUE +0.
          .....
 LINKAGE SECTION.
 01    IO-PCB-MASK.
       05   ORIGIN-TERM-NAME      PIC X(8).
       05   IO-RESERVED           PIC X(2).
       05   IO-STATUS-CODE        PIC X(2).
       05   IO-PREFIX.
            10 JULIAN-DATE        PIC S9(7) COMP-3.
            10 CURRENT-TIME       PIC S9(7) COMP-3.
            10 SEQUENCE-NO        PIC S9(7) COMP.
       05   IO-MODNAME            PIC X(8).
 PROCEDURE DIVISION.
 .....
 0400-GET-SPA.

       CALL 'CBLTDLI' USING GU
                            IO-PCB-MASK
                            SPA-IO-AREA.

*
*   IF STATUS CODE 'QC' IS RETURNED SET END-SWITCH ON
*
       IF IO-STATUS-CODE EQUAL 'QC'
          MOVE '1' TO END-SWITCH
       ELSE
       IF IO-STATUS-CODE NOT EQUAL SPACES
          PERFORM 1000-ERROR-ROUTINE.
 0400-GET-SPA-EXIT. EXIT.
*
*   RETURN THE SPA TO IMS/VS
*
 0600-RETURN-SPA.

       CALL 'CBLTDLI' USING ISRT
                            IO-PCB-MASK
                            SPA-IO-AREA.
       IF IO-STATUS-CODE NOT EQUAL SPACES
          PERFORM 1000-ERROR-ROUTINE.
 0600-RETURN-SPA-EXIT. EXIT.
```

Fig. 12-2. Retrieving and returning the SPA.

comprising the LL, ZZ and CI fields. The transaction code field from position 7 through 14 is required for both input and output.

Terminating a Conversation

A conversation can be terminated either by the conversational program or by an IMS terminal command. Let's examine these two methods individually.

Program Calls. A conversation is normally terminated by the application program. Prior to issuing the ISRT call to return the SPA to IMS, the application program places blanks in the transaction code field of the SPA-IO-AREA. Once IMS recognizes the blank transaction code, it releases the SPA assigned to the logical terminal and the conversation is terminated.

The program can also terminate the conversation by changing the transaction code in the SPA to that of a nonconversational program and returning the SPA.

Terminal Command. While a terminal is participating in a conversation, it cannot send any other messages until the conversation is completed. However, we can enter the /EXIT command from the terminal to terminate the conversation.

The COBOL coding to terminate a conversation is presented in FIG. 12-3.

A CONVERSATIONAL APPLICATION

To better understand the conversational process, let's examine the following example.

First Cycle

The conversation is initiated when the terminal operator enters the CUSTORDR transaction code and the Customer number 00029000 (FIG. 12-4):

```
CUSTORDR 00029000
```

When the conversation is initiated:

1. A SPA is assigned to the original logical terminal, and is connected to the logical terminal name during all cycles of the conversation. (In our example, LTERMAA is the logical terminal.) The SPA resides either on a direct access storage device or in main storage.

   Assume that the SPA for LTERMAA resides in main storage. Consequently, space for the SPA is obtained from the buffer pool when the conversation is initiated. This space is maintained until the conversation is terminated.
2. The SPA prefix is initialized.
3. The transaction code is moved from the input message to the SPA. The SPA is then put on the message queue as the header segment of the message.

```
        WORKING-STORAGE SECTION.
          .....
     *                 SCRATCH PAD AREA
     *    THE SPA-SWITCH IS INCREMENTED BY '1' DURING EACH CYCLE OF
     *    THE CONVERSATION.
     *
      01  SPA-IO-AREA.
          05 SPA-LENGTH                 PIC S9(4) COMP.
          05 SPA-CONTROL                PIC X(4).
          05 SPA-TRANCODE               PIC X(8).
          05 SPA-CUST-NO                PIC X(8).
          05 SPA-ITEM                   PIC X(5).
          05 SPA-QTY                    PIC X(2).
          05 FILLER                     PIC X(10).
          05 SPA-SWITCH                 PIC S9(3) COMP.
             88 FIRST-CYCLE                 VALUE +0.
             .....
      LINKAGE SECTION.
      01  IO-PCB-MASK.
          05  ORIGIN-TERM-NAME          PIC X(8).
          05  IO-RESERVED               PIC X(2).
          05  IO-STATUS-CODE            PIC X(2).
          05  IO-PREFIX.
              10  JULIAN-DATE           PIC S9(7) COMP-3.
              10  CURRENT-TIME          PIC S9(7) COMP-3.
              10  SEQUENCE-NO           PIC S9(7) COMP.
          05  IO-MODNAME                PIC X(8).
      PROCEDURE DIVISION.
      .....
     *  BLANK OUT THE TRANSACTION CODE IN THE SPA AND
     *  RETURN THE SPA TO IMS/VS TO TERMINATE THE CONVERSATION.

             MOVE SPACES TO SPA-TRANCODE
             PERFORM 0600-RETURN-SPA THRU 0600-RETURN-SPA-EXIT.

     *  RETURN THE SPA TO IMS/VS

      0600-RETURN-SPA.

          CALL 'CBLTDLI' USING ISRT
                               IO-PCB-MASK
                               SPA-IO-AREA.
          IF IO-STATUS-CODE NOT EQUAL SPACES
             PERFORM 1000-ERROR-ROUTINE.
      0600-RETURN-SPA-EXIT. EXIT.
```

Fig. 12-3. Terminating a conversation.

4. The USER WORK AREA of the SPA is intialized to binary zeroes. This informs the program that this is the first cycle of a conversation.
5. The message text is left-justified by removing the transaction code.

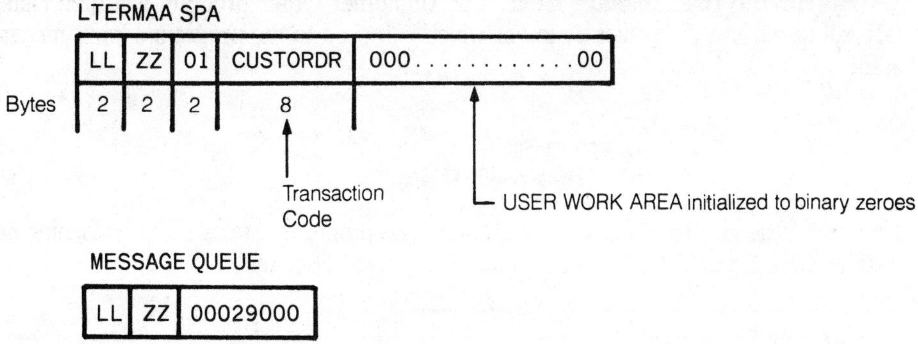

Fig. 12-4. Initiating a conversation.

6. When the conversational transaction is received, IMS/VS chains it to a control block which represents the conversation for the whole duration. The control block contains the conversational identification '01' and three pointers:

   - The first points to the interfacing terminal.
   - The second points to the transaction queue.
   - The third points to the SPA assigned to the conversation.

Retrieving the SPA. When the Customer Order program is scheduled, it issues a GU call to retrieve the SPA:

```
CALL 'CBLTDLI' USING GU
                     IO-PCB-MASK
                     SPA-IO-AREA.
```

The SPA is moved to SPA-IO-AREA which resides in the program's WORKING STORAGE. IO-PCB is initialized with LTERMAA (FIG. 12-5).

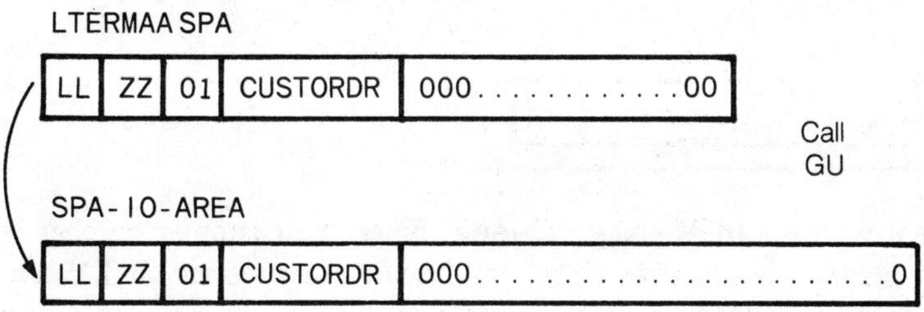

Fig. 12-5. Retrieving the SPA.

Retrieving the Message Text. The Customer Order program will then issue a GN call to retrieve the trailer segment which is moved to the program's input message area:

```
CALL 'CBLTDLI' USING GN
                      IO-PCB-MASK
                      INPUT-MESSAGE-AREA.
```

If the message consists of several segments, the program obtains them by issuing successive GN calls until a 'QD' status code is received (FIG. 12-6).

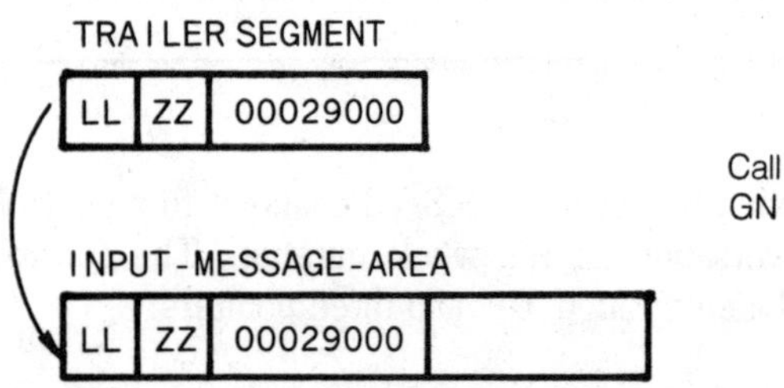

Fig. 12-6. Retrieving the trailer segment.

Call to Access DL/1 Database. The application program issues a GU call (with a qualified SSA to access the customer database) and retrieves the CUSTMSTR segment having the key 00029000 (FIG. 12-7).

```
CALL 'CBLTDLI' USING GU
                      CUST-PCB-MASK
                      SEGMENT-IO-AREA
                      CUST-SSA.
```

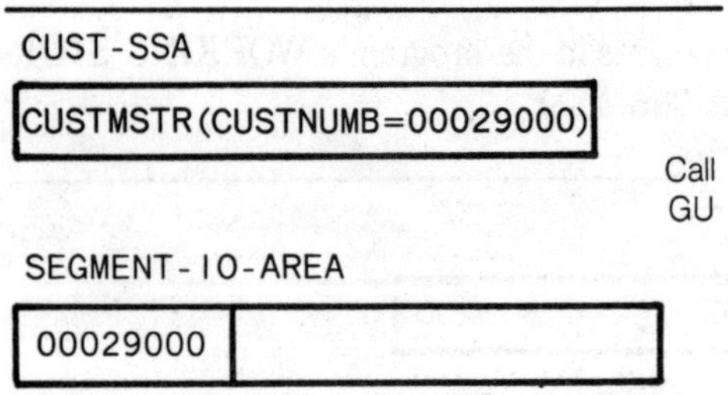

Fig. 12-7. Validating customer number.

Send Response to Message Queue. Since the customer number is valid, the application program builds a response (FIG. 12-8) and issues an ISRT call to place the response on the LTERMAA message queue:

```
CALL 'CBLTDLI' USING ISRT
                      IO-PCB-MASK
                      OUTPUT-MESSAGE-AREA.
```

Fig. 12-8. Response 1.

Save Information in SPA-IO-AREA. The first cycle of the conversation is almost complete. The application program saves essential information in the SPA for the next cycle of the conversation (i.e., the customer number). A switch in the SPA is set to 1. This switch is checked by the program each time an input message is obtained to determine if this is the first cycle of the conversation (FIG. 12-9.

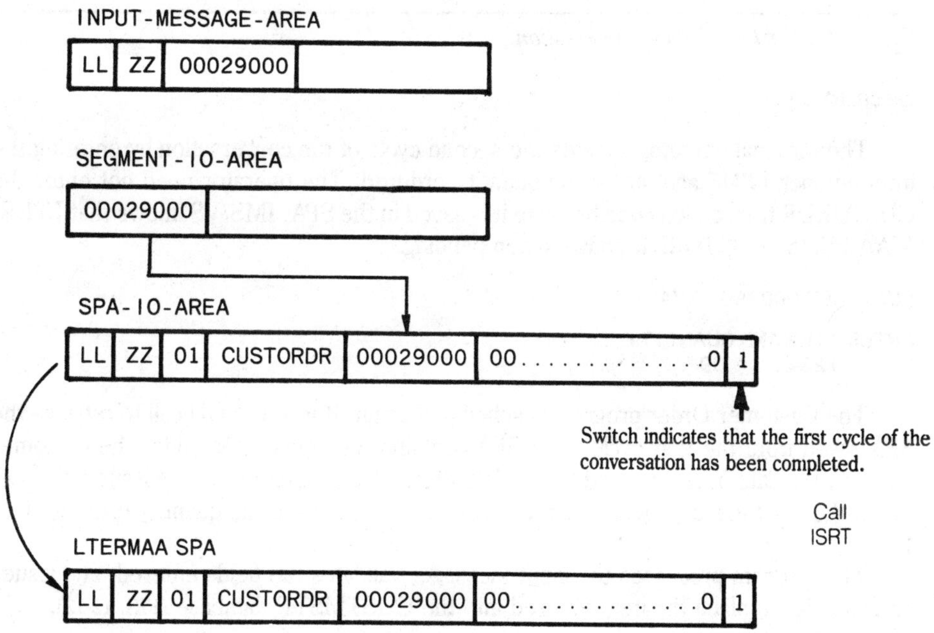

Fig. 12-9. Save information in SPA-IO-AREA.

Returning the SPA to IMS. The program returns the SPA to IMS by issuing an ISRT call to the IO-PCB.

```
CALL 'CBLTDLI' USING ISRT
                     IO-PCB-MASK
                     SPA-IO-AREA.
```

The Customer Order program now issues a GU call against the IO-PCB for the next message in the queue:

```
CUSTORDR 00029000

CUSTOMER 00029000 VALID
ENTER ITEM AND QUANTITY
```

The response is sent to the terminal, and the first cycle of the conversation is completed (FIG. 12-10).

OUTPUT-MESSAGE-AREA

LL	ZZ	CUSTOMER 00029000 VALID, ENTER ITEM AND QUANTITY	ISRT response

Fig. 12-10. First cycle of the conversation.

Second Cycle

The terminal operator initiates the second cycle of the conversation by entering the item number 12345 and 09 for the quantity ordered. The operator need not enter the CUSTORDR transaction code because it is saved in the SPA. IMS/VS knows that LTERMAA has the CUSTORDR conversation pending.

```
CUSTOMER 00029000 VALID

ENTER ITEM AND QUANTITY
      12345     09
```

The Customer Order program is scheduled again. It issues a GU call to retrieve the SPA saved from the first cycle. The SPA contains the transaction code, the customer number, the date accepted, and the cycle switch. The program will then issue a GN call to get the input message which contains the item number and the quantity ordered (FIG. 12-11).

The program processes the input message, validates the fields entered, and issues an ISRT call to place the item ordered into the CUSTMSTR database (FIG. 12-12).

SPA-IO-AREA

LL	ZZ	01	CUSTORDR	00029000	00..............0	1	Call GU

INPUT-MESSAGE-AREA

LL	ZZ	12345	09			Call GN

Fig. 12-11. Second cycle of the conversation.

INPUT-MESSAGE-AREA

LL	ZZ	12345	09		

SEGMENT-IO-AREA

12345	09	

ISRT

CUST-SSA

CUSTMSTR(CUSTNUMB=00029000)

ITEM-SSA

ITEMNUMBb

Fig. 12-12.

The program then saves the item number and the quantity ordered in the SPA-IO-AREA. The cycle switch is now incremented to 2, and the program issues an ISRT call to return the SPA to IMS (FIG. 12-13).

SPA-IO-AREA

LL	ZZ	01	CUSTORDR	00029000	12345	09	00..........	2

Call
ISRT

Fig. 12-13.

The program builds the response consisting of the item number, the quantity ordered, and the status of the order, and issues an ISRT call against IO-PCB to load the response to the message queue (FIG. 12-14).

OUTPUT-MESSAGE-AREA

LL	ZZ	12345	09	ORDER ACCEPTED

ISRT
response

Fig. 12-14. Status of the order.

Third Cycle

The third cycle of the conversation is initiated when the operator enters the second order:

```
CUSTOMER 00029000 VALID

ENTER ITEM AND QUANTITY
        12345      09   ORDER ACCEPTED
        23456      08
```

The processing is similar to that of the previous cycle (FIG. 12-15):

- Retrieve the SPA with a GU call.
- Get the input message with a GN call.
- Validate the input and insert data in the database with an ISRT call.
- Save information in the SPA with an ISRT call.
- Build a response and place it on the message queue with an ISRT call.

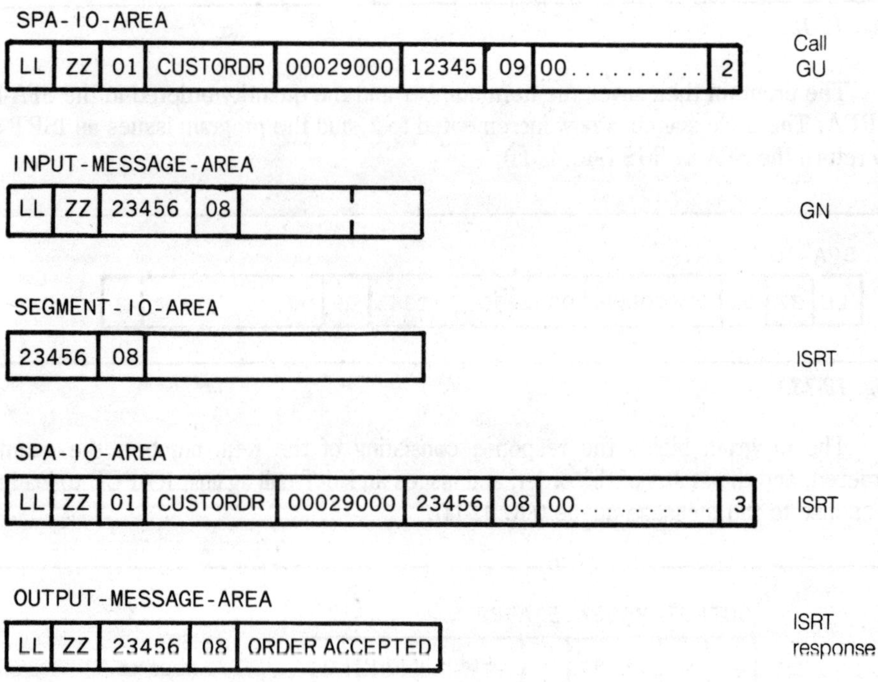

Fig. 12-15. Third cycle of the conversation.

- The contents of the SPA saved in the third cycle are obtained with a GU call.
- The next GN call gets the message END, indicating that there are no more orders by this customer.
- The program builds the fourth response and issues an ISRT call against the IO-PCB to load the response to the message queue.

SPA-IO-AREA

LL	ZZ	01	CUSTORDR	00029000	23456	08	00..........	3

Call GU

INPUT-MESSAGE-AREA

LL	ZZ	END

Call GN

OUTPUT-MESSAGE-AREA

LL	ZZ	CONVERSATION COMPLETE

ISRT response

Fig. 12-16. Fourth cycle of the conversation.

Fourth Cycle

Assuming that no more orders are to be entered, the operator responds by entering END (FIG. 12-16):

```
ENTER ITEM AND QUANTITY
        12345    09  ORDER ACCEPTED
        23456    08  ORDER ACCEPTED
        END
```

Terminating the Conversation

To terminate the conversation, the program blanks out the transaction code in SPA-IO-AREA and returns the SPA to IMS (FIG. 12-17). Since the transaction of the SPA is now blank, IMS frees the logical terminal LTERMAA for a new conversation (FIG. 12-18).

SPA-IO-AREA

LL	ZZ	01	bbbbbbbb	00029000	23456	08	00..........	3

ISRT

↑ Transaction Code (points to bbbbbbbb)

Fig. 12-17.

LTERMAA SPA

	bbbbbbbb	

Fig. 12-18.

The final cycle of the conversation appears below:

```
ENTER ITEM AND QUANTITY
       12345    09   ORDER ACCEPTED
       23456    08   ORDER ACCEPTED
       END
CONVERSATION COMPLETE
```

Note the following before we proceed:

- In each interaction of a conversation, you must send a response back to the terminal user for more data entry. The terminal will be in the waiting mode before a reply is received from the operator. You can send the response via an ISRT call against the IO-PCB or through another conversational program using an alternate PCB.
- If updates to a database are required, you should do these only in the last interaction of a conversation after all data have been collected for updating. This is to maintain database integrity in case a backout is needed for automatic recovery by IMS.

SWITCHING CONTROL BETWEEN CONVERSATIONAL PROGRAMS

In chapter 11, we presented the technique of program-to-program message switching involving nonconversational programs. This section will describe the flexible feature of switching control between conversational programs.

Deferred Message Switching

To accomplish message switching from one conversational program to another, you have to change the transaction code stored in the SPA-IO-AREA before issuing the ISRT call to return the SPA. This is called deferred message switching. When the terminal operator sends the next message, programs related to the new transaction code in the SPA will be scheduled. This transfer of control is transparent to the operator because the new program accesses the SPA saved by the first program, and there is no intervention by the operator.

As an example, let's examine the Customer Order program. The application is now divided into two programs (FIG. 12-19):

1. The CUSTORDR program performs editing and validation of the customer information.
2. The ITEMUPDT program accepts the orders entered and updates the order database.

Cycle One: Processing by the CUSTORDR Program.

1. The conversation is initiated when the operator enters the transaction code CUSTORDR and the customer number 00029000. Program CUSTORDR is scheduled.
2. Retrieve the SPA via a GU call.
3. Obtain the message text via a GN call.
4. Validate the customer number via calls against the customer database.
5. Save the information essential to continuing the conversation in the SPA-IO-AREA (i.e., the customer number). The program also changes the transaction code CUSTORDR to ITEMUPDT before returning the SPA to IMS.
6. Return the SPA to IMS via an ISRT call against the IO-PCB.
7. Send a response to the originating terminal LTERMAA via an ISRT call.

This concludes the first cycle of the conversation.

Cycle Two: Processing by the ITEMUPDT Program. The operator initiates the second cycle of the conversation by entering the item number 12345 and 09 as the quantity ordered. The logical terminal LTERRMAA is now connected to the ITEMUPDT transaction message queue because, in the previous step, the transaction code in the SPA had been changed to that of the second program before the SPA was returned to IMS.

ITEMUPDT is now scheduled. The processing is similar to the previous cycle:

8. Retrieve the SPA via a GU call.
9. Obtain the message text via a GN call.
10. Validate input and insert data to the customer database via an ISRT call.
11. Save the information essential to continuing the conversation in the SPA-IO-AREA (i.e., the item number, the quantity ordered). Increment the SPA switch by 1.
12. Return the SPA to IMS via an ISRT call against the IO-PCB.
13. Build a response and place it on the message queue via an ISRT call. The inputting terminal is informed of the status of the order.

This concludes the second cycle of the conversation.

When the next order is entered, the ITEMUPDT program is scheduled again because the transaction code ITEMUPDT remains in the LTERMAA SPA.

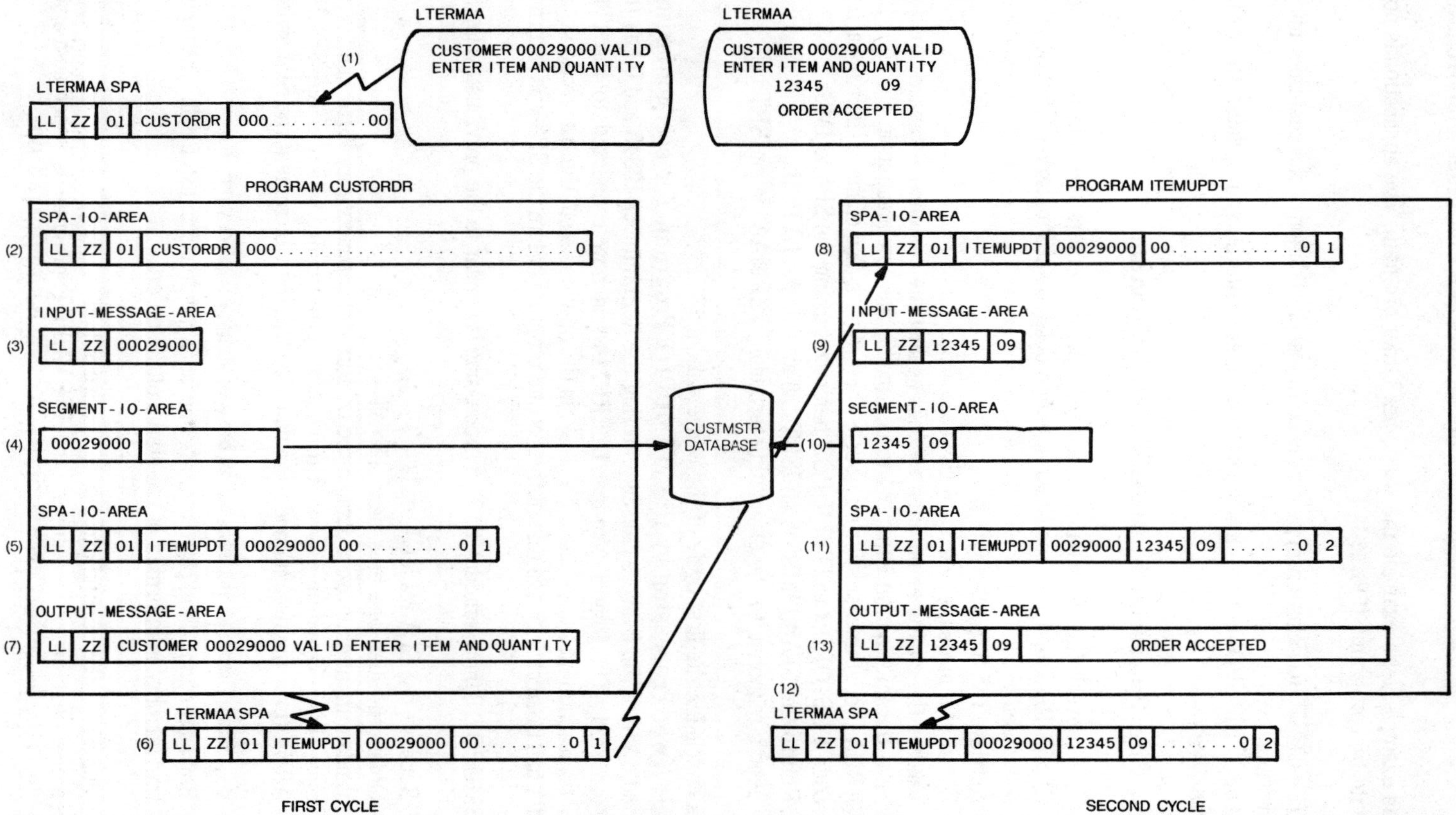
LTERMAA
CUSTOMER 00029000 VALID
ENTER ITEM AND QUANTITY
LTERMAA
CUSTOMER 00029000 VALID
ENTER ITEM AND QUANTITY
12345 09
ORDER ACCEPTED
(1)
LTERMAA SPA
LL ZZ 01 CUSTORDR 000..........00
PROGRAM CUSTORDR
SPA-IO-AREA
(2) LL ZZ 01 CUSTORDR 000.............0
INPUT-MESSAGE-AREA
(3) LL ZZ 00029000
SEGMENT-IO-AREA
(4) 00029000
SPA-IO-AREA
(5) LL ZZ 01 ITEMUPDT 00029000 00..........0 1
OUTPUT-MESSAGE-AREA
(7) LL ZZ CUSTOMER 00029000 VALID ENTER ITEM AND QUANTITY
LTERMAA SPA
(6) LL ZZ 01 ITEMUPDT 00029000 00.........0 1
FIRST CYCLE
CUSTMSTR
DATABASE
(10)
PROGRAM ITEMUPDT
SPA-IO-AREA
(8) LL ZZ 01 ITEMUPDT 00029000 00.............0 1
INPUT-MESSAGE-AREA
(9) LL ZZ 12345 09
SEGMENT-IO-AREA
12345 09
SPA-IO-AREA
(11) LL ZZ 01 ITEMUPDT 0029000 12345 09 ....0 2
OUTPUT-MESSAGE-AREA
(13) LL ZZ 12345 09 ORDER ACCEPTED
(12)
LTERMAA SPA
LL ZZ 01 ITEMUPDT 00029000 12345 09 ....0 2
SECOND CYCLE

Fig. 12-19.

Immediate Message Switching

We can also switch control directly by inserting the current message to an alternate terminal PCB whose destination is the transaction code of another conversational program. This is called immediate switching. To bring this about, we have to insert the SPA-IO-AREA in the alternate terminal before inserting any message segments. Then, the new program will insert responses in the terminal and will return the SPA to the IO-PCB before it terminates.

As an example, suppose Program 1 has received an input message to be processed by Program 2 (FIG. 12-20). To effect immediate program-to-program message switching Program 1 will perform the following steps:

1. Replace the transaction code TRANS001 in the SPA-IO-AREA with that of the new program TRANS002.
2. Return the SPA to IMS by issuing an ISRT against the IO-PCB.
3. Pass the SPA to the new program by issuing an ISRT call against the alternate PCB which has a destination code identical to the transaction of the new program.
4. Pass additional information, if necessary, to the new program by issuing ISRT calls against the alternate PCB.

Now, refer to FIG. 12-21 for an example of new-program processing by the receiving program. To do this, we:

1. Retrieve the SPA with a GU call.
2. Obtain additional information, if any, with GN calls.
3. Process the information obtained.
4. Save the information essential for conversational continuity in the SPA-IO-AREA.
5. Return the SPA to IMS.
6. Send a response to the originating terminal by issuing an ISRT call against the IO-PCB.

The first cycle of the conversation is completed.

Summary of Conversational-Program Switching

Message-switching from one conversational program to another, either deferred or immediate mode, requires that the SPA and the messages be processed by the program that receives control. The first program, which issues the ISRT call to send the SPA to another program, no longer responds to the terminal

Since the same SPA is used by both programs, you have to ensure that the SPAs specified for them are compatible. A conversational program with a fixed-length SPA cannot transfer control to a program with a variable-length SPA; however, a program with a variable-length SPA can transfer control to a program with a fixed-length SPA.

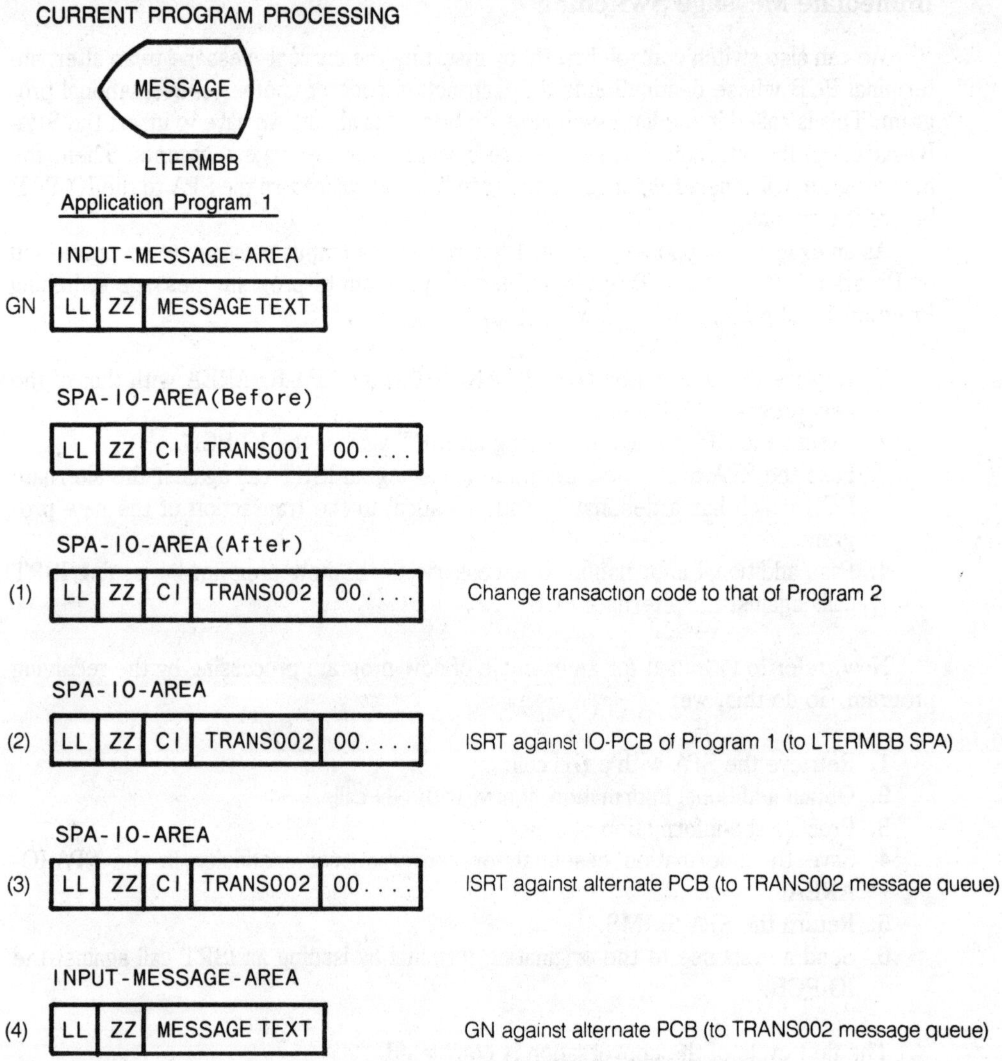

Fig. 12-20. Calls to affect an immediate message switch.

BASIC RULES FOR CONVERSATIONAL PROGRAMMING

Following are the basic rules for conversational programming:

1. Do not modify the SPA control fields.
2. The program must be able to handle a QC status code for the first GU call to the SPA.

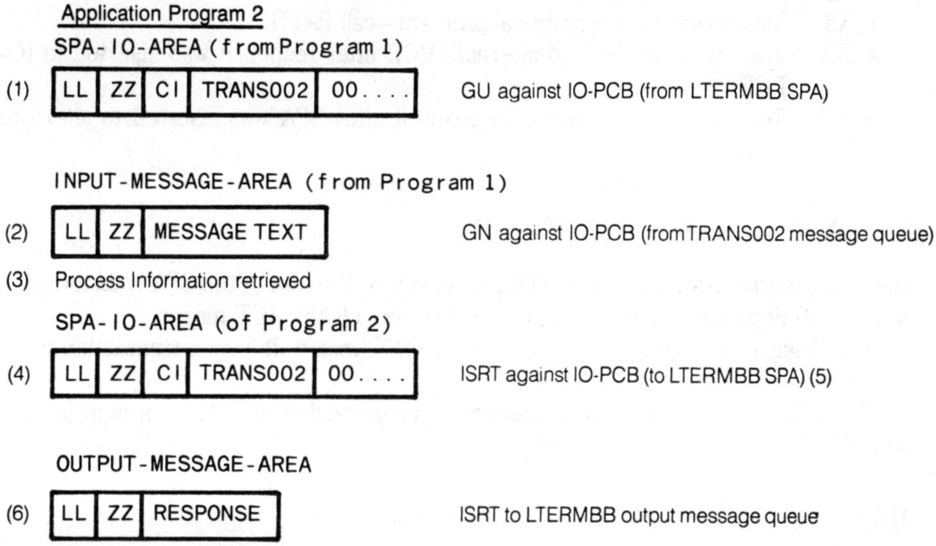

Fig. 12-21. Processing by receiving program.

3. Always respond to the logical terminal with a message, either by inserting a response to the IO-PCB or by passing control to another transaction code that replies to the operator.
4. When message-switching to a conversational transaction, the SPA must first be inserted in the alternate PCB.
5. Return of the SPA to IMS is optional, but if returned, it can be done only once.
6. The PURG call is not allowed. If issued, an AZ status code is returned.
7. The operator may not proceed until a reply has been received.

Status Codes for Calls to the SPA

The status code returned for calls using the SPA-IO-AREA should always be equal to spaces; any other value represents an error. Incorrect status codes returned for calls using the SPA are listed below.

CODE	DESCRIPTION
• X1	I-O error in reading or writing the SPA.
• X2	First insert to a conversational program was not for SPA.
• X3	User modified third through sixth bytes of SPA.
• X4	User tried to insert SPA to nonconversational program.
• X5	User tried to insert multiple SPAs.
• X6	Invalid transaction code placed in SPA.
• X7	Length specification of SPA has been changed (first 10 bytes).

- X8 Error while queuing a SPA.
- X9 Incompatible conversational program—call PATH.
- XA Tried to insert SPA to alternate PCB after response was inserted to IO-PCB.
- XB Tried to insert response to terminal after SPA was inserted to alternate PCB.

SPA STORAGE CONSIDERATIONS

When the program issues the GU call to the IO-PCB, the size of the SPA transferred to the I-O area depends on the length specified on the TRANSACT macro.

Specifying a SPA parameter in the TRANSACT macro defines a transaction to be conversational.

The SPA can reside either on a direct access storage device (DASD) or in main storage (CORE).

DISK

Using DISK allows large SPAs but slows access to the SPA because it involves disk read/write overhead. The read/write buffer is reserved when the conversation begins and is freed after the disk write is completed.

There is less possibility of delay due to buffer fragmentation than with the use of CORE.

CORE

Using CORE is fast and involves no disk read/write overhead. The SPA is obtained when the conversation begins and is freed when the conversation is terminated. Keeping the SPA in CORE saves time but uses more storage.

There is potential fragmentation of the general buffer pool and the fragmentation may degrade service to other terminals.

SPA Usage

- Avoid large scratch pad areas.
- If the SPA is modified, it must be inserted by the application program.
- Do not modify the SPA prefix (control Fields LL, ZZ, CI).
- When you message switch to a conversational transaction, the SPA must first be inserted against the alternate PCB.
- The SPA cannot be inserted against a PCB for a nonconversational transaction code.
- In conversational message switch processing, the first program to get control when the conversation begins determines the type of SPA (disk or core) assigned

to the conversation and, therefore, sets a maximum for the SPA size allowed for any program involved in the conversation.

- If every program involved in the conversation uses the same SPA size, the SPA can be defined as being FIXED.

CONVERSATIONAL PROCESSING OPTIONS

The following table summarizes the various conversational processing options with the types of PCBs referenced and the transaction codes, used in the SPA.

OPTIONS USED	PCB REFERENCED	SPA TRANSACTION CODE
1. Continue conversation	IO-PCB	Same transaction code
2. Deferred message switch (change program)	IO-PCB	New conversational transaction code
3. Immediate message switch (change program)	ALT-PCB	New conversational transaction code
4. Deferred message switch and conversation termination	IO-PCB	New nonconversational transaction code
5. Terminate conversation	IO-PCB	Blank out transaction code

A SAMPLE PROGRAM

Now that you have had exposure to conversational processing techniques, a complete COBOL conversational message processing program appears in FIG. 12-22. This program updates the customer database with new orders entered via a terminal. Here are the key points about it:

- The conversation is initiated when the terminal operator enters the CUSTORDR transaction code and the customer number.
- When the program is scheduled, it issues a GU call to retrieve the SPA and the SPA is moved to the SPA-IO-AREA which resides in the program's WORKING STORAGE.
- It then issues a GN call to retrieve the trailer segment which is moved to the program's input message area.
- The customer number is validated against the database via qualified calls.
- If the customer number is valid, the program saves the customer in the SPA and then sends a message to the operator to continue the conversation.
- If the customer is invalid, the program sends an error message to the operator and terminates the conversation by blanking out the transaction code in the SPA-IO-AREA and returns the SPA to IMS.

```
IDENTIFICATION DIVISION.
PROGRAM-ID. PROGRAM3.
AUTHOR.    ZIEP VUONG.
DATE-WRITTEN. AUGUST 1987.
REMARKS.
    *******************************************************
    *  THIS IS A SAMPLE CONVERSATION MESSAGE PROCESSING   *
    *   PROGRAM.                                          *
    *   . THE PROGRAM UPDATES THE CUSTOMER DATA BASE WITH *
    *     NEW ORDERS ENTERED VIA A TERMINAL.              *
    *******************************************************

ENVIRONMENT DIVISION.
CONFIGURATION SECTION.
SOURCE-COMPUTER.  IBM-370.
OBJECT-COMPUTER.  IBM-370.

DATA DIVISION.

WORKING-STORAGE SECTION.

01  FILLER                        PIC X(27)
                        VALUE 'WORKING-STORAGE BEGINS HERE'.

77  CUST-NOT-FOUND-MESSAGE        PIC X(19)
                        VALUE 'CUST NOT FOUND '.
77  NOTIFY-OPERATOR-MESSAGE       PIC X(14)
                        VALUE 'ERROR, REENTER'.
77  CONVER-COMPLETED-MESSAGE      PIC X(21)
                        VALUE 'CONVERSATION COMPLETE'.

01  END-SWITCH                    PIC X VALUE '0'.
    88  NO-MORE-INPUT                   VALUE '1'.

*****************************************************************
*                                                               *
*                    SCRATCH PAD AREA                           *
*    THE SPA-SWITCH IS INCREMENTED BY '1' DURING EACH CYCLE OF  *
*    THE CONVERSATION.                                          *
*                                                               *
*****************************************************************
*
 01  SPA-IO-AREA.
     05 SPA-LENGTH                  PIC S9(4) COMP.
     05 SPA-CONTROL                 PIC X(4).
     05 SPA-TRANCODE                PIC X(8).
     05 SPA-CUST-NO                 PIC X(8).
     05 SPA-ITEM                    PIC X(5).
     05 SPA-QTY                     PIC X(2).
     05 FILLER                      PIC X(10).
     05 SPA-SWITCH                  PIC S9(3) COMP.
       88 FIRST-CYCLE                     VALUE +0.
*
*  INPUT MESSAGE AREA
*
```

Fig. 12-22.

Fig. 12-22. continued

```
 01  INPUT-MESSAGE-AREA            PIC X(40).

 01  INPUT-MESSAGE REDEFINES INPUT-MESSAGE-AREA.
     05 HEADER-PREFIX.
        10 HEADER-LENGTH           PIC S999 COMP SYNC.
        10 FILLER                  PIC X(2).
     05 HEADER-TEXT.
        10 CUST-NUMBER             PIC X(8).
        10 FILLER                  PIC X(28).

 01  CYCLE-2-INPUT REDEFINES INPUT-MESSAGE-AREA.
     05 CYCLE-2-PREFIX.
        10 CYCLE-2-LENGTH          PIC S999 COMP SYNC.
        10 FILLER                  PIC X(2).
     05 CYCLE-2-TEXT.
        10 CYCLE-2-ITEM            PIC 9(5).
        10 CYCLE-2-QTY             PIC 9(2).
        10 FILLER                  PIC X(29).

 01  END-INPUT REDEFINES INPUT-MESSAGE-AREA.
     05 END-INPUT-PREFIX.
        10 END-INPUT-LENGTH        PIC S999 COMP SYNC.
        10 FILLER                  PIC X(2).
     05 END-INPUT-TEXT.
        10 END-INPUT-MESSAGE       PIC 9(3).
        10 FILLER                  PIC X(33).
*
*  OUTPUT MESSAGE AREA
*
 01  RESPONSE-1.
     05 PREFIX-1.
        10 RESP-1-LENGTH           PIC S999 COMP SYNC VALUE +0.
        10 RESP-1-ZZ               PIC S999 COMP SYNC VALUE +0.
     05 RESPONSE-1-TEXT.
        10 FILLER                  PIC X(8) VALUE 'CUSTOMER'.
        10 RESP-1-CUST-NUMBER      PIC 9(8).
        10 FILLER                  PIC X(5) VALUE 'VALID'.
        10 RESP-1-MESS             PIC X(23)
                         VALUE 'ENTER ITEM AND QUANTITY'.
*
 01  RESPONSE-2.
     05 PREFIX-2.
        10 RESP-2-LENGTH           PIC S999 COMP SYNC VALUE +0.
        10 RESP-2-ZZ               PIC S999 COMP SYNC VALUE +0.
     05 RESPONSE-2-TEXT.
        10 RESP-2-ITEM             PIC 9(5).
        10 RESP-2-QTY              PIC X(2).
        10 RESP-2-MESS             PIC X(15)
                         VALUE 'ORDER ACCEPTED'.
*
 01  COMMON-MESSAGE.
     05 COMM-PREFIX.
        10 COMM-LENGTH             PIC S999 COMP SYNC.
        10 COMM-ZZ                 PIC S999 COMP SYNC.
     05 MESSAGE-TEXT               PIC X(30).
*
```

Fig. 12-22. continued

```
*****************************************************************
*                                                               *
*                 DATA BASE SEGMENT LAYOUT                      *
*                                                               *
*****************************************************************
*
 01  SEGMENT-IO-AREA                  PIC X(30).
 01  CUST-IO-AREA REDEFINES SEGMENT-IO-AREA.
     05 CUST-NUMBER-KEY               PIC X(8).
     05 FILLER                        PIC X(22).
 01  ITEM-IO-AREA REDEFINES SEGMENT-IO-AREA.
     05 ITEM-NUMBER                   PIC X(5).
     05 QUANTITY                      PIC X(3).
     05 FILLER                        PIC X(23).
*
*****************************************************************
*                                                               *
*                 IMS CALL FUNCTION CODES                       *
*                                                               *
*****************************************************************
*
 01  IMS-CALL-FUNCTIONS.
     03  GU                           PIC X(4) VALUE 'GU  '.
     03  GN                           PIC X(4) VALUE 'GN  '.
     03  ISRT                         PIC X(4) VALUE 'ISRT'.
*
*****************************************************************
*                                                               *
*                 CUSTOMER DATA BASE'S SSA                      *
*                                                               *
*****************************************************************
*
 01  CUST-SSA.
     03  CUST-SEGMENT-NAME            PIC X(8) VALUE 'CUSTMSTR'.
     03  CUST-LEFT-PAREN              PIC X    VALUE '('.
     03  CUST-KEY-NAME                PIC X(8) VALUE 'CUSTNUMB'.
     03  CUST-OPRERATOR               PIC XX   VALUE ' ='.
     03  CUST-KEY-VALUE               PIC X(8) VALUE SPACES.
     03  CUST-RIGHT-PAREN             PIC X    VALUE ')'.
*
 LINKAGE SECTION.
*
 01  IO-PCB-MASK.
     05  ORIGIN-TERM-NAME             PIC X(8).
     05  IO-RESERVED                  PIC X(2).
     05  IO-STATUS-CODE               PIC X(2).
     05  IO-PREFIX.
         10 JULIAN-DATE               PIC S9(7) COMP-3.
         10 CURRENT-TIME              PIC S9(7) COMP-3.
         10 SEQUENCE-NO               PIC S9(7) COMP.
     05  IO-MODNAME                   PIC X(8).
*
 01  CUST-PCB-MASK.
     05  CUST-DBD-NAME                PIC X(8).
     05  CUST-SEG-LEVEL               PIC X(2).
     05  CUST-STATUS-CODE             PIC X(2).
```

Fig. 12-22. continued

```
            05  CUST-PROCESS-OPTIONS        PIC X(4).
            05  IMS-RESERVED                PIC S9(5) COMP.
            05  CUST-SEG-NAME-FB            PIC X(8).
            05  CUST-LENGTH-FB-KEY          PIC S9(5) COMP.
            05  CUST-NBR-SENS-SEG           PIC S9(5) COMP.
            05  CUST-KEY-FB-AREA            PIC X(8).
 PROCEDURE DIVISION.

     ENTRY 'DLITCBL' USING IO-PCB-MASK
                           CUST-PCB-MASK.

          PERFORM 0400-GET-SPA THRU 0400-GET-SPA-EXIT.
          PERFORM 0100-MAINLINE THRU 0100-MAINLINE-EXIT
                    UNTIL NO-MORE-INPUT.
          GOBACK.

 0100-MAINLINE.
*****************************************************************
*   FIRST OF ALL, CHECK THE SPA-SWITCH TO DETERMINE WHETHER IT   *
*   IS IN BINARY ZEROES. IF YES, THEN THIS IS THE FIRST CYCLE OF *
*   THE CONVERSATION, ELSE, THIS IS THE SECOND CYCLE OF THE      *
*   CONVERSATION.                                                *
*****************************************************************
     IF FIRST-CYCLE PERFORM 0200-PROCESS-CYCLE-1
                  THRU 0200-PROCESS-CYCLE-1-EXIT
     ELSE
        PERFORM 0300-PROCESS-CYCLE-2
                  THRU 0300-PROCESS-CYCLE-2-EXIT.

*   REPEAT THE MAINLINE LOOP

     PERFORM 0400-GET-SPA THRU 0400-GET-SPA-EXIT.

 0100-MAINLINE-EXIT. EXIT.

 0200-PROCESS-CYCLE-1.
*****************************************************************
*   THIS ROUTINE DOES THE FOLLOWING:                             *
* 1. RETRIEVE ANOTHER MESSAGE FROM THE MESSAGE QUEUE,            *
* 2. VALIDATE CUSTOMER VIA A GU CALL TO THE CUSTOMER DATA BASE,  *
* 3. SAVE THE INFORMATION IN THE SPA AND RETURN SPA TO IMS,      *
* 4. SEND A RESPONSE TO THE TERMINAL.                            *
*****************************************************************

     PERFORM 0500-GET-MESSAGE THRU 0500-GET-MESSAGE-EXIT.

     MOVE CUST-NUMBER TO CUST-KEY-VALUE.
     PERFORM 0950-READ-DATA-BASE THRU 0950-READ-DATA-BASE-EXIT.

*****************************************************************
*  IF CUSTOMER NUMBER IS INVALID, SEND A MESSAGE TO THE OPERATOR,*
*  BLANK OUT THE TRANSACTION CODE IN THE SPA,                    *
*  RETURN THE SPA TO IMS TO TERMINATE THE CONVERSATION,          *
*                 OTHERWISE                                      *
*  SAVE THE INFORMATION IN THE SPA, INCREMENT SPA-SWITCH BY 1,   *
```

Fig. 12-22. continued

```
*  RETURN THE SPA TO IMS,                                          *
*  SEND RESPONSE-1 TO THE OPERATOR TO CONTINUE THE CONVERSATION. *
*****************************************************************

       IF CUST-STATUS-CODE EQUAL 'GE'
          PERFORM 0970-CUSTOMER-NOT-FOUND
                              THRU 0970-CUSTOMER-NOT-FOUND-EXIT
          MOVE SPACES TO SPA-TRANCODE
          PERFORM 0600-RETURN-SPA THRU 0600-RETURN-SPA-EXIT
       ELSE
          MOVE CUST-NUMBER TO SPA-CUST-NO
          ADD +1 TO SPA-SWITCH
          PERFORM 0600-RETURN-SPA THRU 0600-RETURN-SPA-EXIT
          PERFORM 0700-SEND-RESPONSE-1
                              THRU 0700-SEND-RESPONSE-1-EXIT.
 0200-PROCESS-CYCLE-1-EXIT. EXIT.

 0300-PROCESS-CYCLE-2.
*
*  GET SUBSEQUENT MESSAGE SEGMENTS.
*

       PERFORM 0500-GET-MESSAGE THRU 0500-GET-MESSAGE-EXIT.

*****************************************************************
*  IF THE OPERATOR REQUESTS TO END THE CONVERSATION,              *
*  BLANK OUT THE TRANSACTION CODE IN THE SPA TO TERMINATE         *
*  THE CONVERSATION, OTHERWISE ACCEPT THE ITEM ORDERED.           *
*****************************************************************
       IF END-INPUT-MESSAGE EQUAL 'END'
          MOVE SPACES TO SPA-TRANCODE
          PERFORM 0600-RETURN-SPA THRU 0600-RETURN-SPA-EXIT
          PERFORM 0900-SEND-ENDING-MESSAGE
                              THRU 0900-SEND-ENDING-MESSAGE-EXIT
       ELSE
          PERFORM 0960-INSERT-ITEM-SEGMENT
                              THRU 0960-INSERT-ITEM-SEGMENT-EXIT
          MOVE CYCLE-2-ITEM  TO SPA-ITEM
          MOVE CYCLE-2-QTY   TO SPA-QTY
          ADD +1 TO SPA-SWITCH
          PERFORM 0600-RETURN-SPA THRU 0600-RETURN-SPA-EXIT
          PERFORM 0800-SEND-RESPONSE-2
                              THRU 0800-SEND-RESPONSE-2-EXIT.
 0300-PROCESS-CYCLE-2-EXIT. EXIT.
 0400-GET-SPA.

       CALL 'CBLTDLI' USING GU
                            IO-PCB-MASK
                            SPA-IO-AREA.

*
*  IF STATUS CODE 'QC' IS RETURNED SET END-SWITCH ON
*
       IF IO-STATUS-CODE EQUAL 'QC'
          MOVE '1' TO END-SWITCH
       ELSE
```

Fig. 12-22. continued

```
     IF IO-STATUS-CODE NOT EQUAL SPACES
        PERFORM 1000-ERROR-ROUTINE.
 0400-GET-SPA-EXIT. EXIT.

 0500-GET-MESSAGE.

     CALL 'CBLTDLI' USING GN
                          IO-PCB-MASK
                          INPUT-MESSAGE-AREA.

     IF IO-STATUS-CODE NOT EQUAL SPACES
        PERFORM 1000-ERROR-ROUTINE.
 0500-GET-MESSAGE-EXIT. EXIT.

 0600-RETURN-SPA.

     CALL 'CBLTDLI' USING ISRT
                          IO-PCB-MASK
                          SPA-IO-AREA.

     IF IO-STATUS-CODE NOT EQUAL SPACES
        PERFORM 1000-ERROR-ROUTINE.
 0600-RETURN-SPA-EXIT. EXIT.
 0700-SEND-RESPONSE-1.
*
*   SEND OUTPUT MESSAGE TO ORIGINAL TERMINAL.
*

     MOVE CUST-NUMBER        TO RESP-1-CUST-NUMBER.
     MOVE +48                TO RESP-1-LENGTH.
     MOVE +0                 TO RESP-1-ZZ.

     CALL 'CBLTDLI' USING ISRT
                          IO-PCB-MASK
                          RESPONSE-1.

     IF IO-STATUS-CODE NOT EQUAL SPACES
        PERFORM 1000-ERROR-ROUTINE.
 0700-SEND-RESPONSE-1-EXIT. EXIT.

 0800-SEND-RESPONSE-2.
*
*  INFORM THE OPERATOR THAT THE ORDER HAS BEEN ACCEPTED
*

     MOVE CYCLE-2-ITEM       TO RESP-2-ITEM.
     MOVE CYCLE-2-QTY        TO RESP-2-QTY.
     MOVE +26                TO RESP-2-LENGTH.
     MOVE +0                 TO RESP-2-ZZ.

     CALL 'CBLTDLI' USING ISRT
                          IO-PCB-MASK
                          RESPONSE-2.

     IF IO-STATUS-CODE NOT EQUAL SPACES
        PERFORM 1000-ERROR-ROUTINE.
```

Fig. 12-22. continued

```
 0800-SEND-RESPONSE-2-EXIT. EXIT.

 0900-SEND-ENDING-MESSAGE.
*
*  INFORM THE OPERATOR THAT THE CONVERSATION IS COMPLETE
*

     MOVE CONVER-COMPLETED-MESSAGE TO MESSAGE-TEXT.
     MOVE +34                  TO COMM-LENGTH.
     MOVE +0                   TO COMM-ZZ.

     CALL 'CBLTDLI' USING ISRT
                          IO-PCB-MASK
                          COMMON-MESSAGE.

     IF IO-STATUS-CODE NOT EQUAL SPACES
        PERFORM 1000-ERROR-ROUTINE.
 0900-SEND-ENDING-MESSAGE-EXIT. EXIT.

 0950-READ-DATA-BASE.
*
*  READ CUSTOMER DATA BASE TO VALIDATE THE CUSTOMER NUMBER
*

     CALL 'CBLTDLI' USING GU
                          CUST-PCB-MASK
                          CUST-IO-AREA
                          CUST-SSA.

     IF CUST-STATUS-CODE EQUAL SPACES OR 'GE'
     NEXT SENTENCE
     ELSE
        PERFORM 2000-DB-ERROR-ROUTINE.
 0950-READ-DATA-BASE-EXIT. EXIT.

 0960-INSERT-ITEM-SEGMENT.
*
*  BUILD ITEM SEGMENT AND INSERT INTO THE DATA BASE
*

     MOVE CUST-NUMBER          TO CUST-KEY-VALUE.
     MOVE CYCLE-2-ITEM         TO ITEM-NUMBER.
     MOVE CYCLE-2-QTY          TO QUANTITY.

     CALL 'CBLTDLI' USING ISRT
                          CUST-PCB-MASK
                          CUST-IO-AREA
                          CUST-SSA.

     IF CUST-STATUS-CODE NOT EQUAL SPACES
        PERFORM 2000-DB-ERROR-ROUTINE.
 0960-INSERT-ITEM-SEGMENT-EXIT. EXIT.

 0970-CUSTOMER-NOT-FOUND.
*
*  INFORM THE OPERATOR OF INVALID CUSTOMER NUMBER
```

Fig. 12-22. continued

```
*
         MOVE CUST-NOT-FOUND-MESSAGE TO MESSAGE-TEXT.
         MOVE +34 TO COMM-LENGTH.

         CALL 'CBLTDLI' USING ISRT
                              IO-PCB-MASK
                              COMMON-MESSAGE.

         IF IO-STATUS-CODE NOT EQUAL SPACES
            PERFORM 1000-ERROR-ROUTINE.
 0970-CUSTOMER-NOT-FOUND-EXIT. EXIT.
*****************************************************************
*  THE IO ERROR ROUTINE IS EXECUTED WHENEVER AN UNEXPECTED      *
*  STATUS CODE IS RETURNED; THIS ROUTINE VARIES FROM INSTALLATION*
*  INSTALLATION.                                                *
*  YOU SHOULD CHECK YOUR INSTALLATION'S STANDARDS ON HOW TO     *
*  CODE THIS ROUTINE.                                           *
*  THE CODING FOR THIS ROUTINE IS NOT PROVIDED HERE.            *
*****************************************************************
 1000-ERROR-ROUTINE.
*              CODE ERROR ROUTINE HERE
        .....
        GOBACK.

*****************************************************************
*  THE FOLLOWING ERROR ROUTINE IS EXECUTED WHENEVER A BAD STATUS *
*  CODE IS RETURNED FOR A DATA BASE CALL.                       *
*  MOST INSTALLATIONS REQUEST TO DISPLAY THE TYPE OF CALL, THE  *
*  RETURNED STATUS CODE, THE KEY VALUE OF THE SSA AND THEN CALL *
*  A USER WRITTEN SUBROUTINE TO FORMAT A DUMP FOR DEBUGGING.    *
*****************************************************************
 2000-DB-ERROR-ROUTINE.

           DISPLAY 'GET CALL ERROR TO CUSTOMER DATA BASE'.
           DISPLAY 'STATUS CODE: ' CUST-STATUS-CODE.
           DISPLAY 'CUSTOMER NUMBER:' CUST-KEY-VALUE.
*
*          CALL 'ABENDPGM' TO PRINT DUMP.
```

The terminal operator initiates the second cycle of the conversation by entering the item number and the quantity ordered. The operator need not enter the CUSTORDR transaction code because it is saved in the SPA.

- The Customer Order program is scheduled again.
- The program processes the input message, validates the fields entered, and issues an ISRT call to place the item ordered into the CUSTMSTR database.
- The program builds a response consisting of the item number, the quantity ordered, and the status of the order, and loads the response to the message queue and then returns the SPA.

This concludes the second cycle of the conversation.

The third cycle is initiated when the operator enters another order. Processing is similar to that of the previous cycle.

When the operator responds by entering END, the program terminates the conversation by entering blanks into the transaction code area of the SPA and returns the SPA to IMS.

13

Batch Message Processing

In this chapter, you will learn how to develop Batch message processing applications. Batch message processing (BMP) programs run in online and batch-oriented regions. The BMP region provides partial online processing capabilities: It receives and stores messages from terminals for processing against the databases at a later time.

Like a message processing program, a BMP can process transactions from the message queue and access online databases; however, a BMP is scheduled through an OS JCL job stream. Because a BMP is scheduled through a JCL, it does not begin to run as soon as a BMP region is available; online transactions are batched by IMS for presentation to the BMP whenever it is scheduled to run.

WHY BMP PROCESSING?

One of the advantages of BMP processing is that it can receive input transactions that are sent by MP programs. These transactions are captured and queued for batch-type processing during nonpeak hours. This helps reduce the response time it takes the MP program to process and respond. Unlike traditional batch-type programs, the BMP can access online databases concurrently with MP programs and perform batch-type processing concurrently with message processing. BMPs are generally used to perform batch-type processing online, but can also send and receive messages.

We can distinguish two types of BMPs:

- Transaction-oriented BMPs which access message queues for input.
- Batch-oriented BMPs which do not access message queues for input. They simply access online databases. They can also send output to message queues.

BMPs are commonly large jobs which cannot be effectively done by MP programs. They are used when DL/1 databases must be available online all the time and the volume of transactions is too large to be processed by MP programs. BMPs are also used when tapes are involved, and can process OS/VS data sets.

A BMP TRANSACTION FLOW

Normally, online transactions are immediately processed by the appropriate message processing program. However, it is sometimes more efficient to accumulate all online transactions in a message queue and then process them all at once in a batch mode.

For example, adding new customers to a database may not require immediate processing. The transactions can be entered online via remote terminals and then accumulated in the message queue and processed all at once using a BMP program. This can be accomplished by assigning the associated message queue a priority level of 0. This prevents transactions from being processed online and forces them to accumulate in the message queue. This accumulation can be monitored by the operator and, when the predetermined number is reached, a BMP program is scheduled to execute in a BMP region.

SCHEDULING A BATCH MESSAGE PROCESSING PROGRAM

A BMP program is scheduled via a JCL in the OS job stream.

```
//BMPRUN      PROC PSB=E0620040,MBR=E0620040,
//            IN=,OUT=,OPT=N,SPIE=0,
//            TEST=0,DIRCA=000,PRLD=,STIMER=,
//            CKPTID=,PARDLI=,CPUTIME=,NBA=,
//            OBA=,IMSID=,AGN=,RGN=2048K
                (1)                (2)
//STEP10      EXEC PGM=DFSPROC00,REGION=&RGN,
              (3)  (4)  (5)  (6)  (7)  (8)
//            PARM=(BMP,&MBR,&PSB,&IN,&OUT,
//            &OPT&SPIE&TEST&DIRCA,&PRLD,&STIMER,&CKPTID,
//            &PARDLI,&CPUTIME,&NBA,&OBA,&IMSID,&AGN)
//STEPLIB     DD  DSN=IMSVS.RESLIB,DISP=SHR
//            DD  DSN=PRODLIB,DISP=SHR
//IMSACB      DD  DSN=IMSVS.ACBLIB,DISP=SHR
//IMS         DD  DSN=IMSVS.PSBLIB,DISP=SHR
//            DD  DSN=IMSVS.DBDLIB,DISP=SHR
//SYSPRINT    DD SYSOUT=A
//DFSRESLB    DD DSN=IMSVS.RESLIB.DISP=SHR
```

The following describes the function and use of the parameters contained in the EXEC statement. The numbers next to the parameters correspond to the following explanation.

1. The PGM parameter refers to the IMS/VS region controller DFSRRCOO.
2. The REGION parameter specifies the size of the region.
3. The PARM parameter provides the region controller with the information needed to set up a region.
4. BMP (Region Type) means a Batch Message Processing region is specified.
5. MBR (Program Name) is the name of the program which will execute out of the region just specified.
6. PSB (PSB Name) optional parameter, specifies the name of the ACB for the program. The PSB name needs not be identical to the MBR name. This allows the application program to access different databases during different executions. If PSB is not specified, the default is MBR name.
7. IN (Transaction Code) specifies an input transaction code. This parameter is required when the BMP program accesses the message queue. If this parameter is specified, the OUT parameter is ignored.
8. OUT (Action to be taken) specifies the action to be taken if the batch message region starts and no control program is active.

   N = ask operator for decision. This is the default
   W = wait for a control program
   C= cancel the batch message region automatically.

   A value of N, W or C must appear on the JCL statement generated for this parameter.
9. CKPTID specifies the checkpoint ID at which the BMP program is to be restarted. It can be one to eight characters long for an extended checkpoint ID, or a 12-character "time stamp" checkpoint ID.

For BMP jobs, databases are controlled by IMS/VS and must not be specified in the JCL. The databases to be accessed by the BMP program are specified before execution via an ACBGEN job which combines the associated DBDs and PDBs. This will be discussed in chapter 14.

For other parameters not discussed here, please consult the IMB System Programmer's Reference Manual.

Using a Checkpoint PCB

Since all online PSBs contain an IO-PCB, parameter CMPAT=YES must be specified in the PSB to cause an IO-PCB to be generated for the batch PSB. This will allow the same program to execute in a batch or online mode.

JCL Modifications for a DL/1 Run

Minor JCL changes will allow a BMP job which does not access the message queues to run in a batch DL/1 mode and vice versa. The following program illustrates the JCL changes to our sample BMP procedure so that it can run under the DL/1 mode. Note the change in the PARM= card, and that databases that the program accesses must be specified.

```
//BMPRUN        PROC PSB=E0620040,MBR=E0620040,
//              IN=,OUT=,OPT=N,SPIE=0,                          FOR BMP
//              TEST=0,DIRCA=000,PRLD=,STIMER=,                 FOR BMP
//              CKPTID=,PARDLI=,CPUTIME=,NBA=,                  FOR BMP
//              OBA=IMSID=,AGN=,RGN=2048                        FOR BMP
//STEP20        EXEC PGM=DFSRRCOO,REGION=RGN,
//*             PARM=(DLI,&MBR,&PSB)                 FOR DL/1
                DL/1 specifies a batch region
//              PARM=(BMP,&MBR,&PSB,&IN,&OUT,                   FOR BMP
//              &OPT&SPIE&TEST&DIRCA,&PRLD,&STIMER,&CKPTID,     FOR BMP
//              &PARDLI,&CPUTIME,&NBA,&OBA,&IMSID,&AGN)         FOR BMP
//STEPLIB       DD   DSN=IMSVS.RESLIB,DISP-SHR
//              DD   DSN=PRODLIB,DISP=SHR
//IMSACB        DD   DSN=IMSVS.ACBLIB,DISP=SHR
//IMS           DD   DSN=IMSVS.PSBLIB,DISP=SHR
//              DD   DSN=IMSVS.DBDLIB,DISP=SHR
//SYSPRINT      DD   SYSOUT=A
//DFSRESLB      DD   DSN=IMSVS.RESLIB,DISP=SHR
//*   Databases to be specified for DL/1 run.
//*
//*DDACCAPR DD DSN=P06.IMNI0000.DDACCAPR,DISP=OLD       FOR DLI
//*DDACCAIX DD DSN=P06.IMNI0000.DDACCAIX,DISP=OLD
//*
```

SYNCHRONIZATION OF BMP PROCESSING

A BMP program usually takes longer to run if it has a great deal of DL/1 activity. This may degrade overall performance of all running programs because it can heavily tax system facilities. The Program may cause many database records to be enqueued by IMS/VS, thus preventing online programs from accessing the required data.

Such potential problems can be avoided if the program generates synchronization points at suitable frequencies by issuing CHKP calls. The CHKP call is used to create synchronization points to make reserved resources available to other users and to provide a point for program restart if there is program error.

Due to the large volume of transactions processed by a BMP program, we should issue a CHKP call for every 1,500 update calls. An ISRT and a DLET call are counted as three calls. When a CHKP call is issued, DL/1 writes to the databases all buffers that were modified by the BMP program. A log record is also created which contains the checkpoint ID passed by the CHKP call.

If the program abends, we can restart it from the checkpoint rather than from the beginning. The checkpoint ID is specified in the EXEC parameter of the JCL.

For most data centers, BMP programs are assigned a special scheduling class so that their scheduling can be controlled. This prevents them from using too many resources to the detriment of other program runs. BMP programs can process tapes, but can drastically increase processing time.

THE IMS CHECKPOINT/RESTART FACILITY

The checkpoint/restart facility allows a program to be restarted at a point other than the beginning when the program abends. While the program is running, it issues checkpoint calls which establish synchronization points throughout the program. At such points, IMS sends a message to the console operator and writes information about the database call on the system log. If the program abends, it can be restarted from a sync point rather than from the beginning.

Types of Checkpoint/Restart

There are two types of checkpoint/restart available under IMS/VS: basic and symbolic (or extended). Basic and symbolic checkpoint calls are similar in that the issuance of either in a batch program causes IMS to generate synchronization points. The main differences between these two calls are as follow:

1. The basic checkpoint call must request an OS/VS checkpoint/restart or a user-written program restart because it cannot issue the restart call. When a program issues a symbolic checkpoint call, it must use the restart call which restores user areas that were checkpointed in the program.
2. Another difference concerns access of OS/VS files. If a program issues a symbolic checkpoint call, it can access regular OS/VS files, but these will not be opened or repositioned by IMS during restart. These files must be converted to GSAM files. The advantage of using GSAM files is that, if a program has to be restarted, the restart call automatically repositions GSAM input and output files.
3. No program changes are permitted between the time of failure and restarting if we use the basic checkpoint option. At restart time, the same address space must be made available. With symbolic checkpoint/restart, program changes between failure and restart are permitted.
4. With the symbolic checkpoint, no coding of the data descriptions for OS/VS files is needed, but the coding of a GSAM-PCB-MASK for input or output is required.

Use the symbolic checkpoint/restart whenever possible because then it is easier to restart a program. However, if you can't convert OS/VS files to GSAM, then use the basic checkpoint/restart.

The following sections will present the formats of the basic and symbolic checkpoint/restart calls.

Basic Checkpoint Function

The basic checkpoint call is used if the program accesses OS/VS files that cannot be converted to GSAM. Since the basic checkpoint call can only checkpoint OS/VS files, we must use the OS/VS system restart on the call to restart the program.

To indicate to IMS that we want to use the OS/VS checkpoint, we have to provide the checkpoint DCB on the basic checkpoint call and the data set DD statements. IMS issues the OS/VS checkpoint and takes its own checkpoint.

The format of the basic CHKP call is:

```
CALL 'CBLTDLI' USING CHKP
                        PCB-IO-TERM
                        CP-CKPT-ID
                        [Checkpoint function].
```

PCB-IO-TERM is the checkpoint call that must reference an IO-PCB coded in the LINKAGE SECTION, and CP-CKPT-ID is an area eight-bytes long containing the checkpoint ID.

The checkpoint function causes IMS to request that a checkpoint be taken of the region in addition to the program checkpoint that IMS takes. This is an eight-byte field that contains the value OSVSCHKP. If this parameter is specified, we must supply one or two checkpoint data sets. IMS will provide the DCBs (names CHKDD and CHKDD2), and will issue an OS/VS checkpoint before issuing the basic checkpoint call. The checkpoint DCB cannot be used in COBOL or PL/1; it can be used only in the Assembler language.

Symbolic Checkpoint Function

The symbolic checkpoint call is similar to basic checkpointing but is used along with the extended XRST call in a batch or BMP processing mode. When used together, the symbolic checkpoint and extended restart calls provide an advantage: They allow us to store program data along with the checkpoint record and to retrieve data when it is necessary to restart the program after a failure.

In the BMP mode, an XD status code may be returned, meaning that IMS is terminating and no more DL/1 calls can be issued.

The format of the symbolic CHKP call is:

```
CALL 'CBLTDLI' USING CHKP
                        PCB-IO-TERM
                        CP-LENGTH-IO-AREA
                        CP-CKPT-ID
                        CP-LENGTH-PGM-VAR
                        PROGRAM-VARIABLE-AREA.
```

- PCB-IO-TERM is the checkpoint call that must reference an IO-PCB coded in the LINKAGE SECTION.
- LENGTH-IO-AREA is the length of the largest database I-O area in the program.
- CP-CKPT-ID is an area eight-bytes-long containing the checkpoint ID. IMS uses this ID to identify the checkpoint to the master terminal operator and on the system log. The checkpoint ID is in EBCDIC characters.
- LENGTH-PGM-VAR is the length of the area to be checkpointed.
- PROGRAM-VARIABLE-AREA is the area to be checkpointed.

LENGTH-PGM-VAR and PROGRAM-VARIABLE-AREA form a pair of field names to specify the working storage areas we want to save along with the checkpoint record. In each pair, the first item is the length of the area to be saved, and the second is the name of the data area to be saved. Up to seven pairs of field names can be coded.

Restart Function

The restart call is activated in a batch or batch message processing mode by a checkpoint ID supplied in the EXEC parameter of the JCL. The XRST call must be the first call to IMS and is issued only once.

The format of the XRST call is:

```
CALL 'CBLTDLI' USING XRST
                     PCB-IO-TERM
                     CP-LENGTH-IO-AREA
                     CP-WORK-AREA
                     CP-LENGTH-PGM-VAR
                     PROGRAM-VARIABLE-AREA.
```

- PCB-IO-TERM is the checkpoint call that must reference an IO-PCB coded in the LINKAGE SECTION.
- LENGTH-IO-AREA is the length of the largest database I-O area in the program.
- CP-WORK-AREA is an area 12-bytes-long containing the checkpoint ID on return. The contents of this field determine the type of scheduling:
  - Normal scheduling has blanks.
  - Restart scheduling has an eight-bytes-long checkpoint ID or 12 bytes for the date and time.
- LENGTH-PGM-VAR is the length of the area to be restored.
- PROGRAM-VARIABLE-AREA is the area to be restored.

Note:

1. The number of areas specified in the XRST call must be equal to the maximum areas specified in the CHKP call.
2. The length of the areas to be restored must be equal to and in the same order specified in the CHKP call.
3. The maximum number of areas to be restored is seven.

Checkpoint ID

The checkpoint ID must be provided when a program is to be restarted. This ID is required because, at restart time, IMS reads the system log tape and searches the checkpoint log record with the ID that matches the one provided via the Parm field of the EXEC statement. The first ID that matches the ID thus provided is the restart point for the program.

Checkpoint IDs must be unique even within the same BMP run. We can ensure that checkpoint IDs are unique by using IDs that contain:

- Four bytes of data uniquely identifying the program followed by
- Four bytes of a sequential number incremented by one with each successive CHKP call (see example below).

If the checkpoint IDs on a log tape are not unique, the date/time must be supplied at restart instead of checkpoint IDs.

```
01  WS-CKPT-BUILD-AREA.
    05 FILLER                   PIC X(4)   VALUE 'ZIEP'.   program
    05 WS-CKPT-COUNTER          PIC 9(4)   VALUE ZEROES.  identification

PROCEDURE DIVISION.

    ......
    ADD +1 TO WS-CKPT-COUNTER.          ← increment counter by 1.
    MOVE WS-CKPT-BUILD-AREA TO CP-CKPT-ID.
    CALL 'CBLTDLI' USING CHKP
                         PCB-IO-TERM
                         CP-LENGTH-IO-AREA
                         CP-CKPT-ID
                         .....
```

CHECKPOINT/RESTART DATA FLOW

When a normal start is performed, a flag is set to indicate that all CHKP calls are of an extended type, and when a CHKP call is issued, the following will be done:

- The fully-qualified key of each PCB is recorded on the system log.
- All buffers modified by the application program since the last synchronization point are written to the database.
- The checkpoint ID passed with the CHKP call is recorded on the system log.
- The program variable areas are also written to the system log.
- The current positions of all GSAM databases are formatted into a checkpoint log record and are written to the system log.

When a restart is performed, the following will be done:

- The program variable areas recorded at checkpoint time will be restored.
- The key feedback area and the status code for each PCB is restored.
- GSAM databases are automatically repositioned, other databases must be repositioned by the application program via GU calls.

CHECKPOINT CALL FREQUENCY

How often and where a program should issue checkpoint calls depends on the program's length and the type of processing it does. The main factor to be considered is the time it takes to back out and reprocess after a failure.

A checkpoint call issued every 10 to 15 minutes seems reasonable. The frequency must be easy to change if it is deemed too low or too high. One way to do this is to include in the program a counter to keep track of

- The elapsed time after a CHKP call is issued
- The number of database updates after a CHKP call is issued
- The number of segments read after a CHKP call is issued

If the entire run is to have backout capability, a CHKP call should be issued immediately after the XRST call at the beginning of the program. This establishes a checkpoint ID to specify when backing out the entire run.

The best place to issue a checkpoint call is right after a unit of work is completed and before we start the next unit. Since a GU call normally identifies a new unit of work, issuing a checkpoint immediately before issuing a GU call is preferable.

Checkpoint calls cause the position in the database to be lost, so they should never be issued when the position is important. The position in all databases (except GSAM databases) must be reestablished after each call.

WHEN TO USE CHECKPOINT/RESTART

1. For BMP runs, a checkpoint/restart must be used if the run updates databases or the message queue. This is required because BMP runs issue no synchronizations, resulting in dynamic log difficulties when the log fills. If the BMP does not update databases, a checkpoint/restart may be used so that dynamic backout and restart can take place instead of a batch utility backout and rerun.
2. For DL/1 batch runs, a checkpoint/restart should be used. This will save a lot of processing time by allowing for a restart of the batch run instead of recovery and reruns. A checkpoint also makes backout possible.
3. For MPP runs, logging and synchronization are automatically controlled by IMS, and synchronization points are generated whenever a GU call is issued against the message queue. The only reason to use CHKP calls in MPP runs is to group single messages from the message queue when a single message would generate a considerable number of database changes and message switches. (Here, specify MODE = MULT in the transaction macro.)
4. Most installations require the following of DL/1 update programs:
   - To be checkpoint/restart by IMS to ensure database integrity.
   - To execute in both DL/1 batch and BMP modes, thus allowing simultaneous online processing and BMP updating should job requirements remain unavailable until after online deadlines.
   - To begin execution in a DL/1 batch mode and complete processing in a BMP region, thus allowing an execution of the DL/1 batch update program to be shut down by the console operator and checkpoint/restarted in the BMP region to complete processing. This is used when an executing DL/1 batch update program approaches the online deadline.

HOW TO CODE THE CHECKPOINT/RESTART FACILITY

In the following sections, we will explain how to invoke the checkpoint/restart facility in a COBOL program. First, though, let's consider the source program components.

WORKING STORAGE

In the WORKING STORAGE section, you must code a CKPT-BUILD-AREA which contains the checkpoint information, and the PROGRAM-VARIABLE-AREA which contains all information you would like to restore when the program is checkpoint restarted.

Now, refer to FIG. 13-1 for the following:

- CP-WORK-AREA is a 12-bytes-long area containing the checkpoint ID supplied in the Parm parameter of the EXEC statement. The contents of this field determine the type of scheduling:
  - o Normal scheduling has blanks
  - o Restart Scheduling has an eight-bytes-long checkpoint ID or 12 bytes for the date and time.
- LENGTH-IO-AREA is the length of the largest database I-O area in the program to be restored if the program is to be restarted. The length should be equal to the longest segment of the database being called.
- LENGTH-PGM-VAR is the length of the area to be restored.
- CP-CKPT-ID is an area eight-bytes-long containing the checkpoint ID. IMS uses this ID to identify the checkpoint to the master terminal operator and on the system log.
- PROGRAM-VARIABLE-AREA is the area to be restored if the program is to be restarted. This area contains all the information we would like to have restored. Therefore, before issuing a CHKP call, we have to make sure that all the fields specified in this area are current up to that point.
- WTOR-MESSAGE-CALL-AREA embodies parameters to be passed to a user-written subroutine that issues a message to the console operator, thus allowing the job to be shut down. The contents of this field are set up in the PROCEDURE DIVISION. A sample user-written subroutine named E40REPLY is given in Appendix D.

LINKAGE SECTION

Refer to FIGURE 13-2 for the following:

- PCB-IO-TERM is the checkpoint call that must reference an IO-PCB coded in the LINKAGE SECTION. The IO-PCB enables the program to communicate with the online control region if the program is executing a BMP. This is also required if a DL/1 batch job issues IMS service calls such as CHKP, XRST, or LOG.

```
WORKING-STORAGE SECTION.

01  FILLER                       PIC X(50) VALUE
    '  **  WORKING STORAGE FOR PROGRAM4 BEGINS HERE'.

01  WS-CKPT-BUILD-AREA.
    05  FILLER                   PIC X(4)    VALUE 'ZIEP'.
    05  WS-CKPT-COUNTER          PIC 9(4)    VALUE ZEROES.

01  WS-CHECKPOINT-INFO.
    05  CP-WORK-AREA             PIC X(12).           <=== RESTART IO-AREA.
    05  CP-LENGTH-IO-AREA        PIC S9(8)    VALUE +60. <== LENGTH OF
    05  CP-LENGTH-PGM-VAR        PIC S9(8)    VALUE +71.      FIRST AREA.
    05  CP-CKPT-ID               PIC 9(8).           <=== CHECKPOINT ID
                                                          BUILT BY PROGRAM.
01  PROGRAM-VARIABLE-AREA.
    05  WS-PAGE-NO               PIC S9(5).            <=== FIELDS TO BE
        88  FIRST-PAGE                       VALUE +0.       CHECKPOINTED.
    05  WS-LINE-COUNT            PIC S9(3).
        88  MAX-LINES                        VALUE +54 THRU +59.
    05  WS-FIRST-RECORD-IND      PIC 9.
        88  FIRST-RECORD                     VALUE 0.
    05  WS-FIRST-CKPT-IND        PIC 9.
        88  FIRST-CHECKPOINT                 VALUE 0.
    05  WS-ERROR-COUNTER         PIC 9(6).
    05  WS-RECORDS-READ          PIC 9(7).
    05  WS-RECORDS-UPDATED       PIC 9(7).
    05  WS-DB-END-IND            PIC 9.
        88  DATA-BASE-END                    VALUE 1.
    05  WS-NO-CALLS-BEFORE-CKPT PIC S9(4).
    05  WS-NO-REPL-CALLS-DONE    PIC S9(4).
    05  WS-DATE.
        10  WS-MM                PIC 99.
        10  WS-DD                PIC 99.
        10  WS-YY                PIC 99.
    05  PACKED-NEXT-STMT-DATE    PIC 9(9) COMP-3.
    05  ACCOUNT-INFO.
        10  BANK-NO              PIC 9(3)  COMP-3 VALUE ZEROES.
        10  ACCOUNT-NO           PIC 9(11) COMP-3 VALUE ZEROES.
        10  ACCOUNT-OPEN-IND     PIC X.
    05  WS-WTOR-MESSAGE-AREA.
        10  WS-WTOR-CALL-TYPE    PIC X.
        10  WS-WTOR-PROGRAM-ID   PIC X(8).
        10  WS-WTOR-REPLY        PIC X(3).
```

Fig. 13-1. BMP WORKING STORAGE section.

- DATABASE PCB is the PCB of the database to be accessed by the program.
- GSAM-PCB is the PCB of the GSAM file to be accessed. The file is defined as GSAM so that if the program has to be restarted, the GSAM file is automatically repositioned by IMS when the XRST call is issued.

```
*
 LINKAGE SECTION.
*
*****************************************************************
*  CHECKPOINT/RESTART COMPONENTS:                               *
*    . LINKAGE SECTION: THE IO-PCB ENABLES THE PROGRAM TO       *
*      COMMUNICATE WITH THE ONLINE CONTROL REGION IF THE        *
*      PROGRAM IS EXECUTING BMP.                                *
*****************************************************************
*
 01  PCB-IO-TERM.
     05  IO-LTERM-NAME                PIC X(8).
     05  IO-DLI-RESERVED              PIC X(2).
     05  IO-STATUS-CODE               PIC X(2).
     05  IO-IN-PREFIX.
         10 IO-JULIAN-DATE            PIC S9(7) COMP-3.
         10 IO-TIME-OF-DAY            PIC S9(6)V9(1) COMP-3.
         10 IO-MSG-SEQ                PIC S9(7) COMP.
     05  IO-MOD-NAME                  PIC X(8).
     05  IO-USER-ID.
         10 IO-USER-BANK-NO           PIC X(3).
         10 IO-USER-NO                PIC X(5).
*
*  DATA BASE PCB - REQUIRED BECAUSE PROGRAM REFERENCES THE
*  ACCOUNT DATA BASE.
*
 01  PCB-ACCOUNT.
     05  ACCT-DBD-NAME             PIC X(8).
     05  ACCT-SEG-LEVEL            PIC X(2).
     05  ACCT-STATUS-CODE          PIC X(2).
     05  ACCT-PROCESS-OPTIONS      PIC X(4).
     05  IMS-RESERVED              PIC S9(5) COMP.
     05  ACCT-SEG-NAME-FB          PIC X(8).
     05  ACCT-LENGTH-FB-KEY        PIC S9(5) COMP.
     05  ACCT-NBR-SENS-SEG         PIC S9(5) COMP.
     05  ACCT-KEY-FB-AREA          PIC X(16).
*
 01  GSAM-REPORT-PCB.
     05  GSAMPCB-NAME              PIC X(8).
     05  GSAMPCB-SEG-LEVEL         PIC X(2).
     05  GSAMPCB-STAT-CODE         PIC X(2).
     05  GSAMPCB-PROCOPT           PIC X(4).
     05  GSAMPCB-RESERVED          PIC S9(5) COMP.
     05  GSAMPCB-SEG-NAME          PIC X(8).
     05  GSAMPCB-KEY-FB-LENGTH     PIC S9(8) COMP.
     05  GSAMPCB-NBR-SENSEG        PIC S9(8) COMP.
     05  GSAMPCB-KEY-FB-AREA       PIC X(10).
```

Fig. 13-2. LINKAGE SECTION.

PROCEDURE DIVISION: RESTART DETERMINATION

Issuing a Restart Call

To determine whether a checkpoint restart was specified in the JCL execution, the program will issue an XRST call.

The checkpoint work area is initialized to spaces, and the program issues a restart call (XRST) to IMS. This call must be the first call to IMS and can only be issued once (see FIG. 13-3.).

```
PROCEDURE DIVISION.

    ENTRY 'DLITCBL' USING PCB-IO-TERM
                          PCB-ACCOUNT
                          GSAM-REPORT-PCB.
    .....
0010-CHECK-RESTART SECTION.
    MOVE SPACES TO CP-WORK-AREA.
    .....
    CALL 'CBLTDLI' USING XRST
                         PCB-IO-TERM
                         CP-LENGTH-IO-AREA
                         CP-WORK-AREA
                         CP-LENGTH-PGM-VAR
                         PROGRAM-VARIABLE-AREA.
    IF IO-STATUS-CODE EQUAL SPACES
        THEN NEXT SENTENCE
        ELSE MOVE IO-STATUS-CODE TO WS-ERROR-STAT-CODE
             DISPLAY WS-ERROR-LINE
             MOVE 2000 TO WS-ABEND-CODE
(1)          CALL 'ABENDRTN' USING WS-ABEND-PARMS.
    IF CP-WORK-AREA EQUAL SPACES
        THEN PERFORM 0020-INITIALIZE-PGM-VARIABLES
             PERFORM 0030-INITIAL-PROCESSING
        ELSE
             DISPLAY
         '** CHECKPOINT RESTART REQUESTED - CHECKPOINT ID IS '
                               CP-WORK-AREA '**'.

0010-EXIT. EXIT.

NOTE:
----
(1) THE 'ABENDRTN' SUBROUTINE IS CALLED INTO THE PROGRAM WHENEVER
    AN EXPECTED ERROR OCCURS WHILE EXECUTION OF THE PROGRAM.
    THIS SUBROUTINE IS USED TO DISPLAY AN ERROR CODE ASSOCIATED
    WITH THE CONDITION WHICH CAUSES THE PROGRAM TO TERMINATE.
    IDENTIFYING EACH ERROR CONDITION WITH A UNIQUE CODE FACLILITATES
    DEBUGGING OF PRODUCTION PROBLEMS.
```

Fig. 13-3.

If a Checkpoint ID was specified in the EXEC statement of the JCL execution:

- All GSAM databases will be automatically repositioned where they were when the checkpoint call (CHKP) was issued.
- The PCB key feedback area (concatenated key of the last DL/1 call) of all active databases when the checkpoint call was issued will be restored.
- All program areas (VARIABLES in the example) are restored as they were when the checkpoint call was issued.

If no checkpoint ID was specified in the EXEC statement of the JCL execution, the checkpoint work area will remain blank and normal processing is assumed.

Issuing an Operator Message

Here, a message is issued to the console operator by subroutine E40REPLY being called by the BMP program. The coding of this subroutine is given in Appendix D.

The following parameters passed by the subroutine must be initialized:

- WS-WTOR-CALL-TYPE is a one-byte field that must be initialized to I for the initial call. All following calls must be set to N for normal calls.
- WS-WTOR-PROGRAM-ID is an eight-byte area that must contain a valid program ID (in our example, the program ID is 'E0620040'). It must also be left-justified and padded with spaces.
- WS-WTOR-OPERATOR-REPLY AREA is the field used by the operator to communicate with the program. This area is three-bytes-long and must be initialized to spaces.

An example of the issuing operator message appears in FIG. 13-4.

```
0030-INITIAL-PROCESSING SECTION.
    DISPLAY
       '** NO RESTART SPECIFIED - PROCESSING BEGAN NORMALLY **'.
    ....
    READ CHECKPOINT-FILE
         AT END DISPLAY
            '** FREQUENCY OF CHECKPOINT CALLS NOT SPECIFIED **'
    ....

    MOVE CHECKPOINT-NUMBER TO WS-NO-CALLS-BEFORE-CKPT.
    MOVE 'I' TO WS-WTOR-CALL-TYPE.
    MOVE SPACES TO WS-WTOR-REPLY.
    MOVE 'E0620040' TO WS-WTOR-PROGRAM-ID.
    PERFORM 0350-ISSUE-CONSOLE-MESSAGE.
    MOVE 'N' TO WS-WTOR-CALL-TYPE.

    ....
0350-ISSUE-CONSOLE-MESSAGE SECTION.
        CALL 'E40REPLY' USING WS-WTOR-CALL-TYPE    <=== USER WRITTEN
                              WS-WTOR-PROGRAM-ID        SUBROUTINE
                              WS-WTOR-REPLY.            TO SEND MESSAGES
                                                        TO MASTER CONSOLE

0350-EXIT. EXIT.
```

Fig. 13-4. Issuing operator console message.

Program Synchronization Point

In FIG. 13-5, in the part entitled 0340-CHECKPOINT-CALL, we see an area determined to be the logical point at which the program should issue a CHKP call. This, for example, can be issued when the maximum number of updates is reached. At this point, all activity for the database record being updated is completed.

The WS-WTOR-REPLY is tested to determine whether the operator has requested the program to be shutdown. If the area is set to 'EOJ', processing will be terminated.

Checkpoint Call

In FIG. 13-5 before the CHKP call is issued, the checkpoint ID supplied within the program is set up in the WS-CKPT-BUILD-AREA. This area is eight bytes in length, the first four bytes being unique to the program; in this example, the ID prefix is ZIEP. The last four bytes are a sequential number incremented by one with each successive CHKP call.

When the CHKP call is issued, a test for an 'XD' status code (meaning IMS is terminating) should be made. If this status is received, the program must be immediately terminated without issuing further DL/1 calls. This status is only received in a BMP application. If another DL/1 call is issued, the program will abend.

The operator reply submodule should be called to determine if the operator replied to the console message issued at program initialization. If the operator entered the valid reply 'EOJ', the program will be asked to shutdown at the next synchronization point. If no valid reply was entered, the subroutine will blank out the WS-WTOR-REPLY area and formal processing is continued.

GSAM REQUIREMENTS

Next, we'll discuss the requirements for using GSAM databases. These are non-hierarchical sequential data sets. The use of GSAM databases instead of OS/VS files eliminates the need for checkpointing in the application program. Records are read from and written to GSAM files via DL/1 calls.

For GSAM data sets to be referenced in BMP programs, their PCBs must be included in the program's PSB.

The next display shows an example of GSAM PCBs. The PSB lists one database PCB and two GSAM PCBs. The first GSAM file is an input to the program, and the second is output. Also, note the difference in the PROCOPT parms of the two PCBs, and that the same GSAM database PCB cannot be used in both input and output operations within the same execution. The I-O areas used for GSAM input and output operations must be specified as shown in FIG. 13-6.

```
PCB      TYPE=DB,
         DBDNAME=DDACCAPR,
         PROCOPT=GRP,
         KEYLEN=9
```

```
WORKING-STORAGE SECTION.
.....
01  WS-CKPT-BUILD-AREA.
    05  FILLER                     PIC X(4)   VALUE 'ZIEP'.
    05  WS-CKPT-COUNTER            PIC 9(4)   VALUE ZEROES.

PROCEDURE DIVISION.
.....

0340-CHECKPOINT-CALL SECTION.
    IF FIRST-CHECKPOINT
        THEN MOVE 1 TO WS-FIRST-CKPT-IND
             GO TO 0340-CONTINUE
        ELSE NEXT SENTENCE.
    IF WS-NO-REPL-CALLS-DONE LESS THAN WS-NO-CALLS-BEFORE-CKPT
        THEN GO TO 0340-EXIT
        ELSE MOVE ZEROES TO WS-NO-REPL-CALLS-DONE.

0340-CONTINUE.
    ADD +1 TO WS-CKPT-COUNTER.
    MOVE WS-CKPT-BUILD-AREA TO CP-CKPT-ID.
    CALL 'CBLTDLI' USING CHKP
                         PCB-IO-TERM
                         CP-LENGTH-IO-AREA
                         CP-CKPT-ID
                         CP-LENGTH-PGM-VAR
                         PROGRAM-VARIABLE-AREA.

    IF IO-STATUS-CODE EQUAL 'XD'
        THEN DISPLAY '** CHECKPOINT FREEZE IN PROGRESS **'
             MOVE 2035 TO WS-ABEND-CODE
             CALL 'ABENDRTN' USING WS-ABEND-PARMS
        ELSE NEXT SENTENCE.
    IF IO-STATUS-CODE EQUAL SPACES
       THEN NEXT SENTENCE
       ELSE  DISPLAY 'STATUS-CODE: ' IO-STATUS-CODE
             MOVE 2040 TO WS-ABEND-CODE
             CALL 'ABENDRTN' USING WS-ABEND-PARMS.

    PERFORM 0350-ISSUE-CONSOLE-MESSAGE.
    IF WS-WTOR-REPLY EQUAL 'EOJ'
        THEN MOVE 1 TO WS-DB-END-IND
             DISPLAY
                    '****   OPERATOR SHUTDOWN REQUESTED    ****'
             GO TO 0340-EXIT.
 0340-EXIT. EXIT.

 0350-ISSUE-CONSOLE-MESSAGE SECTION.
        CALL 'E40REPLY' USING WS-WTOR-CALL-TYPE
                              WS-WTOR-PROGRAM-ID
                              WS-WTOR-REPLY.
 0350-EXIT. EXIT.
```

Fig. 13-5. Issuing a checkpoint call.

```
SENSEG  NAME=DLACCT00,
        PARENT=0
....    ....
....    ....
PCB     TYPE=GSAM
        DBDNAME=MNI0014G,           <==== GSAM INPUT FILE
        PROCOPT=GS
PCB     TYPE=GSAM
        DBDNAME=MNI0015G,           <==== GSAM OUTPUT FILE
        PROCOPT=LS
PSBGEN  LANG=COBOL,PSBNAME=UPDATE,
        CMPAT=YES                   <==== BMP
END
```

The length of the record plus the two-byte-length and ZZ fields must be placed in the RECORD-LENGTH field before issuing the DL/1 ISRT call for variable-length records.

The RECORD-ZZ field must be set to binary zeroes.

In the FIG. 13-6 above example, RECORD-LENGTH will contain +104. On read (GN) operations, the record length—including the four-byte prefix—will be set in RECORD-LENGTH by IMS. FIGURE 13-7 is a sample code of a GSAM PCB.

CALLS TO GSAM FILES

The format of a call to the GSAM file is:

```
CALL 'CBLTDLI' USING FUNC
                     GSAM-PCB
                     IO-AREA
                     RSA. ← Optional
```

The functions are OPEN, CLOSE, GU, GN, and ISRT. RSA is the record search argument. It is optional for GN and ISRT calls. However, it is required for GU calls. The contents of the RSA depend on the access method you are using. For BSAM tape data sets and VSAM data sets, the RSA contains the relative byte address (RBA). For BSAM disk data sets, the RSA contains the disk address (TTR). Your program should define an RSA as two fullwords on a fullword or doubleword boundary.

```
FOR FIXED LENGTH RECORDS:

   01  GSAM-FIXED-RECORD-IOAREA.                          <=== FIXED LENGTH
       05  TRANSACTION-DATA          PIC X(100).               GSAM RECORD

FOR VARIABLE LENGTH RECORDS:

   01  GSAM-VARIABLE-RECORD-IOAREA.                      <=== VARIABLE LENGTH
       05  RECORD-LENGTH             PIC S9(4) COMP.           GSAM RECORD
       05  RECORD-ZZ                 PIC S9(4) COMP VALUE ZEROES.
       05  TRANSACTION-DATA          PIC X(100).
```

Fig. 13-6. GSAM I-O areas.

```
WORKING-STORAGE SECTION.
.....
01  WS-REPORT-IO-AREA.                             <=== FIXED LENGTH
    05  WS-RPT-CARRIAGE-CONTROL PIC X.                  GSAM RECORD
    05  WS-RPT-AREA             PIC X(132).
....

01  IMS-CALL-FUNCTIONS.
    03  GU                      PIC X(4) VALUE 'GU  '.
    03  ISRT                    PIC X(4) VALUE 'ISRT'.
    03  OPEN-FUNC               PIC X(4) VALUE 'OPEN'.

LINKAGE SECTION.
01  PCB-IO-TERM.
....
01  PCB-ACCOUNT.
....
01  GSAM-REPORT-PCB.
    05  GSAMPCB-NAME            PIC X(8).
    05  GSAMPCB-SEG-LEVEL       PIC X(2).
    05  GSAMPCB-STAT-CODE       PIC X(2).
    05  GSAMPCB-PROCOPT         PIC X(4).
    05  GSAMPCB-RESERVED        PIC S9(5) COMP.
    05  GSAMPCB-SEG-NAME        PIC X(8).
    05  GSAMPCB-KEY-FB-LENGTH   PIC S9(8) COMP.
    05  GSAMPCB-NBR-SENSEG      PIC S9(8) COMP.
    05  GSAMPCB-KEY-FB-AREA     PIC X(10).
```

Fig. 13-7. GSAM PCB coding.

For VSAM data sets, the RBA is the relative byte address of a specific record within the data set. The RBA is contained in the first byte of the RSA.

For BSAM data sets, the RSA is a doubleword used to locate individual records within a block. The first word contains the references to the BSAM RBA if you are using tape or to the BSAM TTR if you are using disk. The second word gives the volume sequence number in the first halfword and the displacement within the block in the second halfword. The interpretation of the RSA is summarized below:

File	Word 1	Word 2
VSAM	Relative byte address	Not used
BSAM DASD	Actual track address	Volume sequence number/displacement
BTAM TAPE	Relative block address	Volume sequence number/displacement

- OPEN and CLOSE calls are used to initiate and terminate GSAM databases activities. In case they are not used, the GSAM database will be opened when the first call references it and is closed when the program terminates.
- The GU call is used with the RSA for random access to a GSAM direct access data set. For GSAM tape data sets, this type of call is used to position the tape for later sequential processing.

- GN calls are used for sequential processing.
- ISRT calls are used to write to GSAM data sets. If the RSA is specified in a GN or ISRT call, GSAM will return the RSA to the user upon completion of the call. This information must be saved for later GU calls.

FIGURE 13-8 illustrates the OPEN and ISRT calls to a GSAM database.

```
 PROCEDURE DIVISION.

     ENTRY 'DLITCBL' USING PCB-IO-TERM
                           PCB-ACCOUNT
                           GSAM-REPORT-PCB.

     ....
 0030-INITIAL-PROCESSING SECTION.
     ....
*
*  OPEN GSAM REPORT DATA BASE
*
     CALL 'CBLTDLI' USING OPEN-FUNC
                          GSAM-REPORT-PCB
                          WS-OUT.

     MOVE GSAMPCB-STAT-CODE TO WS-STATUS-CODES.
     IF SUCCESSFUL-CALL
        THEN NEXT SENTENCE
        ELSE
            DISPLAY 'BAD OPEN OF GSAM FILE, STATUS CODE: '
                                             GSAMPCB-STAT-CODE
            MOVE 2025 TO WS-ABEND-CODE
            CALL 'ABENDRTN' USING WS-ABEND-PARMS.
 0030-EXIT. EXIT.
     ....
 0100-PRINT-DETAIL SECTION.
     ....
     MOVE .....
     PERFORM 0120-INSERT-PRINT-LINE.
     ....
 0100-EXIT. EXIT.
*
*  WRITE TO GSAM REPORT DATA BASE
*
 0120-INSERT-PRINT-LINE SECTION.
     CALL 'CBLTDLI' USING ISRT
                          GSAM-REPORT-PCB
                          WS-REPORT-IO-AREA.

     MOVE GSAMPCB-STAT-CODE TO WS-STATUS-CODES.
     IF SUCCESSFUL-CALL
        THEN NEXT SENTENCE
     ELSE
          DISPLAY 'BAD WRITE OF GSAM FILE, STATUS CODE: '
                                             GSAMPCB-STAT-CODE
                MOVE 2030 TO WS-ABEND-CODE
                CALL 'ABENDRTN' USING WS-ABEND-PARMS.
 0120-EXIT. EXIT.
```

Fig. 13-8. Call to GSAM file.

Summary of Checkpoint/Restart Coding

- The XRST call must be the first call to IMS and is issued only once.
- The number of areas specified in the XRST call must be equal to the maximum number of areas specified in the CHKP call.
- The length of the areas to be restored must be equal to and in the same sequence specified in the CHKP call. The maximum number of areas to be restored is seven.

```
WORKING-STORAGE SECTION.
....
01  WS-CHECKPOINT-INFO.
    05  CP-WORK-AREA              PIC X(12).
    05  CP-LENGTH-IO-AREA         PIC S9(8)   VALUE +60.
    05  CP-LENGTH-PGM-VAR         PIC S9(8)   VALUE +71.
    05  CP-CKPT-ID                PIC 9(8).

01  PROGRAM-VARIABLE-AREA.
    ....
01  IMS-CALL-FUNCTIONS.
    03  XRST                      PIC X(4) VALUE 'XRST'.
    03  CHKP                      PIC X(4) VALUE 'CHKP'.
*
 LINKAGE SECTION.
*
 01  PCB-IO-TERM.
     ....
 01  PCB-ACCOUNT.
     ....
 01  GSAM-REPORT-PCB.
     .....
 PROCEDURE DIVISION.

     ENTRY 'DLITCBL' USING PCB-IO-TERM
                           PCB-ACCOUNT
                           GSAM-REPORT-PCB.

     CALL 'CBLTDLI' USING XRST                    <=== PERFORMED ONLY ONCE
                          PCB-IO-TERM                  FOR THE DURATION
                          CP-LENGTH-IO-AREA            OF THE PROGRAM.
                          CP-WORK-AREA                 XRST CALL MUST BE
                          CP-LENGTH-PGM-VAR            THE FIRST DL/I CALL
                          PROGRAM-VARIABLE-AREA.       ISSUED BY THE
                                                       PROGRAM.
*    PERFORM OTHER PROCESSING

     CALL 'CBLTDLI' USING CHKP
                          PCB-IO-TERM
                          CP-LENGTH-IO-AREA
                          CP-CKPT-ID
                          CP-LENGTH-PGM-VAR
                          PROGRAM-VARIABLE-AREA.
```

Fig. 13-9. Checkpoint/restart program logic.

- The program must build a unique checkpoint ID each time it makes a CHKP call.
- Define nonhierarchical sequential data sets as GSAM files to take advantage of automatic repositioning by IMS when the XRST call is issued.
- All non-GSAM databases must be repositioned by the program.

FIGURE 13-9 summarizes the checkpoint/restart program logic.

A SAMPLE BATCH MESSAGE PROCESSING PROGRAM

Now that you understand the elements of the batch message processing program that are required by IMS to support batch-type processing in an online mode, let's put these elements together into a complete program. This sample BMP program (FIG. 13-10) illustrates the use of the symbolic checkpoint and extended restart calls in a database update program.

```
                         ACCOUNT DATABASE UPDATE
E.R0620040                                                    PROG E0620040
12/18/85                                                      PAGE        1

      BANK  ACCOUNT       OLD           NEW           STATUS
            NUMBER        STMT DATE     STMT DATE     CODE
      500   00071000479   0093085273    0123185365
      500   00071000675   0093085273    0123185365
      500   00071000833   0093085273    0123185365
      500   00071001007   0093085273    0123185365
      500   00071001150   0093085273    0123185365
      500   00071001564   0093085273    0123185365
      500   00071001605   0093085273    0123185365
      500   00071001760   0093085273    0123185365
      500   00071001916   0093085273    0123185365
      500   00071001930   0093085273    0123185365
      500   00071002128   0093085273    0123185365
      500   00071002283   0093085273    0123185365
      500   00071002295   0093085273    0123185365
      500   00071002568   0093085273    0123185365
      500   00071002879   0093085273    0123185365
      500   00071002893   0093085273    0123185365
      500   00071003110   0093085273    0123185365
      500   00071003146   0093085273    0123185365
       .        .             .             .
       .        .             .             .
       .        .             .             .
       .        .             .             .
```

Fig. 13-10. Sample report.

The program reads the ACCOUNT database, checks for accounts which are active, retrieves the NEXT-STATEMENT-DATE, and resets a new date which comes from a Parm card in the JCL.

Batch Message Processing

Extended checkpoint/restart logic is included in the program's coding to ensure database integrity in the event of program failure. It also allows for a shutdown of the program by the master console operator in a controlled programmatic manner. The program can execute in a DL/1 batch mode and can be checkpoint/restarted in a BMP region.

An audit report is produced for all updates. The report file is a GSAM file to take advantage of automatic repositioning by IMS and to eliminate the need for repositioning by the program. The format of the report is presented in FIG. 13-10.

FIGURE 13-11 presents the complete Batch Message Processing Program with embedded checkpoint/restart statements.

```
IDENTIFICATION DIVISION.
PROGRAM-ID. PROGRAM4.
AUTHOR. ZIEP VUONG.
DATE-WRITTEN. AUGUST 1987.
REMARKS.
    **********************************************************
    *                                                        *
    *   THIS IS A SAMPLE BATCH MESSAGE PROCESSING PROGRAM    *
    *                                                        *
    **********************************************************

ENVIRONMENT DIVISION.
CONFIGURATION SECTION.
SOURCE-COMPUTER.  IBM-370.
OBJECT-COMPUTER.  IBM-370.

INPUT-OUTPUT SECTION.
FILE-CONTROL.
     SELECT DATE-CONTROL        ASSIGN TO UT-S-DATECARD.
     SELECT CHECKPOINT-FILE     ASSIGN TO UT-S-CHECKPNT.
     SELECT PARM-CARD           ASSIGN TO UT-S-PARMCARD.

DATA DIVISION.
FILE SECTION.

FD  DATE-CONTROL
    RECORD CONTAINS 80 CHARACTERS
    BLOCK CONTAINS 0 RECORDS
    LABEL RECORDS ARE STANDARD
    DATA RECORD IS STANDARD-RECORD.
01  STANDARD-RECORD                SYNC.
    05  SR-DATE.
        10  SR-MM                  PIC XX.
        10  SR-DD                  PIC XX.
        10  SR-YY                  PIC XX.
    05  SR-DAY-SPELLED             PIC X(9).
    05  LW-DATE.
        10  LW-MM                  PIC XX.
        10  LW-DD                  PIC XX.
        10  LW-YY                  PIC XX.
    05  LW-DAY-SPELLED             PIC X(9).
```

Fig. 13-11.

Fig. 13-11. continued

```
    05  NW-DATE.
        10  NW-MM              PIC XX.
        10  NW-DD              PIC XX.
        10  NW-YY              PIC XX.
    05  NW-DAY-SPELLED         PIC X(9).
    05  MONTH-NAME             PIC X(9).
    05  FILLER                 PIC X(26).

FD  CHECKPOINT-FILE
    RECORD CONTAINS 80 CHARACTERS
    BLOCK CONTAINS 0 RECORDS
    LABEL RECORDS ARE STANDARD.
01  CHECKPOINT-RECORD.
    02  CHECKPOINT-NUMBER      PIC 9(4).
    02  FILLER                 PIC X(76).
FD  PARM-CARD
    RECORD CONTAINS 80 CHARACTERS
    BLOCK CONTAINS 0 RECORDS
    LABEL RECORDS ARE STANDARD.
01  PARM-RECORD                PIC X(80).
 WORKING-STORAGE SECTION.

 01  FILLER                    PIC X(50) VALUE
     '   **  WORKING STORAGE FOR PROGRAM4 BEGINS HERE'.

******************************************************************
*  CHECKPOINT-BUILD-AREA CONTAINS:                               *
*  1. FOUR BYTE PROGRAM-ID UNIQUE TO THIS PROGRAM, VALUE 'ZIEP'  *
*  2. LAST FOUR BYTES ARE A SEQUENTIAL NUMBER INCREMENTED BY     *
*     ONE WITH EACH SUCCESSIVE 'CHKP' CALL.                      *
*     WHEN A 'CHKP' CALL IS ISSUED, ALL DATA BASE BUFFERS        *
*     MODIFIED SINCE THE LAST SYNC POINT ARE WRITTEN TO THE      *
*     DATA BASE.                                                 *
******************************************************************

 01  WS-CKPT-BUILD-AREA.
     05  FILLER                PIC X(4)   VALUE 'ZIEP'.
     05  WS-CKPT-COUNTER       PIC 9(4)   VALUE ZEROES.

 01  WS-CHECKPOINT-INFO.
     05  CP-WORK-AREA          PIC X(12).
     05  CP-LENGTH-IO-AREA     PIC S9(8)   VALUE +60.
     05  CP-LENGTH-PGM-VAR     PIC S9(8)   VALUE +71.
     05  CP-CKPT-ID            PIC 9(8).

******************************************************************
*  CHECKPOINT/RESTART COMPONENTS:                                *
*  1. PROGRAM-VARIABLES: THE AREA OF THE PROGRAM REQUIRING       *
*     RESTORATION IF THE PROGRAM IS CHECKPOINT/RESTARTED.        *
*     THIS AREA CONTAINS ALL INFORMATION WE NEED TO              *
*     HAVE RESTORED. THEREFORE, BEFORE DOING A 'CHKP' CALL,      *
*     MAKE SURE THAT THE INFORMATION IN THESE VARIABLES IS       *
*     MOST CURRENT UP TO THAT POINT. FAILURE TO INCLUDE IN       *
*     THIS AREA ALL PERTINENT INFORMATION WILL MOST LIKELY       *
*     CAUSE A SOC7 ON A CHECKPOINT RESTART RUN.                  *
```

Fig. 13-11. continued

```
*  2. WTOR-MESSAGE-AREA: PARAMETERS PASSED TO SUBROUTINE          *
*     'E40REPLY' THAT ISSUES CONSOLE MESSAGE TO THE OPERATOR.     *
*     THE CONTENTS OF THIS AREA ARE SET UP IN THE PROCEDURE       *
*     DIVISION.                                                   *
*******************************************************************

 01  PROGRAM-VARIABLE-AREA.
     05  WS-PAGE-NO              PIC S9(5).
         88  FIRST-PAGE                     VALUE +0.
     05  WS-LINE-COUNT           PIC S9(3).
         88  MAX-LINES                      VALUE +54 THRU +59.
     05  WS-FIRST-RECORD-IND     PIC 9.
         88  FIRST-RECORD                   VALUE 0.
     05  WS-FIRST-CKPT-IND       PIC 9.
         88  FIRST-CHECKPOINT               VALUE 0.
     05  WS-ERROR-COUNTER        PIC 9(6).
     05  WS-RECORDS-READ         PIC 9(7).
     05  WS-RECORDS-UPDATED      PIC 9(7).
     05  WS-DB-END-IND           PIC 9.
         88  DATA-BASE-END                  VALUE 1.
     05  WS-NO-CALLS-BEFORE-CKPT PIC S9(4).
     05  WS-NO-REPL-CALLS-DONE   PIC S9(4).
     05  WS-DATE.
         10  WS-MM               PIC 99.
         10  WS-DD               PIC 99.
         10  WS-YY               PIC 99.
     05  PACKED-NEXT-STMT-DATE   PIC 9(9) COMP-3.
     05  ACCOUNT-INFO.
         10  BANK-NO             PIC 9(3)  COMP-3 VALUE ZEROES.
         10  ACCOUNT-NO          PIC 9(11) COMP-3 VALUE ZEROES.
         10  ACCOUNT-OPEN-IND    PIC X.
     05  WS-WTOR-MESSAGE-AREA.
         10  WS-WTOR-CALL-TYPE   PIC X.
         10  WS-WTOR-PROGRAM-ID  PIC X(8).
         10  WS-WTOR-REPLY       PIC X(3).

 01  WS-ABEND-PARMS.
     05  WS-ABEND-CODE           PIC S9(5) COMP.

 01  WS-STATUS-CODES             PIC X(2).
     88  SUCCESSFUL-CALL                    VALUE '  '.
     88  UNSUCCESSFUL-CALL                  VALUE 'GE'.
     88  END-OF-DATA-BASE                   VALUE 'GB'.

 01  WS-OUT                      PIC X(3)   VALUE 'OUT'.

 01  WS-MESSAGES.
     05  WS-GET-ERROR.
         10  FILLER              PIC X(21) VALUE
             '  ** ERROR **       '.
         10  FILLER              PIC X(48) VALUE
             'ACCOUNT NOT UPDATED BECAUSE OF A DB GET ERROR   '.
         10  WS-GET-ERR-STATUS   PIC X(2).
     05  WS-REPL-ERROR.
         10  FILLER              PIC X(21) VALUE
             '  ** ERROR **       '.
         10  FILLER              PIC X(48) VALUE
```

Fig. 13-11. continued

```
                'ACCOUNT NOT UPDATED BECAUSE OF A DB REPL ERROR  '.
            10  WS-REPL-ERR-STATUS  PIC X(2).
        05  WS-ERROR-LINE.
            10  FILLER              PIC X(43) VALUE
                '       DATA BASE CALL UNSUCCESSFUL. STATUS = '.
            10  WS-ERROR-STAT-CODE  PIC X(2).

    01  WS-HEAD-1.
        05  FILLER                  PIC X(5)  VALUE SPACES.
        05  FILLER                  PIC X(10) VALUE 'E.R0620040'.
        05  FILLER                  PIC X(41) VALUE SPACES.
        05  FILLER                  PIC X(20) VALUE
                 'BANK OF NOWHERE N.A'.
        05  FILLER                  PIC X(37) VALUE SPACES.
        05  FILLER                  PIC X(5)  VALUE 'PROG '.
        05  FILLER                  PIC X(8)  VALUE 'E0620040'.
        05  FILLER                  PIC X(5)  VALUE SPACES.
    01  WS-HEAD-2.
        05  FILLER                  PIC X(5)  VALUE SPACES.
        05  WS-H1-MM                PIC 99.
        05  FILLER                  PIC X     VALUE '/'.
        05  WS-H1-DD                PIC 99.
        05  FILLER                  PIC X     VALUE '/'.
        05  WS-H1-YY                PIC 99.
        05  FILLER                  PIC X(41) VALUE SPACES.
        05  FILLER                  PIC X(23) VALUE
                 'ACCOUNT DATABASE UPDATE'.
        05  FILLER                  PIC X(36) VALUE SPACES.
        05  FILLER                  PIC X(5)  VALUE 'PAGE '.
        05  WS-H1-PAGE              PIC ZZZZZ9.
        05  FILLER                  PIC X(6)  VALUE SPACES.
    01  WS-HEAD-3.
        05  FILLER                  PIC X(16) VALUE SPACES.
        05  FILLER                  PIC X(4)  VALUE 'BANK'.
        05  FILLER                  PIC X(5)  VALUE SPACES.
        05  FILLER                  PIC X(7)  VALUE 'ACCOUNT'.
        05  FILLER                  PIC X(9)  VALUE SPACES.
        05  FILLER                  PIC X(9)  VALUE 'OLD      '.
        05  FILLER                  PIC X(7)  VALUE SPACES.
        05  FILLER                  PIC X(6)  VALUE 'NEW   '.
        05  FILLER                  PIC X(10) VALUE SPACES.
        05  FILLER                  PIC X(6)  VALUE 'STATUS'.
        05  FILLER                  PIC X(54) VALUE SPACES.
    01  WS-HEAD-4.
        05  FILLER                  PIC X(25) VALUE SPACES.
        05  FILLER                  PIC X(6)  VALUE 'NUMBER'.
        05  FILLER                  PIC X(10) VALUE SPACES.
        05  FILLER                  PIC X(9)  VALUE 'STMT DATE'.
        05  FILLER                  PIC X(7)  VALUE SPACES.
        05  FILLER                  PIC X(9)  VALUE 'STMT DATE'.
        05  FILLER                  PIC X(7)  VALUE SPACES.
        05  FILLER                  PIC X(5)  VALUE 'CODE '.
        05  FILLER                  PIC X(55) VALUE SPACES.

    01  WS-DETAIL-1.
        05  FILLER                  PIC X(16) VALUE SPACES.
```

Fig. 13-11. continued

```
        05  WS-D1-BANK-NO              PIC X(3).
        05  FILLER                     PIC X(5)  VALUE SPACES.
        05  WS-D1-ACCOUNT              PIC 9(11).
        05  FILLER                     PIC X(6)  VALUE SPACES.
        05  WS-D1-OLD-STMT-DATE        PIC 9(10).
        05  FILLER                     PIC X(6)  VALUE SPACES.
        05  WS-D1-NEW-STMT-DATE        PIC 9(10).
        05  FILLER                     PIC X(9)  VALUE SPACES.
        05  WS-D1-STATUS-CODE          PIC X(2).
        05  FILLER                     PIC X(56) VALUE SPACES.

    01  WS-TOTAL-1.
        05  FILLER                     PIC X(3)  VALUE SPACES.
        05  FILLER                     PIC X(28) VALUE
                 '*  TOTAL ACCOUNTS READ:      '.
        05  WS-T1-RECORDS-READ         PIC ZZZZZZ9.
        05  FILLER                     PIC X(95) VALUE SPACES.

    01  WS-TOTAL-2.
        05  FILLER                     PIC X(3)  VALUE SPACES.
        05  FILLER                     PIC X(28) VALUE
                 '*  TOTAL ACCOUNTS UPDATED:   '.
        05  WS-T2-RECORDS-UPDATED      PIC ZZZZZZ9.
        05  FILLER                     PIC X(95) VALUE SPACES.

    01  WS-TOTAL-3.
        05  FILLER                     PIC X(3)  VALUE SPACES.
        05  FILLER                     PIC X(28) VALUE
                 '*  TOTAL ERRORS:             '.
        05  WS-T3-TOTAL-ERRORS         PIC ZZZZZZ9.
        05  FILLER                     PIC X(95) VALUE SPACES.

    01  WS-REPORT-IO-AREA.
        05  WS-RPT-CARRIAGE-CONTROL PIC X.
        05  WS-RPT-AREA                PIC X(132).
   *
   *    DATE FORMAT MMDDYYJJJ
   *
    01  WS-PARM-CARD.
        05  WS-NEXT-STMT-DATE          PIC 9(9).
        05  FILLER                     PIC X(71).
 01  IMS-CALL-FUNCTIONS.
*****************************************************************
*    RETRIEVAL CALLS                                            *
*****************************************************************
     03  GU                          PIC X(4) VALUE 'GU  '.
     03  GN                          PIC X(4) VALUE 'GN  '.
     03  GNP                         PIC X(4) VALUE 'GNP '.
     03  GHU                         PIC X(4) VALUE 'GHU '.
     03  GHN                         PIC X(4) VALUE 'GHN '.
     03  GHNP                        PIC X(4) VALUE 'GHNP'.
*****************************************************************
*    UPDATE CALLS                                               *
*****************************************************************
     03  ISRT                        PIC X(4) VALUE 'ISRT'.
```

Fig. 13-11. continued

```
     03  DLET                         PIC X(4) VALUE 'DLET'.
     03  REPL                         PIC X(4) VALUE 'REPL'.
     03  OPEN-FUNC                    PIC X(4) VALUE 'OPEN'.
*****************************************************************
*    CHECKPOINT CALLS                                           *
*****************************************************************
     03  XRST                         PIC X(4) VALUE 'XRST'.
     03  CHKP                         PIC X(4) VALUE 'CHKP'.
*
*****************************************************************
*                                                               *
*                  DATA BASE SSA'S                              *
*                                                               *
*****************************************************************
*
*    ACCOUNT SEGMENT SSA
*
 01  SSA-ACCOUNT.
     05  ACCOUNT-SEG-NAME             PIC X(8) VALUE 'ACCOUNT '.
     05  ACCOUNT-LEFT-PAREN           PIC X    VALUE '('.
     05  ACCOUNT-KEY-NAME             PIC X(8) VALUE 'ACCOUNTQ'.
     05  ACCOUNT-RO                   PIC XX   VALUE ' ='.
     05  ACCOUNT-VALUE                PIC X(8).
     05  FILLER REDEFINES ACCOUNT-VALUE.
         10  KEY-ACCOUNT-BANK-NO    PIC 9(3)  COMP-3.
         10  KEY-ACCOUNT-ACCT-NO    PIC 9(11)  COMP-3.
     05  ACCOUNT-RIGHT-PAREN          PIC X    VALUE ')'.
*
*    BALANCE SEGMENT SSA
*
 01  SSA-BALANCE.
     05  BALANCE-SEG-NAME             PIC X(8) VALUE 'BALANCE '.
     05  BALANCE-LEFT-PAREN           PIC X    VALUE SPACE.
*****************************************************************
*                                                               *
*                  DATA BASE SEGMENT LAYOUT                     *
*                                                               *
*****************************************************************
*
*    ACCOUNT ROOT SEGMENT
*
 01  ACCOUNT-IO-AREA.
     03 ACCT-KEY.
        05 ACCT-BANK-NO                 PIC 9(3)  COMP-3.
        05 ACCT-NO                      PIC 9(11) COMP-3.
     03 ACCT-COMMON-AREA.
        05 ACCT-BRANCH                   PIC S9(7) COMP-3.
        05 ACCT-NAME                     PIC X(24).
        05 ACCT-TAX-ID                   PIC X.
        05 ACCT-TAX-NO                   PIC S9(11) COMP-3.
        05 ACCT-OPEN-DATE                PIC S9(9)  COMP-3.
        05 ACCT-OPEN-IND                 PIC X.
        05 FILLER                        PIC X(10).

*
*    BALANCE SEGMENT
```

Fig. 13-11. continued

```
*
 01  BALANCE-IO-AREA.
         05 BALANCE-LAST-WRITTEN        PIC S9(9)          COMP-3.
         05 LEDGER-BALANCE              PIC S9(11)V9(2) COMP-3.
         05 CURRENT-BALANCE             PIC S9(11)V9(2) COMP-3.
         05 BAL-NXT-STMT                PIC S9(9)          COMP-3.
         05 FILLER                      PIC X(17).
*
 01  FILLER                             PIC X(26) VALUE
               ' WORKING STORAGE ENDS HERE'.
*
 LINKAGE SECTION.
*
*****************************************************************
*  CHECKPOINT/RESTART COMPONENTS:                               *
*    . LINKAGE SECTION: THE IO-PCB ENABLES THE PROGRAM TO       *
*      COMMUNICATE WITH THE ONLINE CONTROL REGION IF THE        *
*      PROGRAM IS EXECUTING BMP.                                *
*****************************************************************
*
 01  PCB-IO-TERM.
     05  IO-LTERM-NAME                  PIC X(8).
     05  IO-DLI-RESERVED                PIC X(2).
     05  IO-STATUS-CODE                 PIC X(2).
     05  IO-IN-PREFIX.
         10 IO-JULIAN-DATE              PIC S9(7)        COMP-3.
         10 IO-TIME-OF-DAY              PIC S9(6)V9(1) COMP-3.
         10 IO-MSG-SEQ                  PIC S9(7)        COMP.
     05  IO-MOD-NAME                    PIC X(8).
     05  IO-USER-ID.
         10 IO-USER-BANK-NO             PIC X(3).
         10 IO-USER-NO                  PIC X(5).
*
*  DATA BASE PCB - REQUIRED BECAUSE PROGRAM REFERENCES THE
*  ACCOUNT DATA BASE.
*
 01  PCB-ACCOUNT.
     05  ACCT-DBD-NAME              PIC X(8).
     05  ACCT-SEG-LEVEL             PIC X(2).
     05  ACCT-STATUS-CODE           PIC X(2).
     05  ACCT-PROCESS-OPTIONS       PIC X(4).
     05  IMS-RESERVED               PIC S9(5) COMP.
     05  ACCT-SEG-NAME-FB           PIC X(8).
     05  ACCT-LENGTH-FB-KEY         PIC S9(5) COMP.
     05  ACCT-NBR-SENS-SEG          PIC S9(5) COMP.
     05  ACCT-KEY-FB-AREA           PIC X(16).
*
 01  GSAM-REPORT-PCB.
     05  GSAMPCB-NAME               PIC X(8).
     05  GSAMPCB-SEG-LEVEL          PIC X(2).
     05  GSAMPCB-STAT-CODE          PIC X(2).
     05  GSAMPCB-PROCOPT            PIC X(4).
     05  GSAMPCB-RESERVED           PIC S9(5) COMP.
     05  GSAMPCB-SEG-NAME           PIC X(8).
     05  GSAMPCB-KEY-FB-LENGTH      PIC S9(8) COMP.
     05  GSAMPCB-NBR-SENSEG         PIC S9(8) COMP.
```

Fig. 13-11. continued

```
       05  GSAMPCB-KEY-FB-AREA      PIC X(10).
 PROCEDURE DIVISION.

     ENTRY 'DLITCBL' USING PCB-IO-TERM
                           PCB-ACCOUNT
                           GSAM-REPORT-PCB.

 0000-MAINLINE.
     PERFORM 0010-CHECK-RESTART.
     PERFORM 0040-PROCESS-INPUT.
     GOBACK.

*****************************************************************
*  RESTART DETERMINATION:                                       *
*   . BEFORE ANY OTHER CALLS ARE ISSUED TO IMS, A TEST MUST     *
*     BE MADE TO DETERMINE WHETHER A CHECKPOINT/RESTART WAS     *
*     SPECIFIED VIA A PARAMETER SPECIFIED IN THE EXECUTION JCL. *
*     THIS SECTION IS PERFORMED ONLY ONCE FOR THE DURATION OF   *
*     THE PROGRAM.                                              *
*   . INITIALIZE THE CHECKPOINT-WORK-AREA TO SPACES, THEN ISSUE *
*     A RESTART CALL TO IMS. THIS MUST BE THE FIRST CALL TO IMS *
*     AND CAN ONLY BE ISSUED ONCE.                              *
*****************************************************************
 0010-CHECK-RESTART SECTION.
     MOVE SPACES TO CP-WORK-AREA.
     MOVE SPACES TO WS-DETAIL-1.
     CALL 'CBLTDLI' USING XRST
                          PCB-IO-TERM
                          CP-LENGTH-IO-AREA
                          CP-WORK-AREA
                          CP-LENGTH-PGM-VAR
                          PROGRAM-VARIABLE-AREA.
     IF IO-STATUS-CODE EQUAL SPACES
         THEN NEXT SENTENCE
         ELSE MOVE IO-STATUS-CODE TO WS-ERROR-STAT-CODE
              DISPLAY WS-ERROR-LINE
              MOVE 2000 TO WS-ABEND-CODE
              CALL 'ABENDRTN' USING WS-ABEND-PARMS.

*****************************************************************
*  THE 'ABENDRTN' SUBROUTINE IS CALLED INTO THE PROGRAM WHENEVER *
*  AN EXPECTED ERROR OCCURS WHILE EXECUTION OF THE PROGRAM.     *
*  THIS SUBROUTINE VARIES FROM INSTALLATION TO INSTALLATION.    *
*  YOU SHOULD CHECK YOUR INSTALLATION'S STANDARDS ON HOW TO     *
*  CODE THIS SUBROUTINE.                                        *
*  IN THIS PROGRAM, 'ABENDRTN' IS USED TO DISPLAY AN ERROR CODE *
*  ASSOCIATED WITH THE CONDITION WHICH CAUSES THE PROGRAM TO    *
*  TERMINATE. IDENTIFYING EACH ERROR CONDITION WITH A UNIQUE    *
*  CODE FACILITATES DEBUGGING OF PRODUCTION PROBLEMS.           *
*****************************************************************

*****************************************************************
*  IF A CHECKPOINT-ID WAS NOT SPECIFIED, THE CHECKPOINT-WORK    *
*  AREA REMAINS BLANK AND NORMAL PROCESSING IS ASSUMED          *
*****************************************************************
```

Fig. 13-11. continued

```
     IF CP-WORK-AREA EQUAL SPACES
         THEN PERFORM 0020-INITIALIZE-PGM-VARIABLES
              PERFORM 0030-INITIAL-PROCESSING
         ELSE
              DISPLAY
           '** CHECKPOINT RESTART REQUESTED - CHECKPOINT ID IS '
                                CP-WORK-AREA '**'.

 0010-EXIT. EXIT.
 0020-INITIALIZE-PGM-VARIABLES SECTION.
     MOVE ZEROES TO WS-PAGE-NO
                    WS-FIRST-RECORD-IND
                    WS-FIRST-CKPT-IND
                    WS-ERROR-COUNTER
                    WS-RECORDS-READ
                    WS-RECORDS-UPDATED
                    WS-DB-END-IND
                    WS-NO-CALLS-BEFORE-CKPT
                    WS-NO-REPL-CALLS-DONE
                    BANK-NO
                    ACCOUNT-NO.
 0020-EXIT. EXIT.
 0030-INITIAL-PROCESSING SECTION.
     DISPLAY
         '** NO RESTART SPECIFIED - PROCESSING BEGAN NORMALLY **'.
     OPEN INPUT DATE-CONTROL CHECKPOINT-FILE PARM-CARD.
     READ CHECKPOINT-FILE
          AT END DISPLAY
               '** FREQUENCY OF CHECKPOINT CALLS NOT SPECIFIED **'
                  MOVE 2005 TO WS-ABEND-CODE
                  CALL 'ABENDRTN' USING WS-ABEND-PARMS.

****************************************************************
*  THE FOLLOWING PARAMETERS MUST BE INITIALIZED IN THE          *
*  SUBROUTINE ISSUED TO THE OPERATOR:                           *
*  1. WS-WTOR-CALL-TYPE = 'I' FOR AN INITIAL CALL AND ALL       *
*     SUBSEQUENT CALLS SET TO 'N'.                              *
*  2. WS-WTOR-PROGRAM-ID: EIGHT BYTE AREA, LEFT JUSTIFIED       *
*  3. WS-WTOR-REPLY AREA: USED BY THE OPERATOR TO COMMINICATE   *
*     WITH THE PROGRAM.                                         *
****************************************************************
     MOVE CHECKPOINT-NUMBER TO WS-NO-CALLS-BEFORE-CKPT.
     MOVE 'I' TO WS-WTOR-CALL-TYPE.
     MOVE SPACES TO WS-WTOR-REPLY.
     MOVE 'E0620040' TO WS-WTOR-PROGRAM-ID.
     PERFORM 0350-ISSUE-CONSOLE-MESSAGE.
     MOVE 'N' TO WS-WTOR-CALL-TYPE.

     READ DATE-CONTROL
          AT END DISPLAY '**** NO CONTROL DATE RECORD ****'
                 MOVE 2010 TO WS-ABEND-CODE
                 CALL 'ABENDRTN' USING WS-ABEND-PARMS.
     MOVE SR-DATE TO WS-DATE.

     READ PARM-CARD INTO WS-PARM-CARD
          AT END
```

Fig. 13-11. continued

```
              DISPLAY '**** NEXT STMT DATE PARM-CARD MISSING ****'
                      MOVE 2045 TO WS-ABEND-CODE
                      CALL 'ABENDRTN' USING WS-ABEND-PARMS.

        IF WS-NEXT-STMT-DATE NOT NUMERIC
              DISPLAY '**** NEXT STMT DATE NOT NUMERIC ****'
                      MOVE 2050 TO WS-ABEND-CODE
                      CALL 'ABENDRTN' USING WS-ABEND-PARMS.

        MOVE WS-NEXT-STMT-DATE TO PACKED-NEXT-STMT-DATE.

        CLOSE DATE-CONTROL CHECKPOINT-FILE PARM-CARD.
*******************************************************************
*  OPEN GSAM REPORT DATA BASE                                     *
*******************************************************************
       CALL 'CBLTDLI' USING OPEN-FUNC
                            GSAM-REPORT-PCB
                            WS-OUT.

       MOVE GSAMPCB-STAT-CODE TO WS-STATUS-CODES.
       IF SUCCESSFUL-CALL
          THEN NEXT SENTENCE
          ELSE
              DISPLAY 'BAD OPEN OF GSAM FILE, STATUS CODE: '
                                                   GSAMPCB-STAT-CODE
              MOVE 2025 TO WS-ABEND-CODE
              CALL 'ABENDRTN' USING WS-ABEND-PARMS.
 0030-EXIT. EXIT.
 0040-PROCESS-INPUT SECTION.
       IF DATA-BASE-END
          PERFORM 0330-PRINT-TOTALS
          GO TO 0040-EXIT.
       PERFORM 0070-UPDATE-PROCESSING
          UNTIL DATA-BASE-END.
 0040-EXIT. EXIT.

 0070-UPDATE-PROCESSING SECTION.
       MOVE BANK-NO         TO KEY-ACCOUNT-BANK-NO
       MOVE ACCOUNT-NO      TO KEY-ACCOUNT-ACCT-NO
       MOVE '>'             TO ACCOUNT-RO
       PERFORM 0250-GET-ACCOUNT-SEGMENT.

       IF DATA-BASE-END
          PERFORM 0330-PRINT-TOTALS
          GO TO 0070-EXIT.

       PERFORM 0260-GET-BALANCE-SEGMENT.
       IF ACCT-STATUS-CODE EQUAL 'GE'
          GO TO 0070-EXIT.

       IF ACCT-STATUS-CODE EQUAL SPACES
          PERFORM 0150-UPDATE-BALANCE-SEGMENT.

 0070-EXIT. EXIT.

 0100-PRINT-DETAIL SECTION.
```

Fig. 13-11. continued

```
    PERFORM 0110-PRINT-HEADINGS.
    MOVE ' '              TO WS-RPT-CARRIAGE-CONTROL.
    MOVE WS-DETAIL-1      TO WS-RPT-AREA.
    PERFORM 0120-INSERT-PRINT-LINE.
    MOVE SPACES           TO WS-DETAIL-1.
    ADD +1                TO WS-LINE-COUNT.
0100-EXIT. EXIT.

0110-PRINT-HEADINGS SECTION.
    IF FIRST-PAGE OR MAX-LINES
        THEN NEXT SENTENCE
        ELSE GO TO 0110-EXIT.
    ADD +1                TO WS-PAGE-NO.
    MOVE WS-PAGE-NO       TO WS-H1-PAGE.
    MOVE ZEROES           TO WS-LINE-COUNT.
    MOVE WS-MM            TO WS-H1-MM.
    MOVE WS-DD            TO WS-H1-DD.
    MOVE WS-YY            TO WS-H1-YY.
    MOVE '1'              TO WS-RPT-CARRIAGE-CONTROL.
    MOVE WS-HEAD-1        TO WS-RPT-AREA.
    PERFORM 0120-INSERT-PRINT-LINE.
    MOVE ' '              TO WS-RPT-CARRIAGE-CONTROL.
    MOVE WS-HEAD-2        TO WS-RPT-AREA.
    PERFORM 0120-INSERT-PRINT-LINE.
    MOVE '0'              TO WS-RPT-CARRIAGE-CONTROL.
    MOVE WS-HEAD-3        TO WS-RPT-AREA.
    PERFORM 0120-INSERT-PRINT-LINE.
    MOVE ' '              TO WS-RPT-CARRIAGE-CONTROL.
    MOVE WS-HEAD-4        TO WS-RPT-AREA.
    PERFORM 0120-INSERT-PRINT-LINE.
    MOVE ' '              TO WS-RPT-CARRIAGE-CONTROL.
    MOVE SPACES           TO WS-RPT-AREA.
    PERFORM 0120-INSERT-PRINT-LINE.
    ADD +6                TO WS-LINE-COUNT.
0110-EXIT. EXIT.
*****************************************************************
*  WRITE TO GSAM REPORT DATA BASE                               *
*****************************************************************
 0120-INSERT-PRINT-LINE SECTION.
     CALL 'CBLTDLI' USING ISRT
                          GSAM-REPORT-PCB
                          WS-REPORT-IO-AREA.

     MOVE GSAMPCB-STAT-CODE TO WS-STATUS-CODES.
     IF SUCCESSFUL-CALL
        THEN NEXT SENTENCE
     ELSE
         DISPLAY 'BAD WRITE OF GSAM FILE, STATUS CODE: '
                                            GSAMPCB-STAT-CODE
               MOVE 2030 TO WS-ABEND-CODE
               CALL 'ABENDRTN' USING WS-ABEND-PARMS.
 0120-EXIT. EXIT.
 0150-UPDATE-BALANCE-SEGMENT SECTION.
     PERFORM 0300-REPL-BALANCE-SEGMENT.
     IF ACCT-STATUS-CODE EQUAL SPACES
        ADD +1                  TO WS-RECORDS-UPDATED
```

Fig. 13-11. continued

```
           PERFORM 0100-PRINT-DETAIL
           PERFORM 0340-CHECKPOINT-CALL.
 0150-EXIT. EXIT.

 0250-GET-ACCOUNT-SEGMENT SECTION.
     CALL 'CBLTDLI' USING GN
                          PCB-ACCOUNT
                          ACCOUNT-IO-AREA
                          SSA-ACCOUNT.
     IF ACCT-STATUS-CODE EQUAL 'GB' OR 'GE'
        MOVE 1 TO WS-DB-END-IND
        GO TO 0250-EXIT.
     IF ACCT-STATUS-CODE EQUAL SPACES
     NEXT SENTENCE
     ELSE
          DISPLAY 'GN ERROR ACCOUNT ROOT'
          DISPLAY 'STATUS-CODE: ' ACCT-STATUS-CODE
          DISPLAY 'ACCOUNT NUMBER: ' KEY-ACCOUNT-ACCT-NO
          MOVE 2020 TO WS-ABEND-CODE
          CALL 'ABENDRTN' USING WS-ABEND-PARMS.
     ADD +1               TO WS-RECORDS-READ
*
*     UPDATE PROGRAM VARIABLE AREA
*
     MOVE ACCT-BANK-NO    TO BANK-NO
     MOVE ACCT-NO         TO ACCOUNT-NO
     MOVE ACCT-OPEN-IND   TO ACCOUNT-OPEN-IND.
 0250-EXIT. EXIT.

 0260-GET-BALANCE-SEGMENT SECTION.
     MOVE BANK-NO         TO KEY-ACCOUNT-BANK-NO
     MOVE ACCOUNT-NO      TO KEY-ACCOUNT-ACCT-NO.
     CALL 'CBLTDLI' USING GHU
                          PCB-ACCOUNT
                          BALANCE-IO-AREA
                          SSA-ACCOUNT
                          SSA-BALANCE.
     IF ACCT-STATUS-CODE EQUAL 'GB' OR 'GE'
        GO TO 0260-EXIT.
     IF ACCT-STATUS-CODE EQUAL SPACES
     NEXT SENTENCE
     ELSE
          DISPLAY 'GHU ERROR BALANCE SEGMENT'
          DISPLAY 'STATUS-CODE: ' ACCT-STATUS-CODE
          DISPLAY 'ACCOUNT NUMBER: ' KEY-ACCOUNT-ACCT-NO
          MOVE 2020 TO WS-ABEND-CODE
          CALL 'ABENDRTN' USING WS-ABEND-PARMS.

     MOVE BANK-NO         TO WS-D1-BANK-NO
     MOVE ACCOUNT-NO      TO WS-D1-ACCOUNT
     MOVE BAL-NXT-STMT    TO WS-D1-OLD-STMT-DATE
     MOVE PACKED-NEXT-STMT-DATE    TO BAL-NXT-STMT,
                                      WS-D1-NEW-STMT-DATE
     MOVE ACCT-OPEN-IND   TO WS-D1-STATUS-CODE.
 0260-EXIT. EXIT.
```

Fig. 13-11. continued

```
0300-REPL-BALANCE-SEGMENT SECTION.
    CALL 'CBLTDLI' USING REPL
                         PCB-ACCOUNT
                         BALANCE-IO-AREA.
    IF ACCT-STATUS-CODE EQUAL SPACES
        DISPLAY 'REPL ERROR BALANCE SEGMENT'
        DISPLAY 'STATUS-CODE: ' ACCT-STATUS-CODE
        DISPLAY 'ACCOUNT NUMBER: ' KEY-ACCOUNT-ACCT-NO
        MOVE 2020 TO WS-ABEND-CODE
        CALL 'ABENDRTN' USING WS-ABEND-PARMS.
0300-EXIT. EXIT.

0330-PRINT-TOTALS SECTION.
    PERFORM 0110-PRINT-HEADINGS.
    MOVE WS-RECORDS-READ TO WS-T1-RECORDS-READ.
    MOVE '-'             TO WS-RPT-CARRIAGE-CONTROL.
    MOVE WS-TOTAL-1      TO WS-RPT-AREA.
    PERFORM 0120-INSERT-PRINT-LINE.
    MOVE WS-RECORDS-UPDATED TO WS-T2-RECORDS-UPDATED.
    MOVE ' '             TO WS-RPT-CARRIAGE-CONTROL.
    MOVE WS-TOTAL-2      TO WS-RPT-AREA.
    PERFORM 0120-INSERT-PRINT-LINE.
    MOVE WS-ERROR-COUNTER TO WS-T3-TOTAL-ERRORS.
    MOVE ' '             TO WS-RPT-CARRIAGE-CONTROL.
    MOVE WS-TOTAL-3      TO WS-RPT-AREA.
    PERFORM 0120-INSERT-PRINT-LINE.
0330-EXIT. EXIT.
0340-CHECKPOINT-CALL SECTION.
    IF FIRST-CHECKPOINT
        THEN MOVE 1 TO WS-FIRST-CKPT-IND
             GO TO 0340-CONTINUE
        ELSE NEXT SENTENCE.
    IF WS-NO-REPL-CALLS-DONE LESS THAN WS-NO-CALLS-BEFORE-CKPT
        THEN GO TO 0340-EXIT
        ELSE MOVE ZEROES TO WS-NO-REPL-CALLS-DONE.

0340-CONTINUE.
    ADD +1 TO WS-CKPT-COUNTER.
    MOVE WS-CKPT-BUILD-AREA TO CP-CKPT-ID.
    CALL 'CBLTDLI' USING CHKP
                         PCB-IO-TERM
                         CP-LENGTH-IO-AREA
                         CP-CKPT-ID
                         CP-LENGTH-PGM-VAR
                         PROGRAM-VARIABLE-AREA.

*****************************************************************
*  ONCE THE CHKP CALL IS ISSUED, A TEST FOR 'XD' STATUS CODE    *
*  INDICATING IMS IS TERMINATING SHOULD BE MADE. IF THIS STATUS *
*  IS RETURNED, THE PROGRAM MUST BE IMMEDIATELY TERMINATED.     *
*  THIS STATUS CODE IS RECEIVED ONLY BY BMP APPLICATIONS.       *
*  IF ANOTHER DL/I CALL IS MADE, THE PROGRAM WILL ABEND.        *
*  THEN TEST FOR THE OPERATOR-REPLY.                            *
*****************************************************************
    IF IO-STATUS-CODE EQUAL 'XD'
        THEN DISPLAY '** CHECKPOINT FREEZE IN PROGRESS **'
```

Fig. 13-11. continued

```
                 MOVE 2035 TO WS-ABEND-CODE
                 CALL 'ABENDRTN' USING WS-ABEND-PARMS
             ELSE NEXT SENTENCE.
         IF IO-STATUS-CODE EQUAL SPACES
            THEN NEXT SENTENCE
            ELSE  DISPLAY 'STATUS-CODE: ' IO-STATUS-CODE
                  MOVE 2040 TO WS-ABEND-CODE
                  CALL 'ABENDRTN' USING WS-ABEND-PARMS.

*****************************************************************
*  THE OPERATOR-REPLY AREA IS TESTED TO DETERMINE WHETHER THE    *
*  OPERATOR HAS REQUESTED THE PROGRAM TO SHUT DOWN.              *
*  IF THIS AREA IS SET TO 'EOJ', PROCESSING SHOULD BE TERMINATED.*
*****************************************************************
         PERFORM 0350-ISSUE-CONSOLE-MESSAGE.
         IF WS-WTOR-REPLY EQUAL 'EOJ'
             THEN MOVE 1 TO WS-DB-END-IND
                  DISPLAY
                         '****   OPERATOR SHUTDOWN REQUESTED   ****'
                  GO TO 0340-EXIT.
     0340-EXIT. EXIT.

*****************************************************************
*  CALL USER WRITTEN SUBROUTINE TO SEND MESSAGES TO THE MASTER   *
*  CONSOLE.                                                      *
*****************************************************************
     0350-ISSUE-CONSOLE-MESSAGE SECTION.
           CALL 'E40REPLY' USING WS-WTOR-CALL-TYPE
                                  WS-WTOR-PROGRAM-ID
                                  WS-WTOR-REPLY.
     0350-EXIT. EXIT.
```

14

JCL Requirements for the Checkpoint/Restart Facility

You should remember from the beginning of chapter 13 that a BMP application is scheduled through an OS JCL job stream. Certain JCL requirements must be satisfied before you can schedule a BMP job to run and to restart at a later time.

The following sections illustrate the JCL required to invoke the checkpoint/restart facility. We will show you how to set up a job to run our BMP program in both DL/1 batch and BMP modes. First, though we'll discuss the GSAM requirements and log tape specifications for a restart run, then we'll walk you through the sequence of events to restart a DL/1 run, and finally we'll show you how to restart a BMP run.

GSAM JCL REQUIREMENTS

To be repositioned by IMS in the event of a restart, all output files defined in GSAM databases must be preallocated by IEFBR14, IEBGENER, or IEHPROGM:

```
//*-----------------------------------------------------------------
//*
//*      IEFBR14 CREATES GSAM REPORT DATA SET
//*
//*-----------------------------------------------------------------
//STEP10   EXEC PGM=IEFBR14
//DD1      DD  DSN=&STATO.06.D2040001.REPORT&GEN1,DISP=( ,CATLG,DELETE ),
//         SPACE=&RPTSPC,UNIT=&UNIT1,
//         DCB=( E.MODELDCB,LRECL=133,BLKSIZE=6118,RECFM=FBA )
//*
//*-----------------------------------------------------------------
```

Output SYSOUT files should have RECFM=FBA, with subsequent printing performed by IEBGENER or a user-written program:

```
//*-----------------------------------------------------------------
//*
//*       IEBGENER PRINTS GSAM REPORT
//*
//*-----------------------------------------------------------------
//STEP30    EXEC PGM=IEBGENER,COND=EVEN
//SYSPRINT DD SYSOUT=A
//SYSUT1   DD DSN=&STATO.06.D2040001.REPORT&GEN2,DISP=OLD,
//            SPACE=&RPTSPC2,UNIT=&UNIT1
//SYSOUT   DD SYSOUT=&SYSOUT,DCB=(LRECL=133,BLKSIZE=1330,RECFM=FBA)
//SYSIN     DD DUMMY
//*
//*-----------------------------------------------------------------
```

Output GSAM files must have a disposition of MOD or OLD in the update step to be expanded (continue writing after previous EOF) in the event of a checkpoint/restart:

```
//*-----------------------------------------------------------------
//*
//MNI0006G DD  DSN=&STATO.06.D2040001.REPORT&GEN2,DISP=OLD
//*
//*-----------------------------------------------------------------
```

Log Tape Specification

For DL/1 batch or BMP jobs restarted from a DL/1 batch, the IMS LOG tape containing the checkpoint from which it is restarted is allocated via the IMSLOGR DD statement. The JCL as shown below must be used.

When using the online IMS log data set to restart a BMP job, the IMSLOGR DD statement must specify a data set name greater than 17 characters to avoid OS/VS allocation conflicts. This technique is based on the fact that OS/VS enqueues on the full data set name in the DD card, but only the last 17 characters are actually recorded on the tape label.

```
//*-----------------------------------------------------------------
//*
//***  FOLLOWING LOG DATA SET IS NEEDED FOR CHKPT RERUN AND DLI RUN ***
//*
//*IMSLOGR DD DSN=&STATO.06.D2040001.IMSLOG1,DISP=OLD       CHKPT RERUN
//*
//*-----------------------------------------------------------------
```

HOW TO RESTART A DL/1 RUN

This section shows how to restart a job which has executed in a Dl/1 batch mode, that is, the job executed when the databases were offline.

As an example, let's assume that our installation requires us to run our BMP account update program E0620040 in the following manner:

1. Begin to run in a batch DL/1 mode.
2. Allow the program to be orderly shut down by the console operator.
3. Checkpoint/restart the program in the BMP region to complete processing.

Catalogued Procedure

Catalogued procedure 'BMPRUN' has been set up to run our program in both DL/1 and BMP batch modes (FIG. 14-1). To allow an orderly shutdown by the console operator, OUT= is specified at the beginning of the procedure parameter. This parameter defaults to N to specify that the job will ask for the operator's decision when to shut down the execution of the job. As you will see later, the 'EOJ' reply by the operator will shut the program down.

```
//BMPRUN   PROC PSB=E0620040,MBR=E0620040,
//              IN=,OUT=,OPT=N,SPIE=0,                       <=== USED FOR BMP
//              TEST=0,DIRCA=000,PRLD=,STIMER=,
//              CKPTID=,PARMDLI=,CPUTIME=,NBA=,
//              OBA=,IMSID=,AGN=,RGN=2048K,
//              GEN1='(+1)',
//              GEN2='(+1)',
//              CTLLIB='E.CONTROL',
//              STATO=P,
//              IMSVS='IMSVS.',
//              LIB1=PRODLIB,
//              UNIT1=SYSDA,
//              RPTSC='(6118,(5000,2500))'
//              RPTSC2='(6118,(5000,2500),RLSE)',
//*-----------------------------------------------------------------
//*
//*      IEFBR14 CREATES GSAM REPORT DATA SET
//*
//*-----------------------------------------------------------------
//STEP10    EXEC PGM=IEFBR14
//DD1      DD  DSN=&STATO.06.D2040001.REPORT&GEN1,DISP=(,CATLG,DELETE),
//             SPACE=&RPTSPC,UNIT=&UNIT1,
//             DCB=(E.MODELDCB,LRECL=133,BLKSIZE=6118,RECFM=FBA)
//*
```

Fig. 14-1. Sample DL/1 job.

Fig. 14-1. continued

```
//*------------------------------------------------------------------
//*
//*       BMP/DLI STEP TO UPDATE DATA BASE
//*
//*------------------------------------------------------------------
//STEP20    EXEC PGM=DFSRRC00,REGION=&RGN,
//          PARM=(DLI,&MBR,&PSB)                  <=== FOR DLI ONLY    (A)
//*         PARM=(BMP,&MBR,&PSB,&IN,&OUT,
//*         &OPT&SPIE&TEST&DIRCA,&PRLD,&STIMER,&CKPTID,        FOR BMP   (D)
//*         &PARMDLI,&CPUTIME,&NBA,&OBA,&IMSID,&AGN),COND=(0,NE)
//STEPLIB  DD  DSN=&IMSVS.RESLIB,DISP=SHR
//         DD  DSN=&LIB1,DISP=SHR
//IMSACB   DD  DSN=&IMSVS.ACBLIB,DISP=SHR
//IMS      DD  DSN=&IMSVS.PSBLIB,DISP=SHR
//         DD  DSN=&IMSVS.DBDLIB,DISP=SHR
//SYSPRINT DD  SYSOUT=A
//DFSRESLB DD  DSN=&IMSVS.RESLIB,DISP=SHR
//DATECARD DD  DSN=&CTLLIB(DAILY),DISP=SHR
//CHECKPNT DD  DUMMY,DCB=BLKSIZE=80                                 (E)
//PARMCARD DD  DUMMY,DCB=BLKSIZE=80
//MNI0006G DD  DSN=&STATO.06.D2040001.REPORT&GEN2,DISP=OLD          (F)
//IMSERR   DD  DUMMY
//SYSOUT   DD  SYSOUT=A
//SYSUDUMP DD  SYSOUT=A
//ABNLENAB DD  DUMMY
//*
//***  FOLLOWING LOG DATA SET IS NEEDED FOR CHKPT RERUN AND DLI RUN ***
//*
//*IMSLOGR DD DSN=&STATO.06.D2040001.IMSLOG1,DISP=OLD       <===  CHKPT RERUN
//*
//***  FOLLOWING JCL IS NECESSARY FOR DLI RUN                         ***
//*
//IEFRDER DD DSN=&STATO.06.D2040001.IMSLOG1,DISP=(,CATLG,CATLG),
//         UNIT=SYSTP,DCB=(BLKSIZE=11976,LRECL=11972,RECFM=VB)      (B)
//DFSVSAMP DD DSN=&CTLLIB(DPAMS#00),DISP=SHR
//*
//***  JCL SPECIFYING DATA BASES NEEDED FOR DLI ONLY                ***
//*
//DDACCAPR DD  DSN=P06.IMNI000.DDACCAPR,DISP=OLD                    (C)
//DDACCAPR DD  DSN=P06.IMNI000.DDACCAIX,DISP=OLD
//*
//*------------------------------------------------------------------
//*
//*       IEBGENER PRINTS GSAM REPORT
//*
//*------------------------------------------------------------------
//STEP30    EXEC PGM=IEBGENER,COND=EVEN
//SYSPRINT DD SYSOUT=A
//SYSUT1   DD DSN=&STATO.06.D2040001.REPORT&GEN2,DISP=OLD,
//         SPACE=&RPTSPC2,UNIT=&UNIT1
//SYSOUT   DD SYSOUT=&SYSOUT,DCB=(LRECL=133,BLKSIZE=1330,RECFM=FBA)
//SYSIN     DD DUMMY
//*
//*                    LAST CARD OF PROCEDURE
```

STEP10 executes the program IEFBR14 to create a GSAM report data set for our audit report:

In STEP20, program E0620040 updates the account database and writes report records to the GSAM file. Now:

- (A) specifies the parameters needed to run in a DL/1 mode.
- (B) specifies the log data set to be created in the DL/1 run.
- (C) specifies the databases to be updated. (B) and (C) are needed for DL/1 runs.
- (D) specifies the parameters needed to run in a BMP mode. Note that the log data set name and the database names are not specified for a BMP run. These are commented out in the JCL.
- (E) specifies the checkpoint frequency. To allow flexibility in changing this frequency, CHECKPNT is dummied out in the Proc and will be specified in the execution JCL (shown below).
- (F) specifies the data set name of the GSAM file to be updated.

STEP30 executes program IEBGENER to print the GSAM report data set.

Since we cannot run both DL/1 and BMP modes at the same time, the JCL statements needed for BMP are commented out to allow the JCL statements for DL/1 to take affect.

Execution JCL

The execution JCL of our BMPRUN is:

```
//EX1051BT   JOB  (0006,TEST,,0020),'ZIEP ACCOUNT UPDATE',
//           MSGLEVEL=(1,1),CLASS=I,MSGCLASS=T
//PROCLIB  DD  DSN=E.D9800000.PROCLIB,DISP=SHR
//EB062040  EXEC PROC=BMPRUN,
//          IMSID=IMSA,
//          STATO=T,
//STEP20.CHECKPNT DD *                        <=== CHECKPOINT FREQUENCY
1500
/*
//STEP.20.PARMCARD DD *
12318563
/*
//
```

Note that the checkpoint frequency is specified at 1,500 DL/1 calls per CHKP call.

Now, let's submit the JCL execution to invoke our DL/1 job to run. At the beginning of the execution, program E0620040 displays the following message because no restart action has been requested in the JCL:

```
** NO RESTART SPECIFIED—PROCESSING BEGAN NORMALLY **
```

Each time it issues a checkpoint call, the program sends a message to the console operator asking for a reply:

```
***   ZIEP0000 E0620040 ACTIVE — REPLY EOJ TO END ***
           ↑
           Checkpoint ID
```

Now, to shut down the program, the console operator replies 'EOJ' to request shutdown at synchronization point 'ZIEP0004'. At this time, the program shuts down and displays the following message:

```
****   OPERATOR SHUTDOWN REQUESTED ****
```

The execution job log is presented in FIG. 14-2; note the remarks on the log.

Let's recall that when a CHKP call is issued, the following is done:

- The fully qualified key of each PCB is recorded on the system log.
- All buffers modified by the application program since the last synchronization points are written to the database.
- The checkpoint ID passed with the CHKP call is recorded on the system log.
- The program variable areas are also written to the system log.
- The current positions of all GSAM databases are formatted into a checkpoint log record and are written to the system log.

FIGURE 14-3 gives a snapshot of the system log at the start of program E0620040. The program variable areas at the start of the program correspond with the first page of the update report displayed in FIG. 14-4.

FIGURE 14-5 gives a snapshot of the system log at shutdown time. At checkpoint ID 'ZIEP0004', the last account updated is 00305088781; this is reflected by the last line of the update report displayed in FIG. 14-6.

How to Restart a Job

Now that the databases are online, our program can be restarted to continue processing. FIGURE 14-7 presents the JCL to restart the program in a BMP mode.

Step10 is not executed (commented out) because the GSAM report file already exists from the DL/1 run.

STEP20 (the numbers below correspond to the parenthesized numbers in the figure):

1. Specifies the checkpoint ID at which the program will be restarted.
2. Specifies the parameters needed to run in a BMP mode.
3. Specifies the GSAM update report which will be repositioned by IMS before processing.

JES2 JOB LOG – SYSTEM BB33 – NODE N1

```
11.24.17 JOB 905  $HASP373 EX1051BT STARTED - INIT L -CLASS I - SYS AK
11.24.17 JOB 905 &IEF403I EX1051BT - STARTED - TIME=11.24.17
11.24.18 JOB 905 *IEF233A M 482,002891, ,EX1051BT,STEP10
11.24.18 JOB 905  IEF234E K 482,002892,PVT,EX1051BT,STEP10
11.24.23 JOB 905 *IEF233A M 482,PRIVAT,SL,EX1051BT,STEP30,T06.D2040001.IMSLOG1  <—— IMS batch log to be used in BMP restart
11.24.23 JOB 905 &IEF188I PROBLEM PROGRAM ATTRIBUTES ASSIGNED
11.24.28 JOB 905  +DFS2207I SYSTEM LOG(S) BLKSIZE=11976, BUFNO=002.          IMSA
11.24.28 JOB 905  +DFS692I EX1051BT.STEP30          BUFFER CONTROL – BUF=1DE000   IMSA
11.24.43 JOB 905  IEC705I TAPE ON 482,008216,SL,6250 BPI,EX1051BT,STEP30, T06.D2040001.IMSLOG1
11.24.43 JOB 905  +DFS034I BATCH INITIALIZATION COMPLETE   IMSA
11.24.44 JOB 905 @82 ***          ZIEP000 E060040 ACTIVE – REPLY EOJ TO END ***  <—— WTOR to console operator
11.24.46 JOB 905  +DFS0540I *EXTENDED CHECKPOINT*PROGRAM= E0620040,CKPTID=ZIEP0001,REGID=01,DAY=350,TIME=1124461   IMSA
11.24.46 JOB 905  +DFS681I - CHKPT DLI PSB E0620040 ID ZIEP0001 SER 008216        IMSA
11.25.08 JOB 905  +DFS0540I *EXTENDED CHECKPOINT*PROGRAM= E0620040,CKPTID=ZIEP0002,REGID=01,DAY=350,TIME=1125083   IMSA
11.25.08 JOB 905  +DFS681I -CHKPT DLI PSB E0620040 ID ZIEP0002 SER 008216         IMSA
11.25.16 JOB 905  +DFS0540I *EXTENDED CHECKPOINT*PROGRAM= E0620040, CKPTID=ZIEP0003,REGID=01,DAY=350,TIME=1125167   IMSA
11.25.16 JOB 905  +DFS681I - CHKPT DLI PSB E0620040 ID ZIEP0003 SER 008216        IMSA
11.25.29 JOB 905  R 82,EOJ
11.25.35 JOB 905  +DFS0540I *EXTENDED CHECKPOINT*PROGRAM= E0620040,CKPTID=ZIEP0004,REGID=01,DAY=350,TIME=1125354   IMSA
11.25.35 JOB 905  +DFS681I - CHKPT DLI PSB E0620040 ID ZIEP0004 SER 008216        IMSA
11.25.36 JOB 905  +DFS092I IMSV/S LOG TERMINATED IMSA
11.25.36 JOB 905 &DFS627I IMSV/S RESOURCE CLEANUP COMPLETE FOR JS EX1051BT.STEP30
11.25.39 JOB 905  IEF234E K 482,008216,PVT,EX1051BT,STEP30
11.25.41 JOB 905  IEF404I EX1051BT - ENDED - TIME=11.25.41
```

Fig. 14-2. Sample DL/1 job log with shutdown requested.

```
UTILITY PRINT PROGRAM                                  HEX                                                            REC-NO

     %Y              EX1051BT              Y          W    W    0   8           &          Q       **              1
4F08006E083012200000CEFFFFCE000001E001E001E0081008100EB00EB00BF00BF008900890045004500 9D089D00000
2F0000C8055F14800000571051230000D000100018002000280060006800200028002000280070007800B000B800001

   IMSA                        **                                                                                 2
0000CDECFFF00000083012200000
60009421FFF50000055F14800002

  DDACCAPRE0620040       @ @        |DDACCAPR     **                                                              3
20CCCCCCDDCFFFFFFF0000044747083012 44CCCCCCDD0000
014413317950620040011160ACAC055F144F441331790003

  DDACCAIXE0620040                 |DDACCAIX      **                                                              4
20CCCCCCCECFFFFFFF0000040000083012 44CCCCCCCE0000
01441331975062004002 11C00E80055F144F441331970004

      H     E0620040DDACCAPR          ?                                                                 .         5
5119000C0B44CFFFFFFFCCCCCCDD083012460000000000000282200029820002982000000000000000000000000000000002
102204281700506200404413317915 5F145F0000022000009957C000246C000246C00C00C00000C00000C00000C00000C002

   ZIEP0001E0620040                DDACCAPRDDBAL000D&               MNI0006G                       MNI0006G  *    9
1400ECCDFFFFCFFFFFFF0830124100000 0CCCCCCDDCCCCDFFFC50001049030000DDCFFFFC44444444000000005DDCFFFFC00
80109957000150620040055F146509090044133179442130004 0F07007F030000459000670000000000110100145900067 00

                    **     Checkpoint ID                       Program variable area at start of program
00000000000000
00000000000009

   ZIEP0001E0620040 <----                  0000A00G01000000000000200000010050  000A121385       &       N*   10
1800ECCDFFFFCFFFFFFF083012410004000 40000FFFFOFFCFFFFFFFFFFFFFFFFFFFFFFFFFFCFFFCFFFFFF13835500010494D
811099570001506200 40055F14650007000701010000010070100000000000020000001005000001121385 2156F0F07007F05
                                                                                        First account number
E0620040              **                          Line number                        "00071000479" in the account
CFFFFFFF4440000                                                                      database was updated (6 columns).
50620040000000A                              Page number

   ZIEP0001E0620040                 ?                       **                                                   11
4000ECCDFFFFCFFFFFFF00000000083012460044444444444444440000
110099570001506200400C000000055F145F0400000000000000000000B
         .
         .
         .
         .
         .
```

Fig. 14-3. System log at start of program.

```
E.R0620040          ACCOUNT DATABASE UPDATE               PROG E0620040
12/18/85                                                  PAGE        1
 BANK  ACCOUNT         OLD            NEW            STATUS
       NUMBER          STMT DATE      STMT DATE      CODE
 500   00071000479     0093085273     0123185365 <---- First account number
 500   00071000675     0093085273     0123185365       "00071000479" in the
 500   00071000833     0093085273     0123185365       account database was
 500   00071001007     0093085273     0123185365       updated at the start of
 500   00071001150     0093085273     0123185365       the program (see FIG. 14.3)
 500   00071001564     0093085273     0123185365
 500   00071001605     0093085273     0123185365
 500   00071001760     0093085273     0123185365
 500   00071001916     0093085273     0123185365
 500   00071001930     0093085273     0123185365
 500   00071002128     0093085273     0123185365
 500   00071002283     0093085273     0123185365
 500   00071002295     0093085273     0123185365
 500   00071002568     0093085273     0123185365
 500   00071002879     0093085273     0123185365
 500   00071002893     0093085273     0123185365
 500   00071003110     0093085273     0123185365
 500   00071003146     0093085273     0123185365
  .        .               .              .
  .        .               .              .
  .        .               .              .
  .        .               .              .
```

Fig. 14-4. Sample report at start of program.

4. Specifies the log data set to be used to restart the program. This log contains the checkpoint data.

Additionally:

5. As this is a BMP run, there is no need to specify a new log data set name; these statements are required for DL/1 runs only so they are commented out.
6. The databases need not be specified for BMP because they are specified in the ACBGEN job.

You may recall that when a restart is initiated, the following will be performed:

- The program variable areas recorded at checkpoint time will be restored.
- The key feedback area and the status code for each PCB is restored.
- GSAM databases are automatically repositioned.

When we are ready to restart the shutdown program, we supply IMS with the checkpoint ID from which the program is to be restarted via the Parm field in the JCL EXEC statement. In our example, the restart checkpoint ID is 'ZIEP0004', and this supplied to the program via the symbolic CKPTID specified in the JCL.

IMS places this ID in the I-O area which the XRST call points to. Then, IMS reads the system log and searches for the checkpoint record with the ID thus supplied. Once it is found, IMS restores the program variable areas specified in the symbolic checkpoint and restart calls.

After the program has issued an XRST call, it displays the following message:

```
** CHECKPOINT RESTART REQUESTED — CHECKPOINT ID IS ZIEP0004 **
```

```
UTILITY PRINT PROGRAM
                                        HEX,BEGIN=5448                                              REC-NO

   ZIEP0004E0620040                 DDACCAPRDDBAL000D&    &          MNI0006G             MNI0006G    *        6014
1400ECCDFFFFCFFFFFFF08301234000000CCCCCCDDCCCCDFFFC50035871030000DDCFFFFC44444444000000005DDCFFFFC00
80109957000450620040055F155109090044133179442130004OF00088F030000459000670000000005210100145900067 00

            =**
0000000000000017
000000000000007E

   ZIEP0004E0620040                         0003B01H010000000000687700015000050 000 121385     -&    &     N*        *6015
1800ECCDFFFFCFFFFFFF0830123408040004000OFFFFFOFFFCFFFFFFFFFFFFFFFFFFFFFFFFFFFCFFFCFFFFFF138355003587140
8110995700045062004005SF1551000700070101000320180100000000068770001500005000000121385215 6F0F00088F05

E0620040      ,,**
CFFFFFFF4440017
50620040000007F

   ZIEP0004E0620040                ?          ,        **                                              6016
4000ECCDFFFFCFFFFFFF000000000830124617444444444444444440018
110099570004506200400C000000055F145F730000000000000000070

  DDACCAPRE0620040        @ @        ?DDACCAIX    **                                                   6017
20CCCCCCDDCFFFFFFF00000447470830123 6CCCCCCDD0018
114413317950620040011160ACAC055F155F441331790071

  DDACCA XE0620040                   ?DDACCAIX    **                                                   6018
20CCCCCCCECFFFFFFF00000400000830123 6CCCCCCCE0018
114413319750620040021 1C00E80055F155F441331970072

   IMSA                        **                                                                      6019
0000CDECFFF000000830123 00018
60009421FFF60000055F15600073
```

Checkpoint ID

Program variable area at shutdown time

Line number

Page number

Last account number "000305088781" in the account database, was updated

-329-

Fig. 14-5. System log at shutdown time.

```
E.R0620040                                                    PROG E0620040
12/13/85              ACCOUNT DATABASE UPDATE                 PAGE       32

   BANK     ACCOUNT        OLD            NEW            STATUS
            NUMBER         STMT DATE      STMT DATE      CODE

   500      00305049371    0093085273     0123185365
   500      00305050332    0093085273     0123185365
   500      00305054003    0093085273     0123185365
   500      00305058619    0093085273     0123185365
   500      00305063418    0093085273     0123185365
   500      00305072902    0093085273     0123185365
   500      00305072938    0093085273     0123185365
   500      00305076245    0093085273     0123185365
   500      00305080911    0093085273     0123185365
   500      00305081616    0093085273     0123185365
   500      00305087335    0093085273     0123185365
   500   -->00305088781    0093085273     0123185365
         |
         L Last account updated at shutdown time (see FIG. 14.5)
```

Fig. 14-6. Sample report at shutdown time.

The program establishes a position in the database by getting the identity of the last segment occurrence that was processed—in our example, it is account number 00305088781—and restart processing continues. FIGURE 14-8 illustrates the update report after the checkpoint restart.

HOW TO RESTART A BMP RUN

The previous sections showed us how to restart the account update program E0620040 which began to run in a batch DL/1 mode before being shut down by the console operator. Now, let's see the requirements to restart the program if it begins to run in a BMP mode.

Catalogued Procedure

There is no requirement in JCL to restart a BMP job which began in a DL/1 or BMP batch mode.

The catalogued procedure 'BMPRUN' as presented in FIG. 14-7 remains unchanged. Again, here are the main points you need to specify in the JCL:

1. Specify the checkpoint ID at which the program will be restarted.
2. Specify the parameters needed to run in a BMP mode.
3. Specify the GSAM update report which will be repositioned by IMS before processing.

```
//BMPRUN    PROC PSB=E0620040,MBR=E0620040,
//            IN=,OUT=,OPT=N,SPIE=0,
//            TEST=0,DIRCA=000,PRLD=,STIMER=,
//            CKPTID=ZIEP0004,                      <--- CHECKPOINT ID SPECIFIED (1)
//            PARMDLI=,CPUTIME=,NBA=,                    FOR RESTART RUN
//            OBA=,IMSID=,AGN=,RGN=2048K,                               ^
//            GEN1='(+1)',                                              |
//            GEN2='(+1)',                                              |
//            CTLLIB='E.CONTROL',                                       |
//            STATO=P,                                                  |
//            IMSVS='IMSVS.',                                           |
//            LIB1=PRODLIB,                                             |
//            UNIT1=SYSDA,                                              |
//            RPTSC='(6118,(5000,2500))'                                |
//            RPTSC2='(6118,(5000,2500),RLSE)',                         |
//*-------------------------------------------------------------        |
//*                                                                     |
//*      IEFBR14 CREATES GSAM REPORT DATA SET                           |
//*                                                                     |
//*-------------------------------------------------------------        |
//STEP10    EXEC PGM=IEFBR14                                            |
//DD1      DD  DSN=&STATO.06.D2040001.REPORT&GEN1,DISP=(,CATLG,DELETE), |
//         SPACE=&RPTSPC,UNIT=&UNIT1,                                   |
//         DCB=(E.MODELDCB,LRECL=133,BLKSIZE=6118,RECFM=FBA)            |
//*                                                                     |
//*-------------------------------------------------------------        |
//*                                                                     |
//*      BMP/DLI STEP TO UPDATE DATA BASE                               |
//*                                                                     |
//*-------------------------------------------------------------        |
//STEP20    EXEC PGM=DFSRRC00,REGION=&RGN,                              |
//*         PARM=(DLI,&MBR,&PSB)                                        |
//          PARM=(BMP,&MBR,&PSB,&IN,&OUT,                               |
//          &OPT&SPIE&TEST&DIRCA,&PRLD,&STIMER,&CKPTID,        <-------+ (2)
//          &PARMDLI,&CPUTIME,&NBA,&OBA,&IMSID,&AGN),COND=(0,NE)
//STEPLIB   DD  DSN=&IMSVS.RESLIB,DISP=SHR
//          DD  DSN=&LIB1,DISP=SHR
//IMSACB    DD  DSN=&IMSVS.ACBLIB,DISP=SHR
//IMS       DD  DSN=&IMSVS.PSBLIB,DISP=SHR
//          DD  DSN=&IMSVS.DBDLIB,DISP=SHR
//SYSPRINT DD  SYSOUT=A
//DFSRESLB DD  DSN=&IMSVS.RESLIB,DISP=SHR
//DATECARD DD  DSN=&CTLLIB(DAILY),DISP=SHR
//CHECKPNT DD  DUMMY,DCB=BLKSIZE=80
//PARMCARD DD  DUMMY,DCB=BLKSIZE=80
//MNI0006G DD  DSN=&STATO.06.D2040001.REPORT&GEN2,DISP=OLD                (3)
//IMSERR   DD  DUMMY
//SYSOUT   DD  SYSOUT=A
//SYSUDUMP DD  SYSOUT=A
//ABNLENAB DD  DUMMY
//*
//*** FOLLOWING LOG DATA SET IS NEEDED FOR CHKPT RERUN AND DLI RUN ***
//*
//IMSLOGR DD DSN=&STATO.06.D2040001.IMSLOG1,DISP=OLD      <=== CHKPT RERUN (4)
//*
```

Fig. 14-7. Sample BMP restart.

Fig. 14-7. continued

```
//***  FOLLOWING JCL IS NECESSARY FOR DLI RUN                         ***
//*
//*IEFRDER DD DSN=&STATO.06.D2040001.IMSLOG1,DISP=(,CATLG,CATLG),
//*          UNIT=SYSTP,DCB=(BLKSIZE=11976,LRECL=11972,RECFM=VB)           (5)
//*DFSVSAMP DD DSN=&CTLLIB(DPAMS#00),DISP=SHR
//*
//***  JCL SPECIFYING DATA BASES NEEDED FOR DLI ONLY                  ***
//*
//*DDACCAPR DD  DSN=P06.IMNI000.DDACCAPR,DISP=OLD                          (6)
//*DDACCAPR DD  DSN=P06.IMNI000.DDACCAIX,DISP=OLD
//*
//*-----------------------------------------------------------------
//*
//*       IEBGENER PRINTS GSAM REPORT
//*
//*-----------------------------------------------------------------
//STEP30   EXEC PGM=IEBGENER,COND=EVEN
//SYSPRINT DD SYSOUT=A
//SYSUT1   DD DSN=&STATO.06.D2040001.REPORT&GEN2,DISP=OLD,
//            SPACE=&RPTSPC2,UNIT=&UNIT1
//SYSOUT   DD SYSOUT=&SYSOUT,DCB=(LRECL=133,BLKSIZE=1330,RECFM=FBA)
//SYSIN     DD DUMMY
//*
//*                    LAST CARD OF PROCEDURE
```

4. Specify the old log data set to be used to restart the program. This log contains the checkpoint data.
5. There is no need to specify a new log data set name for a BMP job.
6. The databases need not be specified for BMP because they are specified in the ACBGEN job.

Log Tape Identification

We have noted in number 5 above that, for a BMP run, we do not have to specify the log data set name which is used in case we do a restart; this specification is required for a DL/1 job only. You may wonder how to identify the right log tape to be used to restart the program. This explanation follows.

Each installation has a unique data set name assigned to the IMS log tape. Each time the IMS log tape becomes full, a tape copy is created with a unique time stamp affixed to the log data set name. This stamp is used to identify the log tape copy which contains the restart information. FIGURE 14-9 shows how to identify the log tape of our BMP program which was shut down at 23.00.43 hours. If we want to restart a job which was shut down at 23.00.43, we feed the following statement into our JCL:

```
//IMSLOGR DD   DSN=IMSLOG.T3472300.IMSA.IMSVS.SECDARY.LOG,DISP=OLD
```

This tells IMS to get the restart information from this tape.

E.R062C040 PROG E0620040
12/13/85 ACCOUNT DATABASE UPDATE PAGE 32

BANK	ACCOUNT NUMBER	OLD STMT DATE	NEW STMT DATE	STATUS CODE
500	00305049371	0093085273	0123185365	
500	00305050332	0093085273	0123185365	
500	00305054003	0093085273	0123185365	
500	00305058619	0093085273	0123185365	
500	00305063418	0093085273	0123185365	
500	00305072902	0093085273	0123185365	
500	00305072938	0093085273	0123185365	
500	00305076245	0093085273	0123185365	
500	00305080911	0093085273	0123185365	
500	00305081616	0093085273	0123185365	
500	00305087335	0093085273	0123185365	
500	00305088781	0093085273	0123185365	
500	00305089644	0093085273	0123185365	
500	00305091271	0093085273	0123185365	Restart from this point ↑
500	00305092665	0093085273	0123185365	
500	00305093140	0093085273	0123185365	
500	00307500020	0093085273	0123185365	
500	00307500032	0093085273	0123185365	
500	00307500044	0093085273	0123185365	
500	00307500056	0093085273	0123185365	
500	00307500082	0093085273	0123185365	
500	00307500094	0093085273	0123185365	
500	00307500109	0093085273	0123185365	z
500	00307500111	0093085273	0123185365	
500	00307500123	0093085273	0123185365	
500	00307500147	0093085273	0123185365	
500	00307500161	0093085273	0123185365	
500	00307500173	0093085273	0123185365	
500	00307500197	0093085273	0123185365	z
500	00307500226	0093085273	0123185365	
500	00307500238	0093085273	0123185365	
500	00307500240	0093085273	0123185365	
500	00307500264	0093085273	0123185365	
500	00307500288	0093085273	0123185365	z
500	00307500290	0093085273	0123185365	
500	00307500305	0093085273	0123185365	
500	00307500317	0093085273	0123185365	
500	00307500329	0093085273	0123185365	
500	00307500355	0093085273	0123185365	
500	00307500381	0093085273	0123185365	
500	00307500393	0093085273	0123185365	
500	00307500408	0093085273	0123185365	
500	00307500410	0093085273	0123185365	
500	00307500446	0093085273	0123185365	
500	00307500458	0093085273	0123185365	
500	00307500460	0093085273	0123185365	
500	00307500472	0093085273	0123185365	
500	00307500501	0093085273	0123185365	

Fig. 14-8. Sample report after checkpoint restart.

```
85.347   12.54.50   VOL 29   006156          IMSLOG.T3471254.IMSA.IMSVS.SECDARY.LOG
85.347   13.34.50   VOL 30   002097          IMSLOG.T3471334.IMSA.IMSVS.SECDARY.LOG
85.347   14.16.41   VOL 31   004511          IMSLOG.T3471416.IMSA.IMSVS.SECDARY.LOG
85.347   15.01.06   VOL 32   001695          IMSLOG.T3471501.IMSA.IMSVS.SECDARY.LOG
85.347   16.00.56   VOL 33   005838          IMSLOG.T3471600.IMSA.IMSVS.SECDARY.LOG
85.347   16.56.58   VOL 34   007573          IMSLOG.T3471656.IMSA.IMSVS.SECDARY.LOG
85.347   17.34.43   VOL 35   004732          IMSLOG.T3471734.IMSA.IMSVS.SECDARY.LOG
85.347   18.03.30   VOL 36   000880          IMSLOG.T3471803.IMSA.IMSVS.SECDARY.LOG
85.347   18.56.43   VOL 37   005337          IMSLOG.T3471856.IMSA.IMSVS.SECDARY.LOG
85.347   20.03.21   VOL 38   007741          IMSLOG.T3472003.IMSA.IMSVS.SECDARY.LOG
85.347   21.09.26   VOL 39   006816          IMSLOG.T3472109.IMSA.IMSVS.SECDARY.LOG
85.347  [23.00.43]  VOL 40   008123          IMSLOG.[T3472300].IMSA.IMSVS.SECDARY.LOG
85.348    3.38.53   VOL 41   (005796,005720)     IMSLOG.T3480338.IMSA.IMSVS.SECDA
85.348    4.38.10   VOL 42   (005887,005191)     IMSLOG.T3480438.IMSA.IMSVS.SECDA
85.348    5.00.02   VOL 43   (001588,001381)     IMSLOG.T3480500.IMSA.IMSVS.SECDA

                                              Time stamp
```

Fig. 14-9.

Sample ACBGEN JCL

We have learned that, in BMP jobs, we do not specify the databases accessed by the application program. You may wonder how the BMP job accesses the correct files required by the program which executes it. Actually, the specification of the databases is done in advance in a separate process called ACBGEN.

The following illustrates a sample ACBGEN required for BMP jobs:

```
//EX10MDAA          JOB          (0040,TEST,,5),'ZIEP ACBGEN',
.//                 MSGLEVEL=(1,1),CLASS=J,MSGCLASS=T
//***********************************************************************
//*        THIS JOB DOES ACBGEN FOR A BMP PSB - A SAMPLE
//***********************************************************************
//COPY        EXEC   PGM=IEBCOPY
//SYSPRINT       DD   SYSOUT=T
//OUTPUT         DD   DSN=&&ACBLIB,DISP=(,PASS,DELETE),
//                   DCB=IMSVS.ACBLIB,UNIT=SYSTEST,  ← ACB library
//                   SPACE=(CYL,(15,,250))
//INPUT          DD   DSN=IMSVS.ACBLIB,DISP=SHR
//SYSUT3         DD   UNIT=SYSDA,SPACE=(TRK,(1))
//SYSUT4         DD   UNIT=SYSDA,SPACE=(TRK,(1))
//SYSIN          DD   *
   COPY    OUTDD=OUTPUT,INDD=INPUT
/*
//ACBGEN EXEC ACBGEN,SOUT=T
//G.IMS          DD   DSN=IMSVS.PSBLIB,DISP=SHR          ← Concatenate these
//               DD   DSN=IMSVS.DBDLIB,DISP=SHR            two libraries.
//G.IMSACB       DD   DSN=&&ACBLIB,DISP=(OLD,DELETE)     ← ACBLIB
//SYSIN DD *
   BUILD PSB=(EB0620040) ← PSB name
/*
//
```

The ACBLIB stores control blocks required for a specific program. The blocks are called ACBs, and each is a combination of DBDs and PSBs in an internal format required by DL/1 for database system execution. The ACBLIB is referenced in the BMP job via an ACBLIB card as shown below.

```
 ......
//STEPLIB      DD  DSN=IMSVS.RESLIB,DISP=SHR
//             DD  DSN=PRODLIB,DISP=SHR
//IMSACB       DD  DSN=IMSVS.ACBLIB,DISP=SHR
//IMS          DD  DSN=IMSVS.PSBLIB,DISP=SHR
//             DD  DSN=IMSVS.DBDLIB,DISP=SHR
//SYSPRINT     DD SYSOUT=A
//DFSRESLB     DD DSN=IMSVS.RESLIB,DISP=SHR
```

Appendix A

MFS Compilation Statements

This appendix covers the most commonly-used MFS compilation control statements. These statements are used to control the way the MFS language utility works. We will discuss four types of compilation control statements. These are:

Sysprint Control	Miscellaneous	Substitution	Repetition
TITLE	COPY	EQU	DO
PRINT	END	RESCAN	ENDDO
SPACE			
EJECT			

SYSPRINT CONTROL STATEMENTS

The Sysprint control statements are not required but are recommended for improving the readability of output.

The TITLE statement is used to specify the heading to appear on the Sysprint listing. For example:

```
TITLE 'CUSTOMER INQUIRY'                    *** Title ***
PRINT NOGEN
```

The PRINT statement provides printing specifications for the Sysprint listing.

```
PRINT [{ON  }] [{GEN  }]
       {OFF }    {NOGEN}
```

<u>ON</u> OFF	Specifies whether (ON) or not (OFF) a listing should be printed. Default is ON.
<u>GEN</u> NOGEN	Specifies whether or not the intermediate text blocks (ITBs) should be printed in hexadecimal following the statement at the left margin.

By default, the MFS Language Utility produces a listing of the control statements along with the hexadecimal ITBs. An example of an MFS listing with the ITBs printed is presented in FIG. A-1. You can suppress the printing of the ITBs by specifying:

```
PRINT NOGEN
```

The SPACE statement specifies the number of lines to skip when output listing is printed. The default is 1.

The EJECT statement is used to eject a page in an output listing.

MISCELLANEOUS CONTROL STATEMENTS

The COPY statement is used to name a member in a partitioned data set that is copied into the MFS format input steam for compilation:

```
COPY Member-name
```

Member-name specifies the name of the partitioned data set member to be copied into the input stream of the utility preprocessor.

The END statement is used to define the end of the input to Sysin processing. It is defined as the last statement in a MFS input stream. If you omit the END statement, the MFS Language Utility will generate an error message.

SUBSTITUTION CONTROL STATEMENTS

There are instances when long character strings are used many times in the process of defining MFS control blocks such as field attributes. The coding can be simplified through the use of a shorter symbol which represents a much longer string.

The EQU statements defines a symbol to be used to substitute a number, alphanumeric identifier or symbol:

```
SYMBOL  EQU  Number
             Alphanumeric Identifier
             Literal
```

- SYMBOL is one- to eight-character identifier; the first character must be alphanumeric.
- Number specifies the value to be represented by the symbol and consists of one to 256 decimal digits.

- The Alphanumeric Identifier specifies the value to be represented by the symbol and consists of one to 256 alphanumeric characters; the first must be alphanumeric.
- Literal specifies the literal value represented by the symbol and consists of one to 256 valid characters enclosed in quotes.

Here is an example of the EQU statement:

```
HISKIP  EQU     '(PROT,HI)'
        ....
        DFLD    'CUSTOMER INQUIRY',POS=(02,29),LTH=16,  *
                ATTR=HISKIP
```

A period (.) may be used to concatenate two equated values or one value and specific data.

The following example shows how to define concatenated EQU statements:

```
DIF
         TITLE   'CUSTOMER NAME AND ADDRESS CHANGE'
         PRINT   NOGEN
ATRYE    EQU     'ATTR=YES'
JUSTR    EQU     'JUST=R'
FILLO    EQU     'FILL=C"0"'
JUSTRO   EQU     'FILL="0"",JUST=R'
L        EQU     'LTH='
A        EQU     'ATTR='
N        EQU     '(NUM,NOPROT,NORM,NOMOD)'
P        EQU     '(MOD,PROT,NODISP)'
         .....
CUSTUP   FMT
         DEV     TYPE=(3270,2),FEAT=IGNORE,SYSMSG=MESSAGE
         DIV     TYPE=INOUT
         .....
TRANCD   DFLD    POS(04,5),L.8.A.P ← Concatenated EQU values
         ....
         FMTEND
```

The above DFLD definition with concatenated EQU values will produce the same result as:

```
TRANCD   DFLD    POS=(04,5),LTH=8,ATTR=(MOD,PROT,NODISP)
```

The RESCAN statement controls the replacement of symbols specified in the EQU statement.

```
RESCAN  [{OFF}]  [,{  5   }]
        [{ON }]  [ {Number}]
```

(OFF and 5 are underlined as the defaults.)

```
MESSAGE/FORMAT SERVICE PREPROCESSOR                                  86.097 PAGE 0002

ITB OBJECT CODE ERRORS                        STMNT    SOURCE STATEMENT                                  COPY/STK

                                              1              TITLE 'CUSTOMER ENTRY'
                                              2 HISKIP       EQU   '(PROT,HI)'
                                              3 FMT002       FMT
 00000 - FMT002
00140100   C6D4E3F0   F0F24040   80000000
00000000
                                              4              DEV  TYPE=(3270,2),FEAT=IGNORE
 000014 - DEV00004
00680200   C4C5E5F0   F0F0F0F4   F8000400
00000000   F3F2F7F0   40F24040   00180050
80000000   40404040   40404040   40404040
40404040   40404040   40404040   40404040
40404040   00000000   00000000   00000000
00000000   000000000  00000000   00000000
00000000
                                              5              DIV  TYPE=INOUT
 00007C - DIV00005
00460300   C4C9E5F0   F0F0F0F5   80000000
C0000000   00000000   00000000   40404040
40404040   00000000   40404040   40404040
00000000   40404040   40404040   40404040
40404040   0000
                                              6              DPAGE  CURSOR=((08,18))        *** CURSOR POSITION ****
```

```
 0000C2 - DPG00006
00420400   C4D7C7F0   F0F0F0F6   21080000
00000000   40404040   40404040   00000001
00340000   00000000   00000000   00050000
00000000   00010008   00124040   40404040
4040
                                              7          DFLD 'CUSTOMER ENTRY',POS=(02,29),LTH=14,   *
 000104 - DFL00007                                             ATTR=HISKIP
004D0500   C4C6D3F0   F0F0F0F7   F6000000
00000000   00010002   001DD02C   40404040
40404040   000E003F   000E0000   00004040
40404040   4040001D   00000000   00FF00C3
E4E2E3D6   D4C5D940   C5D5E3D9   E8
                                              8 TRANCD   DFLD POS=(04,5),LTH=8,ATTR=(MOD,PROT,NODISP)
 000151 - TRANCD
003F0500   E3D9C1D5   C3C44040   FC000000
00000000   00010004   000549A4   E3D9C1D5
C3C44040   00080000   00000000   00004040
40404040   40400005   00000000   00FF00

                                              9          DFLD 'CUSTOMER NO:',POS=(06,5)
 000190 - DFL00009
004B0500   C4C6D3F0   F0F0F0F9   E6000000
00000000   00010006   0005C03C   40404040
40404040   000C003F   000C0000   00004040
40404040   404000005  00000000   00FF00C3
```

Intermediate Text Blocks

NOTE: By specifying GEN rather than NOGEN, the compiler prints on the left side of the listing a hexadecimal listing of the code generated for each source statement.

Fig. A-1. MFS listing with ITBs printed in hexadecimal.

OFF — The default is OFF unless a number is specified in the operand field.

ON — Specifies that replacement texts should be rescanned for further substitution.

5 / Number — Specifies how many times further substitution is allowed in single RESCAN substitution. Here, 5 is the default.

The following example shows how to issue a RESCAN statement:

```
DIF
         TITLE   'CUSTOMER NAME AND ADDRESS CHANGE'
         PRINT   NOGEN
P        EQU     'POS=(06,22)'
L        EQU     'LTH=20'
A        EQU     'ATTR=MP'
MP       EQU     '(MOD,PROT)'
         .....
         RESCAN ON,2
         .....
LASTNM   DFLD    P.L.A
         ....
         RESCAN OFF
```

In this example, after the first substitution, the following DFLD statement will be generated:

```
LASTNM   DFLD    POS=(06,22),LTH=20,ATTR=MP
```

The number 2 was specified for further substitution. 'ATTR=MP' was substituted by 'ATTR'=(MOD,PROT)' in the second RESCAN:

```
LASTNM   DFLD    POS=(06,22),LTH=20,ATTR=(MOD,PROT)
```

REPETITION CONTROL STATEMENTS

The DO and ENDDO statements cause the repetitive generation of DFLD and MFLD statements. The DFLD labels must be six characters in length so that a two-digit number (01 to 99) can be appended. Longer labels will be truncated.

The format of the DO statement is:

```
[LABEL]  DO  COUNT
             [ ,{ 1                  } ]
             [  { line-increment     } ]
             [  { position-increment } ]
             [ ,{ MAX              } ]
             [  { column-increment } ]
             [ ,{ SUP= 01     } ]
             [  {      number } ]
             [ , BOUND={ LINE  } ]
             [         { FIELD } ]
```

The DO and ENDDO statement can be used in DIF/DOF and MID/MOD. Here is an example in DIF/DOF:

```
DLABEL  DFLD  POS=(nn,n),LTH=n,ATTR=
        .
        .
        ENDDO
```

- LABEL is a one- to eight-character alphanumeric name that may be specified.
- COUNT specifies how many times to generate the statements between the DO and ENDDO statements.
- Line-increment specifies how much to increase the line position after the first cycle. The default is 1. For example, if we want to generate 10 detail lines, and each line is to start at the same column position of each line, then the line-increment is 1.
- Position-increment specifies how much to increase the position parameter after the first cycle. The first cycle uses the nnn values specified in the POS= operand of the DFLD statement. The position-increment is used for input device format when MODE=STREAM is specified.
- Column=increment specifies how much to increase the column position after the first cycle. This parameter is used to define an array with many entries, and each entry is separated from the last entry by one or more blanks.
- MAX specifies the line-increment to be used at the end of each cycle. (The column values in the DFLDs remain the same for each cycle.)
- SUF= specifies the two-digit suffix to be appended to the DFLD name of the first group of generated DFLD statements. The default is 1. MFS increments the suffix by 1 on each subsequent generation of statements. So, the DFLD names of the second generation will have 02 as a suffix.

  If the specified suffix exceeds two digits, MFS uses the rightmost two digits.
- BOUND= specifies when updates to line positions and column positions occur. The default is LINE.

  LINE specifies that all fields are to be examined before repeating. If too many fields do not fit into one line, the column position for all fields will reset to the initial value, and the line position value will be increased by the line-increment value.

  FIELD specifies that each time the statement(s) is repeated, the column position value is increased by the column-increment value. If MAX is specified, or the new column position value reaches device-length capacity, the line position value is increased by the line-increment value and the column position value is reset to the initial value.

In MID/MOD the DO statements will cause the repetitive generation of MFLD statements between the DO and ENDDO statements.

The ENDDO statement terminates the group of DFLD/MFLD statements that are to be repetitively generated. The generated DFLD statements are printed immediately following the ENDDO statement. The ENDDO statement is shown in the example below.

```
         DO 18
LINE     DFLD      POS=(06,02),LTH=78,ATTR=(ALPHA,PROT)
         ENDDO
         DFLD      'INTDIS',POS=(24,73)
         FMTEND
INPUTA   MSG       TYPE=INPUT,SOR=FMT004,OPT=1,NXT=INTDIS
         SEG
         MFLD      PFK,LTH=14,FILL=NULL
         MSGEND
INTDIS   MSG       TYPE=OUTPUT,SOR=(FMT004,IGNORE),OPT=1,NXT=INPUTA *
                   PAGE=YES,FILL=NULL
         SEG
         DO 18
         MFLD      LINE,LTH=78
         ENDDO
```

ISSUING DO AND ENDDO STATEMENTS

Suppose that you are required to generate a screen format as presented in FIG. A-2 (note that there are 18 identical lines on this screen). The MFS control statements are given in FIG. A-3.

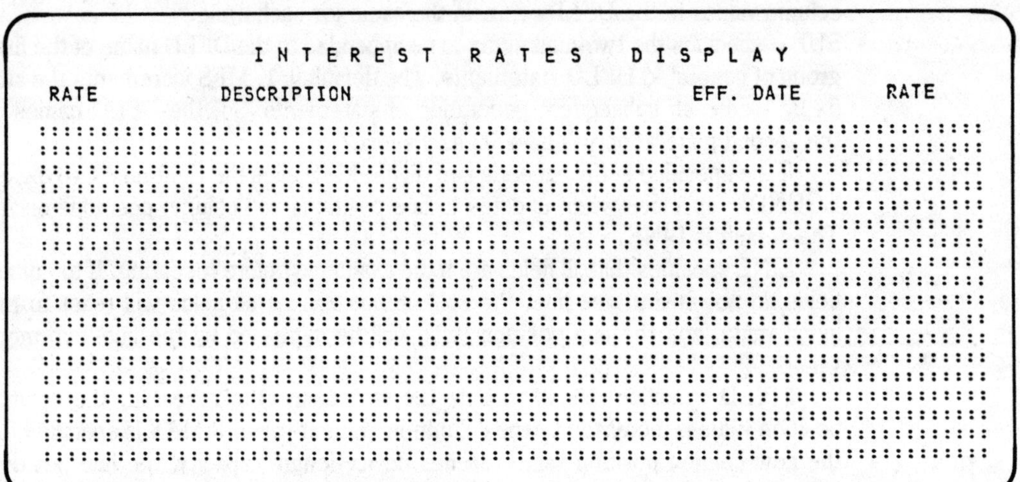

Fig. A-2.

```
FMT004    FMT
          DEV       TYPE/(3270.2),FEAT=IGNORE
          DIV       TYPE=INOUT
            .
            .
            .
          DFLD      'INTEREST RATES DISPLAY',                    X
                    POS=(02.21)
          DFLD      'RATE',POS=(04.03)
          DFLD      'DESCRIPTION',POS=(04.17)
          DFLD      'EFF. DATE',POS=(04.56)
          DFLD      'RATE',POS=(04.72)
          DO  18
LINE      DFLD      POS=(06,02),LTH=78,ATTR=(ALPHA,PROT)
          ENDDO
          FMTEND
INTDIS    MSG       TYPE=OUTPUT,SOR=(FMT004,IGNORE),OPT=1,NXT=INPUTA, X
                    PAGE=YES,FILL=NULL
          SEG
          DO        18
          MFLD      LINE,LTH=78
          ENDDO
          MSGEND
          END
```

This area specifies 18 generations between the DO and ENDO statements.

Fig. A-3.

The following shows the DFLDs and MFLDs generated by MFS as a result of the DO statement:

```
STMNT          SOURCE STATEMENT

    1             TITLE   'USING SYSTEM LITERALS'                          FMT004
    2             PRINT   NOGEN
    3 FMT004      FMT
    4             DEV     TYPE=(3270,2),FEAT=IGNORE,                            X
                          PFK=(PFK,'/FOR DDAINQ.','/FOR SVGINQ.'.               X
                          '/FOR ADDCUS.','/FOR OUTMSG.','/FOR EMPLOY.',         X
                          '/FOR E1061500.'','/FOR PAYROL,','/FOR INDEXF.'.      X
                          '/FOR INDEXD.','/FOR INDEXA.','/FOR INDEXB.'),        X
                          DSCA=X'00C0' ** ERASE CURRENT DISPLAY BEFORE WRITE**
    5             DIV     TYPE=INOUT
    6             DPAGE   CURSOR=((01,02,CURSOR)),FILL=NONE
    7 TIME        DFLD    POS=(01,08),LTH=08,ATTR=(ALPHA,PROT)
    8             DFLD    'COMMERCIAL  LOAN',POS=(01,26)
    9 DATE        DFLD    POS=(01,60),LTH=08,ATTR=(ALPHA,PROT)
   10 PAGEID      DFLD    POS=(01,70),LTH=10,ATTR=(ALPHA,PROT)
   11             DFLD    'INTEREST    RATES   DISPLAY',                        X
                          POS=(02,21)
```

```
12              DFLD    'RATE',POS=(04,03)
13              DFLD    'DESCRIPTION',POS=(04,17)
14              DFLD    'EFF. DATE',POS=(04,56)
15              DFLD    'RATE',POS=(04,72)
16              DO 18
17 LINE         DFLD    POS=(06,02),LTH=78,ATTR=(ALPHA,PROT)
18              ENDDO
19+LINE01       DFLD    POS=(6,2,1),LTH=78,ATTR=(...)
20+LINE02       DFLD    POS=(7,2,1),LTH=78,ATTR=(...)
21+LINE03       DFLD    POS=(8,2,1),LTH=78,ATTR=(...)
22+LINE04       DFLD    POS=(9,2.1),LTH=78,ATTR=(...)
23+LINE05       DFLD    POS=(10,2,1),LTH=78,ATTR=(...)
24+LINE06       DFLD    POS=(11,2,1),LTH=78,ATTR=(...)
25+LINE07       DFLD    POS=(12,2,1),LTH=78,ATTR=(...)
26+LINE08       DFLD    POS=(13,2,1),LTH=78,ATTR=(...)
27+LINE09       DFLD    POS=(14,2,1),LTH=78,ATTR=(...)
28+LINE10       DFLD    POS=(15,2,1),LTH=78,ATTR=(...)
29+LINE11       DFLD    POS=(16,2,1),LTH=78,ATTR=(...)
30+LINE12       DFLD    POS=(17,2,1),LTH=78,ATTR=(...)
31+LINE13       DFLD    POS=(18,2,1),LTH=78,ATTR=(...)
32+LINE14       DFLD    POS=(19,2,1),LTH=78,ATTR=(...)
33+LINE15       DFLD    POS=(20,2,1),LTH=78,ATTR=(...)
34+LINE16       DFLD    POS=(21,2,1),LTH=78,ATTR=(...)
35+LINE17       DFLD    POS=(22,2,1),LTH=78,ATTR=(...)
36+LINE18       DFLD    POS=(23,2,1),LTH=78,ATTR=(...)
37              DFLD    'INTDIS',POS=(24,73)
38              FMTEND
39 INPUTA       MSG     TYPE=INPUT,SOR=FMT004,OPT=1,NXT=INTDIS
40              SEG
41              MFLD    PFK,LTH=14,FILL=NULL
42              MSGEND
43 INTDIS       MSG     TYPE=OUTPUT,SOR=(FMT004,IGNORE),OPT=1,NXT=INPUTA, X

                        PAGE=YES,FILL=NULL
44              SEG
45              MFLD    CURSOR,LTH=04     *** Cursor position ***
46              MFLD    TIME,LTH=08
47              MFLD    DATE,LTH=08
48              MFLD    PAGEID,LTH=10
49              DO 18
50              MFLD    LINE,LTH=78
51              ENDDO
52+             MFLD    LINE01,LTH=78
53+             MFLD    LINE02,LTH=78
54+             MFLD    LINE03,LTH=78
55+             MFLD    LINE04,LTH=78
56+             MFLD    LINE05,LTH=78
57+             MFLD    LINE06,LTH=78
58+             MFLD    LINE07,LTH=78
59+             MFLD    LINE08,LTH=78
60+             MFLD    LINE09,LTH=78
61+             MFLD    LINE10,LTH=78
62+             MFLD    LINE11,LTH=78
63+             MFLD    LINE12,LTH=78
```

```
         MFLD    LINE13,LTH=78
         MFLD    LINE14,LTH=78
         MFLD    LINE15,LTH=78
         MFLD    LINE16,LTH=78
         MFLD    LINE17,LTH=78
         MFLD    LINE18,LTH=78
         MSGEND
         END
```

Now, the following example shows how to issue the DO and ENDDO statements with MAX, SUF=, and BOUND= operands.

The DFLD DO statement is more versatile than the MFLD DO statement since you can specify both line and column increments. When you specify BOUND=LINE, MFS ensures that all the DFLDs included by the DO and ENDDO statements can fit on the screen before they are mapped. Suppose that you are required to generate a screen format as presented in FIG. A-4 (note that there are 17 identical lines on this screen). The MFS format for this screen is given in FIG. A-5.

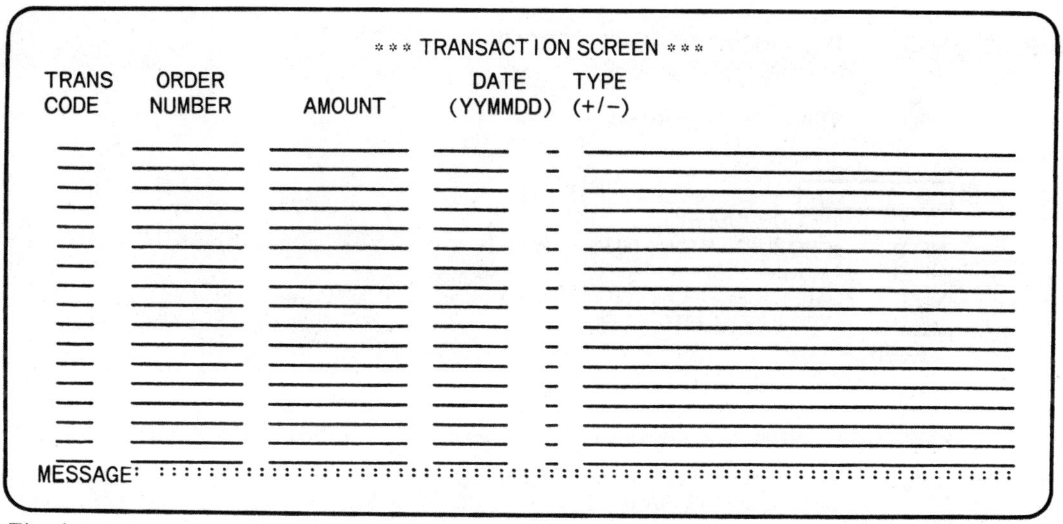

Fig. A-4.

```
         TITLE   'USE OF DO AND ENDDO STATEMENTS'
         PRINT   NOGEN
FMT07    FMT
         DEV     TYPE=(3270,2),FEAT=IGNORE
         DIV     TYPE=INOUT
         DPAGE   CURSOR=((07,03))
         DFLD    '***  TRANSACTION SCREEN  ***',POS=(02,25),ATTR=PROT
```

Fig. A-5.

Fig. A-5. continued

```
         DFLD     'TRANS  ORDER                      DATE  TYPE',          $
                  POS=(04,02),ATTR=PROT
         DFLD     'CODE  NUMBER  AMOUNT  (YYMMDD) (+ -)',                  $
                  POS=(05,02),ATTR=PROT
*
         DO       17,1,MAX,SUF=01,BOUND=LINE
TRCODE   DFLD     POS=(07,03),LTH=03,ATTR=(HI,MOD)
JOBO     DFLD     POS=(07,09),LTH=09,ATTR=(HI,MOD)
AMOUNT   DFLD     POS=(07,20),LTH=11,ATTR=(HI,MOD)
DATEA    DFLD     POS=(07,33),LTH=06,ATTR=(HI,MOD)
TYPE     DFLD     POS=(07,42),LTH=01,ATTR=(HI,MOD)
MESSG    DFLD     POS=(07,45),LTH=35,ATTR=(HI,MOD)
         ENDDO
*
*
         DFLD     'MESSAGE:',POS=(24,02),ATTR=PROT
REPLY    DFLD     POS=(24,11),LTH=69,ATTR=PROT
         FMTEND
*
*
INTRANS  MSG      TYPE=INPUT,SOR=(FMT07,IGNORE),
                  NXT=OUTRANS
         SEG
         MFLD     'TRANS006  ',LTH=09
*
*
         DO       17
         MFLD     TRCODE,JUST=L,LTH=03,FILL=X'40'
         MFLD     JOBO,JUST=R,LTH=09,FILL=X'40'
         MFLD     AMOUNT,JUST=R,LTH=11,FILL=X'40''
         MFLD     DATEA,JUST=L,LTH=06,FILL=X'40'
         MFLD     TYPE,JUST=L,LTH=01,FILL=X'40'
         ENDDO
*
         MSGEND
*
*
OUTRANS  MSG      TYPE=OUTPUT,SOR=(FMT07,IGNORE),
                  OPT=1,NXT=INTRANS
         SEG
*
         DO       17
         MFLD     TRCODE,LTH=05,ATTR=YES
         MFLD     JOBO,LTH=11,ATTR=YES
         MFLD     AMOUNT,LTH=13,ATTR=YES
         MFLD     DATEA,LTH=08,ATTR=YES
         MFLD     TYPE,LTH=03,ATTR=YES
         ENDDO
*
         MFLD     REPLY,LTH=71,ATTR=YES
         MSGEND
         END
```

Appendix B

JCL to Generate MFS Control Blocks

MFS control blocks may be generated in any of three operational modes—standard, batch, and test.

- In the standard mode, normal processing occurs to create blocks and to place them into the staging format library, IMSVS.FORMAT. The MFSUTL procedure is used for this mode.
- In the batch mode, the MFSBTCH1 procedure creates the control blocks and accumulates them in a special library, IMSVS.MFSBTCH. The MFSBTCH2 procedure then moves the batched control blocks into the staging library.
- In the test mode, the MFSTEST procedure creates the control blocks and places them into the IMSVS.TFORMAT library.

FIGURES B-1, B-2 and B-3 present these procedures. Procedures MFSUTL and MFSTEST have two steps, S1 and S2. Procedures MFSBTCH1 and MFSBTCH2 have one step each, S1 and S2. In all three modes, step S1 checks and generates the skeleton module for each source control block and step S2 cross-checks the related control blocks and completes the MFS generation.

SYMBOLIC PARAMETERS

The following explains the symbolic parameters specified in the EXEC statement's PARM keyword of step S1. The default parameters are underscored.

PXREF = NOXREF, / XREF (NOXREF underscored)	Specifies whether (XREF) or not (NOXREF) a sorted cross reference listing should be provided for all labels and related references.

```
//              PROC  RGN=360K,SOUT=A,SNODE=IMSVS,
//                    SOR=NOLIB,MBR=NOMBR,PXREF=NOXREF,
//                    PCOMP=NOCOMP,PSUBS=NOSUBS,PDIAG=NODIAG,
//                    COMPR=NOCOMPRESS,COMPR2=COMPRESS,
//                    LN=55,SN=8,DEVCHAR=0
Step 1 ---> //S1          EXEC  PGM=DFSUPAA0,REGION=&RGN,
// PARM=(&PXREF,&PCOMP,&PSUBS,&PDIAG,&COMPR,
// 'LINECNT=&LN,STOPRC=&SN,DEVCHAR=&DEVCHAR')
//*SYSLIB - USER OPTION
//SYSIN         DD     DSN=&SNODE..&SOR.(&MBR),DISP=SHR
//REFIN         DD     DSN=IMSVS.REFERAL,DISP=OLD
//REFOUT        DD     DSN=IMSVS.REFERAL,DISP=OLD
//REFRD         DD     DSN=IMSVS.REFERAL,DISP=OLD
//SYSTEXT       DD     DSN=&&TXTPASS,UNIT=SYSDA,
//                    SPACE=(CYL,(1,1)),DCB=BLKSIZE=800
//YSUT3         DD     UNIT=SYSDA,SPACE=(CYL,(1,1))
//SYSUT4        DD     UNIT=SYSDA,SPACE=(CYL,(1,1))
//DUMMY         DD     DSN=IMSVS.PROCLIB(REFCPY),DISP=SHR
//UTPRINT       DD     SYSOUT=&SOUT
//SYSPRINT      DD     SYSOUT=&SOUT,DCB=(RECFM=FBA,LRECL=133,
//                    BLKSIZE=1330)
//SYSUDUMP      DD     SYSOUT=&SOUT
//SEQBLKS       DD     DSN=&&BLKS,DISP=(NEW,PASS),
//                    UNIT=SYSDA,SPACE=(CYL,(1,1))
Step 2 ---> //S2          EXEC  PGM=DFSUNUB0,REGION=&RGN,
//                    PARM='&COMPR2,DEVCHAR=&DEVCHAR',
//                    COND=(8,LT,S1)
//SEQBLKS       DD     DSN=&&BLKS,DISP=(OLD,DELETE)
//UTPRINT       DD     SYSOUT=&SOUT,DCB=(RECFM=FBA,LRECL=133,
//                    BLKSIZE=1330)
//SYSUDUMP      DD     SYSOUT=&SOUT
//FORMAT        DD     DSN=IMSVS.FORMAT,DISP=SHR
//DUMMY         DD     DSN=IMSVS.PROCLIB(FMTCPY),DISP=SHR
//SYSPRINT      DD     SYSOUT=&SOUT
//SYSUT3        DD     UNIT=SYSDA,SPACE=(CYL,(1,1))
//SYSUT4        DD     UNIT=SYSDA,SPACE=(CYL,(1,1))
```

Fig. B-1. MFSUTL procedure.

$PCOMP = \frac{NOCOMP}{COMP}$ Specifies whether (COMPOSITE) or not (NOCOMP) the final or composite version of the statement will be printed. If the repetitive generation function for the DFLD and MFLD statements is used, COMP also causes the generated statements to be printed.

$PSUBS = \frac{NOSUBS}{SUBS}$ Specifies whether (SUBSTITUTE) or not (NOSUBS) the substitution variable and its equated value will be printed.

```
                 //              PROC    RGN=360K,SOUT=A,SNODE=IMSVS,
                 //                      SOR=NOLIB,MBR=NOMBR,PXREF=NOXREF,
                 //                      PCOMP=NOCOMP,PSUBS=NOSUBS,PDIAG=NODIAG,
                 //                      COMPR=NOCOMPRESS,LN=55,SN=8,DEVCHAR=0
                 //$1             EXEC    PGM=DFSUPAA0,REGION=&RGN,
Step 1 ------->  //  PARM=(&PXREF,&PCOMP,&PSUBS,&PDIAG,&COMPR,
                 //  'LINECNT=&LN,STOPRC=&SN,DEVCHAR=&DEVCHAR')
                 //*SYSLIB - USER OPTION
                 //SYSIN          DD       DSN=&SNODE..&SOR.(&MBR),DISP=SHR
                 //REFIN          DD       DSN=IMSVS.REFERAL,DISP=OLD
                 //REFOUT         DD       DSN=IMSVS.REFERAL,DISP=OLD
                 //REFRD          DD       DSN=IMSVS.REFERAL,DISP=OLD
                 //SYSTEXT        DD       DSN=&&TXTPASS,UNIT=SYSDA,
                 //                      SPACE=(CYL,(1,1)),DCB=BLKSIZE=800
                 //SYSUT3         DD       UNIT=SYSDA,SPACE=(CYL,(1,1))
                 //SYSUT4         DD       UNIT=SYSDA,SPACE=(CYL,(1,1))
                 //DUMMY          DD       DSN=IMSVS.PROCLIB(REFCPY),DISP=SHR
                 //UTPRINT        DD       SYSOUT=&SOUT
                 //SYSPRINT       DD       SYSOUT=&SOUT,DCB=(RECFM=FBA,LRECL=133,
                 //                      BLKSIZE=1330)
                 //SYSUDUMP       DD       SYSOUT=&SOUT
                 //SEQBLKS        DD       DSN=IMSVS.MFSBATCH,DISP=(MOD,KEEP)
                 //               PROC     RGN=360K,SOUT=A,COMPR2=COMPRESS
Step 2 ------->  //S2             EXEC     PGM=DFSUNUB0,REGION=&RGN,PARM='&COMPR2'
                 //SEQBLKS        DD       DSN=IMSVS.MFSBATCH,DISP=(OLD,KEEP)
                 //UTPRINT        DD       SYSOUT=&SOUT,DCB=(RECFM=FBA,LRECL=133,
                 //                      BLKSIZE=1330)
                 //SYSUDUMP       DD       SYSOUT=&SOUT
                 //FORMAT         DD       DSN=IMSVS.FORMAT,DISP=SHR
                 //DUMMY          DD       DSN=IMSVS.PROCLIB(FMTCPY),DISP=SHR
                 //SYSPRINT       DD       SYSOUT=&SOUT
                 //SYSUT3         DD       UNIT=SYSDA,SPACE=(CYL,(1,1))
                 //SYSUT4         DD       UNIT=SYSDA,SPACE=(CYL,(1,1))
```

Fig. B-2. MFSBTCH1 and MFSBTCH2 procedures (Batch mode).

PDIAG = NODIAG / DIAG — Specifies whether (DIAGNOSTIC) or not (NODIAG) the XREF, COMP and SUBS options should be used and if the diagnostic information should be printed.

PCOMPR NOCOMPRESS / COMPRESS — Specifies whether (COMPRESS) or not (NOCOMPRESS) the IMSVS.REFERAL library is to be compressed before the new ITBs are added.

LN = 55 / nn — Specifies how many lines per page should be printed. The default is 55.

```
          //             PROC   RGN=360K,SOUT=A,SNODE=IMSVS,
          //                    SOR=NOLIB,MBR=NOMBR,PXREF=NOXREF,
          //                    PCOMP=NOCOMP,PSUBS=NOSUBS,PDIAG=NODIAG,
          //                    COMPR=NOCOMPRESS,LN=55,SN=8,DEVCHAR=0
Step 1--> //S1           EXEC   PGM=DFSUPAA0,REGION=&RGN,
          // PARM=(&PXREF,&PCOMP,&PSUBS,&PDIAG,&COMPR,
          // 'LINECNT=&LN,STOPRC=&SN,DEVCHAR=&DEVCHAR')
          //*SYSLIB - USER OPTION
          //SYSIN        DD     DSN=&SNODE..&SOR.(&MBR),DISP=SHR
          //REFIN        DD     DSN=IMSVS.REFERAL,DISP=OLD
          //REFOUT       DD     DSN=&&TEMPPDS,
          //                    UNIT=SYSDA,SPACE=(CYL,(5,1,10))
          //REFRD        DD     DSN=*.REFOUT,VOL=REF=*,REFOUT,
          //                    DISP=(OLD,DELETE)
          //             DD     DSN=IMSVS.REFERAL,DISP=OLD
          //SYSTEXT      DD     DSN=&&TXTPASS,UNIT=SYSDA,
          //                    SPACE=(CYL,(1,1)),DCB=BLKSIZE=800
          //SYSPRINT     DD     SYSOUT=&SOUT,DCB=(RECFM=FB,LRECL=133,
          //                    BLKSIZE=1330)
          //SYSUDUMP     DD     SYSOUT=&SOUT
          //SEQBLKS      DD     DSN=&&BLKS,DISP=(NEW,PASS),
          //                    UNIT=SYSDA,SPACE=(CYL,(1,1))
Step 2--> //S2           EXEC   PGM=DFSUNUB0,REGION=&RGN,
          //                    PARM='TEST,DEVCHAR=&DEVCHAR',
          //                    COND=(8,LT,S1)
          //SEQBLKS      DD     DSN=&&BLKS,DISP=(OLD,DELETE)
          //UTPRINT      DD     SYSOUT=&SOUT,DCB=(RECFM=FBA,LRECL=133,
          //                    BLKSIZE=1330)
          //SYSUDUMP     DD     SYSOUT=&SOUT
          //FORMAT       DD     DSN=IMSVS.TFORMAT,DISP=SHR
```

Fig. B-3. MFSTEST procedure (Test mode).

SN = <u>08</u> nn	Specifies the severity code comparison value, MSG, FMT and TABLE control blocks whose error severity codes equal or exceed this value will not be written to the IMSVS.REFERAL library.
DEVCHAR = <u>0</u> X	Specifies the alphanumeric suffix character X to be appended to the name DFSUDT0_ to indicate the desired device characteristics table. The default is 0.

SYMBOLIC OVERRIDES

Most installations use the MFSTEST procedure to generate the MFS control blocks. Once testing is done, the blocks are moved from IMSVS.TFORMAT to the staging format library IMSVS.FORMAT. Following is a sample execution JCL for the MFSTEST procedure.

```
//EX1051MF   JOB   (CGAC,TEST), 'ZIEP MFS GENERATION',.....
//MFSGEN     EXEC   PROC=MFSTEST, PCOMP=COMP,PSUBS=SUBS               (A)
//S1,SYSLIB      DD   DSN=U0912.MFSCNTL.COPYLIB,DISP=SHR              (B)
//S1.SYSIN       DD   *
        TITLE 'CUSTOMER INQUIRY' ← Place control statements here
        PRINT NOGEN
CUSTUP  FMT
        ......
        COPY
        .....
        MSGEND
        END
/*
//
```

Here, two overrides are specified, PCOMP = COMP and PSUBS = SUBS. These are the two most commonly-used overrides. PCOMP = COMP tells MFS to print the statements generated as a result of DO and ENDDO statements. PSUBS = SUBS tells MFS to perform any substitution requested by the EQU statement in the format set.

The partitioned data set containing the member name to be copied is on the third line.

PRINTING GENERATED DFLD AND MFLD STATEMENTS

FIGURE B-5 presents a sample output listing produced as a result of the DO and ENDDO statements and the COMP parameter. The control statements fed into the MFS input stream are those of SCREEN A-2 and FIG. A-3.

Note that the following items are printed for each DFLD and MFLD generated:

- The generated statement sequence number followed by a + sign to indicate that the DFLD statement was generated as a result of the DO iteration.
- The DFLD label or MFLD statement label, if present, including the appended suffix.
- The statement operator, DFLD or MFLD.
- A literal, if present. A literal whose length exceeds 31 characters (20 characters if ATTR= is present) is truncated to 28 characters (17 if ATTR= is present) and is followed by "..." (three periods) to indicate the truncation.

```
                                                                                    0001
MESSAGE/FORMAT SERVICE PREPROCESSOR                                             COPY/STK
ITB OBJECT CODE/ERRORS                STMT   SOURCE STATEMENT
                                 +PARM='NOXREF,COMP,NOSUBS,NODIAG,NOCOMPRESS,LINECNT=55,STOPRC=8'
                                               ↑
                                               └ Using COMP parameter to print the generated
                                                 DFLD and MFLD statements.
```

Fig. B-4.

- The DFLD name, if present, including the appended suffix.
- The system literal name, if present.
- ATTR=(...) if attributes are present.
- The field length in the form of LTH=nnnn.

```
MESSAGE/FORMAT SERVICE PREPROCESSOR                                  86.105 PAGE 0002

ITB OBJECT CODE / ERRORS

STMNT SOURCE STATEMENT                                                        COPY/STK

    1              PRINT    NOGEN
    2 FMT107       FMT
    3              DEV      TYPE=(3270,2),FEAT=IGNORE
    4              DIV      TYPE=INOUT
    5              DPAGE    CURSOR=((07,03))
    6              DFLD     'TRANSACTION SCREEN ***,POS=(02,25),ATTR=PROT
    7              DFLD     'TRANS ORDER                DATE TYPE ',            $
                            POS=(04,02),ATTR=PROT
    8              DFLD     'CODE NUMBER AMOUNT       (YYMMDD) (+-)',           $
                            POS=(05,02),ATTR=PROT
    9 *
   10 *
   11              DO       17,1,MAX,SUF=01,BOUND=LINE
   12 TRCODE       DFLD     POS=(07,03),LTH=03,ATTR=(HI,MOD)
   13 JOBO         DFLD     POS=(07,09),LTH=09,ATTR=(HI,MOD)
   14 AMOUNT       DFLD     POS=(07,20),LTH=11,ATTR=(HI,MOD)
   15 DATEA        DFLD     POS=(07,33),LTH=06,ATTR=(HI,MOD)
   16 TYPE         DFLD     POS=(07,42),LTH=01,ATTR=(HI,MOD)
   17 MESSG        DFLD     POS=(07,45),LTH=35,ATTR=(HI,MOD)
   18              ENDDO
   19+TRCODE01     DFLD     POS=(7,3,1),LTH=3,ATTR=(...)
   20+JOBO01       DFLD     POS=(7,9,1),LTH=9,ATTR=(...)
   21+AMOUNT01     DFLD     POS=(7,20,1),LTH=11,ATTR=(...)
   22+DATEA01      DFLD     POS=(7,33,1),LTH=6,ATTR=(...)
   23+TYPE01       DFLD     POS=(7,42,1),LTH=1,ATTR=(...)
   24+MESSG01      DFLD     POS=(7,45,1),LTH=35,ATTR=(...)
   25+TRCODE02     DFLD     POS=(8,3,1),LTH=3,ATTR=(...)
   26+JOBO02       DFLD     POS=(8,9,1),LTH=9,ATTR=(...)
   27+AMOUNT02     DFLD     POS=(8,20,1),LTH=11,ATTR=(...)
   28+DATEA02      DFLD     POS=(8,33,1),LTH=6,ATTR=(...)
   29+TYPE02       DFLD     POS=(8,42,1),LTH=1,ATTR=(...)
   30+MESSG02      DFLD     POS=(8,45,1),LTH=35,ATTR=(...)
   31+TRCODE03     DFLD     POS=(9,3,1),LTH=3,ATTR=(...)
   32+JOBO03       DFLD     POS=(9,9,1),LTH=9,ATTR=(...)
   33+AMOUNT03     DFLD     POS=(9,20,1),LTH=11,ATTR=(...)
   34+DATEA03      DFLD     POS=(9,33,1),LTH=6,ATTR=(...)
   35+TYPE03       DFLD     POS=(9,42,1),LTH=1,ATTR=(...)
   36+MESSG03      DFLD     POS=(9,45,1),LTH=35,ATTR=(...)
   37+TRCODE04     DFLD     POS=(10,3,1),LTH=3,ATTR=(...)
   38+JOBO04       DFLD     POS=(10,9,1),LTH=9,ATTR=(...)
   39+AMOUNT04     DFLD     POS=(10,20,1),LTH=11,ATTR=(...)
   40+DATEA04      DFLD     POS=(10,33,1),LTH=6,ATTR=(...)
   41+TYPE04       DFLD     POS=(10,42,1),LTH=1,ATTR=(...)
```

MFS generated statements

The suffix 01 is appended to the first group of generated DFLD statements.

The second generation group has the suffix of 02, etc.

Fig. B-5.

Fig. B-5. continued

```
42+MESSG04      DFLD     POS=(10,45,1),LTH=35,ATTR=(...)
43+TRCODE05     DFLD     POS=(11,3,1),LTH=3,ATTR=(...)
44+JOBO05       DFLD     POS=(11,9,1),LTH=9,ATTR=(...)
45+AMOUNT05     DFLD     POS=(11,20,1),LTH=11,ATTR=(...)
46+DATEA05      DFLD     POS=(11,33,1),LTH=6,ATTR=(...)
47+TYPE05       DFLD     POS=(11,42,1),LTH=1,ATTR=(...)
   .              .
   .              .
   .              .
115+TRCODE17    DFLD     POS=(23,3,1),LTH=3,ATTR=(...)
116+JOBO17      DFLD     POS=(23,9,1),LTH=9,ATTR=(...)
117+AMOUNT17    DFLD     POS=(23,20,1),LTH=11,ATTR=(...)
118+DATEA17     DFLD     POS=(23,33,1),LTH=6,ATTR=(...)
119+TYPE17      DFLD     POS=(23,42,1),LTH=1,ATTR=(...)
120+MESSG17     DFLD     POS=(23,45,1),LTH=35,ATTR=(...)
121 *
122 *
123             DFLD     'MESSAGE:',POS=(24,02),ATTR=PROT
124 REPLY       DFLD     POS=(24,11),LTH=69,ATTR=PROT
125             FMTEND
126 *
127 *
128 INTRANS     MSG      TYPE=INOUT,SOR=(FMT07,IGNORE),              $
                         NXT=OUTRANS
129             SEG
130             MFLD     'TRANS006 ',LTH=09
131 *
132 *
133             DO       17
134             MFLD     TRCODE,JUST=L,LTH=03,FILL=X'40'
135             MFLD     JOBO,JUST=R,LTH=09,FILL=X'40'
136             MFLD     AMOUNT,JUST=R,LTH=11,FILL=X'40'
137             MFLD     DATEA,JUST=L,LTH=06,FILL=X'40'
138             MFLD     TYPE,JUST=L,LTH=01,FILL=X'40'
139             ENDDO                                 MFS generated statements
140+            MFLD     TRCODE01,LTH=3,JUST=L
141+            MFLD     JOBO01,LTH=9,JUST=R
142+            MFLD     AMOUNT01,LTH=11,JUST=R
143+            MFLD     DATEA01,LTH=6,JUST=L
144+            MFLD     TYPE01,LTH=1,JUST=L
145+            MFLD     TRCODE02,LTH=3,JUST=L
146+            MFLD     JOBO02,LTH=9,JUST=R
147+            MFLD     AMOUNT02,LTH=11,JUST=R
148+            MFLD     DATEA02,LTH=6,JUST=L
149+            MFLD     TYPE02,LTH=1,JUST=L
150+            MFLD     TRCODE03,LTH=3,JUST=L
151+            MFLD     JOBO03,LTH=9,JUST=R
152+            MFLD     AMOUNT03,LTH=11,JUST=R
153+            MFLD     DATEA03,LTH=6,JUST=L
154+            MFLD     TYPE03,LTH=1,JUST=L
155+            MFLD     TRCODE04,LTH=3,JUST=L
156+            MFLD     JOBO04,LTH=9,JUST=R
157+            MFLD     AMOUNT04,LTH=11,JUST=R
158+            MFLD     DATEA04,LTH=6,JUST=L
159+            MFLD     TYPE04,LTH=1,JUST=L
```

Fig. B-5. continued

```
              MFLD    TRCODE05,LTH=3,JUST=L
              MFLD    JOB005,LTH=9,JUST=R
              MFLD    AMOUNT05,LTH=9,JUST=R
              MFLD    DATEA05,LTH=6,JUST=L
              MFLD    TYPE05,LTH=1,JUST=L
               .          .
               .          .
               .          .
              MFLD    TRCODE17,LTH=3,JUST=L
              MFLD    JOB017,LTH=9,JUST=R
              MFLD    AMOUNT17,LTH=11,JUST=R
              MFLD    DATEA17,LTH=6,JUST=L
              MFLD    TYPE17,LTH=1,JUST=L
 *
              MSGEND
 *
 *
 OUTRANS      MSG     TYPE=OUTPUT,SOR=(FMT07,IGNORE),                    $
                                                   OPT=1,NXT=INTRANS
              SEG
 *
              DO      17
              MFLD    TRCODE,LTH=05,ATTR=YES
              MFLD    JOBO,LTH=11,ATTR=YES
              MFLD    AMOUNT,LTH=13,ATTR=YES
              MFLD    DATEA,LTH=08,ATTR=YES
              MFLD    TYPE,LTH=03,ATTR=YES
              ENDDO
              MFLD    TRCODE01,LTH=5,ATTR=YES
              MFLD    JOB001,LTH=11,ATTR=YES
              MFLD    AMOUNT01,LTH=13,ATTR=YES
```

Appendix C

The APPLCTN and TRANSACT Macro Statements

This appendix explains in detail the symbolic parameters specified in the APPLCTN and TRANSACT macro statements.

APPLCTN MACRO

The APPLCTN names the application program that processes the transaction code specified in the TRANSACT macro. RESIDENT specifies that the PSB associated with this application program is to be made resident at system initialization time. DOPT specifies that the PSB associated with this application program is to be located dynamically. RESIDENT and DOPT are mutually exclusive.

PSB=	specifies the name of the PSB associated with this application program definition. Each local PSB must be unique.
SYSID=	specifies the identification of the system in the multiple system configuration where the application program will be executed and specifies the system identification which will be used to route the response back to the originating system. The values specified must be numbers in the range from 1 to 255.
PGMTYPE=	specifies the application program characteristics. The first parameter has a default value of TP which specifies that IMS/VS schedules the program when messages processed by the program exist. A program defined as BATCH can use DL/1 in the IMS/VS control program region and can refer to the message queues. The OVLY is no longer used by the system but is retained for compatibility. The third parameter specifies the class to which the transactions specified in the TRANSACT macro are to be assigned. It must be a decimal number from 1 to 255.

The default is 1.
Example:

```
APPLCTN    PSB=UPDATE,PGMTYPE=(,,1)
```

FPATH= specifies if YES or NO this macro is a Fast Path exclusive program. The FPATH=YES and PGMTYPE=TP specifications define a Wait-for-Input (WFI) application program.

SCHDTYP= specifies whether (PARALLEL) or not (SERIAL). This application program can be scheduled into more than one message region or batch message region simultaneously. The default is SERIAL.

TRANSACT MACRO

The TRANSACT macro is used one or more times with each APPLCTN macro instruction to identify the transaction code. The transaction codes cause the application program named in the preceding APPLCTN macro to be scheduled for execution in an IMS/VS message processing region.

WFI= specifies that this is a Wait-for-Input transaction. If WFI is defined, the application program is allowed to remain in main storage after it has processed the available input message(s).

CODE= specifies one or more 1 to 8 character alphanumeric transaction code(s) or remote transaction code(s). Each character of transaction codes and logical terminal names must be an alphanumeric character (A through Z, #, $, @ or 0 through 9). An example of this code is:

```
CODE=(TRANS001,TRANS002,TRANS003)
```

PRTY= specifies the values to be used to determine the scheduling priority of this transaction. This priority also controls the priority of messages created by this application and sent to a destination in a remote system.

Normal: The priority assigned to this transaction when the number of input transactions enqueued and waiting to be processed is less than the limit count value. This priority can range from 0 to 14. The default is 1.

Limit: The priority to which this transaction is raised when the number of input transactions enqueued and waiting to be processed is equal to or greater than the limit count value. This priority can range from 0 to 14. The default is 1.

Limit Count: Associated with each Limit priority is a limit count. If the number of transactions accumulated in a message queue is equal to or greater than the limit count, then the priority level of this queue is temporarily given the value of its limit priority. The limit count can range from 1 to 65535. The default is 65535. For example:

```
TRANSACT CODE=TRANS001,PRTY=(1,1)
```

MSGTYPE= specifies the kind of input message (single or multiple segment) and whether or not the communication line, from which the transaction was entered, is to be held until a response is received.

MULTSEG: specifies that the input message may consist of one or more segments. It cannot be scheduled to an application program until an end-of-message indication is received or a complete message is created by MFS. An example of MULTSEG is:

```
MSGTYPE=(MULTSEG,,)
```

SNGLSEG: specifies that the input message consists of one segment. The end of the segment is assumed to be the end of the message. Scheduling can occur when the first segment is received.

NONRESPONSE: specifies that if the communication line is available for transmission, the terminal can continue to enter messages. For example:

```
MSGTYPE=(,NONRESPONSE,,)
```

RESPONSE: specifies that the communication line to which the input terminal is attached cannot accept further inputs until a response to this message is received.

CLASS: The third parameter specifies the Class to which this input message is to be assigned. It must be a decimal number from 1 to 255. The default is 1. The defaults are MSGTYPE=(MULTSEG,NONRESPONSE,1)

PROCLIM= specifies the number of messages (count) of this transaction, the number of messages an application program can process in a single scheduling, and the amount of time (in seconds) allowed to process a single message. The count value may range from 1 to 65535. If no limit is to be placed upon the number of messages processed at a single scheduling cycle, use value 65535. The time value may range from 1 through

65535. The value assigned is used for the purpose of controlling application program looping. The defaults for PROCLIM are 65535 for all parameters. The PROCLIM parameter is ignored for transactions processed by a BMP program. BMP transactions are assigned a count of 65535 and a time of 24 hours at program scheduling time.

PARLIM= specifies the threshold value to be used when SCHDTYP=PARALLEL was specified in the preceding APPLCTN macro instruction. An additional region will be scheduled whenever the current transaction enqueue count exceeds the PARLIM value multiplied by the number of regions currently scheduled for this transaction. Valid values for PARLIM are from 1 to 32767. The PARLIM value applies to MPP programs only, it is not supported for BMP programs.

MODE= specifies that database buffers are to be written to direct access upon each request for a new message (SNGL) by the processing program or upon program termination (MULT). This operand affects emergency restart. When MODE=SNGL is coded, the emergency restart only reprocesses the last input message, otherwise with MODE=MULT, the emergency restart reprocesses all messages that were scheduled and processed by the application program since the previous checkpoint. The number of messages to be reprocessed depends upon when the last checkpoint was issued. The default is MULT. Conversational and WFI transactions must be defined as SNGL.

SPA= defines that the transaction is a conversational transaction. The first parameter specifies the size of the Scratch Pad Area. When the second parameter is coded as DASD, it specifies that the SPA should be kept on direct access device, CORE specifies that it should be kept in main storage. The default is DASD. The third parameter FIXED specifies that the transaction does not pass control to other transactions with different SPA sizes during the course of the conversation.

SEGSIZE= specifies the maximum size allowed in any one output segment. It must be a decimal number from 0 through 65535. The default is 0. If 0 is specified, the segment size is not checked by the online system at execution time.

SEGNO= specifies the maximum number of output segments allowed into the message queues per Get Unique call from the application program. It must be a decimal number from 0 to 65535. The default is 0. If 0 is specified, the number of segments is not checked by the online system at execution time.

Appendix D

Sub-routine to Issue Operator Console Message

```
E40REPLY START 0
*********************************************************************
*                                                                   *
*          SUBROUTINE 'E40REPLY' ALLOWS THE CONSOLE OPERATOR        *
*       TO SHUT DOWN AN EXECUTING PROGRAM IN A CONTROLLED           *
*       PROGRAMMATIC MANNER.                                        *
*                                                                   *
*       WHEN CALLED BY ANOTHER PROGRAM, THIS SUBROUTINE WILL DISPLAY*
*       ON THE MASTER CONSOLE A MESSAGE WITH A PROMPT ADVISING THE  *
*       OPERATOR THAT THE CALLING PROGRAM IS ACTIVE AND WITH AN     *
*       INSTRUCTION TO REPLY 'EOJ' TO THE PROMPT IF HE OR SHE WANTS *
*       THE PROGRAM TO BE SHUT DOWN.                                *
*                                                                   *
*       THIS SUBROUTINE IS TO BE CALLED BY IMS BATCH PROGRAMS,      *
*       WHICH UPDATE THE DATA BASES, EXECUTE IN A DLI/BATCH MODE,   *
*       AND CAN BE CHECKPOINT/RESTARTED IN A BMP REGION.            *
*       THIS FACILITY WILL ENABLE THE DATA BASE TO BE BROUGHT UP    *
*       ONLINE WITHIN PROCESSING TIME REQUIREMENTS IN THE EVENT     *
*       THE DLI/BATCH UPDATING PROGRAM RUNS BEYOND PROCESSING       *
*       DEALINES.                                                   *
*                                                                   *
*                        PASSED PARAMETERS                          *
*                                                                   *
*         REG       CALL TYPE 'I' - INITIAL CALL (FROM CALLER)      *
*                             'N' - NORMAL CALL          1 BYTE     *
*         REG7      PROGRAM ID OF DRIVER (FROM CALLER)   8 BYTES    *
*                   PROGRAM DESCRIPTION OF CALLER       20 BYTES    *
*                   THIS FIELD FOLLOWS THE PROGRAM ID               *
*                   IN THE CALLING BMP PROGRAM.                     *
*         REG8      OPERATOR REPLY (PASSED TO CALLER)    3 BYTES    *
*                                                                   *
*********************************************************************
```

Sub-routine to Issue Operator Console Message

```
         SAVE  (14,12)              LINKAGE
         BALR  3,0
         USING HERE,3,4
HERE     L     4,BASEADDR
         B     FIRST
BASEADDR DC    A(HERE+4096)
FIRST    ST    13,SAVE+4
         LA    13,SAVE
         LA    5,RETURN             LOAD ADDRESS OF RETURN ROUTINE
         LM    6,8,0(1)             LOAD ADDRESSES OF PASSED PARAMETERS
         CLI   0(6),C'I'            TEST FOR INITIAL CALL
         BE    CONSMSG              BRANCH TO CONSOLE (WTOR) ROUTINE
         CLI   0(6),C'N'            TEST FOR NORMAL CALL
         BE    NORMAL               BRANCH CHECK FOR OPERATOR REPLY
         ABEND 4000,DUMP            ABEND IF INVALID CALL TYPE
CONSMSG  EQU   *
         MVI   IRPTECB,X'00'        RESET WTOR FOR OPERATOR INTERRUPT
         MVC   REPLY(3),BLANKS      BLANK OUT OPERATOR REPLY AREA
         MVC   COMMON+41(8),0(7)    MOVE PROGRAM ID TO WTOR MESSAGE
         MVC   COMMON+20(20),8(7)   MOVE PROGRAM DESCRIPTION TO WTOR
COMMON   WTOR  '*** -------------------- -------- ACTIVE -- REPLY EOJ T*
               O END ***',REPLY,4,IRPTECB,DESC=6,ROUTCDE=14
         BR    5
NORMAL   EQU   *
         TM    IRPTECB,X'40'        DETERMINE IF OPERATOR REPLIED
         BO    CHKIRPT              VALIDATE OPERATOR REPLY
         BR    5                    BRANCH TO RETURN IF NO REPLY
CHKIRPT  EQU   *
         OC    REPLY(3),BLANKS      SET OPERATOR REPLY TO UPPER CASE
         CLC   REPLY(3),EOJDC       TEST REPLY FOR EOJ
         BE    EOJ                  YES, BRANCH TO EOJ
         B     CONSMSG              SEND CONSOLE MESG, IF INVALID REPLY
EOJ      EQU   *
         MVC   0(3,8),REPLY         MOVE VALID OPERATOR REPLY TO LINKAGE
         BR    5                    BRANCH TO RETURN ROUTINE
RETURN   L     13,SAVE+4            LOAD SAVE REGISTERS
         RETURN (14,12),RC=0        RETURN
SAVE     DS    9D
IRPTECB  DC    F'0'
REPLY    DC    CL3' '
BLANKS   DC    CL3' '
EOJDC    DC    CL3'EOJ'
         END   E40REPLY
```

Index

M